T.C. Mulvihill

Killed By A Passing Snowflake

Killed By A Passing Snowflake

First Edition 2008

Published by Snowflake Publications Ireland

Copyright© T.C. Mulvihill 2008

Typeset by My Word! Warwickshire

Printed in Finland by Bookwell Ltd.

Cover design by David Thany

ISBN 978-0-9557499-0-2

*Dedicated with love to Neil and my own
seven wonders of the world.*

*Also to Mom who would never have assumed,
and with love and in memory of my own
eight brothers and two sisters.*

To him who was killed by a passing snowflake. R.I.P.

Then cherish pity, lest you drive an angel from your door.

William Blake's Holy Thursday,
Songs of Innocence.

Chapter One

Sinead O'Connell was not mad, but anyone caught in the whiplash of one of her sudden furies such as her assistant Carolyn now was, seldom realized it.

There was no disguising the fact that Sinead (or Phoenix as she preferred to be known) was just one generation removed from the wilds of North Kerry, for the tenacity of a Kerry farmer and the audacity of a Kerry publican were etched on her very soul and face.

She was the daughter of parents who had both left Ireland for London during the Second World War, a fact which always puzzled Phoenix, since she was brought up in an era where the tendency was for people to flee war zones rather than to seek refuge in them. Her father had regularly declared a bombed out London to be preferable to perpetual cold and hunger on the small patch of land his father farmed in Listowel. As for her mother, she had always declined to give any real indication as to why she had left the family pub in Ballybunion, other than to send money home for brothers who needed educating.

Though strangers in Ireland, they met in Paddington only weeks after Bridget McCarthy had been warned by a gypsy, to beware of a red headed man from the West. She had ignored the warning and less than a year after arriving in England found herself married to Frank O'Connell.

The pair of them settled in London, to a life every bit as restrictive and hard working as the one each had left behind in Ireland, until Frank O'Connell was offered a job on the Kent coast. With the prospect of fresh clean air, distant views of France (a good Catholic ally) and the possibility of affordable housing, they made the move South East. Along with her brothers and sisters; Phoenix was born and brought up in what her father referred to as 'the arse end of England,' the cold Kent coast, where she became known as 'the Irish girl with the red hair.'

Now married to a fair haired Irish man, she was routinely referred to by some of the more suspicious members of his family as 'the tally ho English woman,' a comment designed to

1

offend, but which never hit the mark, for it was not her habit to listen or take note of anyone for whom she had the slightest contempt. Many years previously, she had learned that a lack of sensitivity was a prerequisite for surviving, and that worrying and fretting about what other people thought of her was a waste of time and effort since it seldom affected the outcome of anything she set her mind upon doing.

Carolyn Larkin, Phoenix Ashton's long suffering personal assistant, was well aware of the red headed woman's lack of sensitivity. She listened impassively that cold January morning, to the curses and obscenities Phoenix uttered, as she randomly opened some of the early morning post. It was a familiar routine, but one which far from inspiring boredom or contempt, only evoked from Carolyn a feeling of affection and a fierce desire to protect. Intuitively, she knew Phoenix was deeply unhappy and this knowledge troubled her, for she felt a great debt of unnecessary gratitude to Phoenix.

She would however have been traumatised, if she'd had the faintest inkling, that not only were her feelings not reciprocated, they were deeply despised. As far as Phoenix was concerned, Carolyn was a loser, as feeble as 'a meercat's piss,' working for her when she could have her own business up and running, calling the shots instead of dodging them. Quite unreasonably, Phoenix despised Carolyn, she despised her gratefulness, her inability to take offence and more than anything, she despised Carolyn for throwing away something she had once desperately wanted, - a university education.

The fact that a crisis of confidence, brought on by a cruel and public jilting at the hands of a two timing cheat, was behind Carolyn's decision to walk away from Cambridge at the end of her second year, did nothing to elicit sympathy from Phoenix. It merely convinced her entirely of Carolyn's runt status. The only thought, that had run swiftly through the red headed woman's head, when Carolyn had confided her secret, was that if the girl had, had the balls of a butterfly, she would have got even, not gone mad, and most certainly, she could have made a better fist of things than ending up a dogsbody.

All things considered though, Carolyn had done well for herself, particularly since her exit from university had taken place during a time when recession, repossessions and unemployment were the hallmarks of Britain. She was afflicted with a meek and benign manner which added to her predicament for it hid the many qualities she had to offer, thus making her a prime candidate for being walked over and taken advantage of. After a long search, the only job she had been able to secure, was that as a cashier at a turf accountant in South London, something she aimed to do only until she could save up and buy a ticket for Australia and a new life.

But unlike Phoenix who staunchly believed God never shuts a door without thoroughly bolting all the windows too, Carolyn's natural optimism and desire to believe the best was rewarded. Her stint at the bookies revealed a multitude of hidden talents. Not only did she display a flair for crude on the hoof economics, but she also proved herself more than capable of handling abusive punters, who regularly threatened a rumpus when the three legged horses they backed, never found their way home. In the face of her genteel calm and sympathy, they either took their argument elsewhere or succumbed to her gentle commiseration.

Her smooth management skills and ability to soothe were soon acknowledged, and she was rapidly promoted to the position of personal assistant, from where she was promptly and slyly poached by Phoenix Ashton, who instantly recognised in her someone who had all the attributes she proudly lacked, but prized so highly in others; namely honesty, dedication and tact.

While it may generally be true, that the quiet horse is suspect and that still waters do run deep and dangerous, such clichés do not tell the whole truth. Carolyn Larkin had a distinct feeling, that for all the vocal, direct speaking and apparent candour that emanated from Phoenix Ashton, she really didn't know the woman at all.

And that was exactly how Phoenix wanted it to be. She could not bear sentimentality and the general assumption society has that women want to be friends with each other. She hadn't shared a secret or a confidence with another female since she had left school, for she had no interest in the private life of anybody and it perplexed her when anyone appeared to be interested in hers. There was more chance of a mullah eating a pork pie in a public square in Saudi, than of Phoenix sharing a girl's night in. She found other women's obsession with men and their habits boring and banal. Sometimes when she heard her employees share their personal dilemmas and domestic dramas she felt nothing but confusion and irritation with their apparent inertia. The nature of any problem was always plainly obvious to her - with walking away being the simple and succinct answer to any failed relationship. The belief that you can't make somebody love you was the bedrock of her life and she couldn't understand why women in particular, failed to grasp this simple reality.

But on the morning of the 6th January 2001, it wasn't the personal dilemmas of her staff that was troubling Phoenix. She had returned to work after the Christmas break, to find the annual, unwanted seasonal rush of government circulars intermingling with her regular post. They sat awaiting her in all their pompous glory, together with their naïve, presumptuous advice and veiled threats (delivered under the guise of care,) concerning the fate of employers who failed to salute the omnipotence of the health and safety deity. She stood beside her desk feeling considerably more aggravated and aggrieved than usual, seething for someone or something to vent her frustration on. A letter stamped with the insignia of the Inland Revenue suddenly caught her eye, and a searing heat went through her as she thought of the tax bill she had sought to evade. 'Inland Revenge chasing my arse again,' she thought irritably, picking the letter up and sliding it into her handbag, for private consumption at a later date. Not wanting to dwell on such a nauseous subject, she deliberately turned her attention elsewhere, seizing at random one of the despicable government brochures, she usually binned on sight. Featured on its front cover, was a vibrant group of happy looking people, some in wheelchairs, some in ethnic dress, a microcosm of Britain's contented workforce, all smiling at her.

'They have good cause to look smug,' she said aloud, holding it closer to her face as if scrutinizing it for every detail, 'It would take a murder charge before you could fire one of the fuckers.'

And with a contemptuous shrug, she slapped the brochure with the happy looking people down upon the table.

All the while, Carolyn her gaze averted, continued photocopying rota sheets, as impassively as if it were the radio and not an angry woman droning on in the background. Her quiet, tranquil composure drifted across to Phoenix and the very presence of someone, so cool, so reasonable, so self satisfied only served to infuriate her further.

'Well, what's with the Trappist monk demeanour?' she demanded.

Carolyn, very aware that she was a sitting target for the clearly frustrated woman, looked up with a sense of dread, only to be saved by the telephone. She had consciously remained silent, for extreme views on anyone or anything were alien to her. Also, she knew from experience that although Phoenix might beg to differ, Phoenix really didn't like listening to another point of view.

But she was wrong; Phoenix didn't merely dislike the idea of seeing two sides of an argument, she hated it. In fact, if there was one thing she detested above all others, it was a fence sitter; they stirred in her a desire to push, to make them come down on one side or the other. When it came to views on the world and the people in it, Phoenix's vision was strictly limited to monochrome. Uncertainty in her opinion, was a luxury enjoyed by those who did not want to lead, but who sought to undermine those who did, by constant carping and pointless questioning

It was that urge to *push* that seized her now. She watched Carolyn replace the receiver and the longing to say something so biting and cutting that Carolyn would be forced to sit up and take notice overwhelmed her; but when she opened her mouth to speak, the words refused to be found. Almost instantly the fire within her died and feeling faintly confused she turned and looked out of the window, to Clapham Common, a scene that usually placated her.

The feeling of space that emanated from that great open expanse, so close to the heart of London, was one that she loved, but the usual green blanket of grass was currently well hidden. During the night, an unexpected shower of snow had stealthily fallen, leaving behind a scene more reminiscent of a photograph than reality. It clung in soft heaps on the bare branches of the trees beautifying them, defining their shapes, giving the entire scene the perfection of an airbrushed picture. Phoenix did not see the cool beauty. She saw only the aggravation of delayed travel, the filthy grey slush that would soon develop, and the possibility of slipping onto her backside and making a fool of herself.

There was work to be done, but she had neither the heart, nor the inclination to do it.

'I hate this time of year,' she told herself, following with her eyes, a hunched figure as it made its way warily across the common. 'I hate the emptiness and the thought of the year stretching ahead like a blank cheque to be written on, who can even guess what the balance is going to be by the end of it?'

This sentiment was not a new one; it had been with her for most of her adult life. She dreaded Christmas and feared the New Year and no amount of tinsel or joviality could ever disguise the unhappy memories the season always bought with it.

But this year was different, the apprehension hadn't disappeared into a box like the dismantled Christmas lights and decorations, and the fear far from disintegrating had taken on a tangible threat. When Big Ben had loudly and provocatively chimed in the New Year of 2001, Phoenix had known instinctively, that her goose was cooked, both literally and metaphorically. Work was usually her salvation; her means of escape since there were always crisis's to be dealt with and people to bully, the very things that could be relied upon, to take her mind off the one thing she didn't want to think about.

But standing in her office that cold January morning, stuck for words because her fear had choked them, she realized the charm no longer worked.

Turning back to her desk she picked up her bag and the coat that lay tossed across it and announced to a surprised Carolyn. 'I don't care anyway. I'm going to the bank, I might call back later.' And with that, she made her way to her car, and oblivious to the treacherous icy conditions, drove swiftly home

Chapter Two

Nothing gave Phoenix more pleasure or calmed her fears so thoroughly, as the sight of her house. 'The house that Jack built,' was how her husband Jack referred to it, but since he wasn't around in the 1800's, it was more a case of 'the house Jack renovated.'

It was the most open obvious and tangible sign that she had made a go of things, that she hadn't been beaten, and far from ever getting used to it, her affection felt renewed every time she set her eyes upon its restful countenance. The warm mellow brick, the graceful perfectly proportioned windows and ornate high ceilings, all of them never failed to satisfy and inspire her. But best of all was the warmth which without question or hesitation never varied from room to room, all of it - every bit filled her with pleasure and a sneaky pride in her own cleverness.

Nothing had been spared, when Jack had set out to satisfy her every desire, by creating a modern day masterpiece, with ideas, wood and ivory imported from around the world. The planning application, and subsequent renovation of the landmark house, had caused several eyebrows to be raised and many people in the locality, egged on by fear of change, had ferociously voiced their objections in the local press.

The criticism in all its forms had done nothing to deter her. It had simply made her more determined than ever to do exactly as she pleased with her own house and money.

'Why not,' she had asked Jack, 'Enjoy the world's resources while they are still around and available, rather than waste time fretting about a time when they won't be?'

As the restoration grew bigger and grander, the objections and criticisms had grown nastier and more personal, and Phoenix's cup of joy, had truly runneth over when Jack further enraged the local population by changing the name of the property from Silcock Villa to Fuchsia House (in deference to the emblem of his native West Cork.) The house had borne the name of Silcock for over a hundred years. Silcock apparently, had been a well known local thespian from the Victorian era, although to hear some people in the locality speak, one might be forgiven for thinking he was merely retired rather than deceased.

'Here's one old fucker whose had his day,' Jack had said as he ripped the old sign down, breaking the hearts of every conservationist and closet luvvie within a ten mile radius as he did so.

But the hand placing the key in the lock of Fuchsia House that cold January morning was not one of a confident pioneer, in fact it trembled so violently that Phoenix had to press her other hand against the frame to steady the application. The huge strong red Georgian door swung slowly and silently open and Phoenix half expected to hear her three year old daughter Daisy run out to greet her, before remembering that the little girl was spending the day with a friend. This snow was the first Daisy had ever seen and led on by Jack she believed it to be a spectacle laid on especially for her.

'Look at this,' he had said, as he carried her from her bed to the window that morning. 'Look what Daddy spent the entire night making, just for you to have fun with.'

'Don't fool the child Jack,' Phoenix had snapped, but he'd just laughed and replied,

'But sure doesn't she think I'm God almighty already?' and Phoenix had remained silent, fearful he was nearer the mark than he realised.

There was no doubting the love Phoenix felt for her daughter, indeed the intensity of it, occasionally even frightened her, but somewhere within her a barrier existed that prevented her from being as loving and jovial as she wanted to be. Seeing Jack act the carefree way she imagined herself doing in the privacy of her mind exasperated her, making her only too aware of her shortcomings. Life was always so full of constraints.

She dumped her bag down on the polished yew wood hall table and made her way to the kitchen, stepping over a huddle of dolls abandoned by Daisy at the last minute earlier that morning.

The butternut kitchen was warm and welcoming and best of all, it was empty. She made her way to the cupboard beside the range and from habit glanced around surreptitiously as she opened it. It was full of all the unwanted Christmas food gifts she had shoved in there. Bottled fruits and multi coloured liqueurs stood shoulder to shoulder with boxes of wrinkled sun dried vegetables; reminiscent in Phoenix's opinion of some long lost Australian relatives she had once seen. Placing her hand in she reached for the bottle she needed, desire making her hand shake as she did so, but instinct guided her hand and it emerged triumphant, clutching a long slender bottle labelled 'Apple Cider Vinegar from Normandy.'

She uncapped the bottle with practised ease and poured herself a glass of the pale brown liquid. It wasn't vinegar at all-that had been unceremoniously poured down the sink some weeks previously, it now contained just pure Jameson Irish whiskey; for Phoenix was a consummate secret drinker, who preferred to keep her drinking confined to private sources. Bottles of whiskey and brandy sat untouched in various locations around the house, all part of her strategy to keep secret the real extent of her drinking habit. Her biggest secret fear, apart from being caught short was being caught red handed.

Of course Jack knew she drank but he didn't know how much or how often and in a bid to keep him in the dark, Phoenix had to engage in a number of rituals. Concealing her drinking habit was far more difficult than hiding her reliance on valium which being small and odourless caused no such logistical problems. Taken together for extra effect, she referred to her helpers as her faithful VW and they were as natural a part of her life as breathing or eating.

In the secrecy of her handbag, whiskey masqueraded as Coco Channel, while on her shelf in the bathroom it brazenly donned the appearance of Head and Shoulders. For reasons best known to her, the magical properties of the firewater seemed to be enhanced when consumed in some form of disguise.

Litter bins all over Clapham, Wimbledon and beyond held the cast offs from her various de-canting exercises, she had all eventualities covered. Like an athlete who uses anabolic steroids, she used whiskey in the certain knowledge that participation and success were not achievable any other way.

Although her whiskey habit did not bother her, her consumption of the mint products she used to disguise it did, and she was mighty grateful for the discovery of aspartame. 'I'd be a tooth-less soup drinker by now without it,' she once told herself as she rinsed her mouth with a minty wash before meeting a client. She used such products as one might use garlic to ward off vampires, certainly the last thing she needed was some dangerous 'bad mouther' taking a sniff and killing her reputation with one word or knowing look. Even in the ladette culture of the twenty first century, the world is singularly unkind to women in suits who smell of drink.

She leaned with her back against the sink and inwardly sighed with relief as the warming liquid flooded her senses with a familiar sense of well being, and it was with some reluctance that she remembered the purpose of her trip home.

Taking her glass with her she headed for the study, an oak panelled room beside the kitchen that served as an office; pausing briefly to switch on the radio, the sound of silence not being one she found soothing. Sitting down purposefully on a leather chair she took from the top drawer of her desk a red, felt bound writing journal.

Daisy had given it to her as a Christmas present, and the moment she had set eyes upon it, she had recognised it as an omen to do the unthinkable. Opening the book she ran her hand across the smooth white page, before writing in her bold, clear, script.

January 6th 2001.

The feast of the Epiphany, and as usual, there wasn't a wise man in sight. Her confidence suddenly felt diminished. She was like someone poised above Beachy Head, contemplating the final jump and in a way what she was about to do felt like a final attempt at a final solution. She tried to concentrate on the reason for this rendezvous with a writing journal, but her mind shied away from the memory she tried to thrust upon it, like a skittish horse refusing a jump. But she fought for control, steering her mind back to New Year's Day and the promise she had made to herself.

New Years Eve, was not an occasion Phoenix enjoyed. The whole festival in her opinion carried the stench of false sentimentality. In particular, she couldn't bear the forced joviality of strangers joining hands and singing a ridiculous mawkish song about 'cups of comfort,' and 'meeting again.' The celebrations, struck her as nothing more, than opportunity knocks for weird or repulsive looking men to sneak a few kisses and gropes before the drink and darkness wore off and exposed them for what they were. But since her marriage to Jack, celebrating the arrival of the New Year had became unavoidable, for Jack loved the razzmatazz and the extended drinking hours and general bonhomie that went with it. No longer could she escape by going to bed early with whiskey and a video like she used to do when she was single.

The recent New Year celebrations however, had been different. Since they no longer had a resident babysitter, following their au pairs decision to return to Italy, going out together had not been an option. For too long they had relied on Carmen always being there and had failed to make wider contacts. It had seemed for a while Phoenix might be granted her wish. But Jack was not to be cheated.

They stayed at home and threw a party, which meant Jack did the inviting and Phoenix did the organising. Though she begrudged the time and deeply resented feeding some of the guests Jack had seen fit to invite, she acted like a gracious and hospitable hostess, keeping herself so busy offering food and drink, that she was simply unable to stop for a prolonged talk with anybody.

All part of her plan of course. The New Year's Eve tradition of reminiscing on the departing year depressed her. Looking back was something she personally avoided; it was so pointless, so fruitless and most of all, so incredibly frightening. The chiming of Big Ben, the resolutions and promises made regarding the coming year were all rituals she despised, for she was by nature superstitious. It struck her as utter folly for anyone to claim the New Year a done deal, before it had even started.

Nevertheless when the party had drawn to a successful conclusion and she and Jack had finally flopped into bed, she had allowed her mind to wander back on the past year, the gateway to the New Millennium. It had opened to such hype and hypocrisy, with so many proclamations of a new dawn, but it had been no different to any other year. No different of course, except for the rising tide of panic that had swept her through it. Anxiety and fear had long been her silent unwanted accomplices, but throughout the year 2000, they had developed a new verve.

Why had the anxiety got worse? Was a breakdown of some sort inevitable? Such a thought made her tremulous but there was no end in sight and lying in bed on that cold, first morning of the year, she didn't see how she could hold on much longer. Briefly, she had wondered about the power of prayer. There had been a time when that would have been her first port of call, but that was a long time ago. All the saints of her childhood felt diminished and so very far away. They remained cracked and chipped, somewhere on a shelf in a back bedroom, in deepest, darkest Kent.

On and on her mind had drifted until she became aware of the rhythmic snoring of Jack growing louder and louder as he plunged deeper and deeper into sleep. Instinctively, she had turned to look at him, irritated by this interruption to her train of thought, but as she done so, she had noticed a tingling sensation that affected her entire body. At first she had put it down to tiredness, for she was exhausted, but when she had tried to lift her head to free her tangled hair, she had been unable to do so. Frantically she had sought to move her arms and legs but they wouldn't move either; she was completely numb.

Only one thought had filled her mind and that was death. She was dying on the first day of the year. She had lain as still as the night, cowering in the darkness, remembering Jack's eerie tale about an old woman who had died in bed in Donegal with a look of abject terror on her face. 'Judging by that look,' he had remarked 'the devil himself must have come to collect her.'

Thinking about the devil, had only served to whip up a frenzy of fear and a fierce desire to be free from the torment pursuing her. With an enormous effort, she managed to turn and turn, until she finally rolled out of the bed with the duvet wrapped around her. Terrorised, she had reached out to the bedside table in an attempt to break her fall, but as she did so, it too tumbled over and went crashing to the floor. Reaching Jack was the only thought that had possessed her, if she could reach him all would be well, he would take control and shake her free from this nightmare. She made one last effort to raise her arm up and found thank God, that not only could she pull herself up, she could open her eyes and raise her head.

But when she did so, she had seen with great alarm; that she wasn't on the floor, she was in fact, still in bed, and not only was Jack still sleeping, but the table was still standing. There was a fate worse than death and it was happening, she was going mad. Whiskey was what she needed, but the moment she attempted to stand up, a new calamity arrived. An aura of impending doom engulfed her so thoroughly, that it swamped the panic that caused her heart to beat in such a peculiar way. With no fight left, she had sat back down on the bed and waited for the calamity to wash over her.

She recognised it for what it was. A premonition of what was to come. For years she had feared the dawn of the year 2001 and the unhappy anniversary it would mark. It hadn't sneaked up on her but even so, in the same way an expected death still manages to shock; she now felt profound grief that the inevitable had arrived.

She had stumbled across to Jack, contrition and desperation sweeping through her in turn. She only had to shake him awake and within minutes the burden of deception could finally be unloaded from her back. But as she had reached out to touch him, the cool hand of reason that had steered her for over twenty years, took control again.

Honesty was not the best policy, she more than anyone knew that. Why throw everything away for the sake of an old adage she didn't even believe in? Honesty was the route to madness and she'd take Beachy Head first. She had sat, shaken and trembling, watching the sleeping face of her husband, calm in repose after a night of singing and laughing, unaware of the madness all around him. She couldn't tell him, it would only destroy his peace and do nothing whatsoever to pervert the course of justice that was coming her way.

Eventually, she had walked dejectedly out of the bedroom and into the en-suite bathroom, pausing for a moment, to look over again briefly at the sleeping figure of her husband. In the safety of the bathroom, she sought her faithful VW which she took along with a silent vow of silence.

She had to overcome her fear; she was in retreat and fear was pursuing her, now was the time to turn and pursue it, face it like she had faced everything else that had been thrown at her. Sitting on the floor, with her back to the wall, she had waited for the faithful VW to take affect and when the trembling had ceased and the feeling of doom had withered into a dull acceptance of reality, she had made a promise.

'I'll take the shrink's advice, because September 11th 2001 isn't going to go away and I'm going to be ready for it when it comes.'

That slip of the tongue, was either the first sign Phoenix was getting better, or the first real indication, that she was becoming so confused, she no longer even knew what she was saying. Inadvertently, she had admitted aloud for the first time, a fact she sought to deny even to herself.

For months Phoenix had kept a regular, sacrosanct, appointment booked. According to her diary she was visiting a specialist tax advisor; some particularly difficult VAT returns were giving her cause for concern. At least that is what she told Jack and Carolyn. She even began to believe it herself.

However, Shelby Warner based across the river in Fulham though probably a tax evader, was most certainly not a tax advisor. Her profession was psychotherapy and she personally specialised in the treatment of anxiety complexes and compulsive disorders.

Phoenix would have died rather than admit her problem to someone who wasn't paid to help, a compassionate member of the caring profession, looking into her eyes and confirming her worst fear was beyond the bounds altogether.

The only acceptable help was the kind given in exchange for money, such help wasn't help at all - it was a service, a business transaction that could be controlled and censured.

For several weeks, she had travelled with religious regularity to Fulham and the plush terraced house from where Shelby Warner dispensed her advice.

When Phoenix had first sought therapy, she had done so as a novice. The small knowledge she had of the subject, being absorbed unconsciously from she had seen and heard through the media. It seemed to be a process where celebrities on professional death row were rehatched from oblivion, to game show hosts. All they had to do apart from strip themselves of any integrity, was to relay to the world what they had told their therapists in secret. As such it was worth a go, for not being a celebrity Phoenix could at least spare herself the latter half of the deal.

Finding one though had proved more difficult than she had anticipated, what she really wanted was a word of mouth recommendation, particularly since she held a secret belief that anyone who worked in mental health, had to be as mad as the people they were treating. The last thing she needed to encounter was a Nurse Ratchet character, sitting ready with a syringe and a menacing stare. However as she wasn't prepared to advertise her need, she had been reduced to searching both the classified adverts and the Yellow Pages, but the columns of names, some with a list of letters after them meant nothing to her.

Her search had finally ended, when by chance, she had come across an article in the London Evening Standard, concerning overseas professionals living and working in London. Featured amongst a host of doctors, teachers and interior designers was Shelby Warner, a psychotherapist from New York.

Cutting to the chase, as was her habit, Phoenix had deliberately skipped over the details of Warner's education and professional stance, concentrating instead, on the fundamental issue of personality. There was no point pursuing someone with whom she had nothing in common with. Surprisingly, the therapist didn't sound at all intense or weird; in fact, she seemed to be eminently sensible. Warner, according to the article, was scathing on the European green movement, playfully suspicious of men who were bald through choice, and strongly approved of using animal rights fanatics rather than rats, in experiments to improve the human condition.

Phoenix went to the therapist in the same way a sceptic might see a clairvoyant; ready to pick holes and to laugh it off as pure rubbish, all the while, secretly hoping that somehow, she might be proved wrong.

For weeks she had hung in, enduring the unendurable, for nobody disliked self-reflection or contemplative silence more than she did. She cringed as the therapist raked over the same old ground, pulling up the same old weeds, with as Phoenix viewed it 'the occasional helping of shit,' in the form of faint praise, to fertilize an idea, which somehow never took root.

Far from calming her, the sessions wound her up. Being questioned about her past was nauseating, as were the implications regarding her lack of relationships and over fondness for money. The only way she could keep a lid on the whole process was either through silence, or blatant lying, because the therapist she quickly discovered had an amazing knack for twisting her words. By correcting her, Phoenix found herself close to revealing things that she just knew, had to remain secret.

In essence, what she wanted was therapy without the therapy. If she had told Shelby Warner from the start, that it was some kind of miracle cure that she was after; the therapist would have laughed, wished her well and shown her the door. But she hadn't. She had held on to a bizarre belief that healing could be brought about by wishful thinking; that somehow by going through the motions of seeking help, something positive was bound to rub off. When it eventually dawned on her that therapy demanded something from her, high hopes were dashed and her renowned temper had ignited. It had all been for nothing.

Hurt pride refused to let her walk away. She who detested clingy, touchy feely, bleeding hearts more than anyone she knew, had let herself down by seeing the dogs bollocks of the hug me, don't bug me world – a shrink.

She had invested too much time and money, in what had turned out to be a ludicrous idea, and she wasn't going to let Shelby Warner get away with it. No, she had promised herself, she would go along and tell Warner, exactly what she thought of her and her false promises, because as far as she could make out, Shelby Warner was nothing like the woman she had appeared to be in that newspaper article.

But when she went along for what she believed would be her final visit, it had been Shelby Warner who occupied the best ambush position.

Shelby Warner, originally from New York and resident in London for over five years, hadn't once felt at home there. As far as she was concerned, there was nothing cute or quaint about elevators constantly out of order, pubs without ice and shop assistants who sincerely believed they were doing her a favour. She found London dirty and Londoners tiresome, whinging even. 'The Brits might know a thing or two about stiff upper lips but us Yanks could sure teach them a trick or two about the merits of owning a backbone,' was the considered opinion, she expressed to visiting friends and family from America.

Phoenix Ashton however, was an exception. She was different to the other clients Shelby dealt with. Some of them, although incapable of the most basic skills, like rearing their own children, or reversing a car, could talk for England about their attributes, while others, whose very backsides hung with diamonds, drip-fed a litany of complaints against life that ran on forever. These people were neither ill, nor unhappy, they were just dissatisfied. Most of them, in Warner's opinion, didn't need therapy, they needed a bollocking, and how she would love to be the one to administer it.

On the other hand, everything about Phoenix Ashton oozed anxiety; it was etched on her face and echoed in her barbed caustic comments. Phoenix never strutted up the steps like her other clients; in fact she entered the house with the wariness of someone approaching an STD clinic. She paid in cash, declined receipts, and gave both a false telephone number and address; she would have given a false name as well, if Shelby had not spotted a name badge pinned to her jacket.

She exhibited all the trademarks of a freakish personality, whilst remaining grounded in herself, and Shelby Warner slowly became intrigued by the persistent visits from a modern woman, whose belief that a cure could be achieved by what amounted to a visiting ritual seemed positively medieval.

Patience though, according to Shelby Warner, was not a virtue. It was merely a delaying tactic usually employed by the indecisive to give them time to think. After several aimless weeks, the limited amount of patience she had, had been spent. The weekly sessions with Phoenix Ashton were simply becoming predictable as well as frustrating.

So three days before the first Christmas Eve of the new millennium, Phoenix had made her way to her last appointment, determined to make her dissatisfaction known, unaware that Shelby Warner was also braced for a show down.

Lifting the brass lion head knocker, Phoenix had rapped on the door with three smart taps- Morse code for 'I'm Pissed Off' she had told herself. What she had to say wouldn't take five minutes and she'd be off, still limping, but relieved that she hadn't let a shrink get one over her.

Her aggressive arrival, had been greeted by Shelby Warner, with a face so completely devoid of its usual good humour, that in an instant, Phoenix had found her composure knocked askew.

Using cool, calculated words of dismissal, Shelby Warner had set about stripping Phoenix of both her confidence and aggression. The cold, sharp syllables uttered by the therapist had splintered in the chill afternoon air, piercing Phoenix's heart, as she caught an occasional word in isolation.

Phoenix had been confounded by Shelby's reasoning. How could she be accused of time wasting, wasn't she the one paying the therapist an indecent amount of money? As the proprietor of a large cleaning company, Phoenix Ashton was well used to getting paid for jobs that didn't exist, and she never complained.

She had sought to read Shelby Warner's face, but deciphering intent was not a skill Phoenix possessed. Her strength was assertion, or bullying as it used to be known. As she had searched the American woman's implacable face that chill December day, the only thing Phoenix had known for sure, was that Shelby Warner would listen to any tirade she chose to give, before shrugging her shoulders and walking away.

Shelby Warner however, had been more than slightly perturbed at the reaction of the red headed woman. She had been prepared for a long, drawn out, foul mouthed argument, from somebody whom she felt certain, wasn't used to being told to go away. It hadn't even occurred to her that Phoenix would be so wounded by her words, and seeing the shocked, almost fearful look on her client's face, she had been charitable enough to end her speech on a softer note.

'Listen Phoenix,' she had said. 'I don't even know enough about you to know if it is therapy that you need, it might be a waste of time, it could be medical help that you need, perhaps even a spell as an in-patient. I just don't know. But I'm telling you, no one can endure a never ending spiral of panic, it will end in a breakdown of sorts, if you don't face the fact that there is an issue.'

The words, intended as a gentle, compromising finale, had fallen upon Phoenix's ears with more force than several swipes from the right hand of a heavyweight boxer. So, it was true, she had thought, the therapist deemed her mad, so mad, that she couldn't risk seeing her on a one to one basis anymore. The idea of seeing a doctor was now out of the question, she was being asked to face the fact that she had lost control, but she couldn't do it. In an instant she had seen Warner as her last chance slipping away and abandoning her previous conviction concerning the uselessness of the shrink; she had both begged and demanded help.

Shelby Warner though conventionally trained, was not a conventional practitioner and if Phoenix had bothered to read the newspaper article, featuring Shelby Warner in its entirety, she would have realised that the therapist came with a health warning. Shelby Warner was viewed by her profession as a traitor, and she in turn viewed it with cynicism and downright distrust, all of which only served to alienate her amongst colleagues in her adoptive city. She couldn't help thinking and even worse, telling them, that the only way she would ever be able to share their professional perspective was if she managed to stick her head as far up her arse as most of them seemed to have managed to do.

She did not share the belief of most of her contemporaries, that psychiatric intervention was necessarily a good thing; in fact, she was inclined to think that more often than not, it was a process that led to a life - long sprint on a treadmill of ever more bizarre treatments. Therapy was booming thanks to a touchy, feely sound bite media that encouraged people to seek help on the basis of self diagnosis, but once the process was started, there were all too few checks and balances to keep it in its place.

It was her considered opinion, that many people classified as mentally ill were not ill at all. They were in fact desperately unhappy. It was this group of people rather than the depressed who were more likely to engage in destructive behaviour, such as killing themselves. The depressed needed medical help and the unhappy needed therapy, but not a useless, talking shop sound-board therapy, that encouraged them to ramble aimlessly, often into a pit of despair. It was this point that caused the most consternation amongst Warner's colleagues- advice they insisted was not their remit; they were professionals, not agony aunts.

When Phoenix had made her emotional plea for help, Shelby Warner had felt extremely compromised. Part of her desperately wanted to draw a line under a case which was going nowhere, but when she had looked into the anguished face of the figure on the doorstep, her intrigue with the foxy haired woman, and the secret dilemma which undoubtedly controlled her, had once again been rekindled.

Against her better judgement she had partially relented. She would keep Phoenix on her books, on condition that she was prepared to try a different type of therapy, one which would involve less talking, with the added benefit of requiring fewer visits.

'Look Phoenix,' she had said. 'I think asking you direct questions, has simply given you scope to be too literal. I wonder, if you and I were to approach things more lucidly, like say, a story gently unfolding, would we get more fluidity?'.

And Phoenix, who hadn't had the faintest idea what Shelby, was talking about, but was eager to look knowledgeable and keep Shelby on board, had responded by nodding her head enthusiastically.

'We will cut out the question and answer sessions' Shelby had continued, confident that Phoenix both understood and approved of what she was suggesting 'And work on a different type of therapy, one that will require you to find someone you really admire, someone you have empathy with and who you know would have empathy with you. When you are certain you have the right person, I am going to ask you to tell them your story, perhaps in a series of letters, or as…'

She was interrupted by a furious outburst from a scarlet faced Phoenix whose temper she had managed to well and truly rejuvenate.

'Tell a friend?' Phoenix had shouted incredulously. 'Are we going round in bloody circles or what? I can't even tell you, a therapist who doesn't know me, never mind tell a friend. Besides there isn't a friend I've got who wouldn't run a mile or pity me if they heard what I had to say, and if there is one thing I can't stand, it's pity followed by kindness.'

Seriously rattled, Shelby Warner had resisted the temptation to leap forward and shake Phoenix, until her bones jangled. 'For God's sake,' she had replied, through gritted teeth. 'Would you ever think of listening? I'm not suggesting you mail these letters; the therapy is in the writing of them, writing to someone you have a handle on, someone you instinctively know would understand the perspective you are coming from. No therapist can offer you that. Now do you understand?'

At this point, Warner had turned away, furious at having compromised with someone, who she was beginning to suspect was incapable of developing the ability to listen, never mind the ability to confide. 'You refuse to be questioned about your trauma, but perhaps you can write about it and perhaps then, you might be able to talk to me. Now, do you want to give it a go or not?'

The question had hung in the air and Shelby Warner, catching a glimpse through the window of what she reckoned, might be the first star of the early evening, (but what was in fact, the tail end of a Boeing 747 on its way across the Atlantic,) had made a silent, sincere wish. That Phoenix would politely but firmly turn her offer down and walk away. Her wish was not granted.

'I'll think about it,' Phoenix had announced, before taking her leave.

But the words, she had used to the therapist, had followed her home, ringing through her ears like an annoying jingle as she had made her way, through the crowded city streets. 'If there is one thing I can't stand, it is pity followed by kindness'. They sounded so familiar, but she hadn't been able to place them and that had added to her anxiety.

The anxiety didn't disappear either, over the following days. Instead she had grown increasingly frantic, trying to recall recent books she had read, as well as films and programmes she had watched, all to no avail. She had even asked Jack if the words 'pity and kindness,' rang any bells with him and he had replied, 'No,' but that he was sure as hell certain that they didn't come from her, since he couldn't recall a time when she had used either.

She had ignored him, the art of sarcasm was becoming his second nature and his reply was only what she had expected, but on Christmas Day, her search had come to an end. As she and Jack sat down after dinner, to watch television, a trailer had appeared. It was for 'Gone with the Wind.'

'Highly appropriate,' Jack had commented as he sat down heavily on the settee, 'when you consider all the turkey and sprouts that have just been consumed,' but Phoenix hadn't even been listening to him. Instantly she had known where those words came from. There was only one person who detested pity and kindness as much as she did - it was Scarlett O'Hara from Gone with The Wind.

She had watched awestruck, as the scene where Rhett Butler pulls Scarlett out of bed, and forces her to dress like a madam, to attend Ashley's surprise birthday party had unfolded on the screen in front of her. In an instant, she had been transported back to the dismal bedroom in Kilburn, where she had first discovered that book; the one that was to have such a major impact on her life.

How could she have forgotten it? For some people Gone with the Wind is just a rollicking good read, but for Phoenix all those years ago, it had become her rough guide on how to tell the world to go to hell. She had felt a distinct frisson of apprehension as she remembered the time when that book had been her Bible, when she had become so involved with the people of Atlanta and the attributes of a character she loved and admired so much.

Immediately she had gone in search of her copy, the one she had stolen from the wicked witch, eventually finding it on the top shelf of the dining room bookcase. And as her fingers had frantically turned the pages, she was not disappointed. Scarlett, Mammy, Rhett, they were all there like long lost friends - absence had only made her heart grow fonder.

Therefore, when calamity had presented itself on New Year's Day and she had made that promise to obey the shrink, she knew there was only one person she could tell her story to.

The decision made on the brink of despair had been easy, the choice obvious, but now it came to putting it all on paper; she hardly knew where to start. She picked up her pen, took one look at the sky and the snowflakes that were billowing and tumbling on their way to earth and began to write.

Dear Scarlett,

I feel like a snowflake, caught in the dazzle of a headlamp, on my way to oblivion, but it is not a force ten gale that is driving me, just a savage fear that keeps snapping at the ankles of my mind.

Perhaps this letter is proof that I really am insane, because here I am; a thirty something woman with my own business, a child and a man, but my mentor is not some old dame from halcyon Oxbridge days, or a favoured Godmother who is going to remember me in her will.

No, it is a girl from a book written decades before I was even born.

I came across you Scarlett when life was so colourless, pointless and painful, that I hardly knew how to put one foot in front of the other.

I have a picture of you in my mind, sitting on the steps with that dress spread all about you, talking to those Tarleton twins; the centre of attention. I too was the centre of attention once, but for all the wrong reasons, there were plenty of people fighting because of me, but absolutely no one fighting over me.

When I read about you for the first time, I knew I had found someone to measure ideas and actions against. You were so real to me; you didn't know it but you were the only friend I had, and believe me after the 'big assumption' of '79, I needed a friend. I loved your refusal to be beaten, even when you did stupid things like marrying weedy Charles, when smarmy Ashley evaded you. I could never have done something like that when I was sixteen. No, with me it was always a case of 'the meek shall inherit the earth, it that is all right with the rest of you.' I seriously lacked what you would call 'gumption,' and what I now recognise as 'balls.'

I should have given out some serious verbal abuse when I was sixteen, I can tell you. I was spineless, I really was. But in fairness my family and situation was very different to yours Scarlett. For starters, we didn't have a bloody great plantation with slaves running about here and there. There was only one slave in our family and though it felt like me at the time, it was actually Mom.

Just like yours, my Dad was from Ireland; only mine was from the West coast. He wasn't a bit like your Pa though - from what I've heard, my Dad wouldn't have risked a wager on the sun rising, never mind gambling for a house of a lifetime – he wasn't a speculator like yours was. I loved reading that bit about how your Pa won Tara in a game of poker, before landing himself a really posh wife. Wouldn't he have been just a bit pissed though, if he had ever realised, how much contempt his lovely wife had for him?

I'm afraid I have no French aristocracy in me like you did on your mothers' side, not unless my Mom had a mighty big secret too! Still your Pa was pretty smart wasn't he? Leaving Ireland with just the shirt on his back and a few years later there he is, with a massive house, aristocratic wife and a crowd of blacks fetching, carrying, and calling him Sir.

Daddy claimed to be a socialist. He was always banging on about the Brits treating the Irish like shite. We never had cosy heart warming chats like you and your Pa did, but since he died when I was twelve, I don't really know how he and I would have got on.

And frankly Scarlett I don't give a damn anyway.

I loved it when your Pa tried to warn you off fancying Ashley, when he told you that the only thing worth dying for was land and that anyone with a drop of Irish blood in them knows so. When I first read those words back in the early eighties, I lived in a dingy little room in Kilburn and I was so downcast that even Leonard Cohen records irritated me with their upbeat lyrics. But when I read those words, I had this vision of myself astride a white horse, galloping down the Kilburn High Road, past Woolworths and out through sudden acres of lush green grass bordered by rivers.

It was a strange thing for me to fantasize about, since I was thoroughly finished with small town life and just the thought of living in the country would have been enough to send me into hiding...

Actually Scarlett, I don't think it's love of the land that obsesses the Irish, I think it's fear of madness, of losing control. That's the fear that stalks my family. Apparently it's handed down through the generations, like an heirloom. Some women get granny's eternity ring, I got her depression.

But it's not a foolish obsession for the mind is full of trickery and is not to be trusted, it plays games and it deceives. You only have to think of a three stone anorexic who stares at a mirror, just to see a twenty stone elephant gazing back at her, to have the faintest inkling of how powerful the mind is.

Daddy never won a Tara, but he got a decent enough end terrace in a seaside town in a place called Kent. He hated it there; he said it was populated by gawks, dead from the ankles up. Still it didn't stop him and Mom going on to have seven children, which they could barely afford.

Of course you Scarlett only had two sisters. Now the youngest one Carreen sounded like an angel, but that Suellen was a real cow, you were dead right to knock her wedding plans on the head. If old Frank Kennedy had married her instead of you he would have shot himself.

My parents both left Ireland penniless and though they didn't end up with much, there was one thing they never gave up on and that was their ambition for their children. They were driven Scarlett. Somehow the seven of us making it big would compensate for their hard life and we in turn would encourage our children to bigger and better things, so that eventually the branch of the O'Connell's that left Kerry in their coats would end up big shots somewhere in the south of England.

My brothers James and Michael both went to college and became teachers, while Gerry and Joe went into the motor trade. They bought their own garage on the strength of a loan from a family fiend, and no, that is not a spelling mistake. They have been very successful, not going to frighten the shit out of Ford or anything like that, but they are doing O.K.

Neither of my sisters Alice or Eileen gave a bollocks for education. Alice became a nurse and married a doctor, why scramble up a rock face when you can use a ladder? She now leads an incredibly smug and sanctimonious existence. Eileen - she is the middle sister, did a bit of this and that, before marrying an engineer and running off to live in South Africa. Mind you, she scurried back fast enough when she thought the blacks were going to start acting as if they owned the place.

Mom was forty-six when she had me. She could have said, 'I saved the best till last,' but she didn't. Instead she said, 'You were some shock to the system I can tell you.'

Being labelled a shock is bad enough, but bearable, so long as it is kept a secret, but when I came home from school early one day I heard Mom chatting and drinking tea in the kitchen with her horrible obese friend Breda, (what a name for someone with fourteen kids.) They were speaking in low confidential tones, so I refrained from calling out and had a listen instead.

I heard Mom say, 'It's God's own truth Breda, I thought I was going through the change when I had Sinead, some shock she was I can tell you.'

I felt betrayed, Mom talking about me to a great lump like Breda. I also felt unwanted, unneeded and surplus to requirement. It was the sort of thing Oxfam might say to the offerings of the local do gooder, 'Not another bleeding bag of jumble.'

And to cap it all, the horrid obese bumbling Breda said, 'Ah Bridget, you took a terrible risk, you could have had a mongrel.' IGNORANT OLD WOMAN. I went upstairs and sulked for hours, but I still ate my tea, because I'd have to have been dying not to do that when I was fourteen.

I know you hated school Scarlett and I don't blame you for in the world you lived in what could an education do for a girl other than frighten off every prospective beaux in the county? But it was different for me. I loved school and Mom encouraged me, for she felt sold out by the achievements of my older brothers and sisters, she wanted more than o.k. or pretty good considering the starting block. As I was the youngest, the role of redeemer was given to me, the one who would not only succeed at school but who would go on to a proper university, Oxford or preferably Cambridge.

Mom wasn't stupid. It wasn't a case of putting a pin on a race card and hoping for the best. All my teachers said, 'That girl's got aptitude, if she applies herself, the sky will be her only limit.' I knew exactly what I wanted to be. I wanted to be a lawyer. I loved the idea of chasing case histories, getting my act together, saving the world's unfortunates. In the little fantasies that rolled round my head at night, I was always in the defence team, for the prosecuting one struck me as being on a par with kicking a dying dog.

I loved the language of the law, the smart Latin quotes that put everything so succinctly. Mom was forever going to second hand shops and house sales, picking up old clocks and gilt edged books – they looked beautiful, but were usually dead useless. I came home one day to find she had bought a whole set of ancient Law books and I set upon them immediately. The language in them was archaic, one volume dealt exclusively with the legal status of 'the bastard.' I didn't know bastard was a legal term; I thought it was just a term of abuse for incompetent football players or dogs that barked during the night. It kept referring to the bastard, it said, the bastard can inherit if... the bastard can deny... The bastard can claim... But the bit I loved best was, 'however, when the bastard himself dies...'

Mom and I suppose, Daddy, guarded me like a pair of hawk eyed eagles. Nothing was going to side track me and I didn't mind because I wanted to be successful. More than anything I wanted them to be proud of me. Perhaps I wanted to make up for arriving into their world without an invitation. I wanted them to say, 'She was a shock to the system all right, but a bloody great one, - one worth having.'

Certainly, there was no social life to distract me from my studies, for unlike Georgia, Scarlett, Kent in the seventies was bereft of any balls or barbeques to get excited about.

In our town there were a couple of other Irish families that we associated with. There was the O'Dowd's, - they were obese Breda's gang, all fourteen of them, ginger haired boys with snot green eyes and noses. Most of them emigrated to Australia, but years ago they would have been deported for they were always up to no good.

There were also the Moran's, five black haired girls that the O'Dowd's constantly chased along with my brothers. None of them stood a chance. All five girls fled to London and obeyed their father's dictum of 'marry well, marry money.'

Finally, there was the Condon family. Only he was Irish, his wife was Polish. He had been my father's employer for a while. He was the financial shoulder of the church, the pillar of the community and the armpit of the South.

He was a bastard; what am I saying for God's sake, he is a bastard, a piece of shit that should have been flushed out. Just mentioning his name makes me queasy and even whiskey can't obliterate him from my mind.

He was the ruination of my life and I've never told anyone about him, not even Jack, but then, there are many things I haven't told Jack, including just how much whiskey it takes to get me through a day.

For a time he was convinced every bottle we bought leaked, so I've taken to buying my own, because I need it with me, all the time.

You became something of a secret drinker yourself, didn't you Scarlett, after Frank got killed and you felt guilty and afraid. I'm in the same position. Jack isn't involved in the Klu Klux Klan or any shite like that, but I just feel so very low and depressed. Like a thoroughly pissed off guy who sits on Death Row, fearful of getting a reprieve.

I feel angry and frightened, but most of all I feel so guilty, and I can't figure why all the bad feelings have returned with such a vengeance. Once life was so simple, the plot was; work hard, get a good job and get *choices*, then overnight, in fact over one snowy night it became so complicated and now so much unfinished business is calling time. Oh how I wish I was sixteen again and knew what I know now.

Some people Scarlett, are born with the killer instinct, but me, I was born with an instinctive need to protect and now it is killing me. Don't get me wrong, I was never any 'St Sinead of The Shit Scared'. I went to Mass on Sunday's and to the Legion of Mary on Thursdays with my friend Magda; her parents were Polish, from the same region in fact as Condon's wife. Magda was very devout, she had a saintly face with a permanently con-cerned expression on it and her voice oozed care and considera-tion. I felt shabby in comparison with, because while she was always on the look - out for ways of doing a good turn, I was always in search of a way out of being called upon.

Each week the priest asked us to visit the old, the sick and the lonely to see if there was anything they needed or wanted. Magda was dutiful, but me, the minute I was out of the church door, I forgot my intentions. I had great plans to save the world, I just never got round to carrying them out. The following week the priest would ask how we had got on with visiting all the misfits. Well he didn't put it quite like that. I would have been happy to lie, but Magda was shocked at the very idea. 'Lying to a priest is unforgivable,' she said, 'You mustn't do it, you will be cursed.'

She almost convinced me that he had the power to turn us into goat's feet and truthfully that would have been preferable, to telling him that I had stuffed all the neatly folded newsletters he had given me down the drain. When he asked me if the needy required anything, I had to answer in a way that would avoid him thinking I was a lazy arse and Magda thinking I was the devil's assistant. He would say, 'How are things?' and I would reply, 'Fine as far as I know.'

'Did anyone request anything?'

'Not to my knowledge Father.'

'Did they ask for prayers?'

'I didn't ask, I just assumed they did.'

'Did they request a newsletter?'

'I am not aware of any such requests.'

'Did they request another visit?'

'I'm not aware of any such requests.'

Shit it was worse than being on Mastermind. I think he knew I had sat on my backside and was deliberately making me sweat. You of all people, Scarlett would have understood; how a few lies would have saved an awful lot of bother.

I went each week because it pleased Mom, and it was fun walking home with Magda, calling in at the shop, buying a can of Coke and some sweets. Magda was a bit of a holy, holy, but she was funny. Once when we were walking home, a woman in leopard skin shoes walked past and Magda grabbed the can off me, and began singing into it like it was a microphone, 'That's neat, that's neat, that's neat, that's neat, I really love your tiger feet,' The pair of us pissed ourselves, when the woman turned round and shouted in a Scottish accent, 'Piss off Olivia Newton John, or I'll ram that can up your wee smelly arse.'

Since those early carefree teenage years, Scarlett, I have spent almost my entire life in fear of being found out. I know it will happen and when it does, the reality will be worst than anything I've ever imagined.

It always works that way, people say anticipation is worse than reality, but they are wrong. It's like fearing the dentist, but telling yourself the wait is worse than the appointment. You believe it; you really do, until you find yourself in the dental chair with an arm lock around your head, smiling into the face of some bleeding great butcher, who nearly pulls your jaws apart.

Well Scarlett, in 1979, at the age of sixteen, my life changed forever. I was side tracked, derailed, hit the buffers and rolled over. I could have spent the rest of my days hidden in some forgotten sidings, but I didn't. Instead I came upon your story and read all that stuff about buckwheat bending with the wind and being able to stand up straight again when the storm has passed and somehow through sheer balls and circumstance, I got my life back on track. Not the one I had originally set out on, but I didn't care. I had no idea where it would take me but it didn't matter, so long as I was able to put a lot of distance between the present and the past, because I was certain of only one thing, the past was a bloody dangerous place to be. Somewhere I didn't ever want to visit again.

So I buried it and then one day, I can't remember exactly when, I woke up to the definite knowledge that my past may have been buried, but it certainly wasn't dead. It had merely been submerged. I knew instinctively that it was coming back, like a tide on a dangerous beach and any attempt to stem it would be like the proverbial finger in the dyke, which is no longer a politically correct analogy to use, but is a bloody accurate one.

At least by putting pen to paper and writing to you Scarlett, I have made a start. For the first time in my life I will tell someone, who won't tell anyone else, the truth about Christmas 1979.

Phoenix

Chapter Three

Jack Keane was what the world calls a self made man. A euphemism favoured by some to describe others, who start out with less than themselves, but who end up with more, since their skills are in doing, rather than talking.

It is not a description Jack would have used to describe himself or anyone else, for he knew that people are made by both experience and the luck they chance to meet, and that behind every success or failure, there is usually a crowd of people with a hand in the outcome.

His was not a unique story; he had left Ireland in the mid 1970's at the age of eighteen, no better or worse than the average emigrant, tired of his father's outdated way of thinking and acting. As the youngest son he had grown up with the knowledge that the farm would never be his and he had never begrudged Danny his older brother the dubious inheritance that awaited him.

However when his father had refused to listen to the pleas of Jack's mother, that Jack should be given the chance of university, on the grounds that there is poor eating to be had from a book, Jack had decided enough was enough. It wasn't that he wanted to go to university, quick as his brain was he knew his fortune lay in the strength of his hands. Besides, as a family dependent on the hand to mouth existence of a small farm, tucked away in the hilly country of Skibbereen in West Cork, delayed gratification was a nonsensical notion. Choice was a luxury none of them could afford.

No, it wasn't thwarted desire that angered Jack. It was the small mindedness of his father, a man who was capable of thinking only of the here and now and for whom the expression 'the bigger picture' meant nothing but size.

Though Ireland was still a long way from being a fully fledged roaring economic tiger, there were still means and ways to making money from the Common Market when Ireland joined it in the early seventies. Many farmers, though not scholars, willingly took crash courses in learning how to spot both the loopholes and the opportunities.

Jack tried various ways of getting his father up to speed, even though he held a deep suspicion, that old man Keane, in spite of his easy dismissal of education, actually held a doctorate in 'old fartery' and was a fully paid up member of the old school. Like all who belong to that particular organisation he was incapable of thinking for himself. He knew by heart its central philosophy that says change must be resisted at all costs and anything that makes life sweeter should be viewed with distrust and suspicion.

Two of Jacks sisters, tired of the oppressive atmosphere, emigrated in quick succession to America, to Boston and New York and from all accounts they were happy and more than comfortable with the trappings of wealth that their father had once warned them about.

Shocked by this flagrant act of initiative, Jack's father had moved swiftly to bolt the stable door by seeing the local T.D. He succeeded in getting Jack a position with the postal service - a steady one; it offered a pension and a uniform and the firing gun that told Jack to get ready to run. America was too fiddly and expensive to consider for somebody in a hurry, so Jack decided on London. But when his father heard of his plans, he tried in vain once more to lay down the law; no son of his would ever set foot in the devils lavatory and think he'd be welcomed home again.

The sheer arrogance of a man, who in Jack's eyes, had repeatedly shown himself to be in serious want of good sense, thinking he had the right to tell Jack what to do and where to go, was the final straw. He left a note for his mother and after borrowing money from Danny, Jack headed for London. His father remained true to his word and Jack was forbidden to come home and the rest of the family were prohibited from having any contact with him.

Jack kept in intermittent contact with Danny, via friends and neighbours and set about creating a life in London. The lack of contact was no hardship for him during those early days, when he worked night and day on building sites throughout North London, with hardly time to think, never mind regret.

The already established Irish community provided him with both work and companionship and enough warning bells to remind him that if he wanted to make it big, he had to break the mould. If he remained amongst his own there would be more chance of him sinking to the bottom of the pool than rising to the top - he had to move somewhere where he would be more of a novelty.

So taking a chance, he moved south of the river and began seeking work in the leafier suburbs of South London straying into Surrey and Kent. Here he discovered a less established Irish community and a less cynical indigenous one, where he was more able to take advantage of the dubious skills he had learnt across the river.

His open and honest looking face and cheery good nature gave him the prowl-ness of the fox, who reassures a hen house by frequent and benign visits. No one ever suspected Jack of trickery and when they did, he always had a quick and plausible excuse. But Jack was not infallible; he became so tied up with his obsession of making a go of it all that he tripped over himself in his eagerness and walked into his first mistake with his eyes wide open.

The only feasible way of making proper money was by working for Jack Keane, of that he was certain, and long before Bill Gates ever realised that real chips are not edible Jack knew the importance of networking. He was a regular visitor to the Black Swan pub in Clapham, a recognised chamber of commerce for the construction industry in South London and there he watched and integrated with the bosses, the men who had arrived.

There was nothing of the eel about them; they were all invariably solid and dependable. They had something that Jack didn't, something that gave them, gravitas and stability. Jack figured that amongst other things, this aura owed itself to the fact that they were invariably married and nailed down making them steady figures in a notoriously transient business. It was this recognition that heightened his interest to something more than a passing fancy in the barmaid at the Black Swan, Polly March.

She was pretty and perky in a way that girls back home in Skibbereen were not and more importantly, she seemed to know by name every man who mattered in the building trade. He watched as she chatted effortlessly, calming and soothing even the most irate punters. She had a way about her- good customer technique and in Jack's opinion it was going to waste in a pub.

It might well be true that a man with a fortune is in want of a wife, but in Jack's book it was more likely to be a man without a fortune who is in most need of one. In the era before the mobile phone and fax, Jack knew he was missing countless contacts. What he needed was another layer to his business; someone to take messages, someone who would listen sympathetically and massage a few egos. Someone, who wouldn't be above telling a few good honest, straightforward lies.

The more he watched Polly in action, the more convinced he became that with the right tutoring, she could be just what he needed. So he asked her out and less than six months later, they were married. Even as he exchanged vows in Clapham Town Hall, he knew he was making a mistake, but he kept his fingers crossed, that it would be a prosperous one.

However just as he had watched and miscalculated the benefits of having Polly by his side, she in turn had watched and miscalculated Jack. She was tired of being a barmaid. It had started out as fun, her good looks attracted lots of attention but gradually she had grown aware that most of the men on offer weren't worth touching with a barge pole, never mind with her fine, well manicured hands. They were laughs in the pub, but likely to be louts in the home. She was weary of the foul talk and the tension that crackled in the air when a fight was about to break out. She could of course have got another job, but like so many who spend too much time behind bars, she lost the confidence to think she could ever work in a monotonous environment.

What she needed was a respectable way out and Jack Keane looked just the ticket. She wanted a good, wholesome man, who would work normal hours and provide her with a home and children, and just enough money to spend on the little things that gave her pleasure, like a new dress or makeup, and the occasional trip to Clacton.

He was different to the others, he never swore in her presence, even going so far as to reprimand those that did and he never made crude remarks, or passed compliments that sounded less than totally sincere.

Though he seemed light hearted, often when she caught his eye, he'd look lonesome and her heart would go out to him and she'd think how lost he must feel in a tough, alien city. He was just the sort of man who would benefit from a wife who knew how to please, who wouldn't interfere with his work, or pose any threat to him. She'd be more than happy to let him be the man of the house, and in return how she would love to rally around him and take care of all his creature comforts.

So Jack and Polly were married. It was meant to be a small, secret, romantic wedding with just the two of them and witnesses called from the street. He had engineered this idea. He couldn't let his family know about Polly- not until his business was successful enough to justify her as his choice. However, it ended up with the entire extended family on Polly's side present, because as much as Polly loved romance, she loved her family even more. Jack feigned disappointment but the reality was; he didn't mind at all. It was just his family he didn't want present. They would never accept Polly; every time she opened her mouth she condemned herself- for she was south London through and through. He would he assured himself, find a way round the problem another day.

But Polly found out all too quickly that the Jack in the pub was a very different Jack to the one at home. He perplexed her; he turned down work with large contractors offering steady wages and hours and insisted on working for himself. He rose far too early in the mornings and did not return until late at night and when he was at home, the only thing that obsessed him was the phone; who had called and who hadn't. He showed exasperation, rather than interest in the little purchases she made and completely ignored the tantalising bits of gossip, she specifically sought out for him.

To make matters worse he expected her to work. Not in the Black Swan of course, but at home; answering the phone, making appointments in his diary, apologizing for failed appointments and ordering materials from horrible gruff old men in builders merchants who treated her as if she was a fool.

Her constant confusion over terms like skim coat and dry lining irritated him, but what made him seething mad, to the point that she feared a dust up like the ones that constantly broke out in the Black Swan, was when she told the truth. When she reassured customers that Jack had indeed quoted a lower price than the one issued on the final bill, or that Jack had not turned up for a job because he had promised someone else at the last minute. He would rant and rave, shouting and using all the words she had once believed, he was unfamiliar with

All she had wanted was a home and a husband who worked nine to five and who left his work at work, but when she married Jack, it seemed the Black Swan had moved in with them. Builders, rough and ready plasterers and Neanderthal shaped hod carriers called in day and night, smoking and talking into the small hours. And when they weren't around, irate customers were never more than a phone call away.

The marriage, a culture shock to both parties; ended by mutual agreement before they had a chance to celebrate their first anniversary. Within another two years though, Polly had recovered sufficiently to remarry and become the mother of two boys.

Jack used to see her occasionally, pushing a pram along Clapham High Street with her mother and sisters in tow, all struggling with bags of shopping. The sight never failed to make him sweat, as he recalled what a lucky escape he had made.

When Polly eventually left south London to live on the Essex coast, along with most of her extended family and in- laws, nobody was more relieved than Jack Keane. He bid her farewell and wished her good luck, so graciously and with so much apparent sincerity, that for a moment she was almost tempted to think she had misjudged him.

With Polly gone, the scent of his marriage lasted just long enough for him to capitalise on her contacts and the sense of security people once derived from steady, married men. He dedicated himself to his business and when he returned to Ireland in the late 80's for his father's funeral, he went home feted as a very successful man. His only regret was that his father wasn't there to see him, for Jack would have enjoyed telling him, that it was amazing what could be achieved in the devils bathroom, given the right tools.

Home again in Ireland, he confessed both his marriage and divorce to a shocked and disbelieving Danny, who in turn kept it a secret from both Jack's mother and youngest sister who still lived locally. Jack's mother went to her grave two years later; proud of the son who had proved his father wrong, but without ever knowing how Jack had so thoroughly disgraced himself, his family name, and his religion.

Now in the infancy of a new century, Jack on the face of it had everything he had set out to achieve; money, property, a real marriage and a child whom he cherished. Except he didn't. Something had changed. Phoenix was no longer, the woman he had married. She had become cool and distant, constantly preoccupied with something like she was now, shooing him out, urging him to take Daisy to McDonalds on the pretext that she had tax affairs to sort out. Something he knew to be untrue, since she had recently claimed to have found a tax specialist, who knew a way out of the web she had got herself entangled in.

He stared across at her; wondering what possessed her. She had barely responded to the few asides he had made, concerning a teacher at Daisy's school, who had just been charged with drink driving. Usually she would have seized on scandal like this; avid for the grimy details, gleeful for ammunition that could be used the next time she was reprimanded by the self same teacher for parking on the yellow lines outside the school. But all she had done was repeat the mantra, about Daisy wanting the final toy in her collection from McDonalds.

'Well,' he said, finally giving up on the conversation he thought would hold her. 'What do you intend to get up to while we are out?'

Phoenix looked up at him and just the faintest hint of a blush coloured her cheeks, as she thought for a moment about what she really intended to 'get up to.' 'Oh you know, just a bit of this and that, I'm going to start with cleaning Daisy's room, it's a bomb job and I've one or two letters that need finishing,' She spoke carefully, hoping her bored tone would drive him out. Jack hated lazy, ramshackle, grey days that lacked a definite purpose.

It sounded plausible enough but one liar seldom believes another, and to Jack's ears the reply had the whiff of rehearsal about it. He looked at her and took in her slightly anxious demeanour. She certainly didn't look like a woman about to engage in a cleaning frenzy but she looked distinctly like someone who was up to no good.

'So,' he said, deliberately stringing the conversation out in an effort to gauge just how keen she was to see the back of them, 'You are sending me out in traffic, when it's warm in here and cold out there, to queue for bloody hours for a pile of shite.' He walked across to her and circled his arm around her waist and whispered, 'Give me a nice bit of F&C any day.'

'Oh I would Jack, only I know it's not a nice bit of cod you are talking about,' she said wiggling her way out of his grasp before adding quickly, 'Hurry up Daisy, can't you see Daddy is waiting for you?'

The little girl oblivious to her father's frustration and her mother's deception took a running jump into Jack's arms, putting to an end any further detours in the conversation. 'Wave to us from your window Mommy,' she begged and Phoenix realising she was getting her own way, relaxed and smiled.

'Of course I will darling.'

'I'm still mighty suspicious of you,' Jack said, as he slipped his jacket on. 'Is it Paddy or Johnnie you can't wait to get your hands on?'

She ignored the implication and laughingly replied, 'Don't be so ridiculous, go on out before I change my mind, I'll run upstairs and wave from the window.'

He sighed with resignation and followed Daisy out and at the same time Phoenix ran upstairs into her bedroom and opened the balcony windows. She called out to her husband and child and began waving to them.

'I feel like the Pope, giving a blessing,' she said and Jack replied.

'Yes, but he doesn't use two fingers.'

Anxiously she watched, until the car disappeared out of sight down the long drive before pulling the window closed. Thank God, they had gone, for a moment she had feared Jack would play awkward and announce he was not being sent out after all.

She stood for a moment, staring at the bleak beaten down, damp grass. The early crocus she had noted only the day before as a welcomed harbinger of spring, now sat shrivelled and crushed. 'Some reward for being punctual,' she thought, turning her gaze to the bare skeletal branches of the beech tree and the overcast sky that peeped through them. The dull lifeless scene was reminiscent of a dreary day from her childhood Christmas holidays, when all goodwill had evaporated once the family had returned back to school and work. She shivered at the memory.

Random, un-summoned memories of her youth were becoming part of her daily routine. She knew it was writing to Scarlett that caused her to think back to the girl she had once been, to the time when she was still somebody's daughter and still cared about what people thought about her. The urge to find out more had gripped her, but it was tempered by a sense of trepidation. Reading over her letter to Scarlett had been like looking at a faded photograph, only parts of it were recognisable and though she wasn't altogether certain that full recognition was wanted, the quest to find out more had begun.

She was perfectly aware that the easy bit was over. She had merely set the scene with that first letter, writing about her parents and her brothers and sisters. The inconsequential as Shelby would put it. They were just the handrails to guide her back to the time when her life had fallen apart. Now was the time to tell Scarlett what she hadn't been able to tell the shrink or anyone else and just the thought of what she had to divulge made her hands shake a little.

She glanced briefly into Daisy's room. Her description of it to Jack had been accurate, it was a mess, far too big a job for a Saturday afternoon; she would leave it for Helen the housekeeper to contemplate on Monday.

Turning into the bathroom, she reached up for the tiny brown bottle hidden on the wrought iron shelf and washed

down a valium tablet with a swig of whiskey from the bottle of
Head & Shoulders in her cabinet. She then wiped her hands on a
white cotton towel and headed for the red book.

Dear Scarlett,   **17th January 2001**

I have just sent Jack out with Daisy. He knows I want to be
alone and he is very wary of me, but for all the wrong reasons. I
just need some time to think things over with you.

Sometimes I can't believe that I'm married to Jack. When I
left home at sixteen I swore an oath that I'd never have anything
to do with Ireland, the Irish, horseracing; Guinness or anything
that smacked of home again.

Just as you Scarlett, wanted so much to take after your
refined mother, with her French aristocratic ways rather than
your red faced father, I too wanted to be different to what I was.
But I had no escape. It's pure Kerry blood running through my
veins, no matter which side I turn to.

I suppose I just wanted to be English. Completely and unam-
biguously English because I needed to belong somewhere and I
wanted to make a complete break with the old ways. But
somehow I ended up with what I know best. It sounds old
fartish and that's some achievement, since I'm not yet even forty,
but there is a comfort in the familiarity of home. You Scarlett,
more than anyone, can understand where I'm coming from, after
all, weren't you attracted to Rhett precisely because his aura of
alcohol, tobacco and horse leathers reminded you so much of
your home? Poor old Rhett, if he was around today, he wouldn't
even be allowed on a bus, without a whole plethora of passive
smokers and bearded clerics laying siege to him.

When I first met Jack, he'd just won a massive contract to
convert a block of warehouses into luxury waterside apartments.
Mom and Dad are probably spinning in their grave at the
thought of me being married to a divorcee and from Cork at
that.

Sometimes I find myself staring at a letter addressed to Mrs
Keane and I wonder if I've imagined it all, there is no Jack, no
Daisy, but then I'll hear him effing and blinding at the door or

the cat, or something foolish enough to get in his way and I
know that Jack is real.

I'm trying to prepare the way Scarlett for telling you about
the 'great assumption of 79.' I could start with the end of this
particular story, but I'll obey the shrink and stick to tradition
and begin with the beginning...

I was forced to leave home and all my dreams behind at the
age of sixteen; all because of one bastard. A big hairy bastard,
who ruined my life and then made me responsible for everybody
else being able to continue with theirs - it was the ultimate sacrifice really.

But the worst thing about it Scarlett, was the way people just
assumed that I was the one at fault. In fact they didn't just
assume, they practically lined up to denounce me and that's why
when I think back on the whole affair, I call it the great assumption.

The whole caboodle of responsible, bloody adults, whose
mantra was 'Be careful, be mature, don't jump to conclusions,'-
the very people who should have said 'Hang on a minute, something isn't right,' simply marched in and had me tried and found
guilty without so much as a questioning look.

Shelby the shrink says things must always be seen in context
if they are to have any value, so when I look back on my teenage
years, what happened to me is even worse, when put into the
context of time and place. Like I've already told you, there was
no social scene for me in the Kent of the seventies. There was
the occasional school disco and birthday party which usually
consisted of a few stale sandwiches while sitting around listening
to records being scratched to death by dud needles, nothing else.
The highlight of my week was babysitting for the Condon's, the
big knobs of the parish.

Jerh Condon owned an electronics factory. He had once
employed my father and he came from County Louse, or it
might even have been Louth. He was a big man, tall and broad
with thick black hair, that even grew on his head.

After my father died, he'd call round to our house on the
pretext of a quick chat with one of my brothers, but Mom was
always wary of him, she'd say. 'He has the breed of the snipe in

him, make no mistake.' She was convinced he was checking up on us, making sure she hadn't been splashing out on anything new which would convince him that he was over paying her on the pension front. Make no mistake! Oh, but Mom you did.

She'd fuss around him saying things like 'Oh Jerh sit closer to the fire, the place is in an awful state,' and he'd laugh and say.

'Oh for goodness sake Bridget, you know I wouldn't care if you lived in a pigsty.'

Pigsty! He said that Scarlett because that is what he was thinking, it was pure Freudian. Even Mom knew that, he'd kicked into touch years earlier the bits of his roots that were no longer useful to him.

He didn't like cosy family homes with open fires, they were too reminiscent of what he'd come from. He didn't have an Irish wife either because he didn't want big floury spuds piled up on his dinner table just the way his Mammy used to do. He chose a frail pretty woman from Eastern Europe with a figure and an accent for him to show off, someone a long way from home who would be completely dependent on him.

No one at home particularly liked him for he was slimy, but he was admired for having up and go. We all knew he'd cut the legs from under you, even as he spoke, but he had power and none of us were stupid enough to do anything but lick his boots or kiss his arse if the cause demanded it. He was the right hand man of the parish, ready with his cheque book when the church roof leaked. He provided hampers for the elderly and cash for the children's Christmas parties. I can still see his mug shot in the local rag smiling benevolently with an expression of 'Oh it's just great being able to help, thanks aren't necessary, you have my name, my photo, my business card and I'm quite content with that,' plastered all over his self satisfied gob.

As a family we were tied to him. There was Mom's pension that legally speaking he didn't have to honour. It was meant to be a secret, but somehow the whole parish knew about it. He had put the money up for Gerry and Joe's garage and loaned Alice the use of his Rolls for her wedding.

He was a powerful man, a big shark in a paddling pool, but everything he did was done with a view to payback in some form or another. You would never find him donating to famine stricken Africa, unless someone in the planning department had a relative there.

We all recognised him as a chancer, sly and cunning, but no one had him down as a complete bastard. It goes without saying that I didn't like him but I did like his house. It was like heaven with its deep pile carpets and constant warmth. Our house had an open fire in the dining room, that burned from October to March drawing everyone to it like a magnet, for the rest of the house was as cold as the arctic circle. There is an awful misconception in Britain about 'the cold north,' because I can tell you for sheer chill factor nothing beats the Kent coast, in terms of extremities it is definitely Britain's big toe.

The Condon's house was my idea of paradise; it had central heating, a stereo and a colour television. Mrs Condon or Olga as she graciously allowed me to call her was pale and delicate looking. I think she needed a green house environment just to survive.

When I first started babysitting for them they only had one daughter, three-year-old Grace. Now I know you weren't too keen on children Scarlett, if I recall properly, you detested them, crying nuisances you said they were, always in the way, but Grace was lovely. Getting paid to look after her was money for old rope. She was so placid the only job I had to do was demolish the Coke and crisps left out for me by Olga.

I'd spread my school books out on the table, turn the sound down on the television and switch the stereo on and dance to The Clash, Squeeze and even Slade with their advice 'girls grab the boys.'

Some chance, I never had a boyfriend at school, most of my friends did, even Magda, but I was too shy and home loving. I had a friend called Stephen who loved discussing Shakespeare, the failings of the UN and the fortunes of the Labour party, which in Kent were pretty depressing, but he wasn't a boyfriend. He was one of those meek and gentle boys most girls would love as a big sister. It wasn't a case of having no interest in boys; I just lacked the confidence to think they'd be interested in me.

Sometimes while dancing on the Condon's shag pile, I would fantasise about another life. Hot Chocolate would be thrashing it out on the stereo and I'd be dancing with Errol Brown, my eyes closed while he whispered disgusting things in my ear, begging me to join his backing band or he'd simply die, and that would be the end of Hot Chocolate. I'd be on the verge of agreeing, but then I'd catch sight of headlights through the curtains and I'd skid in my speed to turn the stereo off and the television up before sitting at the table gazing at my books nonchantly. Errol Brown was always pretty talented at making himself scarce.

A ritual always ensued. The Condon's would come in. I'd ask if they had a good time, she'd glance round the place as if making sure all was where she'd left it and ask about Grace and he'd rub his hands together briskly and say, 'Shall I take you home again Kathleen, or will we have one for the road?'

Usually he'd have two.

I don't recall either of them ever answering my question. He'd take me home in his big purring Rolls and the minute I arrived; I'd say to Mom 'you will never guess what colour Parkinson's jacket was tonight.' As the only one with access to a colour television, I had real power. Mom liked Parkinson, but she was a bit disappointed when he announced to the world that he'd had a vasectomy. She was convinced it had made him look older, 'Just take a look at those bags under his eyes,' she'd say 'They weren't half that size before he had the job.' She made it sound like a variation of nip and tuck surgery, as if the missing parts were being stored elsewhere.

'No,' she'd say, 'He mightn't be Irish, but he likes his sport and his pint and he seems a normal enough kind of man.' In my family Scarlett there were certain criteria that made a man a man and both sport and alcohol ranked high on the list.

Those early teenage years, were happy days really Scarlett. As a family we were just about getting ourselves together after the shock of Daddy's accident. He was killed as he walked home from work one foggy November night. Knocked over by a car. I was twelve at the time and I don't remember much about it, mainly because I consciously buried the memory. I remember the tears, the guilt, and the constant reiterating of the word 'if.' The only thing I really learnt from it all was that as an O'Connell, the biggest crime you could ever commit was to wear your heart on your sleeve. Speaking to an outsider about your worries or your fears was ranked somewhere between prostitution and murder.

Life picked up again when Alice married her doctor and went to live in a smart, new build house. She continued to visit almost every day, but Eileen the middle sister who married just six months later, fled to South Africa with her fascist husband, big hearted Harry. There she amassed a massive collection of wooden reptiles and cried crocodile tears for the natives.

Joe and Gerry remained true Kentish boys and like all bad apples they never rolled far from the tree. Their garage was in the town centre and they were always popping in for tea and slander. It was almost as if they had never married.

Mike, the oldest brother taught in Devon, he'd gone to college in the West Country where he had met and married a French girl called Michelle. I remember her as small and fair haired with startling blue eyes, she reminded me of a goose because of her ability to look both haughty and wary at the same time. Mike spent most of his holidays in France so we hardly saw him and that caused Joe and Gerry to brand him a jumped up fart, because he seemed happy with his wife and capable of living outside his brother's pockets.

Only James and I lived at home; he taught at the local Catholic secondary school and was a real Mommy's boy. He spent his entire twenties engaged to Rosemary, an anaemic specimen of a girl. Everyone knew he didn't want to marry her; he just lacked the balls to be straight. He was more like a schoolboy than a teacher. It was Mom who got him up every morning, practically dressing him and urging him to do his books. It makes me weep to think he has the audacity to stand in front of children and tell them how to get their act together.

I was fourteen when I started babysitting for the Condon's; they had previously employed a string of au pairs, but none of them ever stayed long. One in fact left in less than twenty four hours. Rumour had it that Olga was a tyrant in the home and that earned the ape some sympathy.

They employed me as the trusted daughter of good Irish Catholics and they paid me well. They were always going out to fancy dinners. Mom told me once that Dad had suspected Condon was a mason, in spite of all his church crawling and genuflecting. She said that if she had proof, she'd forbid me to go in their house again, for it was well known that masons were in league with the devil. I remember thinking, 'Thank God you don't have proof Mom,' for it would have broken my heart to have lost my well-paid job. If she did though Scarlett, I wouldn't be sitting here now, writing this recollection of my slide down the chute into insanity.

Easter 1979, the Condon's went to Ireland and when they came back, Olga announced she was pregnant. How delighted she was, telling everyone how keen Jerh was to have a son. I worried briefly whether my funds would dry up, for Olga looked frail. That however, was just part of her attraction, when it came to doing things she liked, such as dressing up, she had the constitution of an ox. So my services stayed in demand. However after a hectic summer even Olga began to flag and the ape would phone up and leave messages for me like, 'Would Sinead be a total angel and look after Grace today after school?' I didn't mind, I loved the little girl. I did shopping for Olga, I fetched and carried, in fact Scarlett I was bit like your maid Prissy, except I never squealed, or gave out any bull about being a dab hand at childbirth.

I was fascinated with Olga, she was so different to anyone else I knew, she was so small, so neat and petite with wistful looking eyes that looked capable of shedding tears at the drop of a hat. I thought she was romantic, a lonesome woman from a far country. Now I recognise that look of hers as the trade mark of a woman who had sold her soul for a bit of Ming that turned out to have 'Made in Taiwan' stamped on its arse.

I used to wonder if she ever thought about Poland and if she was homesick, but I never asked her, because there was an aloofness about her, that made personal questions taboo. You could talk about films and books, but really interesting questions like 'Why did you marry that gobshite?' were a definite no go area. She was a mystery, considering that she had a fresh open looking face but a totally closed personality. Her accent also sounded more Swedish than Polish and that swelled the old bullfrog of an ape up even more.

Sometimes though when I played with Grace in the garden I'd see Olga pacing round and round the kitchen or wherever she was, stopping briefly before setting off again. Thinking about it now I think she probably suffered from panic attacks. In those far off days the only things that I thought could create panic were things like snarling dogs or juggernauts out of control. I didn't know that real panic only comes from within.

Yes, I think Olga must have suffered from anxiety; that is why she was so slim. Life is unfair and that is not a complaint Scarlett, just a statement of fact. Sometimes when I see something like say, a woman with a pert backside pushing a buggy uphill in the rain I think, 'That backside is her compensation for not owning a Shogun,'. But then, on another rainy day, I'll see a fat woman with a droopy arse sweeping the floor behind her, struggling up the same hill and I think, 'Bang goes the compensation theory.'

Olga never pushed prams in the rain, the ape wouldn't have approved, it would have reflected badly on him, and in turn when he entered the room well, Scarlett, Olga could have been one of your slaves from Tara, she fetched and carried and laughed to order. Was it love? Or was it a case of 'fair exchange is no robbery.' I didn't know then and I don't know now. But what I do know is that if I'd been her, I'd have settled for plain robbery.

Anyway, at the end of the Christmas term back in 1979, my school held a disco, and luckily for me it was to be held on a Friday, so it wouldn't clash with my Saturday night babysitting. I really thought my luck was in because a boy called Kevin had joined the sixth form and everyone fancied him, but he always paid particular attention to me. He too wanted to be a lawyer and his grandparents were Irish, so we had things in common.

I saved the money that I earned from babysitting for the Condon's and I bought a pair of high heeled black boots, a scarlet red halter neck top and a black satiny skirt.

My friend Clare and I went shopping on the afternoon of the big event, we did Littlewoods, British Home Stores and London Babe, a dingy little boutique that played loud music and had communal dressing rooms, a novelty in the back of beyond. We shopped there mainly because we liked the name, it made us think we were in London, not wind - swept Kent. Afterwards we went to Mario's an Italian owned café and ordered two frothy coffees and two coffee choux buns, they cost a fortune but they were delicious. If Mom had known we'd gone to Mario's she would have been furious; 'Giving your money to that dirty old man,' she'd have said, 'when you could have got soup and rolls for a fraction of the price in Littlewoods café.'

Mario the owner came over to us and sat down and began nosing through our bags and flirting in his usual dirty Mac manner. He made suggestive comments about Clare's eyes and my mouth. He said it was a known fact that women with long hair lasted longer in bed. Both Clare and I laughed but we had no idea what he was talking about. His words made us shiver because he cast his eyes up and down in a very strange manner and gave out gravelly sounding little laughs. A customer came in and Mario immediately leapt to his feet, because it was always a case of business is business with him. But before he disappeared, he bent over and picked the head of a poinsettia that was growing furiously in a pot behind me and said 'Take this my dear, wear it tonight and life will never be the same again.'

Clare laughed like a lunatic, when he pushed the red poinsettia into my hair, just above my left ear. I caught my reflection in the mirror opposite and the beauty of it shocked me, only it wasn't beauty really Scarlett, just the combination of a happy face, auburn hair shinning in the light and a startling flower.

That night, Mom helped me with my hair and I gave her the poinsettia with a clip to hold it in place, but I didn't tell her what Mario had said, she would have thrown the lovely flower in the fire if I had. She brushed my hair repeatedly until it shone and glittered in the light while James fiddled about hanging Christmas cards above the fireplace.

'Look at those boots,' he had said, 'She'll need a bloody parachute if she comes off them.'

That made Mom laugh, 'Don't be doing the Can Can in them girl,' she had warned.

Just before I left, Gerry popped in. His head had a smattering of snow on it and he gasped when he saw me. 'Eat your heart out Legs & Co' he said. It was the first time Scarlett that I had dressed like a normal teenager, in modern clothes ready for the big night out. I felt so excited, so grown up, this is what it was all about and it was so wonderful, intoxicating almost, the way all my family were rooting for me, telling me how lovely I was.

'You'll have to keep her under lock and key after tonight Mom,' said Gerry, 'She'll have a string of blokes after her,' and Mom replied.

'Of course she will, if she is anything like her mother.' Everyone was in such good form on my behalf. Looking back now, I find it incredible to think that the catastrophe awaiting me was silently and slowly unfolding in the wings.

Clare's mother drove us to the school hall. As I left the house, Mom dabbed some Chanel perfume on me from a tiny bottle that Dad had given her years before. She told me to be good, to be lucky and to be back by eleven o'clock. I made my way to the car with my coat pulled up over my head like a tent, feeling like a film star making an entrance.

Oh Scarlett, you set out to conquer Rhett dressed in your mother's curtains and the tail feathers of a dead cockerel, but me, I set out with a red poinsettia and my mother's perfume, to conquer my shyness and have fun in the real world. As I look back on that momentous occasion, I can see how riddled with irony it all was.

Other than Kevin, the boy I fancied, practically the entire school had turned up for the do. All of us were out to impress, I can still see loud-mouthed Julie Poulter bursting out of her blue sequinned top screeching, 'My God it's so embarrassing.' That's the wonder of Christmas Scarlett; even cretins like Julie become momentarily acceptable. I was downcast when I heard that

Kevin had to help out in his parent's pub, but since discos were rarer than hen's teeth in that backward little town, I put him to the back of my mind and set out to have fun.

All the hits from Christmas past were wheeled out for their annual outing, along with the hits of '79, The Pretenders, 'Brass in pocket' and Pink Floyd's 'Another brick in the wall.' But the song that will remain etched on my heart until I die was The Eagles 'There's gonna be a heartache tonight.' It had been a hit a few months previously and I barely remembered it. Clare and Sally and a few other girls who went to the same youth club, had a dance routine sorted out for it that involved a lot of hand clapping above the head and stamping of feet. It didn't take me long to join in. I sang along like a moron, unaware that I was foretelling my own future. Forever the lyrics of that night remain in my heart, a testimony to a time when life was simple.

But the thing is Scarlett, did it all change that night or were the events that happened, just a catalyst for a life that was simply destined to be lived out through a veil of mist?

I remember once when I was a child, playing in the garden, throwing an old tennis ball against the house. I told myself that if I could catch the ball in five consecutive throws, Joe or Alice would take me out to the cinema and relieve the crushing boredom. But, there was a bloody great drainpipe that ran down the middle of the wall, and on the fifth throw every time, the ball struck the pipe and went flying into the garden next door. I kept making excuses, saying this is the go that really counts, but no matter what I did, I couldn't get the ball to land in my hands on the throw that really mattered, so finally I flung the ball in the hedge and sat on the back door step.

The kitchen windows were steamed up because Mom was using the baby burco boiler, to boil the shirts and sheets clean. I hated Mom washing clothes. I hated the steam and the heat and her preoccupation and I detested that little boiler that belched out so much ugliness. It seemed impossible that something so small could contain so much. I used to watch as an endless stream of shirts, vest, towels and sheets emerged steaming hot. It was like that scene in the film Oliver when crafty old Fagin sets the idiot boy up to steal a never ending line of hankies from his pocket. On this particular day, I just sat and moped, picking the paint of the door. And then it suddenly struck me, that one day I'd look back and remember that boring day as a good day, because one day Mom would die. And that day would be so terrible that every day would be a good one in comparison to it.

Don't get me wrong Scarlett, I wasn't obsessed with death, in fact I hardly ever thought about it. The only reason I mention all this now, is that in writing to you, hedging around, trying to tell you my big secret, it dawns on me that it was always there, this fear of, well I don't know, just the fear of calamity being around the next corner.

But anyway, on the night of the big disco there wasn't a fear in my head. It must seem strange to you Scarlett, someone getting so excited about a piddling little dance, because you were always the centre of attraction, but that night all eyes were on me and that was definitely an exception to the rule.

The DJ put on a 70's version of the Can Can and we all linked arms and a contest started as to who could kick their legs the highest, I remember my legs going higher and higher and the drama teacher's backside being within an inch of my boot. I called out to Clare that Mr Simons was coming perilously close to getting a boot up the arse, and the rumour ran along the line and all eyes were fixed on my boot and Mr Simon's rear. As my line swayed forward the one he was in swayed back and the collision occurred. He let out a yelp and Clare who could barely stand for laughing lurched forward and pulled me down and we landed in a heap on the floor. For one fearful moment, I thought I might shame myself for eternity and piss myself laughing. I begged God to save me from disgrace and thankfully He obliged. But getting up in those boots was like getting a turtle of its back. I whispered to Clare that I was glad I had clean knickers on and she shouted back 'What, clean knickers, I'm just grateful I wore any.'

When I clambered up and turned round, I saw Mr Simons standing right in front of me. 'Was that your idea of a joke?' he asked and instantly I was back in the classroom on course for a bollocking. But then I saw the twinkle in his eye and he held out his arm and said 'Dance.'

And I did.

My first proper dance! Holding and being held, not jerking around like an electrocuted chicken to Abba. I was dead conscious of his hand on the base of my back and the slight tickle as his chin passed over my hair. All of us fancied Mr Simons, he was tall and blond and easy going. It was rumoured that he was living in sin with a bank clerk and the fact that he was unattainable made him doubly attractive. He was the first teacher I had ever heard use bad language, and that alone marked him out as a human amongst the aliens that generally taught us.

On one occasion during a drama lesson, we were told to improvise a scene, showing a group of foreign visitors around our town. We all acted very feeble and said there was nothing in that poky town worth showing anyone, but he said 'Rubbish, just put a bit of oomph into it, sound enthusiastic like this,' and he stretched out one hand like a dandy and put the other one on his hip and spoke as if addressing a small crowd. 'See here, our exquisite little harbour. If you look carefully you will see the yachts of many famous people. It's our proximity to London that does it. And well dear me, blow me down, who do we have here, bobbing among the waves? It's our old friend Mr Turd. He's a regular sight on this coastline.' You never knew what he would say except that it would be funny and not aimed at putting anyone down. I couldn't believe he was dancing with me, it was heaven and it was hell, dancing cheek to cheek. I was so conscious of my body skirting his that I nearly froze, but at the same time I was aware that my hand, the one he was holding was becoming increasingly sweaty. I wanted to pull it away and wipe it, but I didn't know how to do it without dragging his attention to it. I thought if he sees me wiping my hand he'll think 'What a grease monkey, I'd be better off sticking to my bank clerk.'

It was a perfect night and I didn't want it to end. Clare's mother, our chauffeur for the evening, was waiting for us outside in her battered old mini. While we had been dancing, snow had been falling and it was beginning to settle on the trees and hedges. I don't know what was wrong with Clare's mother, either she was a banned driver and was driving carefully to avoid detection or she'd been on the bottle. God she drove so slowly. I don't think she changed gear once. I know it was snowing but she was driving as if negotiating hairpin bends in the Alps, and I don't think there was enough snow to stop the trains and that is saying something.

When I got home, Mom was waiting in the hall with her coat on and the happy go lucky atmosphere of the early evening was gone. She was in foul form and set upon me immediately for being late. It had just gone midnight.

Condon had phoned. Olga was going into hospital, the baby was on its way and Mom had feared I wouldn't be home in time and she'd have to do the babysitting for him. She hated going round to his place, or having anything to do with him, beyond a social nod and enquiry. For all her talk about walking tall and looking the world straight in the eye, Mom suffered from a real Irish inferiority complex.

I offered to put the kettle on as a peace offering, but before she even answered, Condon arrived. He was very grave and gracious, he refused tea. 'I think we had better make a move,' he said all sensible and responsible. 'It looks like tonight is the big night.'

As we walked out the door, he called out to Mom, 'I'll run her back in the morning Bridget,' and Mom ever anxious to please said.

'She's more than capable of walking Jerh.'

Driving through the snow in the Rolls was a very different story to crawling through it in the old mini, the silence was incredible and I remember feeling as if I had been submerged under water. The snow fell continuously, twirling and twinkling in the headlights, it mesmerised me. Condon kept silent to begin with, he concentrated on the twists and turns of the narrow streets, but when we got out on to the main road, he turned to me and said.

'So what have you been up to tonight?' I told him about the school disco and he said something about being the belle of the ball and I replied that I hardly thought so. That caused him to tut tut and say, 'I bet you had queues of boys lined up waiting for the honour of a dance with you'. I thought, 'Hang on Mr; it was a disco, not old time music hall.'

No doubt, he was in good form because the birth of his baby was imminent. When we arrived at his place, Olga too seemed in good shape. She was sitting in her usual chair, the television was on with the sound turned down and beside her on the floor was a little floral overnight bag that she had probably packed the night following conception. Olga was organised.

She was breathing heavily and for some ridiculous reason, that made me feel coy and embarrassed. She leant over to pick up her bag and he was on it in a flash. 'Take it easy,' he said, as it were a sack of spuds she was about to heave onto her back. She then went through a whole litany of things I was to do. Grace liked soft but not runny eggs, apple not orange juice. He butted in, it was clear he was getting agitated. He said, 'For the love of God Olga, Sinead knows the routine, you are going away for a day, not a week.' He held her coat open for her like he was a gentleman, and placed it around her shoulders. She leaned forward and kissed me on the cheek. And that shocked me, because she was not a tactile person. I wished her good luck and asked him to phone me as soon as he had news, for I was both excited and anxious for her. In fact I seem to remember my own breathing getting loud and protracted, because I wanted her gone before the snow got any worse.

As soon as they left, the first thing I did was run upstairs to check on Grace, and finding her sound asleep I came back down to the lounge. The silence that night was deafening and for some strange reason the house felt distinctly eerie. I remember looking out of the window and being surprised at the ghostly appearance of the garden. Every tree and bush was thickly lined with snow, even the huge yew tree that Olga had spangled with white Christmas lights. She once told me that when she first came to England, she had been horrified by the garish multi coloured lights favoured by the English, she found them common.

What a snob she was Scarlett. Looking back on her now, I feel real contempt for her. She put it about that she was the daughter of a Polish count who had hit hard times under the communists, but for all any of us knew, she could have crawled out of some hovel in Gdansk.

I'm no poet Scarlett, believe me, but there are occasions when you discover how a poet happens upon a great line and that night was one of them. Watching those everlasting snowflakes, I wondered if they would ever stop. The landscape was beautiful and I don't want poor old Yeats to start spinning in his grave, but there was something terrible about the beauty of it all. It seemed so out of control. Who can prevent the snow from falling or the sea from rising if either of them chose to do so?

I thought about Olga and what she was going through, but I didn't dwell on it. The whole idea of childbirth terrified me. There was a picture of the Black Madonna of Krakow in the Condon's hallway, the only outward sign of Olga's heritage. I stood in front of it and said a quick prayer for her well being.

It was gone half past two in the morning, when Condon came back. I was dozing on the settee when he came in and I nearly died of fright when I heard the lounge door click open. When I saw it was only him, I was mighty relieved.

He came in rubbing his hands together briskly. 'Well Sinead?' he said. 'It's all over in record time too, a grand job, a grand job.'

I asked him if it was a boy and he shook his head. I said, 'Is it a girl?' and that made him laugh.

He said, 'Well I don't think there is any other option is there? It's a beautiful girl with a head of black hair just like her father's; we'll get the boy on another go.'

I asked after Olga and he said she was fine; 'Driving the cows home' was how he put it. There seemed nothing else to say, all was well. Mother and baby were safe. He was home. So, I got up to go to bed, but as I headed for the door, he said, 'Wait a moment Sinead, will we have a little drink to celebrate?'

It was all so innocent, there was no warning of what was about to unfold. If there had been I could have done something, made an excuse and bolted out the door. But I was too stupid, too naive to have any understanding. I hesitated before answering him because I was very tired, but it seemed mean spirited to say no when he so obviously wanted to celebrate his good news. I said I'd have a small one and he went over to the drinks cabinet in the corner of the room and poured two enormous whiskeys.

He handed one to me and said, 'Raise your glass to Olga, and Sinead, the most beautiful babysitter in the world.' I blushed when he said that. How could I possibly toast myself? I put the glass to my lips but the fumes alone almost singed them. I was a novice drinker back in those days. Lager shandy in the summer and piss weak vodka and lemonade at Christmas was my limit.

He finished his in a gulp and began sloshing more into his glass.

I can still see him, one arm resting on the mantelpiece, surveying the room like he was Lord of the Manor, instead of the Lord Fuckhead he really was. He looked across at me and raised his glass. 'Hurry up,' he said, 'there's plenty more where that comes from' and strode across with the bottle poised for pouring. When I put my hand over the glass to signify no more, he said. 'Oh come on, I can't believe old Frank's daughter would turn down whiskey.' But I refused to move my hand.

He slapped the bottle down on the table with a thud, like he was in a huff and made as if to walk back to the mantelpiece and then abruptly changed his mind. He turned and sat down beside me on the settee and began staring at me.

He stared so intently that I thought I must have dirt on my face or something. Finally, he asked me where my flower had gone and when I felt my hair, the clip alone was there, the poinsettia had escaped. I said I must have lost it in the car and he said it was a pity because when he had seen it earlier, he had thought how sexy it looked.

That was my cue to go, I knew less than nothing about men for all that I had four brothers but then they never acted like this old goat. I told him that I was very tired and that I wanted to go to bed. He said 'That sounds all right by me, let's go together.'

The next thing, his arm was around my shoulder. I edged forwards to slip it off, but he just raised it higher. So I stood up, but he immediately sprang up as well with the sudden energy of someone who had just knocked back a bottle of Lucozade and he grabbed my hand. I tried to pull it away, but he held it fast and said, 'Come on Sinead, I've always reckoned you could be something of a goer.'

As I think back now, I am flooded with a sense of bitterness Scarlett, because my mother's teachings were so duff and incomplete. I feel the way you did when you recognised that your mothers entire teaching about how to be a fine lady were useless when it came to getting a life after the war. When you found that lessons on how to be kind and gentle were hopeless skills when foraging for food and warmth, was all that mattered. My mother taught me so thoroughly the virtues of modesty and chastity and in the process, convinced me that women are always the instigator of men going astray. She used to say 'A woman could walk through an army of men and come out clean if she kept her eyes pure.'

That night I felt the responsibility was mine. The onus was on me to keep him straight, not him to behave. I had to leave him in no doubt that his advances were not welcomed. The task was all mine. I told him in a very prim voice not to speak to me in such a way. I reminded him that I was only there to look after his child. He laughed and said, 'Yes but a little fun never harmed anyone,' and began pressing himself towards me, as if his smart little answer had put paid to that objection.

In the following moments I leant two new things, men only hear what they want to hear, and they don't think with their brains. Mom had done a thorough job short-listing the failings of women, but she failed miserably in giving an accurate portrayal of men.

I remember casting my eyes quickly round the room to orientate where the door was because fear was obliterating every sense from my head and as I did so his eyes followed me. He said, 'Do you know Sinead your top is almost transparent in this light, and your breasts are so lovely and big, I can hardly keep my hands off them.' I felt nauseous. What was I supposed to say, 'Poor old you, what a tribulation?'

I tried to break free by stamping on his feet and wrestling my arms out of his grasp and when I finally broke away, I made a rush for the door, but he beat me to it. He leaned against it and

beckoned me towards him but I refused to move. I had no
weapon, other than tears. When he realised that I wasn't
coming, he walked over to me and as he did so, I froze. I
remember thinking, 'Jesus, this is it, this it,' but all he did was
kiss the top of my head. He told me not to be a baby, he hadn't
meant any harm, he was only teasing, and it was Christmas after
all and hadn't he fine news to celebrate. 'Go to bed,' he said,
'and thanks for everything.'

Once I got out of the room, I didn't know whether to go
upstairs or run and hide. Was I blowing it out of proportion?
Did all men act like this following the birth of a child? I tried to
reason with myself. He had apologised, but on the other hand he
had frightened me. I was so confused, I couldn't run and leave
Grace; not when I had been paid to look after her. In the end I
felt the safest option would be to sleep with her. He couldn't
possibly harm me in front of his daughter.

Fright had made me hot and bothered and getting into bed
with Grace was almost impossible because she had her arms
flung out and toys everywhere. When I eventually crept in, I just
lay there, fully dressed, shaking and praying. Every instinct told
me to get out of the house, but I felt powerless to move, it was
almost as if something inevitable was bound to happen. I just lay
there, straining to hear in the darkness.

Moments later I heard his footsteps on the stairs and I
begged God to send him straight to bed, but when I heard the
door of the guest room creak open, I knew I had made the
wrong call.

He called out 'Sinead,' and I kept silent as the dead, hoping
and praying that he'd do the impossible and disappear from the
face of the earth. My heart was beating so fast I felt it might
burst out of my chest and continue bouncing around the floor. I
just lay there, wishing myself invisible, but slowly and eerily the
door brushed open. And I saw him framed in the landing light.
Jesus, Mary and Joseph I have never seen anything more
obscene, he was in the nude, a gorilla on heat, the primate of all
bloody Ireland!

Never mind body hair, this was more a case of hair body. If a
scientist saw him they'd think they had discovered the missing

link. Stripped of his suit, his tie, his Rolls, he was a pure animal. His pelt was one thing but that was nothing compared to his appendage. I thought he was carrying a stick or a broom handle of some kind, but when he came over to the bed, I could tell it was no broom.

He ordered me out of the bed, in a tone of pure disgust, like I was some tramp that had wandered into his house.

I got out, careful not to disturb Grace; and keeping my back to the wall, I edged towards the door, but as I did so, he lurched forward like a puma, putting his hand over my mouth, and dragged me into the guest room, shutting the door with a backward kick. He wound my hair so tightly around his hand that I could feel my roots creaking and he warned me, that if I woke his daughter up, there would be hell to pay. And that is when it happened. He attacked me like a frenzied animal, nipping and growling and uttering such filthy, venomous, words.

It was fear of death that kept me conscious. I was convinced that if I passed out he would kill me. I remember thinking, it is actually happening, I am going to die, and it is worst than I ever imagined it to be. I fought back with my arms and legs, but they felt leaden, I was no match for him. I knew the only fight I could win was the mental one, I mustn't pass out. Eventually he stopped and heaved himself off me, as if exhausted with his efforts and in an instant I was up and out of the room.

When I got as far as the front door I heard him yelling 'Sinead, come back, come back,' but I moved even faster. There was a Chinese rug on the floor that Olga had bought the day before and it slipped under me and I fell and hit my head, but like Mohammed Ali I was down but not out. I leapt up and made for the front door. I yanked the handle but it wouldn't move, so I tore into the kitchen where I found the back door unlocked and unbolted.

I could hear his voice barking orders at me to return as if I were a disobedient dog, and the sound of it drove me on, I opened the door and set off across the snow, slipping and sliding, I had no idea where I was going, I just ran and slid and ran again.

Phoenix stopped writing, but her mind kept running, into the snow, and the dull, dark, starless December night sky. She shivered as she felt the snow crumble and crush beneath her as she slipped and fell repeatedly in her bid to get away from Condon and she clutched her chest, as she felt again, the crushing pain that made breathing almost impossible.

How could it have happened to her? O'Connell's were not fools, but she had acted with no more sense than a guinea hen. She put her hands over her face and though it burned hot from shame and humiliation, it did nothing to remove the chill of despair from her heart.

It was all so futile, why did she think she could escape the past, it was catching up on her and there was no escape route. When she had written her first letter to Scarlett, she had been thrilled with a sense of optimism, overwhelmed with a sense of wonder, of discovery. She wanted to know more about the girl she had been. The light hearted easygoing girl, who laughed with her friends, the girl who went shopping and did every day fun things, the girl who wanted to save the world, but was still capable of lying to priests.

Now, remembering back to that night, the picture was knocked askew. She no longer saw a light hearted girl, the well-meaning baby of the family, she saw only a weak and foolish one and self-hate and contempt bubbled up under her skin.

She closed the red book and locked it away in the drawer and went downstairs, straight to the front door, which she pulled open. It was well below freezing point, but she never even felt the chill air that slunk in around her ankles. She was only aware of a faint feeling of claustrophobia. It was almost as if by opening the door she was providing an escape route for the spirit unleashed by her letter.

But the dark starless January night with its smell of winter and hushed silence, only heightened her fear. She wanted Jack home, she wanted to talk him, hear him laugh; remonstrate with him for being late. And she wanted the distraction of Daisy, she wanted to lift her up and hide from the past behind a barrage of routine as she bathed the child and attempted to listen to her excited chatter.

However, there was no sign of either Daisy or Jack. He had taken her at her word and was giving her a wide berth.

She closed the door and headed for the front room, where she poured herself a whiskey and sat on an armchair, staring morosely at the fire. What she wondered was the point of it all? Why had she raked up the past? Nothing could undo what had been done, the past was coming back and nothing in the world was strong enough to keep it at bay.

A picture of the shrink sitting relaxed and crossed legged flashed into her mind causing a surge of repugnance to sweep through her. Suddenly the idea of seeing a therapist and taking her advice, seemed about as pointless as putting a sticking plaster on an amputation.

Chapter Four

Pointless or not the operation had begun, and though still in its early stages it had already revealed something, Phoenix found difficult to comprehend. Being by nature pragmatic, her pragmatism often extended to effortlessly twisting the facts of any situation to suit her agenda. But somehow, when it came to writing to Scarlett, Phoenix found she was incapable of relaying the past anyway other than how it had been. She took to rereading the letters, often with a forbidding sense of disbelief which caused her hands to shake and her face to redden. Sometimes she felt as if she had stumbled upon the shocking diary of a previously blameless character. Jack had often told her that she would have trouble recognising the truth, even if it leapt up and hit her on the head. Now it seemed he was being proven right.

An overwhelming urge to scribble through a line or exchange one word for another often possessed her, but she never bowed to it. Phoenix who could and frequently did tell bare faced lies without a qualm of conscience, suddenly found herself in the unique position of having to face the truth at her own instigation. An image of her youthful self was beginning to emerge and it was one that filled her with disgust and loathing, but try as she might, she could not alter or tamper with the image one little bit..

For a while, she swore to herself that she would abandon the idea of writing to Scarlett. It hadn't bought her any peace. In fact, since putting pen to paper, she had experienced a higher degree of anxiety, which in turn created an even greater need within her for her faithful VW.

What was more, she felt the distinct possibility that the whole idea was jinxed. Digging up the past had not changed anything, it had merely uprooted and replanted in the wrong place, something that should have been left in the dark.

But try as she might to ignore it, her unfinished letter called out to her through the nights that followed its creation and its siren call drew her back more deftly and ominously than any call of a mermaid, luring sailors to imminent death on the rocks.

By taking up the pen, she had unleashed the demon she had long ago banished to the shadows of her mind. He had been released from his cage and every night he prowled through her dreams like the red fox Jack told Daisy about, who padded softly through the hen houses of his father's farm leaving a trail of destruction behind him. There had to be a way out of this nightmare, it was just unfortunate that the key to it lay in the past. But there was no option, she had to go back.

Chapter Five

When Jack Keane had been sent out to McDonald's with his daughter on that cold January afternoon, he hadn't obediently returned home a few hours later as Phoenix had expected. He had in fact returned after midnight, only to find Phoenix asleep on the settee, the room smelling like a distillery and the television blaring.

So much for tidying up, the room was in disarray with books and magazines strewn around and the chairs and cushions out of place. He smiled when he caught sight of an untouched bottle of Powers cowering under the table like a straight -laced spinster fearful of being asked for a dance. 'The one that got away,' he thought as he replaced it back in the cupboard.

After decanting the sleeping Daisy into her bed, he had descended the stairs braced for a fight, since he knew falling asleep without hiding her evidence had been an oversight, and that Phoenix would curse and swear her way out of admitting she had gone on a bender. When he had woken her up though, there had been no anger, no harsh words, only a momentary look of confusion followed by a resigned look of indifference.

Itching to rub some salt in the wound, Jack had offered her a drink, 'Have one,' he said, raising his own glass. 'I'm sure you've left some,' but she ignored the jibe and brushed past him heading straight for the stairs. There she stopped briefly before turning her head with apparent difficulty in order to flash a look of contempt at him, before promptly tripping on the first step and swearing profusely in the process.

'Jesus falls for the first time,' he said reverently as he bent down to help her up, but she gave no response. Whiskey and valium had dulled her senses she no longer had a need for Jack's company.

Her departure left him feeling cheated, he had come home with the intention of discussing a plan he had hatched that very evening and for a moment he pondered whether to try and cajole her round, but finally he decided against it. When it came to arguing the toss, Phoenix definitely had more stamina than he did.

It was a pity though, Jack had thought, as he slowly removed his shoes, because although he was the undisputed master of cold calling, she was undoubtedly the mistress of consolidation; and he would have welcomed her opinion on what should be his next move.

Jack hadn't taken Daisy to McDonald's; he had abandoned that idea almost the moment he had driven out the gate. Instead he stopped off in Wimbledon, at Hill's department store, where he bought Daisy a toy, much bigger and grander than any freebie from McDonald's before heading to the Black Swan in Clapham. It had been refurbished since the days when he frequented it, now it boasted Sky television, wooden decking and even a children's menu. All part of a desperate attempt to attract a wider clientele.

There was no longer sawdust on the floor, or the all-pervading smell of sweat and dust, that was once its famed trademark. Even the vinyl chairs and stools with the slashed seats had been replaced with softer, more luxurious looking red velour ones. But it takes more than makeup, to disguise a leopard.

The new proprietor was an ex contractor, working his dream and living the nightmare of owning an English pub. He had planned a good old -fashioned London one, 'a touch of the East End in Clapham.' A pub where wives and kids would be welcome, when business was slack, after the real punters, the suited office workers and shop girls had gone home.

But it hadn't turned out that way. Contractors and labourers still flocked to the Black Swan, out of habit; the same habit that caused them to steer their families well clear of it, on account of not wanting to mix business with pleasure.

Jack seldom frequented the place; he hadn't much need of it anymore since most of his gangs came from a steady pool of workers arranged for him by his brother Danny in Cork. Besides that, Jack disliked the association of the Black Swan with the mistake and miscalculation he had made there, all those years ago.

He had gone there on the look- out for one particular person. While Daisy had been checking out the toys, Jack had checked his watch, wondering what to do and where to go. He had no intention of jumping through hoops for Phoenix and there was no way he was going to go back home and allow her to admit him in, like he was some kind of stray dog. It was coming up to almost half past five and being a Saturday that could only mean one thing. The final round up of sports results would be on the television and Shitlegs O'Carolan would be in the Black Swan ready for his Saturday night ritual of tossing his pools coupon and racing slips to the wind.

'Shitlegs O'Carolan,' was a third rate and third generation Irish plasterer, a talisman of prosperity for the London construction business. When he was in work, it was a sure sign London was booming. Nobody called on his services, unless staff shortages had reached critical. In an industry renowned for its lack of refinement, O'Carolan was the uncrowned king of crudity; he was despised for both his animal like habits and foul language.

But these characteristics; were only a few of many reasons why several pub proprietors had banned him from their premises. In an era where pub landlords are expected to be social workers, O'Carolan was too big a risk to livelihood to entertain. Fights, drug dealers and the police; invariably trailed him like a shadow.

The Black Swan only tolerated him for reasons best known to the landlord alone, and on condition that he complied with several agreed terms. Namely, that he stayed away from the restaurant area, declined from asking for credit and kept his bodily functions and fluids under strict control. The only member of staff allowed to serve him was Brian, a one-eared barman from Derry, who had once given O'Carolan a hiding, on account of a sick joke O'Carolan had told about elephants and the size of their ears. O'Carolan was now more likely to attempt lip reading rather than risk asking anyone to speak up in Brian's presence.

Women in particular disliked O'Carolan; for he was never one to underestimate his lack of charm. He held a sad, sincere, conviction that all members of the opposite sex secretly desired him and only ignored him on account of their own lack of self worth.

Jack first met him back in the seventies, a few weeks after setting up his own business. O'Carolan had swaggered across to him one evening offering advice regarding cheap labour in exchange for commission. But armed with the knowledge supplied by Polly, Jack turned his offer down as flatly as he would a chronic case of herpes. He promptly christened him 'Shitlegs' and made a mental note, to avoid him like dog shit on a doorstep.

But now, things had changed, Jack was suddenly very eager to further his acquaintance with O'Carolan, for he had reason to believe O'Carolan might be keen in the near future, to offload some run down garages and sheds in Penge he had acquired years ago in a 'sting' operation.

It was a sting that backfired, leaving O'Carolan badly stung. Instead of cheating a well known South London hood out of property ripe for development, he ended up with a row of ramshackle garages, in a dead end zone that were frankly of no use to man or beast. With the possible exception of the rats that made their nests in them.

But all that was about to change, Jack had recently completed work in the area and had purchased property, with guaranteed planning consent to demolish, paving the way to O'Carolan's lost kingdom.

It was common knowledge that O'Carolan's wife was seeking a divorce - she had spent too many nights in refuges, and this time she meant business. He was devastated; like all bullies the moment the worm turned he professed incredulity and saw himself as the victim. 'Haven't I always kept a roof over her head and food on the table?' he asked anyone who would listen, as if that could possibly make up for years of beating and brutality.

While others speculated as to why it had taken so long for the gentle and refined wife of O'Carolan to see sense, Jack had assumed that disposal of his assets would be O'Carolan's top priority, and he was right. O'Carolan wanted his property sold and out of the equation, before any divorce lawyer saw fit to make sure that his wife and children, benefited from them. It was going to be a long, low key transaction.

After settling his daughter with food and drink, with the aid of some overly interested barmaids, Jack had settled himself to the task of fleecing O'Carolan. A boring night had ensued. He had listened with a commendable show of interest, as O'Carolan detailed his life story. Nothing Jack heard surprised or delighted him. He could have written the script himself, for it was one he had heard, countless times, from a variety of losers, all of whom sang from the same hymn sheet, of missed opportunity.

He listened gravely, with disinterested, honest broker written all over his face, aware all the time that what O'Carolan lacked in intelligence, he more than made up for with cunning. But by the end of the evening, Jack had done a thorough job in confirming O'Carolan's fear, that the property market was shaky at best. The likes of 'poor' O'Carolan with his skills and acumen would be better off relocating to a less expensive part of the country. There he could start again and meet a woman who deserved him - (preferably one with genital warts,) Jack had thought to himself as he raised his glass to O'Carolan's.

The fact that Jack had taken Daisy to the Black Swan did not endear him to Phoenix. There was a time when she would have been suspicious of such a visit, for she knew the history of the Black Swan and its place in Jack's heart. But now she was too preoccupied with her own history, to bother worrying about what part nostalgia played in Jack's decision, to revisit his old hunting grounds.

She was extremely aggravated though, that he had taken Daisy to a place where people knew her. They would surely question what she was thinking off, letting her child stay out so late. When he tried to reassure her that one of the barmaids had taken particular care of Daisy, even taking her into the landlord's living room, to eat her food in a smoke free environment, she had descended into full blown anger. 'Why didn't you invite the NSPCC along as well?' she had shouted, mortified at the damage done to her reputation, 'Or go the full bloody shilling and give her some bloody flowers to sell.'

She was slightly mollified however, when he told her that the bar staff at the Swan had been under the impression that Phoenix was away for the weekend, and she brightened visibly, when he told her about O'Carolan. She detested the man and the thought of cheating him gave her some pleasure.

For a while, peace reigned in a cool atmosphere, and both Jack and Phoenix turned their full attention to work. She had VAT problems to solve and he was taken up with the launch of a new division of his company, one that aimed to specialise in the refurbishment of old and historic houses.

Although Phoenix gave every impression, of being consumed with her work, she was in fact becoming more obsessed with her letters to Scarlett. For the first time it dawned on her that although the memories of Condon had possessed her for most of her life, she had never once looked back on the events of '79 in a systematic manner.

Now, she was like a detective, going back to the scene of an old crime armed with new methods of investigation. What had been revealed was distasteful, but she was practical enough to know that she would never have peace again until she found the source of her newly awakened anxiety.

She had learnt something useful from that night, when Jack had stayed out. Her letters were revealing and bringing back into her life, people and events that had once had control of her. She needed a barrier between herself and the past and that barrier was the people who made up the present.

'I won't make the same mistake,' she told herself. 'I'll only write when Jack or Daisy is around, that way if the fear gets too much, I'll have distraction.'

So Phoenix took to getting up during the night to continue her correspondence, comforted by the thought of Jack and Daisy sleeping nearby, ready to turn to should the past get too heavy. What she would tell Jack if he came looking for her, she didn't know; she would think about that when it happened.

One cold February night, as Jack lay sleeping, after a momentous day which had seen his business extend into Sussex, Phoenix began her next letter.

Dear Scarlett,   **11th February 2001.**

I remember reading, that once you left the Fayetteville Academy
for young ladies, you never read a book willingly in your life
and thankfully Jack has that much in common with you. His
reading extends to bills, statements, estimates and the occasional
glimpse at the Racing Post. So there is little chance of him
reading my letters should he ever come across them accidentally.

He is no Philistine, he's just a man who likes living in the real
world and I think that's what probably attracted me to him in
the first place. When we first met, he took me to the Derby at
Epsom. We went by train so that we could both have a decent
drink and on the way back, we were pissed and began messing
about like a couple of vandals. Jack chased me round the empty
carriage and I had to clamber over several seats to avoid him,
but as I did so one of my heels punctured holes in the fabric.
Jack said he was going to report me to British Rail and not to be
surprised if I saw my mug shot on a poster, wanted, for criminal
damage.

But the train came to a sudden halt and we both fell backwards off the seat. Jack leapt up thinking it was Clapham, but
when he swung open the slam door I heard him shout, 'Shit,
we've missed Clapham, we are on the Thames.' The train was
on a bridge waiting for a signal. It should have been no big deal,
it simply meant we'd have to get a train back out of Victoria.
But I panicked. I began shaking and gasping for breath, all the
time getting more and more disorientated.

I had whiskey in my bag but I couldn't haul it out in front of
a man I hardly knew. Getting stoned in a pub is one thing, but
carrying booze around like some kind of inhaler when you are
past seventeen is hardly a turn on. Jack thought I was playing
about at first, but when he saw it was for real, a flash of panic
swept right across his face. He must have thought, 'What the
hell I have I picked up with here?'

I told him that I had a bit of a thing about the river, I tried to
make light of it, because I didn't want to frighten him off, but it
was true. I did and I still do have a phobia about the Thames. In
a city where every eventuality has been legislated for from
smoking on the tube to leaping off a bus, the Thames is one big

pool of opportunity for instant oblivion. It's a wonder it hasn't been drained.

He said 'You are not the only one, from what I've heard, if the chemicals don't get you, the rats piss will.'

I said 'Oh no, it's not like that,' and then I nearly knocked the entire relationship on the head by asking him if he had by any chance, heard of, The Heart of Darkness' by Joseph Conrad.

He said 'No, but if you are searching for a heart of gold, I know a bloke who might see you right.'

He's incapable of taking anything seriously; it's a condition he was born with. I tried to tell him about this book I had once read. There is a narrator in it who talks about a boat sliding down the Thames on its way to the 'dark continent' but Jack just laughed. I can tell you though, Scarlett, that book did for the hairs on the back of my neck, exactly what Viagra promises to do for every world weary John Thomas in the land. I wanted Jack to know that my panic was based on something, I didn't want him thinking I was some kind of crank who gets excited after a few drinks, but it just went over his head, he wasn't interested in my explanation.

I'm inclined to think Scarlett, that you too would dismiss it as a load of rot. He laughed when I tried to explain this notion about all of us having a heart of darkness. He just said. 'Well now, this Conrad fellow must have been a sad bastard if it took a trip to Africa to find out what an average five year old could have told him in seconds, 'never tell anyone you have Rolo's in your lunch box.'

I don't care what Jack thinks, I love that book Scarlett. Sometimes it is just too easy to close your mind to ideas and possibilities that are unpleasant to face and that is exactly what I tried to do on that early morning, back in 1979, when I fled Condon's house.

That was the start of me beginning to face the world as it is and not how I wanted it to be. It became a marker for all time and everything that has happened to me since, can be traced in one way or another, to that particular time.

What if I had frozen to death in the snow? Would Condon have been charged, or would there have been a cover up? What made me decide to go back to the house? I don't remember making a conscious decision. Sometimes I feel so fatalistic. Is there really any choice in life, we work and plan and yet who knows if it is all preordained anyway. We think we make choices but perhaps we are just following what is already laid out for us.

I just don't know, but back in 1979 there was one thing I did know. I had to get my clothes back. The years of brainwashing had worked. Dignity was much more important than justice; I could go home defiled, but not undressed.

When I left Condon's house, I had no idea where I was going, I just kept moving because hiding from him was all that mattered. Eventually though, I came to a stop near an old disused chapel. There was a low wall around the graveyard and I climbed over it and hid beside a tree. I can't recall what went through my mind. I think part of me thought I was dead and in some kind of after - life and yet in another way I felt like an onlooker watching over someone else's destruction.

There was a phone box across the road, and my first thought was Mom, but I had no money. I needed to speak to somebody and in confusion I phoned the operator but when she answered, I couldn't speak. She kept repeating, 'Caller, what do you want?' and after she had asked about five or six times, all I could reply was.

'I'm here.'

She didn't hang up or berate me, she was very calm. She said, 'Take your time and tell me what is wrong.' Eventually, I told her that I had been attacked, but as I had no clothes, I couldn't get home. The really incredible thing Scarlett is that she believed me. She really did and that fact still astounds me today. There was no doubt in her voice and no probing. She said, 'You sound very young, and if you have been raped, you will be in need of medical attention, so I'm going to divert your call to the emergency services, please hold on and I'll be back.'

But that was it, once she mentioned that dreaded word; I couldn't hold on anymore. It was too terrible to even think about, never mind speak of, as a fact.

I put the phone down and I think it was then that I realised the only way out of the situation with any integrity, was to go back to Condon's house and wait for daylight. Grace would be some kind of bodyguard and I could get dressed and go home and hand it over to Mom to deal with.

The return to Condon's house was hell. Each time I got myself ready to go, a car or milk float would pass, wheels spinning in the snow and at one point a police car went past really slowly and I had to hide behind a hedge. The trip that had taken me less than two minutes to complete Lynford Christy style, took what felt like hours to repeat.

When I reached the ape's place, all the lights in the house were on. I crawled into the porch and must have either fallen asleep or passed out because I recall opening my eyes to see Condon standing there.

He was dressed and he was crying. He kept repeating 'I don't know what happened, I'm so sorry Sinead.' When I didn't answer, he bent down and pulled my arm and immediately leapt back in fright, 'Oh Christ,' he said. 'Get dressed immediately'.

Actor, pretender that he is, even he couldn't conceal the panic in his voice. He must have thought, 'Shit she's going to die of hypothermia and how will I get out of that one?'

Even in the state I was in Scarlett, I was still aware of my lack of clothes and there was no way I was standing up without them in front of my attacker. He caught on eventually, went inside and reappeared with a blanket, which he draped over my shoulders. I stood up, but I was shaking so violently that I promptly fell back down again. I heard him stammer something along the lines of 'there, there,' and I felt his hands on my shoulder as he propelled me into the house, along the hallway and into the lounge. He guided me into the armchair where Olga had sat only hours before. I can't begin to explain what went through my mind but I do remember catching sight of Olga's mules, next to the stereo and an empty coffee cup that looked weirdly forlorn.

I can still remember his touch, because I can still feel it. He cried and he apologised and yet his touch had the feel of belonging to a man who was disgusted by a terrible event that had absolutely nothing to do with him. In Jerh Condon's eyes, I was the defiled - he was just responding like the Good Samaritan to an evil done by somebody else. He made tea, he ran a bath for me, emptying half of Olga's oils and bubbles and God knows what else into it. I remember him, fetching and carrying, and all the while, my eyes and ears searched for a sign of Grace's presence.

I needed somebody, anybody, to break the stifling terror of being alone with him again. I certainly didn't want a bath. I just wanted to be home. Home with Mom, to tell her everything and hand responsibility over to her. But he insisted on the bath, and it was only years later, when I saw a programme on forensics, that I realised why it was so imperative to him.

He set out for me a skirt and top belonging to Olga, since I had forgotten to bring a change of clothes with me. Hidden between the skirt and top were some tights and underwear belonging to his wife.

I stepped into the bath and leapt out again immediately. It was soapy and my entire body felt raw and the foam stung my skin. When I emerged from it, I saw my face in the mirror and the sight of it frightened me. I remembered the reflection I had seen in Mario's café, when I had caught sight of myself with the red poinsettia. That had been a happy youthful face; it bore no resemblance to the beaten dejected one I saw in Condon's mirror.

That was the moment when I fully realised what had taken place.

Up to then, my mind had skirted over what had happened but when I saw my reflection that was the first time, I acknowledged that I had been raped. I had had sex. Did it show on my face? When I got home would Mom open the door and instantly know what had happened. Not the details, but the facts? I sat on the bath and cried and the really mad thing is Scarlett, I held myself to blame. If I had not been there, it would not have happened, it was my fault.

When I eventually got dressed, I went downstairs with my black skirt and torn crimson top in a carrier bag and made for the front door. I had no intention of speaking to the ape again. I wanted to be home, but he must have heard the click of the door because suddenly the lounge door sprung open and he dashed out looking panic-stricken.

'Oh Jesus girl,' he said. 'You can't walk home, I'll drive you', but when he caught sight of my face he stepped back in shock. He took me by the arm and placed me again in Olga's chair.

I didn't have it in me to fight. He bent down and took my right hand in one of his paws and clasped the other one on top. 'Sinead,' he said. 'I just don't know what to say.' I said nothing. I wondered for a moment if I would ever be able to speak again. He tried to get a response by squeezing my hand. 'I've behaved terribly,' he said. 'Please forgive me,' He spoke as if he were apologising for something like reciting an inappropriate joke or belching at a dinner party.

I remember looking down at his thick curly black hair and the shiver of revulsion that ran through me which he must have mistaken for a sign that I was cold because he leaned forward and switched the gas fire up. As he did so, I caught sight of his hands and I found myself looking at them as if I'd never seen them before. They were big, hairy and brutal. I felt an immense desire to scream 'Let me go home you great hairy bastard, I want to see my mother, I want to tell my family about you.' But years of respectability saved the day, you don't give out to strangers or friends, only family.

It has taken me years to articulate the thoughts and feelings that ran through me on that bleak, cold morning, but fundamentally, that was the day when I finished with men forever. If all the flirting, the flowers, the simpering, the kisses, the discos and the car rides, if they were all just a preamble for that grotesque thing that had happened to me, well the world could keep it. I wanted nothing to do with it.

I think the ape must have had some idea of what was going through my mind because he became more persistent. He squeezed my hand yet again and this time he said,

'Sinead, I'm in no position to ask any thing of you, I've acted disgracefully, I really do not know what came over me. It must have been the drink and you looked so lovely, but I beg of you, please don't let Olga ever know, it would break her heart and she loves you so much, I think the shock might kill her.'

He stopped, expecting me to answer but I couldn't speak. So many things were rushing through my mind. I thought about my mother, the shock she would have, my brothers and sisters, the anger, the revulsion and the shame. In my heart though, there was a seed of doubt, a seed that told me that part of the revulsion would be for me too. Mom always referred to sexually experienced people as 'damaged goods.' Did it make any difference how the damage was done?

He was desperate for clues on how to play the situation because he didn't give up in his attempts to get a reaction from me. 'Please Sinead,' he said. 'Tell me you will not breathe a word of this, I am so sorry. I'll do anything. Please Sinead, think of Olga, think of Grace, think of the new baby.'

When he mentioned the baby I was thrown. I had forgotten why I was there and slowly it all swam into focus. Olga was in hospital with the new baby, the new baby girl.

But why should I think about his family when less than hours earlier he hadn't given a fuck for any of them? I couldn't bring myself to speak and I certainly could not bear to look at him. He reached out with his fingers and tried to turn my face round to face him but I closed my eyes, I would not look at him.

He then became insistent, almost aggressive 'Sinead,' he said. 'Say you won't tell.' It was a command, not a request and I nodded, not because I was agreeing, but because I figured it was the only way to shut the bastard up. He squeezed my poor old hand again and raised it to his lips. Jesus he was gross.

'I will not let you down,' he said. 'I will help you in any way I can and when you go away to college, you'll never be short of money.'

Oh that bastard was a pure master of the Freudian slip. The future worried him all right. He was already thinking and hoping there would be a day when I wouldn't be around, reminding him of his actions, not the rape, but his pathetic crawling, begging and pleading.

I was spared more from the gobshite when the lounge door opened and Grace appeared in her pink pyjamas, teddy in hand. He instantly pulled a hankie out of his pocket and flung it at me whispering. 'Dry your eyes, for God's sake, don't let the child see you like this,' He walked over to his daughter and lifted her high into the air and told her that 'poor Sinead' had a terrible cold and had to be looked after.

I sensed rather than saw Grace wriggle out of his arms and the next thing I knew she was pulling herself onto my lap. I felt her soft little hand on my arm and glimpsed her gentle concerned little face. I said, 'Sorry Grace, I have a terrible cold.' It was all I could say but why say it, why didn't I scream and alert the child, alert the world?

I couldn't do it, because she looked so innocent and to destroy her trust would have been an assault on her.

The ape, perhaps sensing danger, came over and picked her up, 'I've some great news for you,' he said. 'Mama has gone and got you a new sister.'

Insensitive brute, up to that point Grace hadn't even been aware that her mother wasn't there. She began to cry and whine and the noise caused my head to throb even more. Eventually the ape took her out of the room.

I can't believe how pathetic I was.

I just sat there, numb and snivelling, unable to speak. Do you know Scarlett, sitting there that bizarre morning, pain shuddering through me, face waxed with snot, I really believed the tears would never stop. But of course they did, just as the snow that I thought would fall forever the previous night ceased, so did the tears, eventually.

It was a very concerned looking ape who crept stealthily back into the room to see me. God he was persistent, he crouched down beside me and started again. 'Please Sinead I know I have no right to expect anything, but please think of Grace, think of Olga and think of your mother.'

I remember thinking 'What has this got to do with my mother?' And if was almost as if the ape could read me, because he said. 'It would break your mother's heart to know what you have gone through.'

He couldn't bring himself to say the word 'rape' anymore than I could. It was the ultimate. Total degradation! It spelt ruin. If voluntary, willingly enjoyed sex leads to second hand status, then rape puts you thoroughly in the 'casualty corner' section of life.

How clever he was. At the time, I genuinely believed that as shite as he undoubtedly was, he was doing his best for everyone given the circumstances. But as the years have rolled by Scarlett, I began to realise just what a predator he was. Every word, every tear, every squeeze, was him manipulating, extracting himself from the misery all around him, passing responsibility for Olga, for Grace, for Mom, for everyone, onto me.

For years I have carried his guilt on my back and his words in my mind word for word, word perfect. And it's not just the injustice of it all that really gets to me, because I'm not a fool. I know enough about the world to know that the good guy doesn't win, that's just Hollywood bollocks to excuse so many 'watch the shit hit the fan' films. Reality is a very different thing. I have never got even with him.

When people strain to say something complimentary about me, they say things like, 'You have to hand it to Phoenix, she's to the point, she takes no messing, it's just her way,' But what they don't know Scarlett is that it is all learned. And the learning nearly cracked me. I couldn't remain the same, I had to change just to survive, like you did when you returned to Tara and found nothing but ruin. You didn't want to be a bully Scarlett, but when you are uncertain of who you are and the authority you have, sometimes the only way forward is to frighten people, from ever questioning you.

Twenty years later the events of that night are still a secret. Jack hasn't the faintest idea what I'm hiding. Sometimes when he starts effing about Tosh his ganger or some other helpless creature that works for him he explodes and says, 'Tell me, do you know of a bigger arsehole than that bum?' and I have to swallow, because I want to yelp. 'Jerh Condon wins hands down.'

But I stop, because I could never tell Jack about the ape. He'd never be able to handle it, he can't even watch films with ambiguous endings; the bastard always has to get the bullet for Jack to be satisfied.

No, Scarlett, I can't tell Jack what happened and if I'm truthful, which I seldom am, it has nothing to do with Jack's fine sense of justice, but everything to do with his concept of me. I just can't do it.

Phoenix

Chapter Six

The year 2001 unravelled slowly, as a bleak and dismal one, with the weather by turns wet and blustery. There was little for anyone to be upbeat about. January had brought the revelation that the mass killer Dr Shipman far from killing a few old ladies had in fact probably killed hundreds and that the killers of a Liverpool baby whose name and face was etched on the conscience of the entire country, were to get anonymity for life.

Even Phoenix, never one to have great interest in news that didn't affect her personally, grew more agitated at the daily recitation of yet more grim tidings. It made her feel as if a mist of doom was enveloping not just herself but the whole of Britain. She callously rebuked Carolyn for wasting time when she bought up the case of a little West African girl who had been murdered by her carers 'right under the noses' of London social workers. She felt she would go mad if anyone broached her with more details of misery and death. She was drowning in despair as it was and the last thing she needed was a parcel of lifeboat puncturers around her.

But the news in Britain during the early part of 2001 was grim, and no matter how Phoenix might want to escape reality there was no hiding from it. In an effort to find something, if not light –hearted, at least not death orientated to focus on, the news media began to speculate about the timing of the next election. Would Blair be daring they pondered and announce an April poll. Or would he play safe and opt for June like most of the political pundits predicted?

But soon all talk of an election was hushed, as a disaster of gigantic proportions afflicted the British psyche.

One February morning as Jack and Phoenix lay in bed lulled into dreaminess by the lashing rain that hurled itself against the window; they heard the first mention of something that was to dominate the news for most of the following year.

Foot and Mouth had been found in an abattoir in Essex. There was nothing in that first broadcast to indicate how serious that find was to be, but within weeks, the true horror became apparent. All over the country, new cases popped up like mushrooms in a forest and vast areas of the countryside, were cut-off in a bid to stem the growth.

Night after night, the news ran stories concerning people in Wellington boots, whose entire livelihoods were being destroyed in front of their very eyes, as masses of afflicted sheep and cattle were burnt like ritual offerings. For a nation that proclaimed to be animal loving to its very core, the sight of such overwhelming suffering in the animal kingdom was almost too much to bear.

Initially Phoenix was sceptical. She dismissed the whole drama as a ruse by farmers, to get compensation for cows they couldn't dispose of on account of them being mad, thanks to the cannibalistic diet they had been reared on. But as the outbreak grew and the media began focusing on stories of personal ruin, her opinion changed.

Tales of people head, neck and tail in debt, due to already difficult farming conditions alarmed her, as did reports of people fighting to keep a business that had been in their families for generations. The bigger picture of agricultural ruin she dismissed out of hand. It was the undercurrent of fear she detected in the individuals interviewed that concerned her, and bought too readily to mind; the fear she was fighting. How could people face a future without their home and income when they were qualified to do nothing but feed and kill animals for a living? There was a lack of control underpinning the whole drama and that worried her.

She could understand the terror most farmers were feeling, she could not however, understand the grief of her workers, who shed tears over the culling of cattle. In her eyes, they were only animals who were going to die anyway. Foot and Mouth simply meant they would never reach the dizzy heights of sitting in a supermarket fridge.

What does it matter to a cow or a sheep how it dies? She thought querulously as she listened one day to a group of workers discussing the culling of sheep, with more empathy than they had ever shown towards events in Bosnia or anywhere else. And ever insensitive to the feelings of others, she expressed her opinion on the subject, vehemently.

'How can you say such things?' asked Betty, a recent recruit, dabbing her eyes with a crumpled tissue, 'It's so cruel and undignified for animals to be stacked in heaps like rubbish.'

But to Phoenix, who viewed the whole disaster from the point of view of the farmer, such an opinion was ridiculous.

'Oh come on, they are only stacked when they are dead,' she said incredulously, 'So what does it matter, it's not as if a sheep leaves instructions for its own funeral, psalm 23 if you please, but nothing from the book of Job.'

'I think you are wrong,' ventured Pauline, Betty's sidekick, 'Animals do have souls that's why people like Betty are vegetarians.'

The thought of a sainted sheep made Phoenix laugh, 'Oh yes,' she said. 'I can just imagine a sheep praying, Lord; make me a kebab, but not just yet. Honestly Pauline, tell me this, if God intended us to be vegetarians, why did he make animals out of meat?'

But she had misjudged the mood. These were women who liked their killing confined to abattoirs and cinemas. They did not share Phoenix's opinion that the suffering was confined to farmers and their bank managers.

A subdued muttering and exchanging of dark looks, followed her question to Pauline, generally few people cared to contradict Phoenix, but this was serious, this was about animals. They were gathered at the Clapham office for a training exercise, but so far very little training was going on. Carolyn, desperate to intervene before vegetarian Betty put her foot any further in her mouth said, 'It's the children I feel sorry for; it must be terrible for them to see their animals taken away.'

But it was the cruelty of Phoenix, not the plight of children that concerned Betty. Why should that unfeeling red haired woman think she could say what she wanted just because she was boss? Betty hadn't been working long enough as a 'Phoenix Maid,' to know there was a good reason why anyone seldom challenged Phoenix. She also rather liked the idea of taking Phoenix on; this was a winnable situation, it was about animals and no else appeared to approve of Phoenix's cavalier approach to them. So feeling she was taking on the mantle of Martin

Luther King, the small rather doe eyed woman rose to the challenge. 'I think you are cruel and unfeeling, if you or yours were personally affected by this blight, you'd be singing a different tune.'

But Phoenix didn't really care what Betty thought. She had merely thrown in an idle comment to a conversation that bored her the moment it commenced. She was taken aback though at Betty's reaction. How could anyone, she wondered, get that excited about animals. She glanced across at her opponent taking in the other woman's short stubby legs and larger than average eyes. 'No wonder she's scared shitless by foot and mouth,' she thought scornfully, 'after all, she looks like a bloody cow.'

Then casting her eyes fully upon Betty, she said airily. 'You're wrong, I'm not unfeeling, I've been known to employ some real old cows in my time, as Carolyn here will verify, so I'd be very worried if foot and mouth showed up in this office.'

And Betty; not sure if the insult was personal did nothing other than chew her sandwich without her usual gusto.

The outbreak of disease had far-reaching consequences beyond the farming community. Britain's reputation for poor husbandry grew and along with it, the number of countries who refused to accept British exports of meat. Dead meat could not get out and live meat would not come in, as foreigners cancelled holidays in Britain for fear of taking home with them more than they bargained for.

Even Jack who lived by the philosophy of 'tough shit' expressed concern. The ancient house of a renowned entrepreneur that he was booked to renovate was situated in the middle of prime Sussex farming country and visits to it brought him face to face with the restrictions and hard reality of a community under siege.

March brought even worse news with twenty five new cases in eleven different areas being reported on one day. Phoenix did what she always did when faced with things she didn't like, she ignored it. Somehow, the mood of a community in the grip of despair matched her own. There was nothing but pessimism and hopelessness and no matter what solution was put forward be it culling or mass vaccination there seemed to be no end in sight. It was out of control.

She went about her work, with a growing sense of unease, and all about her took on a tainted feel; nothing appeared to be the way it should be. She thought about the countryside, open and silent to the onlooker when in reality it was a heaving mass of disease.

One night she found herself staring across the room at Jack, as if he was a stranger so unreal did he suddenly seem. 'What do I really know about him?' she asked herself. 'What a crazy situation that puts strangers who know nothing about each other living together.'

It did not occur to her that her concern was out of proportion and out of keeping for a person who had the art of turning a blind eye shaped to perfection. Even her colleagues; who shed easy tears over the plight of the four legged victims, never let the disaster impinge on their life, once the television was switched off.

Oblivious to what was really happening, depression was slowly catching a firm grip on Phoenix. It was not a nasty, grey, mist shrouded world that was shaping her outlook. It was in fact her outlook that was disfiguring the world. The events in the news were simply confirming what she had long believed, life was a shit sandwich.

If there had been someone Phoenix could confide in, the slide into despair might have been halted. But there was no one. She wanted to turn to Jack; but it was too late. Her deception had gone on for too long, by unburdening herself now she would simply burden him.

There were no friends she had that she could turn to either, for part of the price of getting her life back together had precluded close friendships. She had learnt a long time ago that nobody was to be trusted. There was of course the shrink. She could see Shelby, she wouldn't have to tell her everything, but she could tell her how perturbed she was by the revelations that were unfolding.

In the end she decided against it. She would continue to write to Scarlett and find what else her memory could unravel from the past. Especially about the most important part of all

Dear Scarlett,   **27th February 2001**

Life feels very bleak.

Right now disease is rampant throughout this country and all anyone can do, is point a finger of blame at someone else. No one seems to be in control.

When I discovered your story, I began to feel in charge again. I knew immediately that I had come upon a fantasy that I wanted to make real. I wanted to be like you, I wanted to take life by the balls, be confident and go ahead, fearless of consequences and reputation. I had spent so much of my life wanting to please and appease until it dawned on me that unless I took my life firmly in hand, I would sink without trace into the land of worn out survivors. Just barely alive but grateful.

So I changed. I had to let go off the past and using you Scarlett as my template, I did it so thoroughly that there isn't a person I know, who would associate me with the meek and self-effacing person I once was.

I never use a nice word when a sharp one will do. Words are my machete; they keep people from getting too close to me because I can handle anything, except sympathy. I live in fear, that one day, a gentle voice, a gentle hand will break me and everything I have built up, will collapse.

When the ape dropped me home that fatal day back in 79, it was like being at the Oscars. His performance was flawless. He was gallant, grave and overwhelmingly grateful, thanking me, my mother; his parents for conceiving him, anything and everything. Any onlooker would have been fooled into thinking he was just a normal decent man. It was one almighty act and he risked all with it.

He led me to the front door and when Mom opened it, he did the practical, perennial thing that deceivers everywhere do, he started with the truth. 'Ah, Bridget, I've an apology to make. I've been shameful, taking poor Sinead out on such a freezing night, she has a terrible cold, could even be flu; and I'm entirely responsible. I feel dreadful.'

I kept my head down and walked past Mom, the doorstep was not the place for an accusation. She said 'Ah nonsense Jerh, don't be apologising, did you see the get up of her last night? Sleeveless top in December and all for the sake of the disco, tell me how is Olga?'

'Oh she's grand, thank you Bridget, we've another baby girl thanks be to God. I'm taking Grace to see her now.'

'Send her my love Jerh.'

'Oh I will Bridget; I must dash now, I have Grace in the car, thanks for everything.' When he turned to go, apprehension was written all over his face. He paused for a moment and then said very softly. 'Thanks for everything Sinead. I'll be round later to square up.'

Square up. Square up. He said that, he really did. The bastard, how did he think he was going to square up? Sorry love I know I've frightened the shit out of you, turned your world upside down, guaranteed you a pair of legs like a vice when it comes to sex and a chip on your shoulder the size of a sumo wrestlers arse when it comes to blokes, but here's a fiver and a box of milk tray. We can call it quits now can't we?

Is that what he had in mind?

Well he didn't come round later with a fiver or a box of chocolates, at least not to my knowledge because for the next twenty four hours I was out of it. 'A bad bout of flu,' the doctor said when Mom called him out in the early hours. Mom told him that I'd been at the school disco and that was his cue for a bad tempered lecture. 'I suppose she went dressed for the beach eh? Young fools gadding around like it's the height of summer in the depths of winter.'

He was an old git. He tutted and said something about young girls asking for trouble with the get up they wore. If it wasn't the foolish shoes they tortured their ankles with, it was the skirts or lack of them that caused untold mischief. 'They expose their chests,' he said, 'and then complain when they get bronchitis.'

He was a real bundle of Christmas cheer. I was barely conscious but even so, it was clear from his terse comments and abrupt poking about that he wasn't a man who loved his job.

I thought I was dying. My head pounded, my bones throbbed and when I got up to go to the lavatory I found myself walking like John Wayne. I began to doubt the memory of what had happened, because weird and absurd things kept darting in and out of my head. I was delirious, but I didn't know that at the time. I didn't know whom or where I was what was reality and what was nightmare. I'd wake up to hear myself screaming and overcome with panic.

Mom sat with me. She must have been frightened because Mom didn't like doctors or the police or any harbingers of doom coming into the house. She had called the doctor out of fear. She told me later that I had been hallucinating; screaming out in my sleep to be left alone and she had began to suspect that somebody might have spiked my drink at the disco. But the doctor had reassured her, that I was merely reaping the benefits of having gone out half naked on the coldest day of the year.

If only he, that hopeless doctor had done a proper job Scarlett, everything might have been different. If he had taken the time and looked at me properly, he might have spotted that I was suffering from shock. He might even have examined me further and seen the bruises on my body, and then he might have put two and two together, and called the police and so absolve me of responsibility. But the miserable old bastard was too obsessed with the warm bed he had left. He had listened to Mom, taken one look at me, and written me off as a timewaster.

He was the first to assume.

The following day when my fever started to decline, the ape came round to see Mom. He didn't ask to see me. Mom got real agitated when she saw his car. 'What does that old blackguard want now?' she had muttered. She was frazzled, what with running about after me and trying to get everything ready for Christmas.

Most of the family were coming for Christmas dinner. She had so much to do and I felt guilty because there was nothing I could do except cry and Mom who was convinced that I was still hallucinating sat and soothed me.

When I felt her hand on my forehead, so warm and calm and capable, its presence made me despair all the more. I longed to tell her what had happened but part of me burned with shame at the idea of having to tell her something so filthy. I wondered if I could get away with telling her just the simple fact, or would I have to tell all the gory details. If I did tell her everything, would I be tarnished in her eyes forever? That was how I viewed the situation. I couldn't comprehend how anyone could listen to my tale and not come to the same conclusion that I had already reached, namely that I was dirty, used and untouchable.

So much for discretion being the better part of valour Scarlett, I'm inclined to think the opposite might be nearer the mark, because more often than not, discretion is just a mask to hide behind. Careful words are never quite what they seem; they can't be used in evidence and they lack the weight to be thrown back, on the turn of the wind.

Jack says his father proposed to his mother with the words 'How'd you like to be buried with my people?' He was obviously another soul of discretion who wasn't up to taking any chances either. But life flees past and before you know it you are dead, and it's all too late. You more than anyone would know exactly what I mean, because if you had really thought about it Scarlett, you would never have let Rhett go. You would have told him straight the moment you realised it, that it was him not Ashley you needed.

But you didn't because you couldn't chance making the first move, you couldn't risk showing your hand and that's just great when you are playing poker but it's a shit way to treat someone you love. If there had been just the slightest inkling of being loved for no other reason than simply being me, I might have been able to believe that Mom's revulsion would be for the attack and the attacker alone and not for me.

I tried to prepare myself for telling Mom what had happened. I went over it several times in my mind because it wasn't something I could just blurt out. I had to prepare her as well as myself and just when the opportunity presented itself, the ape pulled up.

Mom left my room and went downstairs to see him. She was gone ages and I began to panic again. Crazy thoughts went through my mind when I tried to think about what he might be saying to her. Had he told her? Was he consumed with guilt, had he been to confession and rushed round for real absolution? Oh God, how humiliating, the ape describing to my mother what he had done to me. Jesus, I remember thinking would my head never stop pounding; it was just all too complicated. I persuaded myself that the ape wouldn't risk his Oscar performance by telling the truth but as I did so another terrifying thought came to mind. Perhaps the ape realising that I would surely tell Mom, was getting his version in first, I had seduced him.

He had come back from the hospital, tired but elated with his darling Olga and,

'I swear to God Bridget, she set upon me in the hallway. I tried to fight her off, make her see sense, but Bridget she wouldn't heed and well you know she had that red top on and the flower in her hair and well after all Bridget I am a man I should have known better, but she never gave me a chance.'

Oh, for God's sake, how I wanted Mom to come back to my room. Just remembering that wait, makes me feel frantic. Eventually she returned carrying a tray with tea and mince pies and I could tell she was vexed, more vexed than usual because she was singing a hymn. Mom always sang hymns when she was worried, 'Soul of my saviour', Sweet Sacrament Divine or O bread of Heaven, all sang to the same tune.

This time she was singing, 'Oh mother bless whom God bestows on sinners and on just.' She put the tray down and said, 'You're looking very feverish again, you must try and sweat it out and give yourself a chance to be ready for Christmas.'

She then pulled a letter out of her overall pocket and handed it to me. 'Jerh said to give you this, he sends his best and says he hopes you will be right as rain soon.'

I couldn't speak. What could I say? He sends his best after he has given his worst.

Mom sat on the edge of the bed and handed me a cup of tea. She kept saying 'You must keep your liquid levels up,' but strangely enough liquid levels were not high on my list of priorities. I took the cup in my hands but they were shaking so violently that I had to hand it back to Mom.

'Will I open it for you,' she asked and I nodded because a feeling of fatigue had washed over me and I felt beyond caring. I was too taken up with the thing I wanted to tell, cups and cards were beyond me. I didn't know where or how to begin.

She ripped open the envelope and pulled out a Christmas card, it was a green one with two gold foil bells on it and when she opened it, two fifty-pound notes fell out like playing cards. I could tell by the look on her face that she was shocked at the amount of money. She then read the card to me 'Thank you for all the love and care you have shown for Grace and Olga. You are very special to all of us.'

I closed my eyes, because tears had begun to seep out again, and their constant appearance was beginning to seriously annoy me. How would I ever persuade Mom that I was going to be alright when I was making it patently clear that I was devastated?

Mom said 'I know Daddy always said he was a cunning old bastard, but he means well if he means nothing.' And then she paused, and if only I had spoken up, everything might have been so different.

It was my cue to speak. My father whom I hadn't been particularly close to was reaching out from the grave to help me. The words Mom attributed to him were spot on. It was my chance to tell Mom that not only was he a cunning old bastard; he was also a violent evil one as well.

I said 'Mom, there's something...' but she didn't even hear me.

She just continued talking from where she left off, 'It was good of him to call round because he has troubles of his own right now.' She looked so agitated that I began to dread what she was going to say next. She hesitated and my heart raced, the suspense was killing me and then she said in a tired and resigned voice. 'Olga is not well, they are thinking of taking her into Sharnwood.'

No wonder Mom sounded so down and out. I couldn't believe what I had just heard. Olga into Sharnwood! Shit, I was shocked.

Sharnwood was always spoken of in hushed terms; it was the district mental hospital, stuck out in the middle of nowhere. On Tuesdays, grizzled, vacant eyed old men filled the local shops and they were just the nurses, in town for provisions. Whenever people declared an unhealthy interest such as admitting a liking for Rod Stewart, people would say, 'I bet he's escaped from Sharnwood.' A rumour at school had it that it was a home for Arsenal supporters, it really was the ultimate.

I asked Mom why Sharnwood and she replied 'Well between you and me Olga has always been a bit flaky and another baby has pushed her over the edge.'

A feeling of doom swamped me. I remember thinking, not only were the stairs burning but the bloody lift was out of order too. There was to be no escape route. But one last chance remained. I knew that although Mom was fond enough of Olga, her opinion of her was smeared with contempt. She disliked the Polish woman's fragile attitude to life, and her obsession with doing everything from rearing her child, to cleaning the lavatory, by the book. There was just the chance, that Olga was blowing a feeling of general pissed off ness, into a full blown breakdown.

I asked Mom what she thought, was Olga just attention seeking, or was there more to it? Mom paused and neither she nor I could ever have guessed how much depended on her reply. Eventually, she said Condon had told her that all visiting was forbidden and that going on his description of the way Olga was acting, it was very bad. Very bad indeed, there was talk of taking the baby away from her.

Christ knows it got worse by the minute, but I was persistent, 'What will become of her?' I asked.

Mom said 'Unless he keeps her out of stress, I'm afraid she will lose her mind completely.'

'Do you think she will get better?' I asked and poor Mom not knowing how loaded that question was, sighed and said.

'Who knows? If he can be persuaded to keep her calm and give her a bit of attention she will recover, but if he allows her to get stressed she will end her days locked up. She has to get better, just think of those two little babies if she doesn't.'

In one moment, Mom secured Olga's future, and at the same time sealed my fate.

I knew conclusively at that moment that no matter what other opportunity presented itself, for Olga's sake and that of her two children; Jerh Condon's actions would remain a secret forever. I half expected to hear a cockcrow.

It was an awful Christmas Day, the first in a long line of horrible ones to come. My bones still ached and I felt distant and remote. Joe and Gerry my brothers were full of themselves, they had secured another loan from the ape and were going on and on about their plans for extending the garage. Their laughter and high-pitched jesting grated on my nerves and for the first time in my life, I looked at my family objectively and the thought came to me that actually I didn't like them very much.

I listened to the pair of them arguing and bragging, neither of them having a clue in their head about the person who was funding them. It occurred to me that if I told the world about Jerh Condon, the game would be over for Joe and Gerry too because the ape would retaliate by calling his loans in immediately. I was trapped and slowly it began to dawn on me just how smart the ape was. He was steering a very smart course, boxing me in nicely.

But, and this really is a big 'but' Scarlett, even if I had spoken, how certain could I really be that I would have been believed?

Mom told everyone what a picture I had made at the school disco and that set Joe off wolf whistling and Sally his wife chipped in that she had heard on the grapevine; that I had been dancing with all the teachers.

That is small town mentality for you, one becomes all. Of course a whole barrage of innuendo then ensued and only Alice my sister didn't join in. She shot daggers at me and said. 'Halter necks were made for animals not humans.' She then turned on poor Mom saying, 'I am surprised you let her out of the house dressed like that.'

Alice's husband Guy was on duty at the hospital, if he had been there he would have attempted to pour oil on Alice's seething stormy waters. We called him the 'Quack,' because he was so bumbling and fearful of confrontation, not at all like a real doctor is supposed to be with their well - known panache for throwing paint stripper on open wounds.

Marriage had not improved Alice. She had always been censorious of others and now married with three children and varicose veins to match; she was showing severe signs of bitterness, though God knows why because on the face of it, she had everything she had ever wanted. Later on, she brought the subject of my outfit up again. She said it was no wonder I was half-dead from the cold, going out dressed like a call girl.

I was like a bloody colander, tears sprinkled out at the least command and Sally who had never liked Alice, took one look at me and told Alice to go suck a lemon and bring a smile to her face. There was plenty of drink and that added to the tension. Alice who fully reciprocated Sally's negative feelings cut her dead and said to Mom.

'Is it true that Olga Condon is going into the mental hospital?'

It wasn't a fit subject for discussion at the Christmas dinner table; it was designed to make everyone feel guilty. Gerry instantly turned on Alice. 'Why beat about the bush?' he said. 'Why not ask if she is painting herself blue at the same time?'

But Alice defensive as ever just replied. 'Well, Sharnwood is a mental hospital, and if she isn't coping, that is where she should be.'

Sally then joined the fray, she said. 'I suppose you've never been unable to cope have you Alice?'

But my sister is too tough a cookie to be put in her place by an in-law. She said 'If you mean have I ever given in to self pity at the expense of my children, then the answer is no,' and before Sally could fire back at her, Alice turned to Mom and said.

'Anyway, what about Jerh and the kids, what are they doing for Christmas?'

I nearly choked when she said that, up till then I'd just sat at the table, sullen and snotty, everyone thought I still had the flu. Mom said 'I invited them here, but he wouldn't hear of it, he said something about Grace staying with his brother's family in London while he sorts things out at the hospital, it's all a bit vague though'

When I heard that, my instant thought was 'Fucking hell, he could have been here.' My hands started trembling so much that I knocked a glass of water over right into Alice's lap and that started her off on a tirade about clumsy oafs who catch their deaths by gallivanting half dressed at midnight.

The thing is Scarlett, the night that ape attacked me, it wasn't just my body he assaulted, it was also my mind. Horrible thoughts, words and ideas flooded into my thoughts completely unbidden. The least provocation and my automatic silent response was 'fuck off,' and that word had never passed my lips before, well except for one occasion when I slipped on some dog shit on the way to a party. But it seemed after what the ape did, I became really foul. I was like a trooper, but not outwardly. Lying in bed at night, listening to the persistent barking of the dog next door that barked its balls off at its own shadow, I would think to myself 'Go on choke yourself you little fucker.' I would never have said or even thought something like that before. I just felt so wound up and frustrated because I wanted to let the world know what had happened, but it seemed the world; and everyone in it, was conspiring to keep the lid on this particularly nasty piece of news.

I was like a pressure cooker, silently hissing and God help the person brave enough to release the pressure.

When Big Ben, chimed in the New Year of 1980, Mom tossed her money for luck and I said to myself 'Goodbye worst year of my life.'

But I had jumped the gun. I was wrong, so wrong.

The gates of hell were only just about to swing open.

Phoenix.

Chapter Seven

Jack Keane was a very perplexed man. The diversification of his business was in full swing and he wanted to give it his full attention; but was unable to do so because he was becoming increasingly concerned, about Phoenix.

She was in his opinion, crossing the barrier from assertiveness into pure unreasonableness on a day by day basis and he was powerless to help her. Any enquiry on his part as to her well being, met with instant rebuttal and an invitation to go somewhere he didn't particularly want to visit. It occurred to him that the cause of her anxiety might be genuine fears over tax fiddling, since honesty and parting with money didn't come easily to her, but intuitively he knew it was something personal.

He was at a loss to think what it might be, business was good, they were comfortable, they had Daisy, and they had each other. Or was that the problem? The idea that Phoenix might be unhappy with him was a new and worrying one. He made up his mind to make their wedding anniversary on St Patrick's Day an extra special occasion, and he took the unusual step of asking Carolyn for some ideas as to what Phoenix might want.

But Carolyn was at a bigger loss than Jack to know what Phoenix wanted. She hesitated before answering Jack's question, loyalty to Phoenix made her feel treacherous for even agreeing to Jack's insinuation, that all was not well.

But on the other hand, she liked Jack immensely and was touched by his apparent concern. 'I can't think of anything Phoenix especially wants right now Jack,' she told him, smiling into his warm concerned face, 'But you are right, she does seem very low, perhaps it's just the miserable weather.'

'True, but it hasn't been raining non- stop for a year,' Jack replied. 'Tell me, is she kicking arses left right and centre here as well as everywhere else?' Carolyn blushed at his astute use of words. Only moments earlier Phoenix had phoned her up, incoherent with rage because a cleaner had signed in late for the second time in succession. The conversation had been so peppered with curses and threats of what she was going to do to the poor woman's backside when she caught hold of her, that

Carolyn had trembled with anxiety by proxy. Someone was going to be unemployed by the end of the day.

Jack laughed good naturedly when he saw the look on Carolyn's face, 'It's okay,' he said, 'you don't have to say a word, but let me know if Phoenix drops a hint about anything.' It was a reference to things in general, not just about an anniversary gift and Carolyn knew it, but she also knew the odds of her finding out what was wrong with Phoenix, were greater than any bookie would be prepared to offer.

Buying a present for Phoenix was not an easy task; she spent a fortune on flowers and yet became as touchy as blazes if Jack even so much as bought her a posy from a garage. She declined holidays on the grounds that she couldn't trust anyone to tend her affairs for longer than a few days and resented any attempt to buy her clothes. 'I'm my own person and I don't need help in dressing myself,' she'd say whenever Jack suggested buying her an outfit. That only left jewellery and even that did not really inspire her, beyond its monetary worth. In the end, Jack decided on a diamond eternity ring and to take her to a St Patrick's night ball being held at a private Irish club in Westminster.

Far from cheering her up, Jack's choice of celebration only succeeded in causing more consternation. It was to be a grand affair and Phoenix did not have the heart or inclination for such an occasion. It meant a lot of palaver such having her hair done and pretending to be delighted with the appointment Jack had told Carolyn to make with a Mayfair manicurist, never mind the fuss and bother of buying a ball gown..

It crossed her mind to call it off on the pretext of business commitments or perhaps health. She could feign a migraine attack. But she decided against that route. Jack was already showing distinct signs of agitation with her mood swings, so it would not be a good idea to tweak him any further.

There was nothing for it, she would have to go along with the show and she did. She even bore with fairly good grace, Carolyn's constant utterances about how wonderful it was all going to be. She bought her dress, a long black velvet one with lace sleeves and kept it hidden like a bridal one. She knew it wasn't the kind of dress Jack had in mind when he told her to buy 'something special,' but she had viewed and tried on several of the frothy ball gowns on offer in the West End and had come quickly to the conclusion that pastels were out of the question. They made her feel like a plastic flower, accentuating rather than covering up how artificial she felt about the whole affair.

'It will all be over in a matter of hours,' she told herself and immediately felt more able to cope. It was the mantra she used to get through any ordeal be it awkward customers or tax interviews; she simply did a time check. Anything was bearable when it came with a time limit of hours rather than years.

And all was going well, until well meaning Carolyn, unwittingly dealt Phoenix's fragile serenity a severe blow.

Phoenix, unwilling to leave the office in Carolyn's capable hands, called in on her way back from the beauty salon on St Patrick's Day, to collect a letter she had deliberately forgotten. Though her nerves were jagged, her nails had been shaped and painted to perfection, and her hair was neatly arranged into a French roll on the back of her head. She didn't feel good, but she looked it and Carolyn enthused when she saw her. 'You look absolutely fantastic,' she said. 'Your hair really suits you up, honestly Phoenix you look so elegant.'

Personal compliments made Phoenix suspicious at the best of times and given the way she felt about the coming evening; Carolyn's enthusiasm was difficult to take. 'Oh hush with the bullshit,' she said dismissively, 'Tell me what's got your attention in that rag you are reading?'

'Oh nothing really,' Carolyn replied, putting her newspaper down, well aware of Phoenix's contempt for compliments (which she mistakenly took for modesty.) 'Mind you,' she continued. 'I've just read about this terrible case about an awful woman. I find it difficult to believe.'

Phoenix was barely listening; instead she was sorting through some letters on her desk and glancing at one in particular franked starkly with the insignia of the Inland Revenue. She looked up and replied flippantly 'Don't tell me, some woman has burnt her husband's entire collection of Arsenal stickers. Give her an award.'

'No, I'm not joking Phoenix.' Carolyn replied earnestly. 'This awful woman has just been sentenced for rape, she's the youngest woman ever convicted in Britain. I didn't think such a thing was possible.'

Phoenix stood rooted to the spot, her heart thumping erratically as anxiety rapidly consumed her. She wasn't altogether convinced she had heard Carolyn correctly, but such was the hold panic now had on her, she couldn't speak and therefore clarify the situation. Taking her silence as a go ahead to reveal more, Carolyn continued, this time reading from the paper, 'the prosecution barrister told the jury that the attack which had followed 'a lovely evening out,' had been encouraged by the defendant; therefore she could be convicted of rape.'

She put the paper down and looked across at Phoenix. 'Isn't that dreadful, how could a woman, subject another woman to something like that?'

Still Phoenix said nothing. She stood staring across at Carolyn, with an uncomprehending look on her face and so overpowering was the anxiety that now gripped her that she had to place a hand on a nearby table to steady herself.

Sensing that Carolyn was getting concerned at her reaction, or rather the lack of it, she fought for control of her face, but speaking was the problem, nausea lingered at the back of her throat and she felt the prospect of being copiously sick was a very real one. Finally she managed to speak. 'That is bad,' she said, but could risk no more. Carolyn, seeing how distressed Phoenix was, immediately grew contrite. How wrong people were, she thought, to dismiss Phoenix as heartless and unfeeling; a hard hearted person would never react to the ordeal of a stranger with such horror. She walked quickly across to Phoenix and placed her hand on her arm.

'Oh Phoenix I'm sorry, what an awful thing to tell you about; especially when you are so looking forward to tonight, I guess it upset me so much, I had to tell someone. Don't let it upset you,' she pleaded, 'She didn't get away with it thank God; she'll be locked up for years.'

Phoenix nodded, and abruptly shook Carolyn's hand off her arm. If she spent another second listening to such twaddle, she would take a swing at Carolyn and demonstrate once and for all how much she despised the simpering, twittering woman. She picked up her bag and headed to the door, managing a faint 'See you later,' as she did so.

In the safety of her car she sat and thought over what Carolyn had just told her. She felt both nauseous and inexplicably nervous. Why did that stupid woman have to bring up such a dreadful subject? Nothing was ever straightforward, she spent her life avoiding things that had the ability to forward the past and whenever she put her guard down, something popped up and put her back in her box.

She was twenty years away from her ordeal but someone in London was starting out on the road to recovery, the same one she had first tread all those years ago. There was a time when she had been prepared to believe it was possible to bury the past by keeping up a frenetic pace, 'keep busy, spin the bucket fast enough and the water won't escape' that had been her motto. For awhile it had worked, but now she had to face the prospect of going back in order to face the future.

She sat silent and subdued, oblivious to the noisy traffic of the south circular road. To the depths of her heart she felt sick and oh so very weary. There had been countless rape cases over the years and she had turned a blind eye and a deaf ear to all of them, for the prospect of knowing the details was just too frightening. Every headline she had ever glimpsed had caused a shiver to run through her body, but even so, there had been something different about the case Carolyn had just informed her about.

Of course, the fact that the poor woman was assaulted after an evening out, just as she herself had been, was a coincidence much too close for comfort. But there was she felt certain, something more to it than that. She just couldn't place it.

When she arrived home she was greeted by an over excited Daisy who patted and pawed her hair, until it almost collapsed. She sneaked a quick drink and vowed to do her best to look happy and play along with her little girl, keeping up the pretence that just like Cinderella she was going to a ball. Daisy ran and fetched like a golden retriever, bringing first one than another pair of shoes, make up and every possible accessory Phoenix could need for a night out. She was excited to see her mother in a long gown, but disappointed that it wasn't a dress like Cinderella or Barbie wore in real life.

She wasn't the only one disappointed with the dress. When Jack came home and peered around the bedroom door, he too was disappointed. 'Oh come on girl,' he said. 'It's a ball I'm taking you to, not a funeral.'

But Phoenix was defiant. 'Black is elegant Jack,' she said, 'It transcends all occasions and it hides a multiple of sins, so I'm staying with it.'

'It's bloody morbid,' he replied as he walked away.

She stuck her tongue out at his departing back. How dare he criticise her? He was going dressed like a bloody penguin himself, so who was he to lecture her about what to wear.

When she descended the stairs; Carolyn who was babysitting, more than made up for Jack's lack of enthusiasm. 'You look magnificent,' she said. 'Just like a film star; so cool and elegant, aren't you proud of her Jack?'

'I will be,' he replied looking at his watch, 'provided she doesn't return to being a rat when the clock strikes twelve.'

Phoenix searched around for something to do or say before making her departure. 'Are you okay with everything?' she asked and Carolyn, who had babysat Daisy on many occasions, reassured her that all was fine.

Phoenix couldn't help noticing rather enviously, how Daisy held on possessively to Carolyn's arm; she never did that to Phoenix. 'Well I suppose it is different with a mother.' she told herself, seeking to justify her daughter's wariness of her, 'I'm always so busy, Carolyn doesn't have any calls on her time, so it is probably relaxing for her to be around a young child.'

But she didn't fool herself completely. She knew the problem lay with her and her constant snappiness and her habit of always thinking ahead to the next thing to be done, a habit which never allowed time for the present to be enjoyed or savoured.

'Well, I don't care anyway,' she told herself defiantly, as she climbed into the waiting taxi.

The scene at the ball took Phoenix by surprise. It was held in a large rather grand room illuminated by several chandeliers that shone and glittered in the evening light. Row upon row of black suited waiters stood in attendance and the whole room was ablaze with white and golden roses decorated to excess with green fern. But it was the quiet, almost subdued atmosphere that made the most impact on her; small groups of people congregated together here and there and the conversations seemed polite and almost reverential.

She had been expecting a teeming mass of frenzy, men showing off their women, and women showing off their dresses. 'I've been thinking too much about Gone with the Wind,' she told herself. 'I really think I half expected to see women being fanned with peacock feathers, and accompanied by their mammies.' At that moment a tall, rather strident, black haired woman brushed past her, with the top half of her dress virtually missing. The sight made Phoenix recall Mammy's words to Scarlett 'You kain show yo' buzzum befo three o clock,' and she smiled at the recollection.

She circulated with Jack, looking suitably demure and supportive and anyone looking on would have sworn she was enjoying it all immensely. However champagne was freely available and Phoenix having quickly sought the personal attention of one young waiter, was never without an overflowing glass in her hand. That together with her determination to 'just go with the flow,' enabled her to keep a calm, impassive persona about her.

They sat down to eat, surrounded by a large contingent from West Cork, who greeted Jack as if he was Sir Robert McAlpine himself. Jack's rise in the London construction business had indeed been meteoric and many were keen to share the secret.

'Never mind nut allergy' Phoenix thought dismissively, as she cut a tender piece of finest Mullingar beef; 'it's allergy to gobshites that I'm suffering from right now'. She listened and watched as several tuxedoed men paid homage to Jack, taking in the hand shaking and smiling, and general good natured back slapping. They were all fellow contractors, who would cut the legs from each other the moment the sun rose on a working day, but to look at them Phoenix thought grimly, you would think they were a registered charity set up with the one aim of helping and supporting each other. She glanced around at the numerous clones of the group Jack was with. Everyone seemed so earnest, and the thought occurred to her, that it was more like a Masonic do designed to re-enforce business contacts, rather than a St Patrick's Night piss up.

For some reason, the thought irritated her. She reached out for her glass of champagne, having declined the wine that was on offer and sat back in her chair, sipping it with no enthusiasm, surveying the other participants with a critical eye.

And it was then, without warning, that something akin to madness; possessed her. It was all wrong. She didn't belong here, with these overdressed, superficial polished jackeens, and she wouldn't tolerate it any longer.

The meal was at an end and the band had already struck up, but only a few lone dancers had taken to the floor. Most people sat huddled in groups around the various tables with their backs to the band, sipping coffee or the last of the wine and talking, talking, talking.

Putting down her glass, Phoenix beckoned across to Jack interrupting his conversation, and smiling at his companions, she said, 'Excuse me, but I have some business to sort out with this old rogue,' and pulling his arm, she led him to the dance floor.

Bewildered, Jack followed and when she put out her hand, he took the cue and held it. She threw her head back and threw herself into action. The band, sensing the energy that possessed her, upped the tempo. Together Jack and Phoenix waltzed and jived and when the Siege of Ennis was announced, Jack spun Phoenix around at a speed he wouldn't have contemplated, if he'd known just how much drink she had taken. But she was well practised in the art of self preservation and remained on her feet, although there were several near misses.

It was almost like the old days when they use to frequent Irish clubs in Battersea and Mitcham; back then Phoenix had been game for anything. Jack was delighted, he hadn't seen her in such form for years, but what; he wondered had got into her?

Something had indeed got into Phoenix; something had flashed into her soul and stirred her up. She didn't want to look grave and sedate; telling people business was grim when really it was flying. She didn't want to be seen to belong to this 'in' crowd of ex pats who sought to distance themselves from their roots.

The Ballybunion publican bubbled under the surface and when the band struck up 'McAlpines Fusiliers,' Phoenix led the way with 'Mother dear, I'm over here...'

The crowd, which initially viewed her antics with a sense of unease, relaxed, abandoned caution, and followed the example of a bearded man from Killarney who began clapping and cheering her on. She returned the compliment by blowing him a kiss and taking a deep bow.

By the time the night was finished, it was Jack not Phoenix who looked more than slightly anxious.

They arrived home in the early hours, to a quiet and peaceful house. Carolyn, who had agreed to stay the night, was already in bed and silence reigned with the exception of the occasional gentle purr of the central heating system on night shift, working away in the dark.

Phoenix followed Jack into the kitchen where out of habit she flicked the radio on. The world service had taken over and a solemn report regarding gangsters from some Baltic state filled the kitchen. Instantly she turned the sound down until only a faint murmur rumbled in the background.

'Will you have a bite?' Jack asked pulling a plate of sliced gammon from the fridge. Phoenix shook her head, the last thing she needed was salt; a raging thirst was already starting to kick in.

'Will you have tea?' she offered. This time Jack shook his head; he picked up a milk carton and drank from it long and nosily.

'My God,' she exclaimed, 'If you drink anymore you'll have to spend the entire night on the throne, King Puck, himself.'

He laughed 'That's great coming from you.' He replaced the carton back in the fridge, wiped his mouth with the back of his hand and kissed her on the cheek. 'I'm due in Sussex in a few hours, so I'm going up, are you coming?'

She walked over to the kettle and took it to the tap from where she proceeded to fill it with the lid still in place, water sprayed everywhere and she cursed the appliance fiercely. 'I'll follow you,' she said, 'but I'm having tea first.'

He waved hazily and left the room and her consciousness. She fixed her attention on the kettle, impatiently willing it to boil. Her mind was still reeling; there was so much she wanted to capture from it before it sank beneath a haze of alcohol. In her haste, she made a disgusting cup of tea from partially boiled water. She took one sip from it before promptly throwing it down the sink. There was something she had to do.

Dear Scarlett.

Since I'm so out of touch with how real people celebrate, I really didn't know what to expect from the ball, but the moment we arrived, I felt an overwhelming desire to panic and run.

I imagined a sickly parade of women showing off their glitzy dresses accompanied by preening men, all trying to surpass each other on the dance floor. But it wasn't a bit like that at all. Instead it was stuffed full of people, taking themselves dead seriously, with numerous raffles for charity and a never ending roll call of the rich and successful.

I was sitting there, staring at a group of black suited men all competing for the title of Pillar of the Community 2001 when this feeling of de ju vu washed over me, I felt as if I'd been in the same situation before. And then it clicked. Jack and me were Olga and Jerh Condon. Over - dressed, over important and out for influence not fun.

It seems I have spent my entire life on the run only to end up becoming what I detest most. I couldn't take it. So I did something, I knew they would never do. I made a public spectacle of myself; I drank and danced and even sang for attention.

All those years ago when I was reduced to nothing by the ape, I vowed I would be someone. I didn't want to sink into oblivion because of him, but tonight it looked like I had become my own nightmare. I wore a black dress to suit my mood, yet all it did was play to the crowd. Jack had the cheek to be annoyed with my choice. He wanted me to look like a painted fool, with hoops and organza, the sort of thing you might have worn

Scarlett. No disrespect, but the world of 2001 is a very different world, to the one you knew.

What a bloody stupid thing to say, of course it's a different world. It's different to that of the late seventies and in real terms they're only around the corner.

I know I'm drunk and becoming garrulous but that mangy era offends my memory. Lots of people born in the 1980's think of the 70's as the glam rock times, when everyone could be someone. Say what you like, dress as you like, so long as its all done in the worst possible taste.

'You've got to laugh at it,' says this ginger git on the telly presenting yet another repeat of a show from the fab decade. 'The 70's were a light-hearted, fun time,' he smirks.

My arse they were. The 70's Scarlett is when sexiness gave way to seediness, freedom got confused with fetish, and pop culture became porn culture. For God's sake half the bloody icons of that decade are doing time now for downloading child porn. Strike up a conversation about the 'fab era' with an average forty year woman today and the chances are she will blank out the posters that once covered grease spots on her bedroom wall and say, 'It's funny you know I always liked the Osmond's. But I never had much time for that turd that was sent down last week for child porn, always knew he was a creep.'

Talk about distancing yourself.

I hate that era Scarlett because I associate it with a time when everybody was so bloody insistent on having fun. It was the era my descent into hell started in and I'll never forget it, and not because it's too good to be forgotten either. I'm aggravated Scarlett. It's probably the drink kicking in, but I feel contaminated, dirty even, having been to the sort of do that the ape specialised in.

It was like being in a zoo and watching a bunch of gorilla's grooming each other. It wasn't a bit like the St Patrick's night benders I use to go on before I met Jack. They were fun for the sake of fun, like the time I met up with some ex flat mates and we went on a pub-crawl through Kilburn.

Two of them weren't up to a serious piss up and that was half the fun of it. They had become teachers and they spent the entire night grousing about practically everything under the sun. No wonder they had discipline problems. If I had to sit listening to them for an hour at a stretch I'd start climbing the bloody wall.

Sally who teaches maths and could give any duck a run for its money in a 'who's got the tightest arse,' competition spent the entire evening flinging filthy looks at anyone who spoke above a whisper, or dared to look as if they were actually enjoying themselves. The other one, Fiona, kept jabbering on about education, education, fucking education until I wanted to scream. We had a meal in a pretentious little restaurant, where the prices gave Sally palpitations. Afterwards we headed for Biddy Mulligan's on the Kilburn High Road- that was the starting gun for the pub-crawl. Mind you, I don't think Fiona and Sally realised what was happening. They thought the search was on for a serious, sober pub where they could bring us all up to date on the crass unfairness of a teacher's lot.

It was fantastic. I have never seen so many fights followed by declarations of undying love in my entire life.

In one crowded pub, I took a bet from Lesley who was up to doing anything, and discovered that I could nip behind the bar and pour a pint unnoticed.

On about the fifth occasion though, I got caught. I was so intent on pulling the perfect pint that I didn't notice this guy come up and stand alongside me. The next thing I knew, a big red angry face was staring into mine shouting. 'What the fuck do you think you are doing?'

The red angry face belonged to a stocky man with rolled up shirtsleeves. I told him I was a representative of Guinness, carrying out a spot check. He looked at me, then at the punters who started clapping, and began wagging his finger in my face. At that point, Sally appeared and started complaining about the time.

He took one look at the dark, tailored suit she was wearing and said. 'Fuck off, we don't do War Cry.' Poor Sally, she always fancied herself as a radical and there she was being taken for a trumpet player. She barked back at him, and began pulling my arm and he just stood there completely perplexed, unable to understand how a raving piss artist could possibly be teamed up with such a stern recruiting officer.

She never asked me what was going on; I think she thought it was an argument about being short changed; something she would have a lot of sympathy with.

They were good days Scarlett, not that good days stopped when Jack came on the scene, but they were different. I was thirty-one years old when I met him, and business was flourishing due to the economic boom that hit London in the 80's.

If it was money, Mom wanted for me after I finished Cambridge, she wouldn't have been disappointed, but the thing is I never did get to Cambridge. In fact I didn't get as far as the North Bank Poly. I didn't become a lawyer, but I still managed to clean up very nicely in financial terms. I became a cleaner. A 1980's version of Mrs Mop.

Remember, I thought the worst year of my life was over when Big Ben rang in 1980? Well it wasn't.

As it turned out it was merely the Hors d' eoveurs or as Janice one of my cleaners would put it, 'the horses duvets.'

Jerh Condon's wife didn't go into the Looney bin; she came home from hospital, looking thin, pale and interesting. Everyone was careful to tiptoe around her. I couldn't bring myself to visit her; nothing on earth would ever get me inside that house again.

There was no call for babysitting because she certainly wasn't up to going out on the batter, and I made it absolutely crystal clear that there was no way I was prepared to look after a new born baby. In fact the first time I saw the child, it must have been about seven or eight weeks old. The ape asked Mom to be its Godmother. She was shocked and I think secretly flattered. He was obviously taking no chances; he had me thoroughly in the bag with the drawstring being pulled tighter by the minute.

I even went to the christening. I told Mom I had homework, but she insisted, saying a break from work would do me good. After the church service, they held a small party at a hotel, which overlooked a stormy dirty sea.

Olga Condon was distinctly frosty towards me and I remember feeling quite aggrieved, because if anyone had a right to act odd it was me. I wonder if in some strange way, she associated me with her illness. Anyway whatever it was she was feeling; I felt completely nauseous when I saw him, pawing her and patting Grace and kissing the baby. I swore on oath that day, that I would never have a baby. I would never become the property of a man, his plaything. Because that is what Olga looked like to me, she had the same, mauled expression that birds wear after a cat has had its fun.

I could barely bring myself to look at the baby. I remember peering into its cot at my mother's insistence and focusing on the soft toy that lay in there because to look at the baby would have been too painful, a solid reminder of that awful night.

Later when we got home, sharp-eyed Alice who misses nothing said to me, 'You were very cool, you hardly looked at the baby at all,' and James who was polishing his shoes ready for school on Monday said.

'Ah, perhaps poor Sinead is jealous, she wants a little baby of her own.'

That started them all off on a teasing bout, some people refer to situations like that as one of the joys of big family life, usually such people are infertile or were dropped on the head as a baby. They haven't got a clue what they are talking about. There is nothing remotely cosy in being teased when you are totally pissed off with the world.

I stormed out of the room, slamming the door behind me and went up into the Arctic Circle that was my bedroom and cried. I had an urge to tear back down the stairs and blurt out what had really happened, shove my face into Alice's and say. 'That arse parading around the church today, assaulted and left me in the snow. So you are bloody well right, I was cool, in fact if I was a brass monkey I'd still be squealing now.'

But I didn't, because a part of me still couldn't even admit that it had really happened and in a perverse way, I felt there was less likelihood of it being true, if nobody else knew. As Shelby the shrink might put it, I was in denial. I didn't have a clever word for it back then. I just knew there was something at the back of my mind that I didn't want to think about.

Oh Scarlett, I can hardly bear to tell you what happened next. I can only bring myself to think about it because I'm so tanked up with champagne and misery. On the feast of the Epiphany, Mom and I went to evening mass and when it was over; an old doll came up and started chatting with Mom. I remember going to take a final look at the crib before it was packed away for another year. When I glanced at the statues of the holy family, a strange feeling came over me, I looked at the child in the manger and for the first time in my life, I doubted his existence.

'Where were you that night,' I thought, 'when I needed you?'

He didn't answer me of course, which is just as well, because if he had, I would have died of fright. But for a moment I sat and stared and it occurred to me, that it was all a load of shite. It was just something I had been born into. I had never questioned it. It was one of those things you did because you were expected to. You are a Catholic and this is what you do. Born a few thousand miles to the East, you'd sit and let a cow wander through your house, or watch the world through a veil.

If Scarlett, I had really understood the meaning of the word epiphany, I would have been very afraid, because staring at that nativity scene, I was aware of two things. The first was an instinctive belief that for all my new cynicism, I was looking at the only rock worth hanging on to. And the second thing; was an almost overwhelming feeling, that something momentous was about to happen. And it did.

The school holidays ended and I went back to school, but throughout January, and February I continued to feel very ill. I felt headachy and lumpy and extremely bad tempered and sick, not as in throwing up but nauseous all the time.

One Tuesday evening, when I came home from school, slightly later than usual, Mom followed me upstairs. She asked me where I had been and I told her that I had been to the library which was true. She looked at me very carefully for a moment, before saying in a very soft voice, 'Sinead, have you been carrying on?'

I was shocked; instantly I thought about the ape, had he said something? I said, 'What are you talking about Mom?'

She began to cry, she said. 'Don't lie to me, I am not stupid, all your play-acting, 'Oh I feel sick, oh my head,' she began mimicking me.

I could only stare at her.

'But I have been feeling terrible,' I said. 'I am not putting it on Mom.'

There followed what I can only call a loaded silence. I knew instinctively that something dreadful was about to follow. Mom took a step towards me and said in a low hushed tone, 'You are pregnant aren't you? When did you last come on?'

I can't tell you how much I wanted to die at that moment. I couldn't reply. Now as a woman approaching forty it seems incredible that I was so naïve, so stupid. The reality was, I had been so wrapped up in the sheer physical horror of the attack, that the thought of another catastrophe following so closely on its heels, was unthinkable. The possibility that I could be pregnant had never entered my head. If it had, I would have definitely stayed out in the snow.

'When did you last come on?' my mother repeated, this time her voice low and menacing.

I opened my mouth to speak but the only word that came out was 'No', but it wasn't the 'No' of denial, it was the 'No' that said 'Please God, don't let it be true.'

My mother recognised it immediately and she set about hitting me across the head and the back, she was shouting and crying at the same time, asking what curse of God had given her a daughter like me. The next thing, the door burst open and James who had just got home from school came into the room.

'What's wrong?' he asked. Mom lifted her head and told him to phone Alice and ask her to come round immediately.

Well that was the start of it Scarlett. The haranguing and the blows and the tears, the real humiliation. It was too late to come clean. I don't think they would have believed me. Mom kept repeating. 'Oh Jesus, Oh Jesus, Oh suffering Jesus,' and what with the distressed mother and the taunting and the jeering, it felt like a crucifixion, my own one.

I couldn't bear to see Mom so distraught, so broken, and so disappointed. 'All the things I have done for you and how have you repaid me?'

There was nothing I could say to that, I knew she had made many sacrifices for me and my intentions had never been other than to make her proud and happy. But I hadn't reckoned on the ape.

Joe and Gerry were bastards; they rounded on me, calling me a filthy little whore. Joe was the worse, poking me with his greasy finger. 'Which little fucker did this?' he kept asking. I think he might have been planning an honour killing. When I said nothing, he said. 'I'm going to find out and when I do I'll break his fucking little neck.'

Watch out Jerk Condon I thought. But do you know something Scarlett; I think if they had known the truth, they wouldn't have attacked the big man, the big J.C. It would have been in their interest to sweep it under the carpet, for the greater good. But a quick up and under with someone my own age and half their size, that was worthy of murder.

They kept on questioning me, who did I go shopping with on Saturdays, and whom did I hang about with at school? I thought of poor weedy Stephen with his white hands and Shakespeare, he'd have a heart attack if one of these brutes jumped on him. I simply refused to speak. It was instinctive.

But what I don't understand Scarlett is why I kept silent. Why against all the threats and tears and shock and shame, didn't I just tell the truth?

I still don't really know why. It wasn't just fear of not being believed.

It was bound up in poor self-concept and the need to protect Mom from a brutal dirty story that had the potential to turn even nastier. She had been through so much since Daddy's death, not just the shock of it, but the inquest and the sheer grinding poverty that followed it all. I couldn't face dragging her into the dreadful mire that an allegation against Condon would have inevitably served up. It wasn't just me, the whole family felt a duty of protection towards Mom. But it seems it was only me who was put to the test of ultimate loyalty.

The only one to act with any honour at all was James. He didn't defend me, but he pulled the others off when a serious beating looked inevitable.

As for Alice, she was cold and unforgiving. She said I had it coming, thinking I was so bloody great, so smart, when really I was nothing but a filthy little trollop who had let Mom down and ruined Daddy's good name. As she left to go home one night, her parting shot was. 'You will be responsible for Mom's death.'

I nearly broke my silence then, I wanted to shout. 'Well I'm fucking well responsible for everything else, keeping Condon's reputation intact, a roof over Graces head and her mother out of the nut house, so throw some more my way.' If I had known that, the Falklands war was just around the corner I would have put my hand up and claimed responsibility for that as well.

I was awarded leper status and remained the untouchable for weeks and as the weeks passed, the safer Condon became. The most chronic, ironic thing of all though, Scarlett was the conclusion they all came to.

Whoever was responsible, God alone and me, 'the scut' only knew, but there was one thing they were all certain of. It must have happened on the night of the school disco when I got home late.

Phoenix

Chapter Eight

As far as Jack was concerned, St Patrick's night had been a raging success. He hadn't seen Phoenix in such form for years and the sight of her dancing and singing, inspired him to think the old Phoenix had made a come -back.

Initially he had been annoyed by the lack lustre response she had made to his efforts to cheer her up, she hadn't even worn the ring he had bought her - in fact she had barely looked at it, before promptly putting it back in its box. He had retrieved it later on from Daisy who was using it as a tiara for Barbie and felt half tempted to take it back and use the money on the Grand National. Phoenix certainly wouldn't notice it missing. But given the way she had acted at the ball, all was forgiven as far as Jack was concerned.

Phoenix was well aware that her reception of Jack's gift and treat had been lacking in warmth and she was sorry, but she wasn't going to apologize. She hadn't asked for anything, she hadn't nagged or hinted for diamonds, and if Jack wanted to act huffy then that was tough.

The morning after the ball, Jack had set off for Sussex before Phoenix was even out of bed. She had awoken with a crashing head and just a vague recollection of the night before. Memory of the ball was swamped by a dull feeling in her chest, as she recalled upon waking, the letter she had written to Scarlett.

She lay in bed, eyes held tightly shut, fearful of the streaming sunlight that had pierced them when she had briefly, flicked them open. After twenty years, she had done it, she had finally told someone. It didn't matter that that 'someone' didn't exist. She had acknowledged in black and white the secret she had kept from everyone that mattered, and she hadn't been struck by a thunderbolt. She couldn't face going to work though. Her head ached and she felt confused and shaky, a condition induced by too much drink and anxiety. It was only when she saw Daisy walking towards the bed, carrying a cup of tea, balanced shakily on a saucer like an offering, that she remembered Carolyn had stayed the night.

Within minutes she despatched Carolyn with the duty of taking Daisy to school and overseeing the office. She said she would call in later, but Carolyn took one look at the circles under Phoenix's eyes, and knew that was highly unlikely.

For the rest of the entire day, Phoenix wandered aimlessly around the house. She had outstanding correspondence to deal with from the Inland Revenue, but when she drifted into her study with the intention of attending to it, an overwhelming sense of insurmountable confusion drove her to promptly leave the room with all the rapidity of someone who has just spied a savage dog sleeping in the corner.

Not only was her mind distracted with matters from the past, but she was beset with a tremulous feeling of anxiety every time she thought about facing Jack, in the cool light of day. She had no clear recollection of what she had said or done at the ball. All she could hope was that she hadn't shamed him in front of his friends and competitors -that certainly had not been her intention.

She made up her mind to quiz him when he came home and find out by stealth, exactly what her actions had been, but when he returned he had his ganger Tosh in tow and her plans were stalled. Tosh had been with Jack off and on for over twenty years and was in Jack's opinion, an astute and capable ganger. Phoenix wasn't enamoured with him, she disliked his ability to constantly turn up when he wasn't wanted, and she greatly resented his refusal to be intimidated by her. He was impossible to insult, he laughed her threats off as smoothly as butter dripped from a hot knife, and smiled when she ranted. Most people described him as irrepressible, but Phoenix settled for defunct. He waltzed into the kitchen behind Jack, tousling Daisy's hair as he did so, snapping a sprig of grapes from a bunch that sat in a bowl on the dresser top.

'So,' he said to Phoenix. 'I hear you've been hob - knobbing with the men in black, that's not a proper way to spend St Pat's night.'

'And what would you know about the proper way to celebrate anything?' Phoenix asked, wary at the mention of the night before.

'Well as it happens quite a lot,' he replied, winking at Jack.

'Oh do tell me Tosh,' she asked sarcastically, 'Or I'll spend my entire life fretting about it.'

'Well,' he began. 'I went to a fantastic party myself, but I drank so much, that when I woke up this morning I couldn't remember where I'd gone.'

'Was it local or did you go across town?' asked Jack pouring himself a glass of water from the tap.

'That's the thing?' replied Tosh, 'I knew it must have been local because I walked, anyway I've spent the entire fecking day phoning round to see if I could find out whose fecking party it was. I didn't have much to go on mind you, because I couldn't remember anything except the bathroom.'

At this point, Phoenix in spite of the fact that it was Tosh telling the story began to feel some interest. 'What was so special about the bathroom?' she asked, turning off the extractor fan in a bid to listen more attentively to the story unfolding, and Tosh replied.

'Well you won't believe it, but it was a gold one, a solid gold one. Anyway I phoned up about six or seven people including Bernie and Jo and all of them like you guys had gone out to celebrate.'

'Did you find out whose it was in the end?' Phoenix asked, puzzled how Tosh could possibly know anyone with a gold bathroom.

'Yes I did. I phoned Pat and Sue, you two wouldn't know them, not your type at all.' Tosh said starting on another sprig of grapes. 'Anyway Sue answered the phone and I said, 'did you by any chance hold a party last night and she said 'yes, why are you asking?' Well, I said 'can you tell me by any chance, if you have a gold bathroom, and do you know what she did? She shouted 'Hey Pat, come here, the dirty bastard who shat in your trombone is on the phone.'

It went against all Tosh's beliefs to ever wait and see how his jokes went down; and this time was no exception. 'Look at him,' Phoenix thought to herself as she watched him snorting with laughter 'he's living proof that a fool always laughs at his own folly.'

Tosh specialised in telling stories that invariably turned out to be long-winded jokes, and no matter how often Phoenix assured herself that she would not be taken in, she always fell for them. This only served to make her dislike him more than ever, for she liked to appear superior in front of him, but he had the knack of fooling her and still managing to make her laugh in spite of herself.

He stayed for dinner and although this was not how Phoenix had planned the evening, she relaxed. It was obvious by Jack's good form, that she hadn't done anything irretrievably bad the night before. He spent the entire meal, talking with Tosh about the new job taken on in Sussex, his first big venture in the renovation of old and historic houses. He wanted a proper gang put together only the very best. Phoenix decided to leave them to it and used the excuse of putting Daisy to bed in order to get away from the table.

What she wanted was a moment's peace. Her nerves were raw – and Tosh was driving her mad with his loud chewing and constant slurping. She watched as he gnawed at a chicken bone like a half starved dog and thought to herself, not for the first time, that he should be under the table not sat at it.

She took Daisy to bed and after peering round the kitchen door and seeing Jack and Tosh well engrossed with their plans, she collected her red book. She would chance sitting in the front room, the settee there made her feel more relaxed and she felt confident she wouldn't be disturbed.

Now that she had broached the unmentionable with Scarlett, she felt an overwhelming need to continue from where she had left off; but she wasn't deaf to the warning bell which rang in her ear. Writing about the past was not without its dangers. There was something she had to ask Shelby Warner. She would write one more letter to Scarlett, and tomorrow she'd make an appointment to see the therapist.

Dear Scarlett,

I wish for Jack's sake I could get myself together again. I feel sorry for him because I know he wants me to be happy. Some men go out of their way to provide their wife with everything, because they want the world to love them, admire them for being a good provider, but that is not Jack's failing.

Since the nineties there has been a lot of hype about 'the new man'. According to papers like the Daily Mail, since women have taken to growing testicles, lots of men have suddenly discovered the joys of domesticity. Not only are they doing their share of the dirty work, they are actually loving it. In surveys, nine out of ten men questioned, said the shittier the nappy the more fulfilled they felt.

What a load of shite. Jack is no new man, he just wants me to be the woman I was when I married him, snappy and together. Well we have something in common then, because so do I, but I just can't find her. I'm seriously beginning to doubt if she existed at all because she has left without trace. I wonder how much longer he can hang on before giving the whole game up because of my moodiness. Jack likes stability, but I have become unpredictable and not in a sexy Eartha Kittish sort of way either.

He's sitting with Tosh now planning his next big move, though why he involves Tosh is beyond me. Jack defends Tosh, he says that he is a first rate foreman, 'Can sniff a good labourer a mile off,' is how he puts it - he must be good at something perhaps he can spin straw into gold. It has to be something spectacular because his personal shortcomings are multitudinous.

He lives in a dismal little bed sit in Battersea, but spends most of his spare time with either William Hill or us. When Jack first introduced us years ago, he said. 'Phoenix this is Tosh, he's from Sligo,' and I thought, yes, he looks sly all right. I don't care what Jack says, as far as I'm concerned Tosh is just a waster, living life through other people with no thought of tomorrow. If he had any up and go in him, he would be running his own business, not playing arse licker in chief to Jack.

When Jack first came over from Ireland, he worked for piss all on building sites throughout London and he could have ended up just like Tosh. He learnt everything he knows about cheating from those days and that is when he found Tosh. Probably under a stone I suspect.

Jack was one of McAlpine's genuine fusiliers for a while, doing jobs here, there and everywhere. He hates songs that glorify that lifestyle; he says it is a mockery to think anyone with a brain would actually choose it.

He is wrong to knock it though, because occasionally the mould can be broken and there is many a labourer who came to Britain with nothing, who ended his days in comfort. But it can come at a cost. Jack tells me that there are loads of blokes he came across with who made a killing, but who got sucked in and married someone they are ashamed to take home. They spend the rest of their lives making an arse of themselves, singing songs like 'The Rose of Tralee' to Dora from Pratt's Bottom who hasn't got the faintest idea what they're rambling on about.

When he first told me this, it was as a preamble to confessing to his first marriage. He married the barmaid at his local pub, and talked her into becoming his receptionist while he set about creating 'B.P' (Battersea Plasterers). She turned out to be as useful as a fart in a hurricane. She got days and dates muddled, mixed her quotes like her drinks, and nearly got him beaten to a pulp on more than one occasion by customers waiting for a skim coat whose details she had forgotten to sketch down.

Jack told me, he needed to be straight about the real reason for his divorce; he didn't want me to think he was involved in any shite like chasing other women. He said Polly nearly drove him mad, he worked his bollocks off, and there had been nothing to show for it

He had a full investigation into her business techniques and discovered she didn't have any. She fell for every sob story thrown at her and gave discounts out left, right and centre, but what really set his arse on fire was her inability to back up his lies.

He said she was pure thick, and shallow with it. A real A&E case, (Jack's short hand for someone who doesn't know their arse from their elbow.)

The marriage was over in less than a year and with the exception of his brother Danny, none of his family knows anything about it. He says he still can't fathom how he could have done it, because he didn't love her; it was one of those things that seemed like a good idea at the time.

In some ways he is a bit like yourself Scarlett, marrying for financial advantage. He was that committed to having his own business, anything was worth a try.

I have no idea if Jack has been totally honest with me, but even if he has peppered the story with a few lies, I don't blame him. The reason why I'm telling you all this Scarlett is because his honesty is part of the problem. By telling me about Polly, he took me into his confidence about his past. I have never returned the compliment. I should have done. I should have been honest with Jack from the start and I wasn't and now it's too late to suddenly play the part of honest Joe.

But the fact remains there is a difference, my secret, is not about a mistake I made, it is not what I did, but what I had done to me. When Mom eventually hauled me off to see the doctor, an old man who kept his eyes firmly on my feet, my fate was sealed. Yes, I was pregnant.

Mom immediately, informed the school that I was leaving, I would not be continuing with my A' level studies. She told them I had been offered a job with my cousin's firm in London. The school was shocked. I had passed ten O'levels the previous year with outstanding grades. They said it would be a tragedy for me not to stay on.

I got a lovely letter from Miss James the head of year, begging me to reconsider. She wrote such lovely things about me, she said I was a beacon of light to the other people in my form with my exemplary manners. She was certain that I had a brilliant academic future ahead of me. Her kind words and good wishes made me cry far more than the taunts and jeers my family threw at me. I showed the letter to Mom, but all she said was, 'If she knew what a dirty conniving little bitch you are, she'd sing a different tune.'

The words Mom spoke to me were always harsh and bitter. Hurt and disappointment fought and won against her urge to reach out to me because I know that somewhere in her heart, she knew I was in hell. But she couldn't let the urge to soothe win, less it made her look as if she was condoning what I had done.

Those days passed so slowly Scarlett, the days were bad but night time was the worst, I still need a television or radio on throughout the night because I have a fear of silence, a leftover from those dreadful days. I remember one dark night lying in my bed and hearing the siren of an emergency vehicle blasting through the cold night air. I wanted to scream out. 'Why are you hurtling on your way to a pathetic burglary or a false alarm when you are passing a real emergency, here in this house, this end terrace where somebody's life is being ripped apart'. For a moment, I thought I really was screaming, but it was only my mind playing desperate games, trying to break out of the terrible situation.

Mom confided the dreadful news to our parish priest, Father Benedict in the hope I suspect; that he could perform some sort of miraculous miracle. He must have been about ninety and I wonder the shock didn't kill him. I have no idea, why she set such store by him; he was after all just a man, and between you and me Scarlett, not a particularly good specimen of one either. Mom thought him small and saintly, I thought him stunted and shifty.

She made me take tea with him in the lounge. I dreaded the thought of it until it occurred to me that it might be an opportunity to put the record straight. Some chance! From the moment he entered the house in his dark overcoat and felt hat, he instantly distanced himself from me.

'Oh Sinead, Sinead,' he said. 'This is a most awfully sad business, your poor, poor mother. What were you thinking of?'

Thinking of? When? Before, during or after? The priest like everyone else just assumed, took it for granted that I was an errant young girl who had got her just deserts. What could I say? 'Well actually Father, I did think a baby born right in the middle of my A' level course would be rather timely and as you can see, Mom here is just bursting to have another baby round the house.'

Where do people like him come from? I kept my eyes suitably downcast. He placed the cup Mom had given him on a little side table and leaned forward, shoulders hunched and I thought he was going to reveal a big secret, but he didn't. 'You know Sinead,' he said, 'You are facing a very big responsibility,' (really I thought, what *could* the good Father be referring to). He cleared his throat; he was obviously finding it all very embarrassing, but not half as much as I was.

'Babies, you know,' he said. 'When they are born, are very small, very small indeed, just about this big.' He held his hands about a foot apart, and I thought, 'Get away with you Father, everyone knows new born babies are enormous, at least six feet.' Just what was this guy trying to do?

Well the top and bottom of it Scarlett, was that he was trying to bring home to me that I might consider myself a young girl, but the fact was, girlhood was over for me. I had responsibilities, something about old skin and new wine. If what he wanted to do was tell me succinctly and in a nutshell, that my life was over, that I had ruined everybody else's, put the world in a worse shape than it was at the end of the last Great War, then yes he did a pretty thorough job. If on the other hand his mission had been to tell me that it was all very sad, but God is merciful and full of hope and the church was there to offer me succour in a dark moment, well in that case he failed miserably.

When he rose to leave, Mom thanked him profusely for coming, and as he turned to whisper 'God bless,' he shot me a look that said. 'See what becomes of bad little girls who lie to their parish priest at the Legion of Mary?'

Mom didn't know what to do with me. She swore the whole family to secrecy; it was her nightmare that other families in the parish would get to hear of my ruin. Whenever I went out she would snap, 'Drop those bloody shoulders down, don't go acting as if you're proud of it.' I didn't understand what she was talking about because there was absolutely no outward sign that I was thoroughly and completely up the spout.

It wasn't just Mom who was hyper; Alice said she didn't know if she would be able to keep it from her husband Guy. She said she would be mortified when he found out that her sister had acted like a common tramp. Alice was Mom's sole confidant and it was her who came up with the idea of sending me to London to live with Aunty Phil in Kilburn.

Aunty Phil was my father's sister, a spinster and a retired nurse. I had only met her once and could remember nothing remarkable about her other than her hatred of cats. She had stayed with us for a few days following Daddy's death, and nearly threw a fit when she saw our tabby cat Candy jump up on my knee. 'For God's sake Bridget, you shouldn't keep that animal in the house, why there was a terrible case just a few weeks back of a child choking to death on a cat's hair in her sandwich.' Just about everyone dropped the ham sandwich they were holding, and began staring at it as if it were a lethal weapon.

She was a fusspot, a bitter old woman but Mom always insisted that her heart was in the right place, which might have been true if she had a heart in the first place. According to Alice she was the perfect choice. Alice had it all worked out, I could stay with Aunty Phil, have the baby, get it adopted and then get a job. Alice loved that last bit because what she really meant was; cut out all this university lark and talk about having a life. That was the source of Alice's discontent, she was so afraid that I was going to get a life, have freedom, while the novelty of being a doctor's wife grew less attractive by the minute.

To begin with, Mom was very reluctant to send me to Aunty Phil; she didn't like the idea of Daddy's family thinking she had made a hash of things. 'Poor Frank dies and Bridget lets the family go to the wall.' That was how Mom believed Aunt Phil would see it, but Alice was quick to soothe, 'Oh Mom, Phil won't judge you because of her, one bad egg doesn't spoil the great job you have done.' By great job of course Alice meant herself, hadn't she bought the bacon home with that fine husband of hers?

Mom looked unhappy, Alice looked defiant and for the first time there was disagreement between them until I reunited them. For the first time, sitting on that hard backed kitchen chair the full implications of what lay ahead hit home, it was Alice's talk of giving birth. After the horror of the attack, the false accusations and clumsy assumptions, here was yet another ordeal to go through, and feeling that enough was enough I remember suddenly bursting out, 'Why can't I just get rid of it, other people do, just let me get rid of it.'

There was a shocked silence, but for one moment Scarlett, one very brief moment I saw a gleam of hope in Mom's eyes before it was dashed by Alice's sharp words. 'For God's sake,' she said. 'You'd have an abortion wouldn't you? You really are low, isn't it bad enough what you have done already, without killing an innocent baby too?'

'An innocent baby,' Mom repeated. 'You can't do that.'

Her words though Scarlett, were addressed as much to herself as to me. But once the idea hit the air and mingled with the fear of birth, I became demented and began screaming and crying, 'Please just let me get rid of it, save me, help me, someone please help me.'

I became so distressed that Mom ordered Alice to fetch the whiskey, which she then forced into my mouth, but I was screaming and shouting so much that I began choking and the whiskey sprayed everywhere. A thought passed my mind that if I got upset enough, it might end naturally, because it always happens that way in books. When I began to calm down, I noticed that Alice looked both frightened and shocked. Perhaps she thought on top of confessing to her husband that her sister was a slut she would also have to add that I was a mad one at that.

For the first time since the nightmare started, there was a softening in Mom's attitude towards me. Perhaps it was a realisation that desperate situations, call for desperate actions, and that a lifetime of belief and faith can go out the window, when self-preservation calls upon it.

More whiskey was poured. Alice sipped and glared, Mom drained and I gulped and a plan was hatched. If Aunty Phil agreed, I was to go to London, have the baby, give it up for adoption and find work in London (said Alice,) go to college (said Mom). Put like that after several whiskies, it sounded easy.

So that Scarlett is how I came to live in London.

Phoenix.

With perfect timing, Phoenix stopped writing just as an enormous bang on the ceiling, sent the chandelier swinging. It came from Daisy, bouncing on the bed in the room up above. She had obviously missed her target and had landed on the floor. Phoenix debated for a moment whether to go upstairs, when another thud clarified her mind, 'If I don't go up to her, she'll come crashing through the ceiling,' she thought. She tucked her book under her arm and went to see her daughter; it was not like Daisy to play around at night.

Daisy's bedclothes were in a mess, they sat in a tangled heap on the floor and Daisy herself was red and flushed from her exertions. Phoenix went into the room and pulled the clothes back on to the bed. 'Be quiet,' she told the little girl sternly, 'it is very late and you should have gone to sleep hours ago.' But Daisy was not in the mood for sleeping. She tugged at her mother's arm and asked for a story. Phoenix caught by a sudden desire for a drink hesitated and Daisy noticing the pause became insistent. Realising she would not get any peace until her daughter had her way; she pulled a book off the shelf and began to read it.

It was a silly book, Phoenix thought, about a stupid child who wanted a real bear for Christmas, but it did the trick, within minutes Daisy was asleep. For a moment, she sat staring at the face of the sleeping child and a flood of bitterness washed over her. Jack was not the only one who knew her mind was elsewhere, Daisy knew something was wrong as well and she wanted her mother's attention back. If she wasn't careful, she would turn her happy go lucky daughter into a clingy whinging brat.

She felt overburdened with responsibility. Too many things were pressing on her, not least the welfare of her husband and child and there was no walking away from them, at least not with a clear conscience. Her mind was conclusively made up, she would see Shelby. She needed advice because although writing to Scarlett was clarifying things, it wasn't offering any solutions.

Chapter Nine

Phoenix kept true to her word and the very next day made an appointment with Shelby Warner; an action that caused her to spend the rest of the entire week, fretting to the point of obsession about what she would tell the therapist.

Although she had told Shelby Warner very little about herself, that 'little' represented far more than she had ever told anyone else. Everyone knew her to be insensitive and sharp, but nobody other than Shelby knew that these characteristics, had been chiselled by events from a far past and were not the result of a genetic inheritance. Most people merely assumed Phoenix to be naturally hard edged and hard driven and since there was a Labour Government stuffed to bursting point with women just like her, she wasn't considered unique.

This need to see Shelby Warner was motivated by a sudden desire Phoenix had to talk to someone and talk, not confess was what she intended to do. There was no way she was seeing Shelby with a view to revealing all. Her past had to be unpacked slowly, there was to be no cutting to the chase with this particular story.

When Phoenix finally arrived at the elegant house in Fulham, on a wet Friday afternoon, she was in a state of great agitation. To her relief, Shelby appeared to be back to her usual friendly form. She smiled and showed Phoenix into the consulting room and cheerily asked to be excused for a few moments, while she finished a telephone call.

Phoenix sat down and looked around her.

Was it a ruse she wondered, was Shelby really on the phone, or was she delaying in a bid to heighten the tension? Was it just a psychological trap to 'sweat her out'? If that was the case it was certainly working for her hands were already damp with perspiration.

While she waited in the comfortable room, with only the ticking of a clock to break the silence, she rapidly came to the conclusion that coming had been a mistake. Anxiety was beginning to make its presence felt by way of a mounting feeling of disorientation. She looked across at the open door and visualised it swinging shut, trapping her inside and the imagery made her feel sickeningly claustrophobic.

Could she sneak out? Would there be time to reach the front door before Shelby heard her? She cocked her head to the side, straining to hear if Shelby was still talking. A faint murmur in the distance rumbled along the hall way and taking heart, she took a firm hold of her bag, her muscles contracting like an athlete, ready to run. But as she stood up, a thought struck her, where would she go? Who could she run to?

She loosened the grip on her bag and sat down again and addressed herself as if she was one of her workers - it was no good wanting what wasn't on offer.

In a bid to distract her negative thoughts she cast her eyes around the room, seeking to fake interest in the furniture and décor. For the first time, she noted the dominance of the colour red and a faint shiver of superstitious fear ran down her back. Red, she sincerely believed was a sinister, unlucky colour. Had the room been redecorated since Christmas? She tried to imagine how it had looked the last time she had seen it, but couldn't bring to mind how it had appeared.

However she did recall a radio programme she had once heard, concerning the effect of colour on mental health. Pastels apparently were the most soothing, with pale green being favoured by most psychologists. It was obvious Shelby Warner hadn't tuned into that particular show; the room Phoenix was sitting in struck her as reminiscent of the red room in Jane Eyre. 'No wonder I'm shit scared,' she told herself, 'All I need now is some satanic Bronte lunatic running in, brandishing a knife in a bid to cut the queue'.

The door shut with a click, snapping her out of her day dream and she looked up to see Shelby standing by the window, her hand half raised by way of apology. 'Sorry to have kept you waiting,' she said.

'No problem,' replied Phoenix, untruthfully.

'Well,' Shelby asked as she walked towards her, 'How are things, have you started writing like I suggested?'

Phoenix replied by nodding her head...

'Do you mind me asking who you are writing to?' she asked, taking a seat opposite Phoenix, and settling back in her usual leisurely pose.

The question caught Phoenix off guard, although she knew Shelby would question her about the content of her writing, it hadn't occurred to her that she would ask for the name of the person she was supposedly writing to. She felt acutely embarrassed at the idea of mentioning Scarlett O'Hara and debated for a moment whether to lie, but when no viable alternative came to her, she thought; what the hell, and replied. 'Scarlett O'Hara from Gone with the Wind.'

Only the cooing of a pigeon roosting in the branches of a lime tree outside the window broke the silence that followed. The pigeon cooed and the counterweights of the carriage clock on the mantelpiece swung effortlessly to and fro, but nothing was forthcoming from Shelby.

Why, wondered Phoenix in a panic, why wouldn't the wretched woman speak? In the end rather than wait for the blow to fall, she pre -empted the therapist. 'Is that proof of madness, writing to someone who doesn't exist?'

'No I don't think it is at all,' Shelby replied, 'but it sure as hell backs up what I said once, about you being creative.' She shifted in her chair before continuing. 'The funny thing is, I'm not surprised at all, but tell me why did you chose her, do you associate yourself with her situation, her personality or what?'

Phoenix paused 'I chose her, because she was strong and determined; something I wanted to be when I first read about her.'

'And when did you first read about her?'

'When I was about seventeen or eighteen,' Phoenix replied with a shrug.

'No offence,' Shelby said, 'but that is a long time ago; she must have made some impression.'

'She did,' Phoenix agreed. 'I wanted to be just like her, I remember reading how she wanted to tell the world to go to hell and thinking that is exactly what I'd like to do. And I did.'

The words tumbled out and Phoenix watched to see the effect of them upon Shelby's face. But the therapist remained impassive.

'Can I ask why you wanted to tell the world to go to hell?'

'You can,' she replied, 'but I'm afraid I can't tell you.'

'Was it the whole world, or just certain people in it?'

Phoenix flicked her eyes from Shelby's face and fixed them on the adjacent wall. A tasteful oil painting hung on it, an original as far as Phoenix could make out. It showed a mountain range, probably somewhere in the West of Ireland, the feet of the sweeping grey mountains were being bathed in rolling waves from the Atlantic and the movement of the water captured so well on canvas, made Phoenix feel slightly dizzy.

She played again in her mind, the question Shelby had just asked, and as she did so, a whole sea of faces from the past, friend and foe flashed in front of her eyes, but it was impossible to differentiate who was who.

'The whole world,' she replied decisively.

'When people tell the world to go to hell, it is usually because they have been let down by someone or a system they once trusted. It is a way of guaranteeing that they will never be hurt again,' Shelby said, pausing for a moment, before getting to the inevitable question. 'Would you agree with that?'

'I think,' Phoenix replied, 'you've just stated the bleeding obvious.'

'That's a bad habit of mine,' Shelby conceded, raising her eyebrows as if to say, 'so what.' 'But tell me- did it work?'

'I don't,' Phoenix said somewhat wearily, 'really understand the question.'

Shelby leaned further back in her chair. 'It is a fairly straight-forward one,' she said, 'You set out to tell the world to go to hell and I want to know, since doing that, has it gotten off your back? Did life get easier, when you decided you didn't care anymore?'

Phoenix made no reply, instead she turned her attention back to the painting on the wall, for she found the sweeping airiness of the mountains mesmerising; it gave her a feeling of space, an antidote to the increasing claustrophobia of the room.

'I'd hazard a guess,' Shelby murmured, 'that since you are seeing me, the answer is no.'

Still silence prevailed, and Shelby not wanting the session to get bogged down with an unanswerable question, moved hurriedly to change the subject.

'Leave this aside for a moment,' she said lightly, 'You mentioned on the phone that there was something you wanted to ask me.'

It was an innocent enquiry but it had a profound and startling effect upon Phoenix. She forced her attention away from the painting and abruptly stood up looking distinctly distraught. For one dreadful moment, an overwhelming desire to blurt out everything swept over her, all control over thoughts, words and actions were it seemed gone from her. So strong did the urge continue; that she had to physically remove herself to the window, away from the line of direct eye contact. But to her alarm, the urge did not decrease and in vain she sought distraction by frantically trying to undo an already undone top button on her blouse.

Not daring to either look or speak to Shelby, she focused her attention on the small back garden which was hardly visible, for the window pane was frustratingly obscured by a mesh of raindrops. All the while Shelby remained passive. No enquiry or soothing noise emanated from her, she just watched silently as Phoenix struggled to regain control of her thoughts. Her lack of interference was gratefully received by Phoenix who was finding the task of calming herself difficult enough without the bother of having to reassure someone else.

When at last the mayhem in her head began to decrease, Phoenix turned towards Shelby 'For a moment,' she said quietly, 'I thought I was going to... but I can't and I mustn't.'

She stopped; too alarmed to continue speaking less the wild words she longed to say re-emerged and overtook the cautious careful ones that had to be said.

There had been a time in the past, when the urge to scream or shout in public had frequently promised to overwhelm her, and on many occasions she had fled out of shops and off buses when the fear of losing control had swept through her. It was this bizarre behaviour that had introduced her to valium. She had seen a doctor with great reluctance, knowing that most were reluctant to prescribe tranquillisers without an inquisition. To avoid interrogation, she had prepared a carefully concocted story, telling the doctor that she would like 'something like a tranquilliser,' just as a 'psychological prop' since she had recently had a bad experience on an aeroplane that had been forced to make an emergency landing. 'I'm sure I'll never use them,' she had said, 'it would just be nice to know they are there'.

To her surprise, the doctor who had viewed her as an extremely 'together' young woman, made no attempt to dissuade her, in fact, as he had written out the prescription, he had given her a trusted tip. 'I had an experience like that once,' he told her, 'and take it from me, the best way to knock a sudden panic on the head, is a quick swig of whiskey'.

Just as she had evaded the issue all those years ago, so she evaded the issue again with Shelby. Rather than face the reality, that something of critical importance was behind her sudden unconscious desire to reveal all to a therapist she had employed with the sole task of helping her, she chose to ignore it.

She sat down and feeling suddenly leaden with bleakness, she spoke, slowly and deliberately. 'I'm not a fool, I know what is behind all these bizarre panic and anxiety attacks but what I really need from you Shelby is help in coping with the symptoms, not deciphering the cause.'

'I'd never take you for a fool Phoenix,' Shelby replied, watching her client intently, 'but to use your terminology, have you ever considered that 'the bleeding obvious' the thing you think is responsible for your anxiety; could actually be a false lead.'

'Oh I'd doubt that,' Phoenix replied emphatically feeling more confident now that the panic was in decline, 'Believe me I've no doubt where my anxiety is coming from.'

'Okay,' Shelby said, recognising that the chance for an open and candid exchange had slipped away, 'You might be right, I'm not going to insist on knowing what happened to you, but the least you can do, is tell me why you can't relay it. Is it embarrassment? Is it because you think I might not believe you, or is some kind of judgement at issue?'

The sudden menu bewildered Phoenix. She turned her face away and thought over the options Shelby had just offered, thinking initially that the choice was obvious, but eventually, feeling very confused, she had to admit, she had no idea.

'I don't know,' she replied, slightly flustered. 'I really don't know. It could be any one of them, I just really don't know.'

'If that is the case,' Shelby said slowly. 'I don't think you have as firm a grip on your trauma, as you think you do, because if you did, it wouldn't be such a difficult question to answer.'

'But you are wrong,' Phoenix insisted, in a voice driven high by the sting of apparent criticism. 'I know what happened, believe me not that many traumatic things have happened to me, but the ones that did, were memorable, very memorable.'

'It isn't a question of doubting your memory,' Shelby replied smoothly, 'But it's a fact; perspective can be open to question. Take sexual abuse for example, there are men and women assaulted as six year olds who never forget what happened, but who spend the rest of their lives asking the wrong questions and so consequently, never recover.'

Not one to be subtle herself, Phoenix instantly took a literal interpretation of the scenario Shelby had used to illustrate her point, and in doing so, felt a chill blast of despair. Was she, she wondered, exhibiting classic abuse symptoms? The thought of being so transparent depressed her, and the urge to reveal all thoroughly died. All she wanted to do now; was bury the tracks she had exposed, but her mind didn't feel up to the task of spinning a misleading yarn.

'Don't be downcast,' Shelby said, sensing the subdued air that drifted across the room, 'It may not feel like it, but you have made great strides.'

Phoenix shook her head despondently 'It doesn't feel like that to me' she said, bending down to retrieve her coat from the back of her chair.

'It's tough,' Shelby agreed, 'but you have to admit, just a month ago the conversation we've just had, wouldn't have been possible.'

Phoenix nodded and glanced at her watch. Now that some kind of equilibrium of mind had returned to her, she felt confident enough to question the way she had acted. Should she have risked telling Shelby something? Not the horror of Condon and all that followed, she could cope with that. But the truth about how she had kept so much from Jack, and how he was bound to walk out the moment he knew her history? Mentally she shook her head. No, she was right to have kept silent. Shelby didn't know Jack, so any reassurance she offered would be pure guess work, or wishful thinking.

'I'd better be making a move,' she said, and Shelby realising there was no more to be said stood up and began to walk towards the door.

'Stay with the writing,' Shelby urged as she opened the front door, 'but do yourself a favour, when you read over your words, double check and check again, that you are asking the right questions, leave assumptions behind.'

Phoenix took her leave, feeling both puzzled and extremely wary. Was it possible that something other than her gross deception of Jack was behind her anxiety? She didn't think so; after all, it was a pretty damming prospect telling her husband that she had had a child by another man. That was bad enough, but when she added another layer, telling him how the child had come about, it was pure bloody disaster.

No matter what spin she put on it, at the very least she was a deceiver. The option of owning up wasn't available; it had been, years ago when she first met him, but it wasn't now. No, she shook her head as she opened her car door, deception was the source of her anxiety, of that she was certain.

And yet! Suppose she was wrong, what then? But I can't be wrong she told herself loudly as she drove straight through a red light scattering petrified pedestrians with more velocity than a beater extracting birds from a bush. She glanced in her mirror at a man standing in the middle of the road, splaying his arms up and down, gesturing towards her with his fingers. 'What the fuck is his problem?' she asked herself, 'Did he have any idea how ridiculous he looked?'

She turned her thoughts back to the problem at hand. For over twenty years she had raked through the aftermath of 79, keeping panic and fear subdued, so why should acute anxiety strike now? It had to be the approaching anniversary that would fall on the 11th September 2001 and the inevitable fall out following on from it. Nothing else made sense.

Chapter Ten

When Phoenix arrived home from her appointment with Shelby, Jack and Daisy were waiting for her, with a surprise in store. On the table sat an enormous bouquet of long stemmed yellow roses - only a small part of a special weekend arranged by the pair of them for Phoenix.

'They were Daisy's idea,' Jack said hastily, when he saw the frosty stare she aimed at the flowers, 'she saw them outside the florist in the village and knew you wouldn't be able to resist them.'

Phoenix instinctively reached out and touched the perfectly formed buds, they were beautiful, but all the same, she shot Jack a suspicious look. 'And that's not all,' Jack announced 'we are going to Brighton for the weekend, Daisy and me both think a bit of fresh air will do you the power of good, don't we puss?' he said, tousling his daughters hair with an affectionate hand. Daisy let out a squeal of delight and began running around the kitchen.

'We are going in the morning Mommy,' she said. 'Daddy said we can play on the beach and have ice cream.' Phoenix said nothing. She felt swamped; what with flowers and talk of the seaside and misguided advice from a secret shrink.

'Well,' Jack said 'what do you think?'

'Does it matter what I think?' she asked taking off her coat. 'You seem to have everything worked out.' He threw his hands up in exasperation, and catching sight of Daisy balancing on top of the dresser in an effort to reach a vase, he went over and lifted her down.

'Run upstairs and get the toys you want to take tomorrow and I'll do that.'

'Will you come up Mommy?' she asked anxiously.

'Just give me two minutes,' Phoenix replied, trying to inject some enthusiasm into her voice.

The moment Daisy was out of earshot Jack turned on her. 'You really are pissing me off, we are all chasing your arse and still it's not enough.'

'Am I asking you to chase my arse?' she demanded. 'Why can't you just get on with your own life and leave me alone?'

'Leave you alone so you can become more miserable than ever?' he asked and before she could answer, he continued, 'take a look at yourself, we tip toe around you, we get you flowers and what do you do? I'd get more reaction out of a headless kipper if I prodded it enough.'

'And why would you want to prod a headless kipper?' she asked, suddenly tired with the arguing. Noting the lighter tone, Jack too became more conciliatory,

'Come on girl,' he said. 'Lighten up, or you will take all of us down with you.'

'I'm trying Jack,' she said tiredly, 'I really am,' and he replied in an equally worn out voice.

'Too bloody right, you are trying, very trying.'

She ignored him and went instead to see Daisy. How strange it was, she thought, that the daughter of a cleaner should be such an expert on how to piss a place up. The room was a mess; Jack had obviously let her run riot from the moment she had arrived home from school. Clothes draped out of drawers and off hangers, while toys with various limbs missing, peppered the floor like a scene from a war film. She sat down on the bed and began the task of folding up some clothes.

They were only staying one night in Brighton, but even so, judging by the huge crowd of bears and dolls Daisy had crammed into a holdall, she obviously wanted plenty of company. After seeing to Daisy, Phoenix packed a small bag for herself and Jack. She took good care to conceal her red book inside her clothes. It was definitely going to be needed. In fact it was her overwhelming need to spend time with Scarlett that made her feel so exasperated with the surprise trip.

They arrived in Brighton the following day, to find the weather had fooled the forecasters at the last minute. The predicted dull skies and drizzle were nowhere to be seen. Instead the sun shone bright from an incredibly blue sky, and although a chill wind blew from the east, the sun went some way to disguise its fierceness.

All arguing put aside, both Jack and Phoenix made an attempt to act civilised. They walked along the sea front hand in hand, Daisy running ahead of them like a terrier, stopping now and then, fear written all over her face when the gap between them and herself, grew too large.

The sudden fine weather had drawn large crowds to the sea. A conference of evangelical Christians was being held and delegates young and old promenaded along the sea front in outfits reminiscent of 'Brief Encounter.' As Jack walked with his family, he pondered on the fact, that although Brighton was close to London, it was so very different. The population seemed much younger than he imagined it to be. He had always associated the British seaside with pensioners and shopping trolleys.

'Do you know something?' he asked pausing for a moment while he checked his mobile phone, and Phoenix, who did not like open ended questions, immediately felt inexplicably anxious. She waited for him to continue, wondering what the big issue was going to be.

'Do you know,' he continued 'Anyone could take us for Daisy's grandparents, because judging by the average mother around here, there can't be one older than fifteen or sixteen.'

The colour drained from her face and she looked carefully at Jack. Perhaps he knew, perhaps he knew everything and his innocent question was nothing more than blarney for 'spit it out while you still can.' The only position she had ever been able to play was that of attack and that is exactly what she reverted to now.

She dropped his hand and turned on him.

'Just what are you trying to imply?' Her voice was louder and more aggressive than she intended and a group of people walking slightly ahead stopped and turned around, startled, as if they had been pelted on the back with a snowball.

Jack too was taken by surprise. 'Oh,' he said. 'So you are touchy about pushing on forty. As it happens I'm not trying to imply anything, other than the fact that all these kids with kids are making me feel like a bloody Granddad.'

Phoenix looked around her, as if searching for evidence to back Jack's opinion up, and luckily for him; at that very moment, a group of extrovert girls, some barely in their teens emerged from the pier, with at least two baby buggies between them. She stared after them, before turning back to Jack. 'Perhaps,' she said, 'If you are finished with your sociological comments, we could get a drink?' She spoke breezily, wanting to disguise the fact, that a sudden overwhelming anxiety was in need of quenching by a glass of whiskey, and led the way to the bar on the pier.

'You take a seat,' she told a perplexed Jack, who felt slightly aggrieved at the prospect of a family day out being squandered in a dark dank bar. He was about to object, but Phoenix was well advanced in her plan. 'Go on,' she said pushing him gently towards a bench of seats. 'I'll bring the drinks over.'

In a low, hoarse voice she ordered a double whiskey, and cursed as the barman drifted lazily across the bar, applying a glass to the optic with all the agility of someone riddled with arthritis. When he returned, she snatched the glass out of his hand, before downing the contents in one gulp and promptly ordering another one along with a pint of Guinness and an orange juice.

The barman, young and inexperienced as he was, sensed an aura of what he took to be hostility surrounding Phoenix and rushed the second order, pouring a sad and beaten looking pint of Guinness. She paid up and grasped the three glasses together, stopping deliberately en route in sight of Jack to take a sip from her whiskey; so to account for the smell on her breath.

They sat together, watching Daisy amass a collection of assorted beer mats, under the eye of far from child friendly bar staff. There was football on the big screen television, and while Jack flicked his attention towards it, Phoenix wondered just how crucial a role whiskey really played in keeping panic under control in situations like this. All the same, she didn't decline another drink when Jack asked with some reluctance if she wanted more, she'd leave it to another occasion, to experiment with that idea.

As she surveyed the passers – by sauntering along, she came rapidly to the conclusion that Jack was absolutely right. There were a lot of young mothers, but as far as she could tell, there were very few young fathers in sight, at least acknowledged ones.

The afternoon was spent on the beach where Phoenix sat in her coat, huddled against the wind like Scott of the Antarctic, while Jack and Daisy skimmed stones into the sea. They were having a wonderful time; Phoenix however was bored and frustrated. Her ears were beginning to ache from grimacing against the wind and she was perplexed as to how Daisy could continue to get excited by the sight of a stone bouncing on the water. In fact the whole place aggravated her. It was cold and full of stupid looking people dressed in sensible clothes, walking their dogs or their spouse, with the same look of indifference. All she wanted was to be sat somewhere warm and dry, from where she could admire the coastline through a window with a glass of something in her hand.

Later that evening, they ate dinner at the hotel. Jack in his effort to please had booked a sea facing suite at The Grand; he was desperate to get the old Phoenix back. For a time at the St Patrick's night ball, he had caught a brief glimpse of her, but she had disappeared and the new disinterested, detached one had taken her place again.

The atmosphere in the dining room was hushed and neither Jack nor Phoenix felt particularly relaxed. For all their wealth; neither had any real desire for either fine dining or fine company, and like a lottery winner who moves from a council flat in the back of beyond to a penthouse in Mayfair, they felt faintly uncomfortable.

A group of waiters dressed in black, hung around them like crows on a washing line, pouncing on their every need. Eventually, when one of them dived so quickly to retrieve Daisy's dropped spoon, that it almost hit him on the head, Jack's patience snapped. 'For the love of God will you back off, you are making me nervous, never mind the child.' The waiter bowed, apologised and after delivering Jack a savage look disappeared into the kitchen.

Jack turned to Phoenix and raised his eyebrows. 'On the strength of that look alone, I think I'll forgo the pudding, I couldn't face any hot snot or bogey pie tonight.' Her loud peal of laughter scattered the remaining group of waiters to the far end of the room and they were finally left in peace.

When dinner was over, they drifted into the bar where Jack ordered coffee and brandy and while they sat at a table overlooking the sea, Daisy sought out the attention of a baby in a buggy at the next table.

'I'm glad we have five minutes together,' Jack said, 'Because there is something I've been wanting to ask you for awhile now, in fact it was my main reason for taking you to Brighton.'

'Go on then,' she said sniffing the brandy from her glass. But to her surprise, instead of firing away, he sat looking at her, almost scrutinising her face, as if trying to read something from it. Alarm rapidly beat surprise into remission, when she realised whatever it was Jack wanted to ask, he wasn't finding it easy to do. She wondered uneasily what it could be and slowly, something too awful to contemplate, occurred to her.

'My God,' she thought, 'he knows. That comment earlier about young mothers, I was right, it was a hint.' Panic now seized her; she felt her heart begin to race and her mouth burn dry. She wanted the brandy, but her trembling hands weren't to be trusted. No longer could she hear the conversation of the people at the table behind, only the hum of anxiety filled her ears. She raised her eyes to his and saw he was still looking at her. 'For God's sake' she thought, 'ask and be damned'.

Eventually, he raised his own glass and after taking a sip, he put it down on the table and turned fully towards her. 'Be honest with me,' he said. 'Tell me what is wrong; this coolness has been going on for too long, is there someone else?'

For a moment, Phoenix was so shocked she couldn't even register the feeling of relief as it flooded through her. Thank God, he didn't know the truth, but how in God's name had he come to such a crazy assumption?

She kept her eyes downcast; aware the longer it took her to respond the more certain he would be that he was right to doubt her. Be honest he had implored her and for one moment she was tempted to be just that and tell him everything- the burning hate in her heart and the fear that dogged her daily; but a voice she had heard many times before; cautioned her to stop.

What, it asked, what if Jack didn't believe her, what if he thought she was just a dirty, tacky liar. Or supposed he did believe her? What then. What was worse, keeping a secret or having Jack know that she wasn't the woman he thought she was at all? Telling the truth would mean Jack knowing she had once walked naked through the snow and had allowed herself to be beaten mentally and physically. He would discover she had crawled her way up, not stomped it, the way he thought she had.

She closed her eyes and opened them again in a vain hope they would look out on an altered world. But nothing was changed. Jack was still there, awaiting her reply, apprehension written all over his face.

She put her hand out and took his. 'I'm sorry to disappoint you Jack,' she said, 'But no, there is no one else, there never could be, while you are around.'

The relief on his face was palpable and Phoenix immediately felt vindicated in not having told him the real truth. 'But something is wrong,' he persisted. 'I know there is.' She hesitated before resorting to the age old lie that cheats have used since the time of Moses.

'It is work Jack,' she said. 'I have one or two problems there and perhaps you were right earlier, I don't relish the idea of getting old.' She added the latter suggestion, because she knew intuitively, that he knew, her anxiety was personal and home based, rather than abstract or financial.

She raised her glass, confident now that she had all trembling under control. 'It is nothing serious,' she reassured him, 'so don't go worrying, just give me time, and I will be fine again.'

He was contented with her reply and they were united again, until later that night, when Phoenix, certain he was asleep, unhooked his arm and took her red book to the chair by the window.

Dear Scarlett,   **25th March 2001**

I'm in Brighton – on a weekend break arranged by Jack as a bit of rest and relaxation and frankly it has proved anything but.

Twice in a row he has forced my heart into my mouth, by commenting on teenage mothers and on the possibility of me having someone on the side.

He is right though about the teenage mothers, I've never seen so many. After my own experience, I find it impossible to think that any young girl might choose to have a baby, but I suppose that is the point, most of them do choose, I never had any option.

Anyway Scarlett, if the right wing press is to be believed, having a baby at sixteen in the New Millennium, is a bit like passing an exam that grants you entry to the bar. You get more money, a bigger house and a fuller figure.

I know Jack is worried, but how I wish he would just leave me alone. When I returned from seeing Shelby, he had an enormous bunch of roses waiting for me, which he tried to palm off on Daisy, but it was his idea. I don't like him buying me flowers Scarlett, because flowers equal guilt. When men have been shits, florists flourish, that's why there are so many flower sellers on the streets of London. Guilt is big business.

I visited Shelby with the one intention of asking her, if she thought writing to you could inadvertently cause me to dig something up I mightn't be able to handle. Sometimes when I pick up my pen, the words just flow and when I read over them, I realise I have written down what actually happened, rather than the censored version I carry about in my head.

But what would happen if I revealed something too terrible to contemplate? That's what I wanted to ask Shelby, but after talking to her, I came to realise, there is no choice, I have to write, whatever the consequences.

Watching the sea outside this window is calming. Although there is only a slight breeze, I can still see the gentle heave of the waves that push on for eternity. The sight reminds me of my childhood home, where life was lived out amongst the constant call of the gulls and the ever present smell of salt in the air. It also brings to mind, how I had came to leave it all behind me.

I left with Mom one bright, cold spring morning and travelled to London on a National Express coach. 007 was its code, but I didn't feel in the slightest bit like James Bond, more like

Miss Moneypenny's granny. All I had with me was a little case, James or Gerry was to bring my big case up at a later date.

When we arrived at Victoria coach station, Aunty Phil was waiting for us. She was very sour with me, but grave and reassuring with Mom, 'Ah Bridget, you poor thing,' she said, sounding all caring and concerned. 'Haven't you been through enough?'

I was almost taken in. Perhaps she did have a heart, but when she flashed me a look that said, 'Well aren't you just about the biggest piece of dead sea shit that's been seen in these parts for years,' I knew it was true, you really could hide her heart under a needle and still have space for her brain.

We had lunch at the Restful Tray on Oxford Street, where Aunty Phil relived all her glory gory days as a Sister at the Charing Cross Hospital, how she had ran the NHS single handed. Mom played up to her, telling her she was the jewel in the crown of the entire health service.

For the most part I was left out of it. I remember flicking my eyes around the restaurant taking in the sheer normality of the other diners. It was so crazy, me a school girl sitting in an old doll's diner when I should have been at school, sympathising with Hamlet's dilemma, not immersed head neck and arse in one of my own.

At one point Aunty Phil mentioned that a spot of hard nursing would be no bad thing for me. 'A turn at making beds rather than jumping into them,' was how she put it. I looked up in time to see Mom give a sharp shake of her head, warning Phil to be quiet. I think Mom felt that enough bitter words had been spoken.

Aunty Phil asked Mom if she cared to take a look at Oxford Street, but Mom declined, she said something about getting back in time so she could baby-sit for Alice. That was news to me, she must have made that up on the hoof. No doubt she was as pissed off as I was with the whole business. She simply wanted to go back home to some normality.

As she boarded the coach for the homeward journey, I remember thinking how unreal it all felt, it was just a terrible dream, but when after some hesitation she put her arms around me and told me to be good, to say my prayers and not to give Aunty Phil any trouble; I knew it was for real. She sat behind the driver and waved from the window, I can still see her face, it looked small and sad and there was something so very lonesome about her.

For all that Mom had left rural Ireland some forty years previously; she was still in the grip of the men in black who had ruled her childhood community. She was fighting both impulse and reason and I think she did what she did Scarlett, not just because of reputation but because... well I don't know.

The wages of sin might usually be death, but for us O'Connell's they were much bloody worse. On top of all the baggage of tradition, she carried the belief that she had let Dad down, because she had treasured in her heart all his hopes and plans for me, and that was her biggest cross. It became my burden as well.

Sometimes Scarlett, throughout the years following this nightmare time, when things got really black, I used to think about Mom and curse her. How could she have let this happen? How could she really believe that me with all my hopes and ambitions, church going and years and years of having the sin of sex before marriage rammed down my throat, how could she believe that I had willingly had sex with a school boy? Was it the case that she knew the truth and wanted to avoid the scandal of Jerh Condon being arrested on a rape charge?

I have never under estimated the consequences of that scenario Scarlett. Not just me but my entire family would have been dragged through the courts and in a small town there is no such thing as anonymity. Jerh Condon had the money for the best brief. Reputations would have been soiled forever. Did she know the truth and simply think it was better for me to carry the blame rather than involve the whole family?

That's what I was tempted to believe during those black moments. But I know that is not the case. People can literally get away with murder simply because no normal person can comprehend their actions.

Even at Tara you had scandal, like the Yankee overseer's oversight with the trashy Slattery girl. That was scandalous for its time but believable. However, would an accusation of child abuse, or interfering with animals have carried any weight? I don't think so. Today though, there have been so many cases of paedophilia; that at times, it seriously looks as if you need at least a GNVQ in child abuse to get into the priest hood, teaching or any form of social work. So many good people have paid the price for failing to spot someone else's perversion...

I think that is how it was with Mom. It would have been beyond her comprehension to think that a rich man like Condon would attack his babysitter, a member of his community, his church. She would reason that if he was that desperate for sex, he would have gone out and bought it. There was no other option for her to believe other than I had gone to a disco, got carried away and lived to regret it.

After Mom's coach pulled away, Aunty Phil and I boarded a bus for Kilburn. We had to wait ages for it and she never uttered a single word to me. She just stood there, bag in hand firing filthy looks at me and I knew she was thinking, 'This guttersnipe thinks she's had a kicking, but she's seen nothing yet.'

By the time we reached her house I was knackered. She lived in a big Edwardian semi, just round the corner from the Catholic Church. It looked impressive enough from the outside, but as soon as she opened the door the illusion of grandeur was shattered.

The place stank both of dampness and overcooked vegetables, with a tinge of mothballs thrown in for good measure, although I don't know why any moths would have frequented that place, unless they were on a suicide mission, because it was that bloody cold.

Lino covered every floor, brown for the hallway, mock wood for the lounge, and for the kitchen she had really sent the boat out with a garish multi coloured covering that reminded me of a migraine attack. From that very first night she was at pains to lay the rules down. She told me to put the kettle on, not as in, 'make yourself at home', but as in 'I'm doing you a bloody great favour and you're going to be my whipping girl.'

145

I made a pot of tea and she went berserk. 'What on earth are ye playing at girl, that tea is so strong ye could stand a spoon in it?'

Rule number one was clear - all tea was to be no stronger than a meercats piss. Sugar rotted the teeth and was expensive, so give up any notion of sugar in tea or on cereal. Baths were to be taken on Friday evenings between seven and eight. No women's magazines were to be bought into the house, what with their filth and carrying on, and finally with a dead straight face she told me to, 'Go easy with the toilet paper and if anyone asks you who ye are, you are the daughter of an ex patient of your aunt's.'

She also informed me that as a girl of sixteen, no longer in full time education, my poor mother had lost her child allowance. I was to go to social security in the morning, and make a claim for national assistance.

That first evening we ate a frosty meal of cold meat, bread and cats piss tea. Some people spend their life saying 'mustn't grumble.' Not Aunty Phil though, grumbling was a way of life for her. She grumbled about everything, the bread was too hard for her poor teeth; the tea was too hot, her neighbour too noisy. The list went on and on and on but then came her biggest gripe, the one I was to hear at least a thousand times.

As she poured herself yet another cup of piss weak tea, she turned to me and said. 'All my life I have worked hard and did I complain, never. Not once. I said to myself, one day Philomena ye can retire and travel to all the holy places, Knock, Fatima and Lourdes and you will do so with a clear conscience because ye've earned it, and what do I get? A bad egg of a niece who shames her mother, her family and her religion, but you don't fool me missy, with that wide eyed innocent 'how could it happen to me' look. I've met your kind before; don't forget I was a nurse for forty years. Like all the other little scuts that hang round dance halls, you just assumed you'd get away with it, but you didn't and now you are paying for it.'

She then told the greatest lie of all time, 'I'm not an unreasonable woman,' she said, 'But in my day, back in Ireland girls like ye would be locked up for the way ye carry on, and I'll tell ye one thing, it worked.'

I bet it bloody well did, in fact as a method of contraception I'd say it would make the pill and condoms look positive amateurs. Sell that idea to China, aren't they the ones teeming with the great unwanted?

My bedroom was at the back of the house and just like the rest of the place it looked as if an over -zealous member of the green party had decorated it. Everything about it was second hand and had the stench of 'make do.' Nothing was surplus to requirement. Magnolia emulsion on the walls, faded green lino, threadbare brown curtains and a bath mat in front of the door to guard against hypothermia. A sad looking picture of the Sacred Heart hung over the bed and a 40-watt bulb drooped wearily out of the ceiling socket, totally nude without even a Woolworth's paper shade to protect its trade- marked arse.

Her entire house reminded me of Johnny Cash's record about the guy who nicks a Cadillac one bit at a time, because there wasn't one towel, spoon or pen in the entire house that didn't have NHS stamped on it. But there was something else Scarlett, which I didn't spot that first evening - at the bottom of the wood wormed old wardrobe, under a pile of old editions of The Kerryman, were two books. 'The Faith of Millions,' by John O'Brien, and 'Gone with the Wind' by Margaret Mitchell.

The next morning she rapped on my door at seven o clock with such urgency that I leapt out of bed, thinking there must be a fire. 'Get up out of that bed, or we'll not make 7.30 mass,' she bellowed. It was a Wednesday and she was hauling me off to mass. That became the routine for every morning and it soon became clear that she had sold her old cronies in the church some very dubious details about me.

Several grey haired coffin dodgers crept up to me and said, 'we've heard all about ye terrible predicament, don't turn ye back on the Lord.' All about my predicament? I wanted to shout, 'you know piss all about it; you don't even know that I am 'Phenomena' O'Connell's niece.'

That crafty, lying, sanctimonious old cow must have spun some crazy line about me, because the one thing all these nosey dolls had in common apart from their grey hair, was a very wary manner. She must have fed them all a dud line, such as I was the mentally unstable daughter of an ex patient of hers who was dying of cancer.

'Sure the poor old critter is wrecked with cancer, and what does that daughter of hers do? She gets herself pregnant, but don't remonstrate with her, she'd pull a knife on you as quick as she'd look at you.'

It had to be something like that, something that would fly round the parish faster than a fart in a lift and kill two birds with one stone, bring her papal medal one step closer, and more importantly, frighten the shit out of any of the old crones from quizzing me about who, what and where.

None of them ever tried to strike up a proper conversation with me; they just whispered little messages like, 'Keep the prayers up.' 'Trust in God.' 'God is good.' The slogan brigade - if they had been Protestants they would have worn sandwich boards and paraded up and down Oxford Street, frightening the shite out of passers by.

I did get national assistance, well rather Aunty Phil did, the government gave me money and Aunty Phil immediately took it off me for board and keep. She gave me a miserly amount for personal things like Mars bars and coffee and I became something of a streetwalker.

Everyday I walked up and down the Kilburn High Road. I loved it and it was with a sense of dread that I returned to that dark dank house.

It must have been early May when I first arrived at Aunty Phil's. I can't have been more than five months pregnant, and it hardly showed. Aunty Phil of course acted as if I were nine months gone with quads.

'Put a coat on for God's sake and don't be advertising your wares,' she barked, every time I ventured out of the house. I don't have a good recollection of what I looked like at that point because thankfully Aunty Phil had never gone to the expense of buying a full length mirror, but I knew I wasn't big, because most of my clothes still fitted me.

There's a line in a song Scarlett that says something about life being what happens while you are taken up with making other plans, and it's absolutely true. It's a crazy idea planning for a future that might never happen, but in those days I just wished my life away at a furious pace.

Before coming to live in Kilburn, I'd only ever been to London for Christmas shopping, and with the school to see Henry IV, and Othello at the theatre. There had also been occasional school trips to museums and art galleries, all of them occasions of great excitement. Looking back on those times and my classmates, I still find it incredible to believe that I was the one to be pregnant at sixteen. There were so many who would have been better candidates, because socially I was very backward.

I remember one occasion, when I went with my class on a trip to the science museum, there had been an IRA bombing campaign in London, organised by 'Sinead's friends' as some people at school put it. As a result every tourist venue made a big fuss of searching all bags.

We had to wait in a queue to enter the museum and my friends Clare and Jill and Magda were ahead of me. The security guard took their handbags and pulled out lipsticks, purses, and address books, all the typical paraphernalia you'd expect to find in a teenagers bag.

When it came to me though, the security bloke pulled up the flap of my bag and shot me a dead suspicious look. Mom had packed some sandwiches for me; she said they would be cheaper than going to a café. She had wrapped them in greaseproof paper, and they just about slid into my bag without an inch to spare. With difficulty the guard pulled them out and the waft of egg sandwiches hit the air.

He looked at me as if I were playing some kind of sick joke and my friend Clare whispered, 'See, he was right to follow his instinct, he's found a stink bomb.'

Everyday rather than sit in Aunty Phil's house I'd trawl up and down the High Road. If I hadn't been in such a terrible fix, I would have thought that I had died and gone to heaven, because for me, Kilburn was fantastic, so busy and varied, with its cafes and pubs and turbaned people.

I was a young girl in a big city completely unprepared for it. My personal money allowed me a daily cup of coffee in a café and there were lots to choose from. There was one I loved best though, a Maltese one where they played great music and never embarrassed me by taking away my empty cup. The staff there were lovely, especially an old fella, who used to call me his little flower. 'How is my little flower today?' he would ask but not in the gropey flirty way that Mario would have asked it.

I'd order my coffee and sit the window, feeling like the last of the big spenders. The dreadful day came though when Aunty Phil told me that she had booked an appointment with the CAA. I would have been less afraid if she had said the CIA. The CAA was the Catholic Adoption Agency. I was to meet a representative to plan the proposed adoption of my baby. I couldn't bear any talk about the reality that lay ahead. Going to see a doctor was bad enough, but at least the one I saw in Kilburn didn't stare at my feet. He was Dr Singh, a Sikh.

That cunning old woman, Aunty Phil, told me her doctor; Dr O'Mara from Tralee was over- subscribed. What she really meant of course was that she didn't want me sullying her good reputation. I didn't care anyway. Dr Singh was fine, just got on with the job, with no sarky comments or assumptions. He told me to lie still on the couch as he pressed his fingers deep into my belly to feel the baby. Christ, how I hated that. I would lie there as stiff as a poker, hands down by my side, fists clenched while a horrid little rhyme from childhood flooded my mind. 'Annie get your gun there's a girl in the garden, laying on her back with her belly to the sun.'

Each exposure, every prod, sealed my fate and brought home to me what the ape had done. I was filled with an overwhelming determination, that one day; someone would pay for the indignity that I suffered.

Right now it is Jack and Daisy who are paying for it. The villain got away and that troubles me.

Phoenix

Chapter Eleven

The weather, throughout March and early April, was change-able, but not as changeable as Phoenix's moods, which swung to and fro more frequently, than the weathercock perched high upon the local church tower, changed direction. She had taken to reflecting more deeply on her letters to Scarlett, and this caused in her moments of great exhilaration, which were often followed by ones of deep oppression.

On the one hand, she recognised conclusively, that progress had been made. For the first time, she was standing up to the past, looking it in the eye and facing it as it was. Knowing the past wasn't sacrosanct was exhilarating, it could she discovered, be examined and held to account.

On the other hand, looking back reinforced how far away the source of her trauma was. How could she realistically believe anything could change? For too long she had merely assumed the past was dead, but now she saw with startling clarity that some issues had never died, they had merely hidden under a barrage of time from where they still managed to direct the action that made up her life.

There was deep within her, a belief as solid as any reality she had ever known; that only when events and misdemeanours from the past had been rectified, would she ever find peace again. Life had been knocked off its natural course and nothing would be well, until it was diverted back on to its proper track.

But she wondered, what if the track couldn't be found, what then? Was she destined to spend the rest of her life in a state of perpetual anxiety? If that was the case, it was more than she could bear.

Jack noted the more peaceful, cheerful exterior, which Phoenix's moments of exhilaration exuded, and gave thanks for it, but failed utterly to see the deeper anguish nestling beneath it, which often masqueraded itself as a calm, contemplative silence.

Carolyn however, recognised the subtle change in Phoenix for what it was and unfortunately she wasn't the only one. Most of Phoenix's employees noted the difference and many of them seized on it with something approaching glee.

'It wouldn't surprise me if she has cooked the books and is against the ropes on account of it,' remarked Olive, a veteran from the early days of Phoenix Maids. Her remarks met with the general approval of her fellow workers, all of whom had experienced more than a sample of Phoenix's caustic tongue. Carolyn however, was outraged at their lack of empathy.

'It is unfair to say things like that,' she said, 'and also extremely dangerous, it is slander.'

Olive and Tracey turned and faced each other, hands raised, both feigning shock and fear. 'Oh no, please don't grass on us Carolyn,' begged Olive, winking at Tracey, 'We don't want to go to Holloway; we might end up sharing a cell with Phoenix.'

Only Carolyn failed to find anything funny with Olive's little rendition and Tracey sensing disapproval, immediately felt a dart of unreasonable aggravation, which she tried to assuage by turning on Carolyn.

'Your trouble' she said vindictively 'Is that you don't live in the real world, Phoenix is vicious, I wouldn't waste any pity on her. She certainly wouldn't waste it on *you*'.

But Carolyn, while recognising the emphasis, Tracey had placed on the word *you* with its implication, that if anyone was to arouse contempt in Phoenix, it was surely Carolyn herself, refused to be deflected, from safe guarding Phoenix's reputation. Although she hated confrontation, she refused to remain neutral.

'All of you receive twice the going rate from Phoenix,' she said in a slightly shaky voice, 'So it seems a bit rich that you are willing to take her money, while talking her down'

At this point, Olive, sick with what she perceived to be Carolyn's attempt at canonising Phoenix, joined forces with Tracey and turned her ire on Carolyn. She had long disliked Phoenix, ever since Phoenix had administered; what she had termed 'an official public bollocking' over some private work Olive had attempted to do with a client. To see Phoenix cut down to size would be a dream come true. Of course the fact that her job and bonuses would also disappear, should the axe fall on Phoenix never occurred to her, because she wasn't a thinking woman, only a poor loser who lived her entire existence on the drama of other people's lives.

'You don't know what you are talking about Carolyn,' she said, stuffing her rota sheet into her handbag. 'Phoenix uses you, and your admiration of her is misplaced, she only got where she is through cheating and lying, as for the wages, they are nothing more than bribery, and I tell you, if it suited her, she'd fire the lot of us without a second thought and personally I'd love to see her swing.'

Carolyn looked at the petite, sallow faced woman and her hands trembled with anxiety. She wished she could find the words to put Olive succinctly in her place, but the art of the 'put down' was beyond her. She was certain though that Olive had always been jealous of Phoenix, she was jealous because Phoenix was good looking and smart, creating a business of her own while Olive had merely tried to steal one and hadn't even managed that properly.

There was no other armour Carolyn had other than to smile. And the other women, recognising the calm serene expression of a woman who refused to believe ill of her heroine, forsook their cause. It didn't increase their admiration of Carolyn, but it made them uneasy about continuing their assault on Phoenix.

Carolyn's empathy, with what she took to be Phoenix's fragile mental state had substance, for she had suffered a break-down herself, and although it had all happened a long time ago, she still retained a painful memory of the signs and symptoms that had lead up to it. She was in little doubt, that the air of detachment and disinterest emanating from Phoenix was symptomatic of something serious.

All those years ago, when she had faced a bleak future, Phoenix had come to the rescue, stepping in and giving her a chance, when few other employers would have given her the time of day. She was in a position now of owning her own flat, she had money in the bank and a decent car and it was all thanks to Phoenix. Now it was Phoenix who was in need of help, and Carolyn was going to make sure she got it.

But how, that was the question. She couldn't risk asking Phoenix what was wrong. Phoenix was so proud and so strong - she'd take an enquiry like that as an insult. She wondered if a reflective book might help, it would be a gentle hint that she knew all was not well, without being intrusive. But what would be suitable reading for Phoenix? Carolyn knew she was a Catholic by upbringing, but then Phoenix never spoke about religion or attended Mass as far as she knew. 'Across the Threshold of Hope,' by John Paul II was making big news, how would Phoenix, respond to that?

But then again, Phoenix looked so Irish, so perhaps a book on Celtic Spirituality might help. She took a sojourn into Waterstones one night and perused the spiritual and self help section. There was one spectacular book which caught her eye; it was full of exquisite photographs of the sun setting on mountains and wheat fields, each one accompanied, with a brief meaningful quote, focusing on the relationship between the ancient Celts and nature. It was awe inspiring, but Carolyn hastily put it down with a guilty smile, for it bought to mind, the dislike Phoenix held for anything to do with the Green movement. She remembered with a silent laugh, the haranguing Phoenix had once given a self righteous member of a green party, who had foolishly canvassed for her vote, after giving her a leaflet declaring war on business.

'Do you think I'd give the time of day, to someone who wants to put me back into a mud hut?' she had demanded, screwing the leaflet up and throwing it into his face.

The politician of course, had attempted to remonstrate, but that had only incensed her and when she had stridden towards him menacingly, he had turned tail and had retreated, apologizing profusely as he did so. But she had pursued him all the way, like a guard dog seeing off an unwelcome intruder. He had mounted his parked bicycle with an agility that he didn't know he was capable of, with Phoenix shouting, 'Do I look the type who would ever take a fecking bike to work, when there is a car available?' ringing in his ears.

No, all in all, perhaps Celtic Spirituality with its emphasis on the natural world would not be a good choice for Phoenix. In the end Carolyn decided on a book of Chinese proverbs, they dealt with a variety of subject matters and there might be one or two Phoenix would find inspirational. She took it away and wrapped it up, ready to give Phoenix the following day.

Phoenix meanwhile, was oblivious to the concern she was causing Carolyn, there was only one concern that bothered her and that was her inability to answer Shelby's question, as to why she couldn't talk about the past; the more she thought about it the more entangled her mind felt.

Was it shame? There was a time when that would have been the obvious answer, humiliation at her treatment by Condon had burned her heart badly but she knew, upon reflection; shame was no longer the burning issue.

Why, she asked herself, did Shelby seem to think the answer should be so obvious? Phoenix spent much time pondering this question, and came to the surprising conclusion that Shelby was right; the only way forward was to drop the assumptions and simply question everything.

It was this new introspection that bothered Carolyn, for Phoenix was the least analytical person she had ever known. It could only mean something drastic was wrong, if Phoenix was not using instinct, as her basic port of call.

When Phoenix prepared to leave the office for home that Friday evening, Carolyn handed her the book of Chinese Proverbs. 'I hope you won't be offended,' she said gently, 'But you've looked so tired recently that I took the liberty of buying you something small that might interest you.'

Phoenix took the package with some surprise. It never occurred to her Carolyn might be watching her and weighing her up. She never did that to Carolyn, she seldom did it to anyone unless there was the possibility of some material advantage in it. 'Do I really look that down and out?' she asked and Carolyn suddenly anxious that her words were going to be misconstrued replied quickly.

'Not at all, it's just that it has been a long dreary winter and I thought you could do with cheering up.'

Phoenix looked at the brightly wrapped package before turning her gaze into the honest and sincere face of Carolyn. There was something unfathomable, in the wide open clear blue eyes that met her narrowed green ones that instantly made Phoenix feel distinctly uneasy.

'Thanks,' she said. 'Should I open it now or later?'

Without hesitation Carolyn replied, 'Oh later, it's nothing much, just something I came across in Waterstones.'

Phoenix took her leave feeling slightly unnerved, why on earth, was Carolyn buying her presents? She arrived home to find Jack looking smug and self satisfied. In his hand he held a letter from his solicitor. It contained the memorandum of sale, concerning Shitlegs O'Carolan's garages.

'I hope you don't mind,' he said, 'But I'm using the name of O'Connell to put the bid in via O'Carolan's solicitor. The trouble is, this O'Connell is a tricky bastard. He's going to give Shitlegs the run-around.'

Phoenix took her coat off and bent down to kiss Daisy.

'Use what you want,' she said, 'you usually do.' Daisy seeing the gaily wrapped package in her mother's handbag, instantly seized on it.

'Oh Mommy have you got me something nice,' she asked. 'Can I eat it now?'

Phoenix laughed. 'I'm afraid you can't darling, it is something for me and I don't think it's eatable.'

'Oh,' said Jack walking towards them. 'What is this about Mommy getting presents, what have I been telling her about secret admirers?'

Phoenix picked up the packet and began to unwrap it, 'I'd hardly classify Carolyn as an admirer,' she said pulling the book out from its wrapper. She paused and read the title 'Chinese Proverbs' before turning the book over, to check its back cover, feeling certain, it was a spoof copy, some kind of joke. But no, it was the real thing.

'What on earth is Carolyn thinking about?' she asked Jack.

She flicked the book open and read silently for a moment, before going on to flick several pages over at a time. 'My God,' she laughed 'this should be called the book of the bleeding obvious, listen to this,' and she began to read at random, in a solemn pseudo Chinese voice, 'do not take the seeds and throw away the melon.' 'Or how about this one, 'the higher the climb, the further the fall.'

She threw the book down on the table and turned to Jack. 'Well, I'm sure glad I had a read of that, or I might have made the mistake of attempting suicide by jumping out the basement window.'

Jack laughed and picked the book up and began flicking through it, just as Phoenix had done. 'Carolyn must be pretty concerned if she was willing to risk giving you this,' he said, 'So take this warning and listen, 'when drunk, the truth tumbles out.' 'Or,' he continued, 'try this one from the Western Han Dynasty, 'if there is a fire, I can put it out by pissing on it.'

He snapped the book shut. 'Makes you think doesn't it?'

Phoenix walked away exasperated, it never took Jack long to get down to basics, but he was right about one thing, she would heed the warning about the truth tumbling out.

After dinner, when Daisy had been tucked into bed, Phoenix took the book of proverbs with her to the bathroom. In the warmth and comfort of the bath, she closed her eyes and tried to turn her thoughts to things long past, but the image of Carolyn kept flicking in and out like interference on a radio wave. What had possessed the simpleton, to think she of all people, would be interested in Chinese Proverbs?

She reached out and picked up the little book from the side, and began to read from it with more attention. She soon came to the considered opinion, that while most of the proverbs were overwhelmingly banal and pointless, one or two were worthy of consideration.

She emerged from the bath and wrapped her damp hair in a towel and as she did so, she caught a glimpse of herself in the mirror. 'Half a truth engenders a new lie,' she quoted quietly. It sounded meaningful, but she didn't really understand it.

As she began to descend the stairs, she heard voices drifting up from the kitchen. Jack was talking to someone, how annoying when all she wanted, was peace and quiet. She paused for a moment then continued as she recognised the loud guffawing laugh that ricocheted throughout the house. The surprise visitor was Tosh, well at least it wouldn't matter that she wasn't properly dressed properly.

When she entered the kitchen, Tosh looked up and stared at her, his hand on his chin as if in deep thought,

'You reminded me of someone just then,' he said to her.

'Marilyn Monroe possibly,' she replied.

'No,' he said shaking his head, 'The head waiter in the Taj Mahal up the road.'

She ignored him and sat down on a chair beside the range, wondering what she could say that would tell Tosh succinctly, to piss off.

Jack handed her a beer and offered Tosh one at the same time. 'Tosh has just been to seen Mike Wood in hospital,' he informed her by way of apology for the ganger's presence. 'Mike was the guy who did the casino job with us.' She nodded knowledgably although the name meant nothing to her.

'Oh he's in a very bad way,' Tosh said, speaking as if the man in question was on a life support machine, 'the worst case of piles the doctor has ever seen, no wonder he never sat down for a tea break.'

Jack visibly winced. 'How long will he be kept in for?' he asked.

Tosh shook his head. 'No idea, but I tell you, the ward he's in is like a bloody dolphinarian, everyone in it has had a pile job done and not one of them can fart without howling.' Jack laughed and Phoenix threw Tosh a withering look.

'I tell you,' he continued, 'if I made a recording I could make a fortune, I'd sell it to Greenpeace; boost their campaign to save the dolphins.'

'It's not dolphins they want to conserve,' corrected Phoenix. 'It's whales.'

Tosh looked at her aghast. 'Are you mad?' he said. 'Who the bloody hell wants to save Wales, but since you are talking out of your arse, I've only got one thing to say to you.' And with that, he lifted his leg and broke wind.

'Get behind me Satan,' he said, turning his head round and addressing his errant backside sternly.

Phoenix delighted for a viable reason to leave the room, got up and shot a look of disgust at Tosh. 'I have some paint upstairs I want to watch drying,' she said and as she began to walk away, Jack reached out and pulled at her hand.

'Come on girl,' he said. 'Don't leave us.' She smiled at Jack before turning another hostile glare on Tosh.

'Oh don't mind me Jack,' she said. 'Pull up a chair for Tosh, and give his arse a chance to rest, after all he's been speaking through it most of his life.'

She walked out, to the sound of Tosh guffawing. She wasn't in the form for him and it was early yet, so he probably wouldn't be gone for hours. For a moment she debated about what to do, but it was a false debate. She knew exactly what had to be done. She would write to Scarlett, then go to bed and review in the dark of night, what she had written.

Dear Scarlett,   **2nd April 2001**

I've been thinking over the advice Shelby gave me and I realise she is right. I probably do assume too much about the past. How brave psychotherapists are, they take people like me off the street, never knowing what we might reveal. Do they ever panic that one of their clients might flip, and that they'll end up in the freezer?

Since my last letter to you, I have been thinking about the time when I lived with Aunty Phil in London. I wish I had known about whiskey and valium back then. I could have done with them.

At the time I couldn't grasp what had happened – it was just all so unreal. In a way it was like an out of body experience, I felt as if I was a bystander, watching on as my life fell apart. I didn't want to believe that me; Sinead O'Connell, had been assaulted. I was repulsed by the violence and hate men are capable of. I found myself thinking about men in general, bus drivers, doctors, the lot of them. Were they all the same was it just circumstances that kept them contained? I began to understand why there are women like Aunty Phil, who use men solely to mend pipes and deliver coal.

And then there was the fear of giving birth. There were moments that I can only describe as 'flash forwards' when nasty gory images of the imminent birth would screech through my mind. I'd go to bed and dream that the baby had been born during the night. I even used to wake up fully believing that I'd find it in the bed and sometimes I'd find myself searching under the blankets, thinking it must be there.

The fear was so overwhelming and yet in a peculiar way it carried me through those days, there was something to focus on, something inevitable. I remember reading Scarlett, that when the war really came to your doorstep with the shelling of Atlanta, you became less frightened because life became like a dream. Something that couldn't possibly be real. I think that is how it was with me. It was all too terrible to be true, like a really awful film that is too implausible to be bothered by.

After reading your story I remember questioning whether you had really changed Scarlett, or whether the war and all its misery had simply brought out the real you. Now I find I'm asking the same question of myself. Am I, what I was destined to be? Foul mouthed and harsh? Was that gentle obliging Sinead the impostor? And if so, how did the transition happen? I can't be certain but I think it may have started the day Aunty Phil took me to the CAA.

The summer of 1980 was a hot one, most girls my age walked round London half dressed, but Aunty Phil being neurotic about my 'condition' as she called it, insisted on me wearing a jacket at all times. 'Put a jacket on,' she would say. 'Don't go drawing attention to yourself.'

So I'd fetch my tweedy jacket or blue cagoule and I'd face looks and stares as passers- by muttered under their breath, 'She's either from the bleeding tropics or going shoplifting.' For someone who was instructed not to seek attention, I attracted it easier than a stack of shit attracts flies.

We set off for the CAA office one hot and sunny morning at the beginning of July. It was situated behind Paddington station, down a little back street, a tiny office on the ground floor of an ordinary terraced house. It had been freshly decorated in my honour of course; in fact the paint on the front door was still wet. As we approached, two workmen stepped aside. They looked knowingly at each other. I suppose one look at the fierce old woman marching like a soldier with a sweaty puffy looking teenager by her side helped them to weigh the situation up pretty quickly. As we drew nearer, the two men turned their gaze directly on me and something must have snapped, because I remember thinking 'I don't give a shit,' and instead of looking away like I normally would have done, I stared straight back at the younger of the two men. He dropped his gaze first.

'Is this the CAA?' Aunty Phil barked and the older man replied

'It tis, but don't shoot me miss, I'm only the decorator.'

She gave him a filthy look and said 'Hmm not much of one by the look of it,'

The younger of the two burst out laughing and the older one grinned but Aunty Phil was oblivious to them. She really was an obnoxious bitter old woman, when I think now about all the new mothers she must have dealt with in her forty years of nursing, I shudder for them. I bet she halved their joy. She shouldn't have received a gold watch; she should have been taken out and shot for services to inhumanity.

We went inside to a small white washed room that was parti-tioned from a back room by a hatched window and single door. There was a middle aged woman in there fussing about with a drawer that had got stuck in the filing cabinet. When she saw us she left it immediately and came across with an outstretched hand.

'You must be the O'Connell's,' she said really warmly, like seeing us had made her day.

But the old dragon wasn't one bit impressed; she ignored the friendliness and said. 'Tis her, Sinead O'Connell, that has the appointment with you.'

Talk about disassociating yourself, she acted as if being related to a pregnant teenager; would result in her being issued with an armband or being branded on the forehead. The woman was pretty smart; she caught on immediately to the tension and diffused it by introducing herself. Her name was Flora Burnell.

She invited me to meet the case worker and asked Aunty Phil to take a seat. She also offered her a coffee. Aunty Phil was dead huffy, she rudely refused Flora's offer. She was miffed at not being invited in along with me, so she could poke her drad in, and tell yet more people what a scandalous scut I was altogether.

I followed the woman along a dim little passageway until we came to a door at the end of it. I was disappointed at being handed over to someone else, because I liked Flora, she looked kind and I could have talked to her. I also liked the way she sussed Aunty Phil out as well.

My case officer was a Miss O'Farrell. She was younger than Flora and she looked, well like I'd always imagined social workers to look like. You'd certainly never mistake her for Julia Roberts. She was thin, with wispy short hair, cut in a style that accentuated her world cup ears and her pale face was completely devoid of make up. Everything about her made a statement, her denim pinafore dress with its dropped waist, her Milky Bar Kid glasses, the ugly knot of brown beads thrown round her neck as a token of glamour and the flat brown brogues on her feet.

When I entered the room she looked up as if to say. 'Ah, another fool that needs sorting out by clever old me,' and pointed to a chair with her pen.

She basically ordered me to sit down and then very bluntly and officiously, dismissed Flora. I disliked her on sight. I didn't like the way she used my first name, and I didn't like the way she spoke to Flora. She did it in a way to emphasize her seniori-ty; from the way she spoke you'd think she was the Chairman of ICI dismissing a lavatory attendant, not a short-sighted social worker in charge of a team of three. She sat opposite me across a blue table and dispensed with any attempt at chit chat or charm.

'Sinead,' she said. 'I have some bits and pieces here from your doctor, your mother and your parish priest, so I have a good idea of your situation. Is there anything else you'd like to fill in?'

'Your face for starters,' I thought. I was furious. Here was another professional, another person who should know better, making a complete arse of herself with her assumptions. Just what did she know about me, other than what other people had conjectured?

'You seem to know it all,' I replied, dead sarcastically and do you know what Scarlett, she took it as a compliment. She said,' I make it my business to get all the facts, because babies are very precious and its vital that everybody is happy with the arrangements I make.'

She spoke caring words, but she didn't look or sound like a caring person, she sounded like an organiser.

She asked me to confirm my EDD. For a moment I didn't have a clue what she was talking about, - of course she was referring to my estimated date of delivery. Before I could answer, she said. 'The 14th of September and you've been booked into St Mary's Paddington.'

She knew all the facts and none of the details but that didn't deter her from questioning me like the Gestapo.

She went on as if memorising a script. She said she assumed that I must be feeling very nervous and then totally lost me by saying it was an exciting time. Was she mad? Going on holiday or standing up on the big dipper, or doing a hundred miles an hour along a country lane, that's exciting, having a baby is pure bloody hell.

The more I think about it Scarlett, that was definitely the day either I changed, or the real Sinead emerged. I couldn't be bothered anymore with what people thought about me. The very people I had been brought up to respect and grovel to were gobshites, totally unworthy of respect.

It didn't matter what answers I gave to Miss O'Farrell's carefully contrived questions, she had me fixed in a mould. I was a teenage slut, one that should have known better given the reference of the parish priest, but a slut all the same. Why fight it? She, Miss O' Ferret, was completely oblivious to my discomfort, she prattled on about the countless number of people she had on her books, 'good decent honest people' who were desperate for a child.

She told me she would have no problem finding a good Catholic home for my baby, a home that would give it a much better chance in life than a young girl like me realistically could.

She said 'Your sacrifice will be somebody else's silver lining.'

That was the phrase that confirmed her in my mind as a fully developed sheep dropping. There was no sacrifice. It wasn't my baby, I didn't ask for it, it belonged to that great hairy ape and I felt nothing but hate. I couldn't bear all the talk about desperate people. I wanted her to shut the fuck up, let me sign the papers and get out.

If at that point, she had one bone of sensitivity in her miserable body, she would have stopped. She could have contented herself with her own story about wayward teenagers bringing silver linings. She could have continued going happily into churches and schools up and down the country, and telling one and all not to be judgemental of young girls who get into trouble, after all wasn't she herself, a witness to the sacrifices they make by handing their babies over. But she didn't shut up. She didn't notice my agony, she just continued with more claptrap about deserving couples and the need to take care in the future.

On and on she went, until finally, having bored the backside off herself, she said. 'Obviously Sinead we have to make the final decision about where babies go, since we have the facts, the complete picture of each case, but do you have any particular preferences?'

I should have put my head down, shook it or declared an urgent need for the lavatory, but something in me said 'enough.' Her voice grated on me, it was so patently obvious that she didn't and never would have a clue about solving a dilemma like the one I was in and before I knew it, I found myself shouting. 'I couldn't give a monkey's arse where you put it, I never asked for it, I don't want it and I don't give a fuck who does.'

She made the only unrehearsed sound of the entire interview, she gasped, but before she could utter a word, I was up and out of the room.

As soon as I slammed the door behind me, I regretted my actions and the words I'd used.

I felt I had let myself down, confirmed her opinion of me, I could imagine her conferring with a pack of like- minded ugly social workers, telling them, 'Well I did my best, but else can you expect from a guttersnipe?'

I walked back into the reception area where Flora was still fiddling about with that filing cabinet. She looked embarrassed; she must have heard every word of my parting comments. 'Oh

Sinead,' she said, 'Your companion, said to tell you, to make your own way home, she left a little while ago.'

I thanked God for small mercies; at least I wouldn't have to endure that tyrant ranting on about my behaviour, about the disgrace I was to my family, the church, the U.N.

I didn't go straight home; I took the tube from Westbourne Park up to Oxford Circus and wandered up and down Oxford Street. The heat was unbearable, but at least I was able to whip my jacket off without a tongue lashing. I sat for ages like a granny on a bench, eating an ice cream, watching the crowds. There were thousands of foreign students, young, tanned, good - looking and unbearably slim and in aggravatingly high spirits.

A group of Hari Krishna's danced by and I must have been staring into space, because a bald young man began waving furiously at me, trying to get my attention, I was tempted to give him the fingers. I've never understood how people can make such prats of themselves in public.

After awhile I got up and ventured into Selfridges. It took me back to my childhood, because once when I was about nine or ten, Mom and I had travelled up to London for some Christmas shopping and I got lost in Selfridges. It took me ages to find her. I remember sweeping through department after department but because of the Christmas decorations, they all looked the same and I soon lost my bearings. I was fearful at being lost and yet afraid of finding her, because I was certain she'd give me a bollocking for being so stupid. Eventually a really nice West Indian man took me to customer's services and within minutes Mom and I were re-united. Mom wasn't angry at all, just relieved and to prove it, she took me to Littlewoods café and treated me to a chocolate éclair and a glass of coke.

Selfridges was every bit as big as I remembered it and I headed straight for the fashion department. The fashions of 1980 were pale and foamy and all the more beautiful because they were so unattainable .I had gone upstairs on the escalator but heat and fatigue made me decide to take the lift down.

A mistake, it had a full-length mirror in it and I saw myself pregnant for the first time. I looked dreadful, not big, worse than big, puffy and bloated and so red. I looked like a farmer's wife. Jesus I wanted to die, it was fifty times worse than I'd imagined. It put me right off the idea of walking the streets of London. I had a sudden urge to be home, not in that pokey hovel in Kilburn, but home with Mom by the sea with the shriek of the gulls and the smell of salt in the air. Things I had once despised.

When I did get back, Aunty Phil was furious, she had phoned the CAA asking them where I was, and they had told her that I had left, 'a little bit upset.' Aunty Phil had obviously panicked, she probably feared that I would be found dead, and it would be reported on the front page of The London Evening News, and then everybody would know, that the pregnant teenager staying with Philomena O'Connell was her niece.

While I had been out, my brother Joe had called, he had bought up my big case. I cringed when I opened it, because tucked in beside my books and shoes and things, was a Mothercare bag. Mom had bought me two scary maternity smocks. I never wore them, I took them back to the Kilburn branch but because I didn't have a receipt they wouldn't give me a refund, just a credit note.

I nearly cried, what the hell did I want with a credit note for a baby shop? It was money I needed. I screwed it up and threw it in the gutter and later that night I was racked with guilt for having trashed Moms gift. Aunty Phil was furious with me for not being there when Joe called; she'd obviously wanted to put a show on with me for his benefit.

'What kept you?' she grumbled. 'I've been worried sick and your poor brother comes all this way and you not even here to say boo to him.'

I told her that I had no idea he was coming, if I did, I would have come straight back. 'Some chance,' she sniffed. 'You've been too busy gadding round the streets to be bothered thinking of anyone else.'

I asked if Joe had any news and that set her off again. 'No, except your poor mother is beside herself with worry, but when did you last think of anyone but yourself?' Then, as she was apt to do, she changed the subject completely. 'What's this anyway?' she said. 'About you leaving the agency upset. I hope you are not getting any ideas in your head about keeping that baby, I won't stand for it, you've made your bed, now you can lie in it and see how comfortable it is.'

It's a wonder Scarlett I didn't hit her on the head with a saucepan. I looked at her for a moment, and left the kitchen without a word and that really infuriated her. She came after me, shouting that I had no business treating her like dirt in her own house, but I ignored her and went up the stairs to my room.

Going to that agency had changed everything. Suddenly it was all official, there was a baby, it was going to be born, it was going to be given away and when that day came I'd be free.

The atmosphere between Aunty Phil and me took on a new degree of chilliness, she hardly spoke to me at all, unless to complain about some small misdemeanour, such as leaving the light on or letting a towel slide to the floor. I didn't give a meercats piss. Mom wrote to me every now and then, it was cheaper than phoning and besides she didn't want Phil bothered with the phone. I carried Mom's letters with me everywhere I went because I didn't trust the dragon an inch, I knew that the moment I left the house, she headed upstairs, rooting in my room for evidence of sex, drugs and rock and roll. She lived in hope. My life in Kilburn was spectacularly boring.

Looking back now, I find it difficult to comprehend why Aunty Phil was so angry, so nasty. The deed was done, she could have given me a going over when I arrived, and then made an attempt at a civilised relationship with me. She must have been more frustrated and bitter than I had given her credit for - someone, who having lost her chance of marriage and mother-hood, had became insanely jealous of anyone else who hadn't. Even though she had worked as a nurse in a major London hospital, she wasn't a sophisticated woman. In fact I'm tempted to think she was scarcely capable of walking on her hind legs.

What I didn't realise then, but see clearly now, is the impact religion must have had on her life, after all, she was born and raised in the era of hate the sin and kick the arse of the sinner. It was the same with Mom; it's hard to fight tradition. I don't suppose my personality made it easy for Aunty Phil either, all that anxiety and panic must have made me very prickly, but even so, nothing excuses her for her lack of charity or common courtesy. I would have received better care at the cat's protection league. They might have neutered me, but I doubt they would have gone in for the same amount of tail pulling that Aunty Phil did, metaphorically speaking of course.

Writing about all these things that happened years ago, makes me realise how tangled the web is. I feel sorry for anyone sad enough to be a psychotherapist; it must be a tough life listening to tale after tale of human misery. Someone walks in off the street and there is no saying what they'll reveal. I wonder if they ever think 'Shut up for fuck sake, I can't take any more.' It's a wonder really more of them don't flip and put the patient in the freezer.

Phoenix.

Chapter Twelve

Yew Wood School Wimbledon; was a mixed pre preparatory of some repute. It was originally opened in 1945 by two impoverished, genteel, spinster sisters whose dedication to all things pertaining to excellence and eloquence quickly gained an outstanding reputation throughout south west London. When the elderly sisters, retired from the scene in the early 1980's; traumatised by Thatcher's new Britain, the school was duly taken over by a board of management, who faithfully followed the path set in place by the two original founders.

Following Daisy's birth, Phoenix had initially employed an au pair to assist her with child care, for she had already decided to branch into the world of franchises and therefore had the freedom to work her hours around the habits of the new baby. When Carmen the au pair eventually went back to Italy, Phoenix divided care of Daisy between herself and Helen, the woman she employed as a part time house keeper. Although the arrangement had worked, it had not been ideal.

However, a chance meeting one day with Rebecca Swift a near neighbour introduced Phoenix to the idea of Daisy attending the nursery at the rather sedate looking Yew Wood School nearby. Rebecca's own daughter Lily who was just a month older than Daisy had just started there and was by all accounts happy and contented.

On the face of it, Rebecca was an unlikely associate of Phoenix; she was a very successful, cool and contained barrister who lived something of a bohemian existence. Phoenix was intrigued by the woman. She learnt many things from her, chief among them being the knowledge that private education was not as exclusive as she thought, and neither is being as ugly as sin, a pre requisite to being a dyke.

Rebecca had been amazingly frank about her status. She delivered it with style and panache, without the slightest threat of the evangelical fervour that would have sent Phoenix running. She also told Phoenix confidentially, that since she firmly believed fatherhood to be a social invention, she had achieved Lily as the result of AID technology. Phoenix who didn't have the slightest interest or awareness of how babies were manufactured in laboratories declined to express her ignorance and merely responded by nodding her head sympathetically.

Later on of course, she had button- holed Jack on the issue and he had told her that he knew right and well what babies by AID meant. He said he had once known a fellow who regularly donated and as a consequence of his actions, most of the cows in West Meath bore a striking resemblance to him.

After listening to Rebecca's recommendation of Yew Wood School, Phoenix had collected a prospectus with an air of confidence, which dissipated somewhat after she had read the accompanying application form in its entirety. She couldn't help questioning as to how well Daisy would fit into such a hallowed establishment.

Jack, though dismissive of private education in general, had no such reservations. He told Phoenix that Daisy would become 'the stuff of documentaries,' for there wouldn't be many children in Yew Wood who could boast a double bill of builder for a father and a cleaner for a mother. He had seen fit to laugh about it, but for Phoenix, it was no laughing matter.

Anyone (outside her business circle of acquaintances) who enquired about her occupation were told that she was a business woman, if they wanted her to be more specific and it was in her interest to appease them, she told them she ran a house keeping agency. Such reticence on the subject of her occupation was an ongoing source of annoyance to Jack for whom the matter was very simple.

'For God's sake,' he once retorted after she had enviously relayed to him the rags to riches story of a woman who had made a fortune designing chocolate novelties, 'You make money don't you? Art for art's sake girl, money for fucks sake'.

When Phoenix had finally set about filling in the school enrolment form, the subject of her occupation had come up again and irritated with what he considered pointless worrying, he had snatched the pen off her.

'I'll do it,' he had said, 'you are making something out of nothing,' and instead of putting Phoenix down as Sinead Keane, he had written, Doctor Sinead O'Connell. When he told her, she thought he had been joking and he had been of course, but he still sent it in.

'If anyone asks you about their herpes,' he advised, 'Tell them you are a Doctor of Philosophy and you'll have a think about it.'

After her parents had been formally interviewed, Daisy was duly accepted and when she had set off on her first day at school, Phoenix had been aware that she was living her parents dream, the O'Connell's or at least a branch of them were on the up at last.

The Spring Term 2001 drew to a close and to mark the end of it, Yew Wood was putting on a performance; a simple non graphic telling of the Easter story. Neither Jack nor Phoenix wanted to go. Jack detested amateur dramatics in any shape or form, they were always he feared, full of people who muffed their lines, tripped over themselves in their haste to overact or who worst still, sang hopelessly and obliviously out of tune.

Phoenix on the other hand had no such phobia; she simply disliked the thought of being herded into a crowded room and being forced to listen to meaningful words when her mind was in a state of chaos. However since they were expected to go, there was as far as Phoenix was concerned, absolutely no question of either of them skulking out of it.

When they arrived on the opening night, the school hall was every bit as busy as Phoenix had anticipated it being. She picked up a programme handed to her by one of the older children and read through it quickly. Thankfully it was in two parts; so at least she wouldn't have to sit through interminable scenes, before Daisy got on with her business.

Rebecca was there and so were two or three other parents that she vaguely knew. She smiled and waved at them, before promptly steering Jack to the back of the hall, it was less claustrophobic and since the exit was only feet away, there was somewhere to run to if it all got too much.

They took their seats on the benches set out, and glanced in unison around the room. It was very different to the tiny National School Jack had attended many years ago. That had been a two room affair, decorated with a plethora of statues and crucifixes. The only art on show at Yew Wood was that produced by the nursery children. Jack stared long and hard at some of the bizarre images adorning the walls and came to the conclusion that it was like being in the Tate Gallery; he couldn't make head or tail out of any of them.

Phoenix however, was not reminiscing. She was tuned in with more precise concentration than an air traffic controller to a variety of conversations going on around her. In the main people seemed to be obsessed with the prep schools they were seeking on behalf of their children. The key merit of each school appeared to be the size of the fees, and the cost of extra -curricular activities. Phoenix watched and listened turning her head every now and then to trace a comment back to the mouth that had uttered it. Each couple, she discovered, was a replica of the other, with all the men appearing as indulgent cretins being fleeced by scheming, manipulative wives.

And it was all carried out so loudly. What a different world these people occupied, they so badly wanted their business to be known, commented upon and envied; what a different existence it was to a life lived by sleight of hand.

She was disturbed out of her thoughts by a sudden vibration along the bench she was sitting on as a large woman, accompanied by a little string - bean of a man sat down heavily beside her. The woman had clearly modelled herself on Bette Davis. She had the movie stars hairstyle, lipstick and icy stare copied to perfection, but unfortunately not her panache. She threw a disparaging look at Phoenix, who in turn glared back at her, wondering if the woman could possibly have looked at herself in a mirror before setting out for the evening. An opened packet of sweets jutting out of the copycat film star's handbag caught Phoenix's eye, and she felt a surge of aggravation, why did the elephant have to beat a path to her? Turning to Jack, she asked if he would mind swapping seats. He took one look at little and large and seeing the big woman's jaws working out an aerobic exercise as she chewed her treat, decided in the interests of peace and harmony, to agree to the request.

After what seemed an interminable wait, Mrs Williams the head teacher, finally emerged on stage to thank parents and friends for coming, and within minutes the play began.

Daisy's role was minimal; she only had to stand with her arms outstretched in the shape of a cross. She represented the tree which was passed over in favour of other grander ones who were chosen to adorn a King's palace by way of furniture and jewellery boxes, but who in the end, is chosen to be the cross on which the Christ is hanged.

Phoenix watched, her eyes fixed on Daisy, hands clutched tightly together and although she felt her heart would burst, so beautiful did her blond haired daughter look, she couldn't help feeling a sense of despair at Daisy being chosen to be the sacrificial tree.

Surely it was an omen. She glanced across at Jack and caught him smiling, sneaking a sly wave to Daisy; he obviously didn't mind his daughter being chosen as the fall guy, so why did she? As the first act ended, she made a conscious effort to conceal her negative thoughts and applauded long and loudly. Jack meanwhile sighed with relief, at least it was half way over and no embarrassing mishap had befallen anyone. But he relaxed too early. Mrs Williams emerged back on stage and urged the audience to give the players another big hand clap before promptly falling backwards off the stage.

Nothing other than her dignity was hurt. Jack, however, was mortified.

An interval with cheese and wine followed the head teacher's spectacular stage exit, and Jack and Phoenix mixed with the people they knew including an architect Jack had once collaborated with on the construction of a West End hotel. All agreed conclusively, that it was all 'very splendid indeed.'

The second half consisted of the older, more self confident pupils singing seasonal songs, a performance that was guaranteed to disgust Phoenix, who dismissed the naturally exuberant children as nothing more than precocious brats. Since Daisy's role was over, she had no more interest in it and her mind began to wander as it was apt to do when bored. With a sickening surge of fright, she felt a sudden twang of panic beginning to uncoil. She whispered across to Jack that she was in urgent need of the toilet and scampered past him, knocking a small stack of the biscuits that had been served during the interval, off the big woman's knees as she did so.

The school foyer was cool and empty and Phoenix leaned her head against the window, willing her breathing to regulate itself. After a moment of repose she stared around at the closed door to the hall, and decided she would risk a swift drink. Facing the window again, she reached into her handbag for the Coco Channel bottle and opened it in a flash. No sooner though had she finished her first swig, when she heard the click of the hall door opening. Turning quickly, she saw Mrs Williams emerging from the hall, with just the slightest hint of a limp.

'My God,' she thought in a panic, 'Don't say she is popping out for a quick one too.' In her haste to replace the cap on the bottle, she fumbled, and cursed as the liquid leaked on to her fingers. Frantically she poked the bottle back in her bag and moved swiftly towards the next window, praying that the aroma would not accompany her.

Mrs Williams looked up, and seeing Phoenix for the first time, began to walk towards her.

'Are you feeling all right?' she asked, and Phoenix keeping her head aside replied

'Yes, just a little bit hot.'

'Oh dear,' said Mrs Williams, and promptly opened the window. Is that to cool me down, or to let the smell out? Phoenix wondered.

She looked at the head teacher with a critical eye; taking in her functional linen skirt and her oh so sensible 'don't wolf whistle me' shoes, there was nothing prepossessing about her. If I met her in the street, she thought, I would never guess the power she wields as a head teacher, but she'd easily pass as a cleaner or checkout assistant.

'Wasn't Daisy wonderful Dr O'Connell?' Mrs Williams remarked, 'You must be very proud of her.'

For a moment, Phoenix looked startled. Whatever was the woman talking about? She then remembered that thanks to Jack's foolery, she *was* Dr O'Connell.

With perfect composure she replied, that yes, she was indeed proud, the whole play had been wonderful but then with such skilful teachers involved could it be otherwise? 'I'll butter the old baggage up', she thought, 'perhaps then, she won't spread it round that Daisy Keane's mother smells like a wino'.

Mrs William's took the compliment graciously and headed back into the hall and immediately Phoenix relaxed again.

She wondered around the foyer, looking at the photos of all the bright faced happy children and staff. There were photographs of Sports Day, a slimy looking politician and a teddy bears picnic that had been held to raise money for a local hospital.

A feeling of nostalgia overwhelmed her as she walked around; she remembered her own school days, right back to primary school, with the nuns in their long black habits and swinging wooden rosary beads. The Reverent Mother had once told the school assembly that while opportunity only knocks once, temptation leans on the doorbell. Although Phoenix had dismissed the later part of the sermon as being typical of a woman who was rumoured to suck lemons for a treat, she had taken the former part to heart. Long ago she really had believed life was good and that success was there for the taking. But she had bailed out of the race, and the baton was now being passed on to Daisy. The thought made her shudder.

The evening ended successfully with vast amounts of money being raised for even more PE equipment, an expenditure that irritated Phoenix. It was a flagrant waste of money that could be better used for something else, though admittedly, she didn't have the faintest idea what.

All the way home, an excited, exuberant Daisy chattered and recited the entire play and questioned both her parents, to make certain they had been paying attention. When they finally arrived, she proved almost impossible to get into bed and only settled after extracting a promise from Jack, that he would bring her home 'something nice' the next day for being such a clever girl.

After seeing to Daisy, Phoenix came downstairs to find Jack watching Sky Sports. 'I'm going to look through a few things,' she said. 'Do you want anything?'

He shook his head, and she went out of the room closing the door softly behind her. She then headed for the study and her red book.

Dear Scarlett,   **7th April 2001,**

Tonight I watched my daughter perform in a school play, an ordeal Scarlett, since I can't bear being in confined places right now, but she was wonderful, just as I knew she would be. Even Jack enjoyed the show. He thinks he is being indulgent by allowing me to send Daisy to a private school, but frankly he doesn't have a choice. He is very dismissive of the other parents, he refers to them as either gormless wonders, or greasy bollocks and by that he means, they either work in a bank or own a restaurant.

But I feel I owe it to Daisy. I have got an inferiority complex Scarlett. Like I told you, I never did get to university, and for someone who started life with such big plans, ending up as a cleaner is hardly something to boast about. Would you ever have stooped so low? I think you might have, after all you did some pretty ropey things yourself to earn a buck, like owning saloons in a Baptist stronghold, and working convicts.

You understood that when the going gets tough, the tough get nasty. That's what I loved about your story, the way you faced things as they are. You picked cotton, offered sex for sale, and even murdered an intruder, but sometimes you have to be what the times demand.

Being in a school again, took me back to my school days. I find it incredible to believe that I was once a Kentish school girl. Look how far I've come. All that talk about waving the machete of words around to keep people at bay, didn't stop me getting involved with Jack and then getting Daisy, and now I've got them, I can't bear the thought of losing them.

How did I ever let my guard down and become involved with anyone?

It wasn't done consciously. I really thought every feeling died in me the night I gave birth to Condon's off spring.

My estimated date of delivery was the 14th of September 1980 but on the 4th Mom broke her golden rule and phoned me up. She said she would come up on the 12th to be with me, although she was certain that the baby would be late.

As the big day drew nearer I became very anxious. Mom sounded more resigned and gentle and in some ways I was happy that she was coming up to be with me, because I really needed support. But I dreaded her seeing me in a state of torment. When I was about thirteen, my school showed us a film about the birth of a baby, it was disgusting and it frightened the life out of everyone. I think it was shown for that purpose, to stem the rising tide of teenage mothers.

The worse bit was when it was all over, the camera shot to a picture of the new mother drinking a cup of tea and a smarmy voiceover said. 'Most new mothers appreciate a good cup of tea because after all labour is very hard work.' They made it sound as if she'd just painted the house or shifted a piano, not taken part in a thoroughly disgusting deed. For weeks after seeing that film, I walked round staring at any woman mad enough to be pushing a pram, thinking 'well she's still alive.'

When I told Mom about it, she said I was crazy, because if having a baby was that bad, no woman would ever have more than one. It sounded logical at the time. Now of course, I know it as total tripe.

Mom was so pleased when August gave way to September. 'Thank God,' she said, 'it didn't come early; at least it's not going to be an August baby.' I don't know why she had such a hatred of August, whenever I asked her she would only reply. 'August is a wicked month and nothing good ever comes out of it.' I don't want to sound like a superstitious whinge Scarlett, but since my birthday is on August the fifteenth, (the feast of the Assumption) two days before Mom's wedding anniversary, I can't help but wonder if her hatred was personal.

Anyway on the 10th of September, just before midnight, I woke up with a start. I felt funny, not as in ha bloody ha, just very peculiar. I sat up aware of a tightening, contracting pain and I knew the moment had come. I begged God to make the pains go away but they didn't, they got worse. I paced the room, reluctant to go waking Aunty Phil because she was like a bear at seven o clock, so what on earth would she be like at two o clock, but in the end I knew I had to wake her.

She asked me how long the pains had been coming and I knew by the way she spoke that she was expecting me to say, 'Oh just now,' so I lied out of fright and said. 'Oh only for about an hour or so.'

She said I was a 'Fool of a la Tom', why hadn't I woken her immediately? She leapt out of bed and began asking about broken waters and timing the contractions. At about half past three, she decided it was time to go to the hospital in Paddington and that's when the nightmare became real.

She called a taxi and I have a vague recollection of a quiet, smooth ride through a very deserted looking London. When we arrived at the hospital a really young nurse booked me in and took me to a cubicle. She was cheery and good-natured. She said a midwife would be along in a few minutes, which for some reason made me think of a number 52 bus trundling up a hill.

I was lucky; it had been a fairly quiet night. After about ten minutes the same nurse popped back, she said she was going to fasten a monitor on me so that the baby's heartbeat could be tracked. Aunty Phil kept strangely quiet. As the nurse clipped the monitor to me, the noise of the baby's heartbeat filled the room. It sounded like the 3.20 was being run at Epsom, the thud, thud of the heart slowing down then speeding up. The nurse then turned to me and said 'You are doing fine, well done,' and like a fool, I thought that was all there was to it. How stupid I had been to imagine agony and torment.

The fact is, the moment I got on that bed, the contractions practically disappeared, and I was left for ages just listening to the galloping heartbeat. But when the night shift changed over to the day shift, that's when the shite began heading for the fan.

The young kind nurse popped her head round the curtain to say goodbye and good luck and in her place came a vixen, a red haired fox like creature with a pointy nose and red complexion.

Aunty Phil had gone home by this point; her experience probably told her that it was going to be a long haul. The fox marched straight in didn't say hello, kiss my arse or anything, just went up to the monitor had a look at it and flipped through my notes. Her opening words were 'you are very young for this caper, what does it take for you young girls to realise that having a baby is no picnic?' She said that last bit, because the contractions had started again with a vengeance and I was contorted with pain and unable to speak.

When the pain eased she said 'Right, now lets have a look to see how much progress you've made,' and with that she whipped off the blanket that had been placed on me so gently by the young nurse.

The second she placed her hand on my leg that was it, I was off in a pincer movement up the bed. I could take her sarcasm, I could even take the pain up to a point, but there was no way, anyone was putting their hand in *that* place.

She was furious; you'd think I had insinuated that she fancied me by the way she stormed. She said 'Don't be so ridiculous, if you can get yourself pregnant you can take an examination.'

She made it sound as if I'd used a D.I.Y. kit, how to get yourself pregnant in three easy steps, and she had the nerve to talk about young girls walking around with their head up their arse. She attempted to examine me again, but the same thing happened. I didn't consciously clam up, it was spontaneous. In the end she got exasperated and stormed out, returning a few minutes later with another midwife.

This one was more approachable; at least she tried to talk me through it. 'Just relax Sinead, look at the ceiling and it will be over in a moment, we just need to see how much progress the baby has made.' It made no difference, I couldn't do it.

She said that if I let her examine me, she'd arrange for me to have an epidural and that would relieve all the pain. It was a tempting proposition, but she was incapable of copping on to the simple fact, that she could have promised me anything. Even Condon's head on a plastic platter, but it would have made no difference, it was out of my hands.

Eventually just like the fox, she got huffy and took my refusal as a personal insult. The two of them walked out and left me alone and for that I was very grateful. After a while a doctor came in, but she didn't look much like one, she was young and casual. 'Hi Sinead,' she said. 'How are you doing?' I said I'd rather be on the beach, and she laughed and said. 'I don't blame you, so would I.'

I remember her walking over to me and standing with her arms folded. She said a lot of women didn't like internal examinations, it was no big deal, but if I let her have a go, it would be better for everyone. She then leant down and brushed my hair away from my face and said very gently 'You are very young and very brave, let me examine you and as soon as it's done I'll get some effective pain control for you.'

She was so kind and spoke with such concern that for some stupid reason tears filled my eyes. I had held them at bay for so long but I couldn't take her kindness, I would have preferred the sharp tongue of the fox. She asked if I would give it a go and I nodded, but it was no good, she made several attempts but all to no avail, the moment her hand touched one of my thighs, the other thigh shot across and held it in a clamp, it was like trying to sneak a bone away from a savage sleeping dog.

She didn't get at all angry, she just said after each failed attempt, 'Lets try again.' Eventually even she had to admit defeat. She stood for a moment just watching me and then she said. 'Sinead, did you have sex often before you got pregnant?' I didn't answer her. She said 'Lots of women hate these examinations, but they don't react in quite the same way as you have.'

She paused and I knew what was coming. 'Sinead', she said, 'did you have sex voluntarily?' All I could do was cry. 'We will talk about this later,' she said. 'I have to go now.' She went and I never saw her again.

All day long the contractions came and went. They gave me a set of earphones to pass the time away and I tuned into hospital radio and found out instantly what people mean when they say 'I took coke once and had a terrifying experience.' It was unbelievably bad.

Aunty Phil turned up again in the afternoon. 'You're taking your time,' she said. 'I thought it would all be over by now.'

That was typical of her to think I was deliberately slowing the show down. I didn't want her anywhere near me. I felt humiliated in her presence. She said she hadn't phoned Mom. 'She'll only go worrying so I'll phone when there is real news.'

She told me that she had gone to Mass and had put a candle on for me.

She sat there, critiquing the state of the place, the round shoulders of the nurses, the price of the tea and the number of black staff. As she did so the contractions started up again, and she went off and fetched a midwife. This midwife was another sour little puss who didn't like being told her job; she told Aunty Phil that I would be seen to in good time.

Aunty Phil left and about ten minutes later the contractions started for real. I was taken into a delivery room, and the first thing that caught my eye was the little plastic cot standing in the corner, it was incredible to think that the baby inside me was destined for that cot. How on earth was it ever going to get out?

The midwife in charge was an Irish woman called Maura, she was cheery and bustling and she had a young student midwife called Jenny helping her. Maura was very competent she had obviously heard about my performance earlier on in the day, and didn't bother messing about with examinations. She said, 'What you need to do is relax,' and without warning, she slapped a big black rubbery smelling mask on my face, it cupped my mouth and nose and for a moment I pictured the ape's hand over my mouth again and I began kicking and screaming.

Maura was shocked. She kept saying, 'Take it easy girl, it's only gas and air it will help you, if you give it a chance.'

I told her I needed a moment to orientate myself, and when I felt a bit calmer Maura persuaded me to give it a try. Jenny held it to my face and Maura took control telling me to take deep long breaths, she said it would be over soon, but how soon was soon, I wanted to know.

I remember glancing at a clock above the door and telling myself, it couldn't last forever. It was coming up to six o clock.

I was a terrible patient; I screamed and carried on like a mad woman. I heard Maura mutter to Jenny something about it not being right at all, and I remember thinking you're absolutely right Maura, it's not right, what kind of God dreamt up this nasty gory spectacle. And just when I thought I couldn't take anymore, it was over.

A couple of other nurses must have sneaked into the room, no doubt wondering what the commotion was, because the moment the baby was born a big cheer went up. They all crowded round and I heard Maura's voice clear as crystal say, 'Oh Sinead, you have a beautiful baby boy, he's pure beautiful, a darling.' She took him over to a type of work surface where she carried out an inspection of him, and then she wrapped him in a blanket and put him in my arms.

She said, 'Oh Sinead you are so lucky, just look at him.'

I did, he had tiny perfectly formed little hands, and a tiny trembling mouth, and oh so sleepy eyes but the only thing my eyes wanted to focus on was his mane of black hair. There was no doubting whose son he was. I felt nothing other than coldness and a terrible fear.

He was given a little blue tag around his wrist, and on it was written. 'Baby of Sinead, born 11th Sept 1980, weight 6lb 3oz.'

Several of the nurses attempted to take him out of my hands, but Maura wouldn't have it, she kept saying. 'Leave him, where he belongs.'

I didn't realise it at the time, Scarlett but now as I write these words I see so clearly that Maura like all the other nurses must have known that this baby was going for adoption. She wanted me to form a bond with him, she wanted a happy ending to this story but the problem was, she didn't know its utterly miserable beginning.

I stayed in hospital for a week, and I fed the baby with a bottle and each night a nurse would come and take him to the nursery. Both Mom and Aunty Phil visited. Neither of them felt it appropriate to bring flowers after all, a bastard in the family is nothing to celebrate. I felt embarrassed because the other women on the ward were sorry for me, my bedside cabinet was the only one completely bereft of flowers or cards. I think they must have thought I belonged to some queer sect, and they weren't that far off the mark.

Aunty Phil as usual put her great big furry foot in it, 'Just look at that head of hair,' she said, 'that's pure O'Connell that is.'

No it wasn't, it was pure bloody Condon. That hair was unmistakeable it was the chief thing that made the baby so distasteful to me. I couldn't hold it in my arms without catching sight of that hair, and the person responsible for it. Despair and hate seethed through me, I was tied to a bed, having gone through hell, and that bastard was getting on with life.

For some reason my hatred began to focus more and more on Aunty Phil. I felt bitter with her for mentioning the baby's hair, talking about it as if it was something to be prized, when I knew the origins of it.

But the really big surprise to me Scarlett was Mom's reaction to the baby. She was captivated with him. She couldn't leave him alone, every day, within seconds of arriving she'd have him out of his cot and she would pace around with him held tightly in her arms. I knew she was being pulled apart. All her instincts said 'Keep it, and to hell with what people think.'

At the age of ten days, I handed Joseph Francis, over to Miss O'Farrell at the CAA office in Paddington. Mom was very downcast, too down to bear the company of in fact. I told her to go home and I asked Aunty Phil to accompany me to the adoption agency instead. When we arrived, all I wanted was to be left alone.

I asked her to go home ahead of me, but she was very reluctant to leave; she kept saying, 'you are not in a fit state to be left alone,' but I was insistent, I wanted to be alone.

Miss O'Farrell told me that she had found the perfect family for Joseph; they lived in the West Country, and had a four-year-old daughter of their own already and intended to keep the name I'd given the baby, they loved it. They were delighted to hear about the safe arrival of Joseph and they wanted to assure me of their intention to give him a 'happy and contented life.' I wondered if Miss O'Farrell remembered my outburst with her the last time we met, if she did and I bet she did, she had the grace not to mention it.

I handed Joseph over, he was dressed in a blue romper suit Mom had sewn, and wrapped in a white shawl that Alice had made; a peace offering? I don't know. He had gone to sleep in my arms in the waiting room, and was still asleep when I handed him over. He never saw me go.

I left quickly and I hardly remember the walk back to Paddington station.

It was over. I should have felt enormous relief, this was the moment I had been waiting and praying for, but I didn't.

I just felt consumed with an immense desire to die, I looked at the arrival and departure boards and saw Penzance, Bristol and Exeter appear and disappear. If only I could jump aboard an express train and accidentally fall out the door. It would all be over. Lingering Catholic superstition ruled suicide out, but anyone can have an accident can't they?

I had sent Aunty Phil home because I wanted to be alone, but Paddington was crowded, and there was no where I could go for five minutes peace to just sit and think it all over. I headed for the only place I knew I'd be alone, the public toilets. I joined a queue and eventually, I was able to slam the door on the world.

I couldn't understand why I felt so low, so empty, I didn't want the baby, I didn't wish him harm, now he was in the world, I just wanted him and me to live our lives in a way that meant our paths would never cross again. If he hadn't been the replica of his father, I might have felt differently, I don't know.

All I knew was that Joseph was a permanent reminder of that terrible night, and I didn't ever want to have to tell him that his father was a rapist who should have been locked up.

I tried telling myself that now I could move on, get a job, or as Mom suggested, go back to school, not my old one of course, but to a 6th Form College in London, but all I could do was cry.

The tears fell for lost innocence, and for all that never would be. No matter what I did or where I went, nothing could change the fact that I was a mother with a son. The past really is the only permanent thing we have in life, nothing can alter that. It can't be changed or moved one single bit. It is fixed. Sitting in that dismal toilet, listening to the clanging of doors, the occasional snatch of the tannoy, I felt like an old hand at life, the future stretched ahead of me as an ordeal to be got through with nothing to look forward to, only regrets at what had gone by. I felt like you did Scarlett when you collapsed on your return to Tara, when the realisation hit you, that a way of life was over and all you could see was the 'harsh vista of the dark future.'

I didn't know then of course, that one day there would be Jack, and I certainly never figured on having Daisy. If anyone had suggested to me the possibility of another baby, I would have rearranged their face on the spot, but Jack and Daisy were still a long way off at that point.

Seeing Daisy perform tonight, so innocent, so totally at the mercy of what life might throw at her, stabbed at my heart. That's the crux of it Scarlett, I've never been able to feel real joy or happiness, because I have always been dogged with fear of what lies around the corner. When you have faced total terror at sixteen you are ready for anything. Nothing can shock you; you live your life prepared for the worse because you have experience of knowing it can happen to you.

Right now the National Lottery is running an advertising campaign that states, 'It could be you,' and every time I see it, I think, 'too fucking right, only there is no 'could' about it.'

Knowing what I know Scarlett has made me feel that I'm never going to be taken by surprise again. I have lived, expecting the worst, hoping that by doing so, I can outsmart fate...

Phoenix dropped her pen and swung round to see Jack standing behind her. She hurriedly closed the book and placed her hand on top of it.

'What are you doing creeping up behind me?' she asked.

'I didn't creep up,' he said. 'I've been calling you for ages and when you didn't answer I came to see if you were ok.'

She felt her face twitch; the anxiety of trying to look nonchalant was almost tickling in its intensity. How long had he been standing behind her and what if anything had he seen?

'Is it too much to ask for five minutes peace before you come chasing me?' she asked, as she casually replaced the top back on her pen, before laying her hands gently across her book.

He walked round to her side and lifted one hand off the red book.

'What do you mean five minutes peace?' he asked, 'you've been gone hours and anyway what are you doing that's taken you so long.'

She shook his hand off hers and replaced it back where it belonged, on top of the book.

'Nothing that would interest you Jack, I'm just trying to account for a few bits and pieces.'

'Your notion of accounting has always intrigued me,' he said. 'I wonder you bother with an accountant because I've yet to meet one that can match you for spotting the loophole.' He paused, and without warning swooped the red book off the desk. 'I'm sure I could learn something from you,' he said, 'but the trouble is - would it corrupt me?'

Phoenix knew she had to play cool, but anger pumped by fear seized her. She had to get the book off Jack without raising any suspicion beyond that of tax fiddling. If she stormed and ranted, he would tease, if she shrugged her shoulders he would take no more than a vague glimpse of interest. That would be her usual strategy, to avoid interest by showing disinterest, but it was a dangerous one to risk right now. The moment he saw the book was full of words not figures, he would be bound to read just a little, just enough to damn her. In the end she decided to go for the role of exasperated put upon wife.

'Why are you always nosing into my affairs Jack?' she demanded. 'I'm telling you, if you don't give me my book back now, I'll never speak to you again.'

He laughed. 'That's a tempting proposition,' he said, 'but you'll have to offer something better than that.'

She paused for a moment, whatever else, he must not open the book, he evidently believed it contained something to do with accounts, she had to keep it that way, by tomorrow he would have forgotten about it.

'Hush,' she said suddenly, placing a hand to her ear and turning away from him. 'Someone is here, did you hear that knock? I'm not expecting anyone, are you?' She made as if to walk to the door, but he overtook her.

'It could be Mike with the van keys,' he said, 'Mind you I told the stupid sod not to bother dropping them in tonight.' He threw the book down on the desk and headed out the door.

'If it's anyone for me, tell them I'm in the bath.' Phoenix called after him.

The moment he left the room, she seized her book and with shaking hands put it at once, under lock and key.

Her face felt flushed with anxiety. What if Jack had read the most revealing letter she had ever written? It was too dreadful to contemplate, it had been a close call and it was a warning. She'd have to be more careful in future.

She switched the light out and went to find a drink and Jack.

He would no doubt, be puzzled when he discovered, there was no one at the door, after all.

Chapter Thirteen

The following day, Phoenix stayed in bed much later than usual. An unexpected burst of April sunshine flooded the bedroom casting a golden glow on the stripped oak floorboards and elegant white satin curtains that gracefully fringed the Georgian windows.

From her bed Phoenix could see the branches of the beech tree stretching into a clear cloudless sky and the two grey squirrels which chased each other up and down, round and round leaping from branch to branch with daring audacity. She watched their amazing agility with absolutely no sense of wonder.

The scene, an idyllic representation of a spring morning in London, did nothing to lift her spirit. She felt nothing other than a heavy sense of oppression. Writing about the birth and handing over of Joseph weighed deeply in her heart and try as she might, she couldn't dismiss it.

Too clearly she saw she had been right all those years ago, when she had known instinctively, that no matter where she went or what she did, nothing could change the fact that she was the mother of a son. How could she have ever believed hiding from reality was realistic?

She put her hand out and picked up the copy of 'Gone with the Wind' which she now kept at her bedside, like a Gideon Bible. She looked at the cover of the hard back edition, eyes fresh to its every detail. It featured a still from the film and showed Scarlett O'Hara in her widow's weeds dancing with Rhett Butler. She opened it, and flicked the pages over until she came to the part, where Scarlett, a widow and a mother, less than a year after getting married is reduced to the depths of depression; bored to tears in her beloved Tara.

'It's no wonder the book made such an impact on me,' she thought, closing her eyes and leaning her head back on the pillow, there are parts in it that could have been written with me in mind.' She sat up and opened her eyes and read again the description of Scarlett in decline, drinking in the utter listlessness and inability, Scarlett had in accepting her new born baby boy was a part of her life. Each word was an echo of how she too had once felt.

She shut the book with a snap. 'I don't care anyway,' she told the empty room. 'I don't care at all.'

Downstairs, Jack was busy eating breakfast in the kitchen with Daisy. It was a Wednesday and Helen the housekeeper was there, waiting for Phoenix. She had come ready to do some steam cleaning that Phoenix had specifically requested, but Phoenix was nowhere to be seen and neither was the steam cleaner.

Not wanting to disturb Jack, Helen started her day's work by removing the kitchen curtains in order to wash them. She had worked for Phoenix for just over two years, and knew better than to prevaricate on account of a bit of missing equipment. The money was good as were the conditions, and although she didn't particularly like Phoenix, she was fond of both Jack and Daisy.

She glanced up at the rustic cuckoo clock, a christening gift for Daisy and clicked her tongue self righteously. The cuckoo no longer called the hour. Instead the little brown carved bird hung down in a drunken pose, knocked off its spring by Jack who had aimed a spud at it one night, when its singing had obliterated the sports results on the radio. It was gone half past eight and in Helen's opinion, it was quite wrong for a man to have to see to a child's needs before a day at work, what was the point in a man having a wife if she didn't see to his needs and those of his offspring? Like many women who were once daring in the 1960's Helen had simply reverted to form on her fiftieth birthday. She had enjoyed her days of liberation, she had even bought Germaine Greer's famous book and had often quoted loudly and vociferously from its back cover. But her two boys were now of an age that placed them in danger of being the recipients of the feminist propaganda she had once preached. So it was all hands to the pump, when it came to protecting men's interests.

Phoenix emerged a few minutes later, fully dressed with her car key in hand; ready to take Daisy to school. 'Good afternoon,' Jack greeted her, as she leaned over to kiss Daisy.

'Pity you never mastered telling the time Jack,' she replied, and looked up with a start as she heard the utility room door click open. For the first time she became aware Helen was there.

'Oh shit,' she said. 'I'd forgotten she was in.'

'It isn't any big deal is it?' he asked, and she told him how she had promised Helen the steam cleaner to do the kitchen with.

'Well let her get on with it,' he replied.

'She can't,' said Phoenix. 'I've forgotten to bring the bloody thing home yet again; you know how particular she is.' She looked at her watch. 'I think I'll forget about coffee and make a move, come on Daisy.' But before she could get out of the room, Helen came back in from the garden.

'Good morning,' she said to Phoenix. 'I'm ready to get on if you have the steam cleaner handy.'

'I'm sorry,' Phoenix said. 'I fully intended to bring it home, just make the laundry a priority today Helen.'

'Okay then,' said Helen, 'but you know what they say about the road to hell being paved with good intentions, don't you?' And with that she disappeared into the laundry room.

'Good intentions my arse,' Phoenix said to Jack 'it's more likely to be paved with sanctimonious half wits like her.'

'Of course it is,' he told her, 'Anyone who dares to put you straight deserves never ending torture, why do you think I always let you have your own way.' He learnt over and kissed her on the cheek. 'Don't forget, you are collecting Daisy tonight. I will be late.'

She turned and left the house, Daisy skipping happily beside her and returned a smile every bit as bright as the one Daisy had flashed at her, but when she caught a glimpse of the girl's tiny hand grasping her doll, a curious dull feeling descended on her. She felt a sudden impulse to wrap her arms around her child for eternity and in an instant, she made up her mind to collect Daisy at lunch time; she'd think up some excuse for the school and she'd spend the time with her little girl.

She arrived at work to be greeted by an excited Carolyn who had two good pieces of news to impart. There had been an excellent response to an advertising campaign she had initiated in the local press, and there had also been several enquiries to the advert regarding franchises in the Dalton's Weekly. Business was certainly looking good. Phoenix smiled, and said it was great altogether, but there was nothing rapturous in her response.

During the course of the morning, Phoenix interviewed three new cleaners and spoke at length to her accountant on the phone. Things were certainly looking up- he would be able to sign off her accounts with just a few more details. She gave a silent gasp of thanks. Thank God, she had an accountant who understood her. He had been recommended by a publican from Hatch End – a native of North Kerry and he had got her out of more holes than John Laing had ever dug.

But even this piece of good news failed to lift her spirits. She went about her work silently and ritually, glancing at the clock, willing, it to reach a time, when she could leave in all decency.

Eventually the clock obliged and she was able to announce to a surprised Carolyn that she was going home; of course she was to be contacted immediately if anything serious cropped up.

Daisy was delighted when she saw her mother enter the class-room, and in an instant, she cast aside the plastic cutter she had recently arm wrestled off another child. Not all was lost, Phoenix told herself; not while she still had Daisy. She took the little girl to an Italian café in Wimbledon, where she further intensified her daughter's joy by agreeing to eat an ice cream decorated with wafers and scattered marshmallows.

They sat by a window and Daisy's loud and excited chatter guaranteed them first class service from a waiter not long in London from Sicily, who was enchanted with the blonde haired 'bambina'. He was also rather struck with Phoenix, something about her face touched his sentimental Sicilian heart and nothing she asked was too much trouble for him.

Afterwards at Daisy's insistence the two of them went for a brief walk on the common, where Phoenix surprised her daughter again by joining in with her game of searching for fairies in the grass. Much as Daisy liked her mother's new habits, she couldn't help feeling just a little confused and bewildered by them, especially Mom's happy agreement to go for a walk.

Perhaps Mom really did believe Daddy's story about fairies owning a crock of gold - now that would certainly entice Mom to go searching for them.

When they eventually arrived home, Helen was in full swing, cleaning the house.

'I wasn't expecting you back,' she said to Phoenix. 'Is Daisy not feeling well or something?'

'Daisy is fine.' Phoenix told her as she flipped her coat onto the coat stand, 'it's just such a lovely day, both of us thought it too good to waste with working.'

'Well it's lucky for some,' Helen said, and instantly Phoenix felt a wave of irritation sweep over her. Why did people always have to be so begrudging?

'You are absolutely right,' she replied sharply, 'but the funny thing is, the harder I work, the luckier I get.'

She felt an almost irresistible urge to tell Helen to piss off, but she swallowed it and went into her study instead. No one, not even an irritating faggot like Helen, was going to knock her off her stride.

Now was a good time to write, with Daisy in the garden and Jack miles away in Sussex. She unlocked the drawer and took out the red book.

Dear Scarlett,

After writing to you about the adoption of Joseph, I am wracked with superstitious fear. I've even taken Daisy out of school early, so I can keep her safe at home with me. But you know Scarlett, there was no way I could keep that baby - it didn't feel a part of me. It wasn't mine. It was simply something that had happened to me. After I handed him over, I went back to living with Aunty Phil.

No one ever said I couldn't go home; it was just assumed that I would stay in London. Mom was convinced that London was the best option for me. 'No point in going back,' she said.

After the birth and adoption, I was without energy or interest in anything. All I wanted to do was sit and think but my thoughts weren't comfortable ones, there certainly wasn't any peace to be found in them. Nobody mentioned post natal depression, but I think that is what it was, life just felt without meaning or purpose.

Aunty Phil must have told Mom about my moroseness, because I received a very severe letter from her. It was just like the one you got from your mother Scarlett, when she wrote to you regarding your conduct with Rhett; when she said you were a disgrace to your family and upbringing.

Mom didn't mention 'disgrace' with me; she had exhausted that subject some months previously. Instead she concentrated her efforts on getting me back to education. It was ridiculous she said, crying for what might have been, the future was what counted now. She instructed me to enrol in a local school or college. 'Aunty Phil will help you,' she wrote, 'you have got another chance; you must take it and not dwell on the past.'

But what she didn't understand Scarlett, was that it wasn't me dwelling in the past, the past was dwelling in me. It stared out at me with every baby I saw, every bleeding heart article I came across, and in that horrendous monster Aunty Phil who felt duty bound to treat me like some kind of debauched hooker.

I read, and reread Moms letter so many times, trying to get impetus from it, because she made it sound so easy. But it wasn't. I felt so low. I couldn't see the point in anything. The thought of going back to school or college and studying again struck me as pointless in the extreme. I wasn't capable of caring about anything and the thought of reading books and discussing people and events in them as if they were real, was enough to drive me mad. I became fixated with the real world and every-thing else seemed trivial.

Even now Scarlett, I can't bear trivia, it's just too risky a pursuit to enjoy when the world is awash with real drama that could come knocking on the door any time of the day or night. I wanted so much to leave behind the dark and weary world that I was enmeshed in, but there wasn't any escape from it, not even in sleep. I began to have a recurring dream; it wasn't a frighten-ing one, just very frustrating. I used to dream about money. I'd be walking down a road or through a park, and I'd come across a coin but when I picked it up, a whole of string of coins would rise from the ground attached to the one I had picked up. All I wanted was a single coin but it was impossible to detach one from the others. I used to wake up tired and sickened from my exertions and I began to dread going to sleep and meeting up with the chained money.

When I told Aunty Phil about Mom's letter she went berserk, 'Am I expected then to keep you in the lap of luxury, while you pursue the education you should have got before you went off gallivanting with other ideas?'

I was speechless when she said that. Mom was the last person on earth to hitch a free ride with anyone. I told her that I was sure Mom would obviously sort something out. She became dead sarcastic then, 'Oh good old Mom will sort it out will she? Don't you think its time ye stopped sponging off people and thought about your mothers welfare, why don't ye get off your arse and find a job and start paying your way.'

It never occurred to me that Mom might really want me out working. Her letter had sounded so persuasive. So the very next day I went down the Kilburn High Road and traipsed in and out of job agencies. I didn't have a clue what kind of job to look for. I told the same story to every agency; I had ten good O'levels, almost half a year of A' level study behind me and I had left school to help out a sick old aunt. I didn't think that last bit was a lie at all, because in my opinion Aunty Phil was very sick.

All the agencies had windows crammed full with jobs and they were all staffed by young women with long hair, painted nails and sweet F.A to offer.

None of the jobs existed. They were all, either withdrawn, gone or undecided. Of course Aunty Phil didn't believe me, she thought I was prevaricating, 'You don't fool me one bit, there are jobs out there if ye would only put your shoulders back and look sharp about ye,' she said.

Eventually one morning she came banging on the bathroom door shouting 'Get down here at once the woman from the agency is on the phone.'

And I ran, my heart thumping, thinking it was the CAA, phoning to tell me that the lovely young couple in the West Country were returning the baby, but it wasn't.

It was a woman called Rosie, from First Post job agency, she said. 'Hi Sinead, I know you've been looking for clerical positions, but I've got a nice little job here, in a canteen in White City, it's only a temporary one but it will bring you in some cash for Christmas. Are you interested?'

I took one look at the shit coloured lino and the dark stairs that led up to my bedroom. Was I interested? I almost kissed the phone.

So one bright frosty morning in November 1980, I set off for my first real job. I wore the only decent clothes I had, a navy skirt, white blouse, and a black velvet jacket that I had bought from Mom's catalogue with the money the ape had given me.

It was totally inadequate wear for mid November, but there was no way I was going to wear my school mac. When I got to Kilburn tube station it was crowded, there had been an incident further up the line and lots of trains had been cancelled.

I couldn't get over how well turned out everyone looked. Lots of men wore suits and the women all seemed to have fitted coats and dainty little scarves tucked around their necks, lots of them carried rolled up umbrellas as well. I felt like a hick who had just rolled in from the country. Even my velvet jacket seemed out of place, as if I was dressed for an occasion, not naturally well turned out. Somehow everyone looked smarter and more together than me.

As the tube stopped along the way, people got off and others got on and I saw they were all well turned out, it wasn't that Kilburn was such a smart place after all, it was just my perception of things. I had spent so long hanging around spinsters, ante natal clinics and social workers and now I was being flushed out into the real world of working people, sales staff, accountants, bus drivers, I had forgotten what it was like. I wondered how I'd ever handle it.

I had to change for White City and I was anxious that I wouldn't be able to fight my way out, but when my stop came so many people swarmed out of the train that I was swept out onto the platform like a bit of flotsam on to the beach at home.

When I finally got to White City, which to my country girl eyes wasn't really white at all, I stuttered and stammered in my attempt to find the industrial estate where the canteen was located. And when I found that, trying to find the canteen was almost impossible. 'You can't miss it, its right in the middle,' was what I was told whenever I asked for directions. There was no heavy industry on the estate, just newspaper distribution centres, furniture wholesalers, and printers. I know, because I visited every bloody one of them.

I eventually found the canteen. I had walked past it several times dismissing it as the communal bogs. It was a single storey prefab building and after setting off that morning with an hour to spare, I arrived late.

It was a dismal building, a bit like an old fashioned transport café. It had a low ceiling and clumps of Formica topped tables scattered here and there with a mish – mash of wooden chairs. At the far end of the room was a counter with glass display cabinets holding sandwiches and sausage rolls and things. Behind it stood a dark haired woman, who was counting rolls from a bag. I went up to her and introduced myself.

I said I had been sent by the agency. She was dead cool. She looked at me as if to say 'so what?'

Her name turned out to be Maria, and she told me in a nutshell what was expected of me. The canteen opened at half nine, serving teas and coffees to the workers on the estate, freshly made sandwiches went on sale between twelve and two, and everything was cleared up by half past three, 'if everyone got their finger out.'

She told me there was one other member of staff, Stella who had just phoned in sick, 'but you won't miss her,' she said, 'because she's useless, soft in the head, does more damage than work, but she's harmless.'

After hearing that I felt a bit afraid of Maria and her obvious tendency to beat about the bush, instead of just saying what she meant!

She looked Spanish, with her dark hair and clear olive skin. She had a brazen good-looking face, one that challenged you to contradict her. She wasn't Spanish though; she was a Londoner, pure Shepherds Bush.

She pointed out a couple of things to me and said. 'I'm not going to go through the whole rigmarole, you'll pick it up as you go along, it's that straight forward, even an idiot could do it.'

Maria then took a bit of time to explain where things were kept, and the general procedure. Most sandwiches were made during the morning, but sometimes people requested particular ones, and they had to be made to order.

When the place began to fill up she worked smoothly and quickly, and didn't bite my head off when I kept asking her things, she was a woman of few words. Things went very smoothly. I didn't scald myself or anyone else, and I don't think I gave the wrong change. My only mishap was with a dopey looking secretary with prominent teeth and orange hair, who ordered a banana sandwich, (what kind of woman eats banana sandwiches?)

Bananas were something I associated with children, like the times when I mashed bananas for Grace and added cream and sugar.

I took out two slices of bread and began buttering them, peeled a banana and began slicing it and that's when the ginger bunny hit the roof

'No, No,' she screamed. 'I never eat white bread and I certainly don't eat butter.'

I apologised and reached for the brown bread, and deliberated for a moment about whether to pick the bits of banana off the sandwich I'd just made. But when I felt the bunny's very hostile stare, I decided not to and reached out instead for another one.

She made me feel so nervous, that my hands shook, and I nearly tore the bread as I was cutting it, when I handed it to her, she snatched it and walked off without paying, muttering to herself. I tell you Scarlett, she wouldn't walk away from me today without a serious verbal kicking.

I worried about what to do with the wasted sandwich. I didn't know what Maria's policy regarding spoilt food was, that is how much of a gawp I was. I didn't have to worry for long though. A fat guy who had been watching the whole spectacle said. 'Here love, I'll take that rather than see it go to waste.' I gave it to him, it was quicker than stuffing it in the bin, and as I watched his enormous jaws slap open and devour it I thought it was the same difference.

The day was over bang on time and I felt an enormous sense of satisfaction. It wasn't great work, it was menial and subservient, but it broke the link with the past. I was back on track, a seventeen year old getting up and out for work.

By the time I bought my travel card and paid my digs I had hardly any money left. But I didn't care. Each passing day bought me more confidence, and working in a temporary job with people I'd never meet again gave me an opportunity to get myself together.

Mom wrote again, she was very unhappy at the idea of me making sandwiches for a living. 'What was the point of it all, the entire trauma if you end up a dogsbody, you must pursue your education, if you don't, mark my words you will regret it for the rest of your life.'

She also mentioned in her letter that Aunty Phil had confided to her that I was reluctant to go back to college.

'Mark my words,' was one of Mom's favourite sayings. When I read that letter, my blood turned cold. I knew Mom was right, it wasn't just a fulfilment of her ambition for me; she knew what my dreams had meant to me. But since the school year started in September I had to fill in the time with something, and frankly making sandwiches was about as far as my confidence went.

From then on, I felt nothing but outright hatred for Aunty Phil. She had tried to stop me from going back to education under the guise of protecting Mom, when really she was protecting herself. Sometimes my bitterness with her almost burns. She was such a twisted woman.

She had once wanted to be a nun, but had lacked the commitment, and she lacked the balls to get married and have a family. She so badly wanted me to pay for the sin of having that baby. To see me educated and successful would have broken her heart and confirmed her worst fear, that it is possible to have it all, so long as you're not fussy about the order.

Returning home to that dark soulless house every night was very depressing. Aunty Phil still refused to give me a key, but never guaranteed to be in when I got home. That way she made me feel like a visitor, not a lodger who was paying for the honour of staying with her.

I never got used to the smell of her house. I can still smell it now, the combination of damp and vegetables and oldness. She would have benefited from keeping a cat. At least the place would have smelt better.

Each night followed the same pattern. Tea in the kitchen, usually pie and beans or mince stew with boiled spuds. Above us on the wall hung an out of date calendar showing a picture of the river Shannon. Looking at my food one night, a plateful of grey gravy with bits of spud and debris floating in it, I wondered if she was homesick, for it resembled nothing so much as the Shannon, after it had burst its banks.

She would ask me a series of questions. 'Was I late'? 'Did I remember to switch the light off?' 'Would I mind closing the door more gently, the dead wanted to remain asleep.' It wasn't a conversation at all just a series of questions and implied criticisms.

I would then wash up and clear the things away; and she would go to the sitting room and switch the telly on, taking the paper with her.

One day she caught me going into the lavatory with the paper under my arm and she went mad. 'For God's sake ye are like a dirty old man, don't take the paper in there, it's the height of bad hygiene.'

I said I was only going to read it not use it, and she said, 'Enough of your smartness, I'd put nothing beyond you.'

Now I think about it, the toilet roll in that house seemed to last forever, she must have been seriously constipated.

Every night I'd go up to my room, and listen to the radio and think and dream of all the good times that were passing me by. Just up the road were the biggest and busiest pubs in London, and what was I doing? The only highlight of the week was Wednesday evenings when the agony aunt was on the radio; answering peoples sexual and emotional problems.

It was the 1980's and the whole bloody world was liberated, and could do what the hell it pleased, but that wasn't what came across on that radio show. People seemed stuffed with problems.

I remember one night, this really hesitant guy phoned in. He stuttered and stammered so badly that I found myself panicking for him. Eventually, he managed to squeak out that he was fearful of being gay. And what did the sympathetic, understanding agony aunt do?

She nearly bit his head off.

'What the hell is there to be frightened of?' she barked, 'Be proud of it, there's nothing wrong in being gay.'

I thought there bloody well is where I come from. It just goes to show, people who set themselves up as experts, often know piss all about reality. What passes as an exciting slice of alternative living in parts of London, can lead to a serious thrashing outside the M25.

It was on one such dark December night around this time that I discovered you Scarlett. I had returned home cold and damp, and rather than attempt to eat the gruel Aunty Phil had placed before me, I had gone straight upstairs. I was almost out of my mind with boredom, and I began rooting in the old wardrobe. You were there in a hardback book. There was a picture of you dressed in black, dancing with a dark haired gypsy-looking fellow on the front cover.

The title 'Gone with the Wind' sounded familiar and I vaguely remembered Mom talking about the time her and Dad had gone to the flicks during the war to see it. I think she had been very taken with it, mainly I suspect because of your Irish ancestry. Mom was not biased but she genuinely did believe ancient Israel was located somewhere on the Cork and Kerry border, and that McGillycuddy's Reeks were none other than the range where the Mount of Olives might be found.

I picked the book up, and almost put it back down when I read the blurb 'set against the backdrop of the American civil war.' I thought 'Thanks, but no tanks.' I hate war stories, but when I flipped open the first page and read the opening line. 'Scarlett O'Hara, was not beautiful but men seldom realised it,' I was hooked.

I raced home every night, desperate for the next instalment. I was mesmerised. I couldn't believe my luck. It was like an omen, as if you were there for a purpose Scarlett. You were my wake up call. Here was a tale, of a young woman facing ruin, a woman with a choice - throw the towel in, or turn and make a stand.

Mom was right. If I stayed in a bum job, I'd drown in a sea of lethargy and hate. I would let Condon destroy me. I'd end up with a miserable downbeat life, and the real crime would be that it didn't have to be that way. I was intelligent; I had looks, not as captivating as yours of course Scarlett. I mean I didn't have a seventeen inch waist, but my figure was good. I told myself that if I set my mind to it, I could do it. I could rise out of this misery, and I promised myself that when I did, I'd make Jerh Condon pay for the night he ruined me.

The fact is Scarlett; he never made any attempt to find out about me.

All that talk he gave out about seeing me right when I went to college, well it never materialised, as far as he was concerned, I was yesterday's news. Anyone who thinks like that deserves to be buried in shit up to their armpits. He would definitely have known about my plight, you can't keep a secret like that in a small town.

Mom had sworn the family to secrecy, but whereas she had a hold over my brothers, that hold did not extend to their wives. One of them definitely leaked it out. Condon obviously thought 'tough shit, she can't prove anything now.'

My pledge to turn things round wasn't as dramatic as yours Scarlett, choking on a radish and swearing to God to get even, but it was just as heart- felt. My aim was to get a better-paid job and move out of that Godforsaken house. I carried on with the job I had, circulating my qualifications to every agency I came across.

The weeks leading up to Christmas flew past, Maria became more talkative, and Stella, the simpleton turned up some days, to break a cup, bang her nose on a broom, and eat more Mars bars than was good for her. When Maria had first mentioned Stella, I had imagined a young girl. She was in fact a middle-aged woman, trapped in a pensioner's body with a child's mind. A living embodiment of what a bitch nature can be.

She loved music, she'd put the radio on full blast and to this day I still can't listen to Blondie, Madness or the Stranglers without thinking back to those surreal times. Maria sometimes played a cassette of Edith Piaf, and I remember singing along to 'Les Amants D'un Jour.'

'Tears in my eyes and tears in my heart, Shine another glass, make the hours past, working everyday in a shit café.'

I learnt after a while, that Maria was in the process of getting divorced. Her husband was a bastard, and she was having a hell of a time trying to get disentangled from him.

'Take my advice; avoid marriage and kids like the plague,' was what she told me one day and I flushed red when she said that, because of my big secret. She mistook my blush for innocence, and said. 'I'm telling you girl, once a bloke saddles you with a kid, he thinks he's got you nailed down. That's when the misery starts.'

Maria had owned a delicatessen before she got married. It turned out she was well qualified, with certificates and all sorts of diplomas and things in food preparation and cellarage. Her husband had encouraged her to begin with, but when she had the baby he took the business over and he ran it full steam into the buffers. Not only was he useless he was violent as well.

I asked her if she regretted having the child, and she said. 'Yes, but only because I am sorry that my daughter had to witness some terrible things' He sounded a monster, a waster, just totally inadequate. God the world suddenly seemed crammed full of monstrous men. Maria said on top of everything else he was off with other women all the time.

'I won't have him coming near me,' she said, 'Bringing disease home, I just pray the cops will find him one day, rotting somewhere in his car.'

When she said that, a mental image of a big bag of pus slumped over a steering wheel flashed through my mind.

She might have been bitter and hurt but she wasn't stupid.

Apart from the franchise running the canteen, she had also set up her own catering business. She said she took the canteen job for two reasons. It persuaded the courts to give her custody of her daughter (the bastard was contesting that,) the hours fitted in with the school day and made her look responsible. And secondly it led to lucrative free lance catering jobs.

She said she didn't declare her evening work, because she was screwing her ex for every penny he had. 'When it's all over and I'm really shot of him, then I'll come clean.'

She was highly sought after as an outside caterer. She seemed to have something on practically every night of the week, of course at that time the Christmas party season was in full swing. I asked her how she managed it, and she replied. 'With difficulty - fancy giving a hand, the money is good.'

So to Aunty Phil's consternation I started working evenings, preparing finger buffets in shops and offices all over northwest London. For the first time I felt that I was really living, mixing with bright sociable people out for a good time. I was working, but it didn't feel like work. More importantly, I learnt so much from Maria, that when it came to running my own business, I was already streets ahead of most of my competitors.

I watched how staff intermingled with each other at the various work parties. The little power struggles that went on. I learnt that some people are like dogs, they respond far more positively to a good kicking than a pat on the back. Time and time I noticed it, friendly egalitarian bosses getting shit thrown at them behind their back, while total shites got hero worship.

Maria was also instrumental in teaching me how to handle people. For these evening parties, she was a completely different person to the rather sullen woman I knew by day. Gone was the dowdy overall she wore in the canteen. She wore slinky black outfits; and being slim and dark she looked elegant and glam-orous.

The first thing she did at every party was suss out the person who had to be impressed, nothing was too much trouble for him or her. Anyone else – well they could kiss her arse.

She told me that company 'do's' where food and booze are plentiful often bought out the worse in people. She hated those who took a freebie, but still acted as if they were footing the bill, she thought they were lower than a boil on a snake's belly.

One night she laid on a very up market function, there wasn't a sausage roll or peanut in sight, just lots of smoked salmon and continental pastas and salads. It was the early 80's and the birth of the sun dried tomato was still awaited in North West London.

Maria was doing her bit again, looking cool and elegant. She looked more like one of the guests than most of the guests did, but a nasty big fly, in the form of a complaining arse was in the ointment. This particular guy made it his business, to moan about everything.

Nothing was to his liking. She came across to me and hissed 'He's the kind of git you've got to watch, give an inch and he'll have you wiping his arse, don't take any crap from him.'

I thought that was pretty funny considering what she had just said about his arse, but she wasn't amused. 'A turd like that can do a lot of harm with his griping, look at him mouthing off.'

I thought she was worrying unnecessarily, because a lot of people were giving him daggers; he was obviously the office pain. But he really upset Maria and when he came up to her, and muttered something about warm champagne, and cold brie, she turned to me and said. 'That does it; I'm going to put something in his coffee that will have him shitting through the eye of a fucking needle for months.'

She was a fighter and she was successful, because she let nothing pass her without an opinion on it. Sometimes at the end of an evening as we were clearing up, we'd chat, she'd tell me about herself, her family and her problems.

My regret Scarlett is that I didn't tell her about mine. If I had told her about the ape - she would have given him a verbal trouncing, 'a decent effing,' as Jack would say. It would have given me a chance to confide and get another perspective on the whole affair. More importantly it would have broken the taboo of never talking about it, and that might have made it more likely that when I met Jack, I would have told him, if not everything, at least *something*.

But I didn't tell her, I gave her the barest of details of my life. I'd had a fall out with my family in Kent, and I lived with a disagreeable old aunt. The ape remained a secret. It must have been pride. I don't know. I just couldn't tell her.

Phoenix.

Chapter Fourteen

The Spring Term drew to an end and the thoughts of Daisy Keane along with most other children turned to visiting velveteen rabbits, fluffy yellow chicks and of course, chocolate. She wasn't the only member of the family with Easter on her mind; it was the one time of year when Jack always felt an overwhelming need to return to Ireland.

There was however, one person in the Keane household; whose mind was not on Easter, and that was Phoenix. Her mind was firmly fixed on events from the far past, and how to make sure they didn't slip into the present. Therefore when Jack came home one night, and announced he had booked a flight for all of them to Cork, it was not met with universal approval.

Daisy received the news with rapturous delight - Ireland meant lots of fuss and attention being lavished on her. She also liked the idea of flying like a bird through the sky. It took Phoenix to put a dampener on things. She didn't want to go. She could barely cope as it was with people she was paid to get along with, never mind making small talk with people she would pay to avoid.

She was about to dismiss it out of hand, when it occurred to her that surely Jack and Daisy could go alone. They didn't need her. She could do with a few days to think things over. She would put writing to Scarlet on hold; for she still had a fear of doing that while alone, in fact she felt strangely more afraid than ever. But a chance to sit and think uninterrupted, well that was different.

She rehearsed carefully what she would say to Jack, since she knew he would be disappointed at her decision to stay in London. She would persuade him that since she was both snowed under with work and very tired, it would be better for everyone if she remained behind. He would surely understand.

But he didn't.

He was furious when she faced him with her proposal, and luckily she had had the good sense to wait until Daisy was safely in bed before she broached the subject with him. Seeing him seated industriously at the kitchen table, with his open diary in front of him had prompted her to collect her own diary. She clutched it to her, as if it were a witness to what she was about to claim.

'I've been thinking Jack,' she said lightly, 'It might be better if just you and Daisy went to Ireland for Easter this year.'

'Oh yeah?' he replied without even looking up. 'Why is that?'

'Because I am so busy, I'm really snowed under. In fact it was probably the wrong time for Carolyn to place that advert.' She placed her open diary on the table, willing him to take a look at it.

He looked up, ignoring it completely, and closed his own diary before pushing it away from him.

'In that case,' he said, 'It might be as well to leave Carolyn to it; you look as if you need a break.'

It wasn't going quite the way she had planned – she didn't want him to work out a strategy for her, or give her a medical opinion. She decided to sound a touch more earnest.

'Actually Jack,' she said. 'It is not just because I'm busy - I really could do with a few days to myself. I need a bit of space.'

He sat calm and still, staring at his clasped hands which now occupied the spot on the table where his diary had sat before he had pushed it away, and she was misled by the aura of tranquillity which seemed to surround him.

'Do you have any idea,' he said. 'What I'm thinking?'

She shook her head. 'About what?' she asked, feeling a little confused.

'I'm thinking you are a fucking liar.'

She flinched, that certainly hadn't been the answer she had been expecting, but she held her ground. 'I am not a liar,' she replied coolly, 'and I'm definitely not a fucking liar. You know how stressed I've been recently, I thought you would be glad for a break yourself.'

'Always making excuses aren't you?' he said. 'Have you any idea how fucking boring you are becoming?'

Fury replaced coolness in her demeanour; it was moving away from Ireland and becoming a discussion about her. 'You are not what I would call riveting yourself,' she replied hotly. 'What is the big deal? It's not as if I'm stopping you from going, go and take Daisy with you, she'll love it, you'll love it, I won't. What's the problem?'

He got up from his chair and walked towards her. 'You,' he said. 'You are the fucking problem. I come home every-day after working my fucking bollocks off and what do I come home to?'

She stared at him, telling herself to keep calm, to keep cool. The only way to deal with Jack in a temper was to face him off. Back down or whimper and he'd wipe the floor with her. The platitudes she reiterated were worthy ones, but even so, she felt her temper beginning to rise seriously close to boiling point. How dare he pass himself off as the only one who worked? She thought about what her own days entailed; the driving around London, the constant phone calls, the pulling together of awkward touchy workers, the accounting, collecting Daisy, on and on it went.

'What about me?' she said clutching a hand to her chest. 'Doesn't what I do count as work?'

'What do you work for?' he shouted. 'We don't need the fucking money but that doesn't stop you working like a fucking scrubber and for what? So you can put more money in the bank and count it.'

The implication about being tight hurt almost as much as the one about being a scrubber. She looked at his face, it looked wild and angry, but it did nothing to deter her.

'You don't complain about the standard of living we have do you?' she demanded. 'Where does all the money come from for you to screw the likes of O'Carolan, or pay for Daisy's school, or all the bloody cars you get through?'

He walked up, so close to her that their noses almost met. 'Running that fucking business ten years ago when you had fuck all going for you was great, but now you make me puke; running off, all the fucking time, chasing every fucking penny, like a fucking Fagin, undercutting every poor bastard that needs a start, then being so fucking cowardly about telling anyone what you do for a living.' He stopped for a moment and then as if remembering the purpose for the pause, he leant over and picked her diary up and began slapping it against the table.

'Why don't you make some attempt at being a mother instead of spending your life shovelling shit?'

He turned his head aside and with a throw like a cricketer, hurled her diary against the wall. It fell to the ground with a clatter, while torn pages and receipts continued to fly through the air.

It was that action that ripped her. Hate every bit as cold and vicious as that she felt for the ape and her family flooded through her. He despised her. He was no different to any of the others. He trashed her character and made her seem like a low life racketeer.

Just like everyone else in her life, he assumed he knew her, knew her motives. Did he think he was just going to walk away from the mess he had created? Leave her to scramble round on her knees like a skivey to pick up the mess he had made? He had another thing coming. She looked into his hard angry face and without warning, delivered an almighty punch, right on his jaw. It stunned him for a moment and while it did so - she took the opportunity to hammer punches and slaps across his face, screaming and shouting abuse at him all the while. When he finally came to his senses, he pulled her arms off and held them tight, drawn up high behind her back, his face red and furious staring into hers.

She was mighty tempted to spit in his eye, but resisted it. 'Don't think,' he shouted, 'Don't think, you'll ever get away with hitting me again, try it and I'll thrash you to a pulp.'

He dropped her arms, shoving her against the wall as he did so and hurried to the front door. An echo of finality rang through the house, as she heard the front door slam shut, not a sound was to be heard in its aftermath. She felt her mouth twitching in preparation for tears to fall but she fought the urge and stood half slumped against the wall, trying to get her breathing back under control.

Anger and hate now had equal possession of her. She hated him. She hated his cruelty, and the words he had used to describe her more succinctly, than she had ever been able to do. She stood head down until a creak on the stairs caused her to look up.

It was Daisy. The noise of the door slamming shut had disturbed her. She walked warily down the stairs, peering through the open kitchen door as she did so, a white teddy in her hands.

'Who is fighting Mommy?' she asked.

'Nobody darling,' Phoenix replied, 'it was just Daddy telling me about an argument he heard at work today.'

'Where has Daddy gone?' she asked

'For a walk.'

'What for?'

'To get something'

'What does he want?'

'Milk, I think,' she snapped irritably, God, would the child never stop asking questions? She took Daisy's hand and led her back to bed.

'I'll tell Daddy to give you a kiss when he comes home,' she promised the little girl as she switched the light off before going back downstairs.

She had managed to calm Daisy down, but she felt far from calm herself. She wondered where Jack had gone, but she didn't care.

Was this the beginning of the end? The end after all has to have a beginning.

Never before in her entire life had she raised her hand to anyone and never before had she used some of the words she had described him with tonight. A shot of self disgust flooded through her as she thought of some of the things she had said, while hammering the living daylights out of him. Could she sink any lower?

She poured herself a drink from a bottle in the drinks cabinet, dispensing with the need to take it from a secret source. It was all so utterly hopeless. What could she do? She glanced down and caught a glimpse from a smiling cool Peggy Lee who stared up at her from the CD rack. She knelt down and took the CD in her hand, looking at it more closely. How shocked she had been, when Jack told her all those years ago, that he liked Peggy Lee. It seemed like a life time ago. So much had changed and yet in a way it hadn't.

Her situation was the same then as it was now, only then she had really believed, she could control the past.

She sat down on the edge of an armchair, too tense to sit comfortably and thought over the words both her and Jack had exchanged, a foolish exercise since it did nothing other than fill her with despair. Everything was falling apart and it was beyond her control to do anything about it, certainly thinking wasn't helping, in fact it was driving her mad.

She got up and walked into the study and collected her red book. The present suddenly felt too difficult to comprehend. Taking the book back to the front room she sat and stared at it. What she would write about, she didn't know- all she was after was distraction.

Dear Scarlett,

Even if Jack apologised for the things he said tonight, it wouldn't make any difference. He has simply put into words what I think of myself anyway. Looking at me, from my angle, I'm even less attractive than from the outside. To others I might just appear harsh and driven, but I can see and feel the festering pool of hate that is the engine, and it is not an attractive sight.

All of this leads me to question Scarlett, why I ever got involved with Jack, for the last thing I need right now, is someone who is prepared to give me an honest reflection of what I'm really like. I could do with just a little dishonest flattery.

My first impression of him was of someone jovial and good humoured. He was always whistling or singing that Peggy Lee song, 'I'm feelin' them too good today blues'. He was, I thought as uncomplicated as a house sparrow, but judging from some nature programmes, sparrows aren't as simple as you'd think. You only have to watch a sparrow nick a piece of bread, from the beak of a brick shithouse of a pigeon, to know that tales of the simple sparrow are spurious.

He used to call for me, knocking loudly on my door and yahooing through the letterbox. He was a little envious of the house I had at the time in Wandsworth. It was a gem of a buy.

The previous owner had been one of my clients, an unlikely one since most of them were yuppies, desperate to pay over the top for everything. Her name was Maud and she was a pensioner. She had spent her entire life working for the advancement of her only child, and the only thanks she got was being sent off to live in a care home.

Her son and daughter in law came up from Sussex to oversee the sale, and to them fresh from their cottage in the country with its roses and wisteria, the end terrace must have seemed like a nightmare. It was 1990 and prices were dropping and I think they could see their nest egg disappearing down a black hole.

I was there when they were visiting and I hinted that I was house hunting in Wandsworth. Maud's son instantly saw an opportunity to cut an estate agent out. A smart move by a smart arse, but he had been out of London too long to realise, that terraces in the capital don't carry the stigma terraces in the provinces often do. He thought he was being cute, but he wasn't as cute as me. I got it for a song and I didn't feel in the least bit guilty, Maud was going into a home and the two gobshites who could have given her a better ending didn't deserve her cash.

Jack was dead impressed when he first saw it.

'How did you get your hands on this?' he asked.

I just shrugged my shoulders and said. 'It's O.K but actually I'm thinking of moving to Barnes.' I had no intention of moving anywhere; it just doesn't pay to appear too content, too grateful.

When I saw his place, I was shocked. It was a ground floor flat in Battersea. A typical builder's place, unfinished -well that's an exaggeration, un- started would be more accurate. He invited me round for dinner; on what must have been our second or third date. When I went inside I met Tosh the ganger for the first time.

After introducing us, Jack left me in the lounge, while he went off searching for a corkscrew. As soon as he went out the door, Tosh turned to me and said 'They're pigs aren't they?'

'Who?' I replied and he said.

'Pinky and Perky' and then he laughed himself senseless.

When Jack came back, he told Tosh to scoot, but Tosh being Tosh began rummaging in his pockets, pretending to search for something. He obviously sniffed food and drink in the air and he didn't want to go. When Jack began to show signs of irritation, he said 'It's all right, I know when I'm not wanted,' but just before he went he said to me. 'Don't let him pass any strange noises off on the dog under the table.'

When he left, I asked Jack if there was a dog under the table, and he said. 'No, because there isn't a table.'

Needless to say Jack didn't cook a dinner, he had arranged for a Chinese to be sent round. The fluorescent colours of the sauce reminded me of a chemistry set I had owned as a child. I couldn't bear the thought of eating it, and Jack was really put out. But I did drink the wine and pick at the rice. Afterwards Jack told me to take a look through his C.D collection, and choose something while he made coffee.

There was plenty to choose from, R.E.M, Oasis, Blondie, The Dubliners, Christy Moore, the Chieftains, he had stacks of them.

I said. 'You choose, surprise me,' and he did.

He said. 'Do you know who has the sexiest voice going?' and for one awful moment I thought that he was about to shatter my illusions and say Madonna, but he didn't. He said 'Peggy Lee.'

I told him that I thought Peggy Lee was a big fat woman who played the piano, and he laughed and said 'you great tick, that was Peggy Mills.'

He showed me a C.D with a picture of Peggy Lee on the front of it. She looked cool and blond, and I got a secret buzz from thinking that Jack was more likely to be turned on by Scandinavian coolness, rather than hot and hairy Mediterranean armpits.

I thought Peggy Lee sounded awful, the sort of droning music you'd hear in Tesco's. Well that was my initial reaction. But as I listened to her clear precise diction, I began to see why Jack rated her so highly. I know jumped up farts go on about the potency of cheap music, but it's a fact, music of any kind can capture a moment and hold it in time forever. Peggy Lee will always be synonymous with that night because, it was the first time in years that I had felt remotely at home with someone.

On the face of it Scarlett our relationship flowed, but in reality each step was calculated and assessed by me. In a way it was out of my control because I liked him and I wanted it to go somewhere. But I was vigilant, constantly on the lookout for signs of him wanting to move on, because I knew the day I got the slightest hint that he was slacking, I'd be off.

I can't play any music tonight Scarlett, anything upbeat would just aggravate me; and something soft or sentimental would simply push me over the edge.

I am so tired of fighting. Every step along the way, since that terrible night at Condon's place has been one more round in a never ending fight. I'm not just talking about the fight for money, and possessions, but the constant fight against the madness that is always lurking in the background. All I want is a break.

Phoenix.

She put her pen down, too tired to bother any more, she felt confused. Why was she telling Scarlett about her first house, what did that have to do with anything? She sat and stared at the closed book for a moment. Was writing to Scarlett making things better or worse? She didn't know, but of one thing she was certain, it was a Pandora's Box. She wouldn't be able to put the lid back on, even if she wanted to.

She got up and locked the book back in its drawer and immediately headed upstairs to her bedroom, where she collected her copy of Gone with the Wind from her bedside table.

Back downstairs, she sat in the kitchen, flicking the pages of the book, until she came to the last page in the novel. As she did so, she raised her head and stared directly at the door, remembering back to the time, when she first read the ending to Scarlett's story. How shocked she had been. She had searched for another page, convinced the story couldn't end with Rhett walking away. In fact, she had been almost frantic in her desire to believe she had it wrong, she'd read and reread the last page searching for clues that would suggest the ending was not as it seemed.

And when it had finally sunk in, that Rhett was gone for good, she had felt real grief for Scarlett.

Now she felt real grief for herself. It was unwinding. Trying to cope with the past and the present simultaneously was like trying to drive forward and reverse at the same time. Impossible!

It was gone midnight when Jack returned home smelling of drink, and cigarettes. He had obviously been to the pub. She didn't even raise her eyes when he entered the room. He came straight up to her and put his hands on her shoulders.

'I'm sorry for the things I said,' he told her quietly. 'I didn't mean a single word of it. I just so badly want you with me wherever I go, you know that don't you?'

She nodded her head, not daring to look at him. The tears she had fought to control all evening were in imminent danger of escaping. He took her hand and they went upstairs, both deciding the least said the better..

Two days later on Holy Thursday they flew to Ireland, all of them. Jack had arranged for a hired car to be ready at Cork airport and they drove south in the evening sunshine. The roads were clear and they sped on at alarming speeds through Bandon, past Clonakilty, all the way down to Skibbereen.

There they stayed with Jack's brother Danny, on the family farm. He gave them a rapturous welcome, and for a moment, even Phoenix was pleased that she had come. The farm was a hilly one, overlooking the Atlantic and the view from the top field was spectacular.

Later that same evening; Jack's sister Eileen; came visiting, dressed in an old jacket and Wellingtons boots; she had come straight from milking the cows, eager to see her brother and niece, with no thought to her appearance, at least not until she saw Phoenix staring at her feet. She returned the stare with an equally disparaging glare at the stilettos Phoenix was wearing.

Both Jack and Daisy received a fierce hug from her. She told Daisy she was bigger and more beautiful than ever; and Jack that he was looking every inch the prosperous trader. Turning her attention to Phoenix, she gave her a brief hug before telling her she looked tired.

As she felt Eileen's arms go round her, Phoenix sensed pure animosity. 'If she was a dog,' she thought to herself. 'I'd be lucky to escape with my ankles intact.'

Most of the night was spent talking about the Irish economy. Jack was enthralled with property prices in the area, especially when he heard that a tumbled down old barn he used to play in was now the holiday home of a well known British TV star. Danny took delight in seeing Jack's surprise, but Phoenix could tell the economy meant nothing to him. He was one of the few people she had ever met whom she genuinely recognised as good. She had never heard him say a bad word about anyone. From the first time he had met her, he had gone out of his way to make her feel special and in his company she felt a glow of warmth and contentment. He complimented her and told her frequently he had never seen Jack look happier. She reciprocated, by always reserving her sweetest smile and warmest hugs just for him.

But she didn't feel so charitable towards Jack's sister Eileen. She always looked at Phoenix with an expression of downright suspicion, dislike even and Phoenix always repaid her with an expression of downright disinterest. It was as if Eileen suspected Jack was up to no good and Phoenix was the back seat driver, steering him to perdition. Phoenix didn't care. As far as she was concerned Eileen could kiss her arse until roses bloomed in January.

The next day, being Good Friday, Jack, Phoenix and Daisy accompanied Danny to church. With the exception of Danny, none of them wanted to go, but to refuse would be an insult. Danny told them they would go to the church where Daisy had been baptised. He preferred it to his local one he said, because the priest there spoke faster.

The little church was in the depths of the country, out towards Bantry and the journey there took them through tiny winding lanes, some leading to the sea, some to rocky common pasture. Everywhere the fuchsia lined the hedgerow, its red sentinels no doubt getting ready to greet the approaching summer

It was almost three o clock when they arrived and the tiny church was full to capacity. Phoenix instinctively headed for the back, where the farmers stood, but a woman who recognised them as visitors, insisted on squeezing up and making room for all the Keane's to sit together. Phoenix grimaced at Jack, before flashing a grateful smile of thanks at the interfering woman. The church was dark and cool and in the silent pauses of the service, the caw, caw of the pagan rooks going about business as usual on Good Friday, was all that could be heard.

The priest had chosen three lay people to read the prolonged Gospel with him. Two men and the token woman partook of the drama. They had attractive voices, and even Jack perked up when he realised it wasn't going to be the long tedious muffled type of reading that had been all the rage when he was young. The congregation were invited by the priest to sit and Phoenix sighed with relief, she could just about bear the Easter story; it was the Christmas one, or more particularly Christmas time, she found difficulty with.

She sat back resigned, waiting for it to be over, wondering what she could turn her mind to that would speed the time away, but to her surprise she found herself listening with rapt attention. She listened as if she had never heard the story before, looking from one to the other of the readers, waiting for the next instalment. Of course, she knew the story well; after all it never changed, but for the first time, she felt some idea of what it was really all about.

Here was a story that felt familiar. She even found herself identifying with it. She recognised and flinched at the pain of being deserted by friends. She felt again the anguish of betrayal and the mental suffering that comes from being caught up in something beyond human understanding. She physically winced as the narrator recalled how the soldiers repeatedly struck the tired and emotionally drained Christ. And a tear almost fell as she recollected that all this was borne by an innocent man.

It was all too desperate and when the priest, acting the role of Christ turned to the good thief and said 'Truly today you will be with me in paradise,' it finally became too much.

She got up abruptly and pushed past Jack dislodging him from his day dream. Grateful for an excuse to get out of the church he got up and followed her, motioning to Danny to keep Daisy back.

She made her way to the door, blinking as the fierce sunshine streamed down upon her, and stumbled across some broken tomb stones until she came to a wooden bench. The whole scenario had been too much to take and her nerves were already overstretched. She had heard those words so many times, but they had been just part of a script that told a bloody and violent story.

But today they proved overwhelming. She found the optimism of Christ's words to the thief, too much to take. They churned up in her such a feeling of loss; that the only thing she could do was run.

A thief, a common criminal had woken up to the worst day of his life. He knew a terrible ordeal stretched ahead of him, a violent end to what had more than likely been a violent and defunct life. And just when all hope, all salvation had gone from him, when he had surely given up caring, it was all turned round.

What started out as the worst day ended up as the best - it was entirely bizarre.

She felt both sceptical and envious. How she longed to be in his place. To know it was all over and that the past no longer counted anymore, to be beyond feeling and hurt- that was where she wanted to be.

Jack sat down beside her, but he didn't say a word. Just an awkward silence interrupted by the incessant rooks sat between them. Both felt incapable of reassuring the other.

Being Good Friday, the pubs in Ireland were closed, so when church was over, they drove home for a drink, well Jack and Phoenix did, Danny settled for tea. In fact Phoenix was so desperate for a drink, she went straight upstairs to her room and had a real one from the bottle in her suitcase, before going back downstairs and demurely accepting 'just a small one' from Danny.

The next few days were spent visiting friends and family, including a brief visit to the McCarthys in Ballybunion and the

O'Connells in Listowel, who welcomed them and did everything in their power to urge them to stay.

A lot of the local labourers were men who had once worked for Jack in London but thanks to the booming economy, they were home again and pleased to be there. They teased Jack and asked him when he was coming back for good.

Daisy too had a wonderful time, chasing chickens out of the kitchen and herding the cows with the help of a big stick. The day before they flew back to London, Jack persuaded Phoenix and Danny to view a disused hotel he considered ripe for development into holiday homes. Danny laughed at him, but went along all the same. They drove through the now familiar fuchsia lined lanes until they came to surely the only village in the whole of Ireland untouched by even the whiskers of the Celtic tiger.

They viewed the ramshackle old building with good natured disinterest before going in search of a bar. The fellow who served them did a good job in talking the area up. He said it was a great area to buy into, as it was definitely on the up.

'We'd be flying,' he said 'if only the feckers round here were up to it. Only a few weeks ago,' he continued, 'A German tourist came in here to me and he said that he'd gone into a bar in the village up above and asked for a sandwich, and do you know what the barman said to him? 'Do you think this is a fucking restaurant?' He handed a pint of expertly poured Guinness over to Jack and stood back, waiting to take in the reaction of the crowd around the bar.

'All it takes,' he said shaking his head, 'is a bit of flexibility and for God's sake the man only wanted a sandwich.'

There was a murmur of approval. One and all, sitting around the bar agreed that it was a terrible image to give of the locality and a very poor showing for Irish hospitality. The talk went on to sport, the weather, the price of Guinness and a few rounds later Danny casually asked if there was any chance of a sandwich. The bartender shook his head and glanced at the clock.

'It's gone three,' he said.

Immediately Jack leapt up and said to Danny 'What do you think this is; a fucking restaurant or something?'

The entire bar erupted into laughter and calls of 'own goal.' The poor barman at least had the grace to look sheepish as his own story backfired on him.

As far as his family were concerned, Jack was in top form and Daisy was a honey pot. Only Phoenix looked less than in top shape. Danny worried about her, but Eileen scoffed at his concern. 'She's a typical English woman, aren't they all mad for the work,' she asked, 'she'll be in top form the moment she hits home.'

For a quiet life, he agreed, but instinctively, he knew Eileen had it very wrong.

Chapter Fifteen

Both Jack and Phoenix returned from Ireland more relaxed but noticeably subdued. Though neither of them mentioned the big row again, the dark cloud that had arisen from Phoenix's reluctance to go away in the first place; sat on the horizon and Jack's sympathy for Phoenix began to rapidly diminish.

Life was good and he wanted to get on with it and here he was being held back and constrained by her negative attitude. It was obvious she was over stressed; he could see it by the shadows under her eyes and in her increasing absentmindedness. But what could he do? God knows he wanted to be understanding. Telling him to go to Ireland with Daisy had been the last straw. He was annoyed with her for making him so angry; driving him to say things he regretted but still fundamentally believed. She had changed so much during the past year, he just didn't understand it.

But from Phoenix's point of view, Jack too had changed. He had once been so proud of her, marvelling in her prowess and energy, giving her credit for the way his business had boomed since meeting her. But that didn't appear to be the case any longer. She wasn't, she told herself, critical of him. There was after all more than a grain of truth in some of the things he accused her of; but the aspects of her character that had once been a source of pride for him, now seemed to be targets for his criticism. She had never claimed to be an earth mother and neither had she ever expressed a desire not to work, or to play fairly.

Since the night of the big row, she had found it difficult, to hold her head up in his company; she was ashamed of her violence and ashamed to think he thought so little of her. Of course he had apologised, but she didn't believe a word of it. Jack simply wanted a quiet life, and if an apology not worth the air it was delivered on bought it about, well Jack was up to that.

The only person, apart from Daisy who remained consistent in her life was Carolyn. She took on more and more responsibility, and though Phoenix was loath to admit it; she coped every bit as well as Phoenix did. She carried out spot checks, investigated complaints, and generally ran the show to nothing but approval from both staff and clients.

Phoenix was grudging in her admiration and being a realist, admitted to a twinge of jealousy. She didn't praise Carolyn, but she refrained from criticism and that alone was a welcome departure as far as Carolyn was concerned.

Although business was going well for Phoenix, it was going even better for Jack. His venture into the restoration of old and historic houses was proving to be a runaway success. A massive double page advert in the South London Press complete with editorial and photographs had paid dividends, and the response took him by delighted surprise. The photographs were of a house he had done up in Wimbledon; his own one of course. Even Phoenix had to laugh when she read the description of him as 'a sensitive and intuitive craftsman,' with 'respect for heritage positively oozing from his every pore.'

'Would that by any chance be the same Jack Keane who once threatened to bury a conservation officer?' she asked.

'Never heard of him,' Jack replied, 'sounds like a jumped up guttersnipe to me.'

There was one downside though to Jacks new burst of success and that was the necessity of entertaining the entrepreneur who had given him his biggest break. Howard Bleasdale had opened shopping malls all over the South East. He was blessed with a unique talent for making each one identical, while selling them to local authorities as 'individually designed.' The same formula was used over and over again; pale pastel colours, plastic gilt mirrors, and plenty of never to die ferns.

He was, Jack informed Phoenix a 'contradictory old fart,' since he was spending a vast fortune having his own Elizabethan Manor, situated out in the bush, somewhere in Sussex, authentically done up to the last pathetic detail.

The relationship between the Eton educated entrepreneur and self made West Cork builder flourished, mainly due to the latter's ability to feed the formers romantic vision of the Irish in Britain. Somehow news of the Celtic Tiger's mighty prowess had escaped Howard Bleasdale's attention, he was sincerely caught in a time warp that caused him to believe that donkeys bearing peat baskets roamed the streets of Dublin, and that most Irish men only worked in London in order to feed their starving families back in the Emerald Isle. It wasn't racism, just good old fashioned, comfortable ignorance. Howard felt good about offering a helping hand to a Paddy who was trying to raise himself out of the mire; he would even do the same for a black, if the opportunity arose.

He knew all about hard times, without a trace of satire or sarcasm he once told Jack about the day, many years ago, when he had gone cap in hand to his bank manager, to ask if his millionaire father would be a good enough guarantor for the bank loan he was seeking. Jack didn't mind what notions Bleasdale liked to entertain in his head, but he did mind consorting with him on a personal level. It was easy to baffle and bluff on mutual territory, but personal entertaining was a very different proposition.

Phoenix wasn't over the moon about meeting him either. 'He sounds like an old hypocrite,' she said when Jack told her about Howard and his wife coming to dinner, 'Living in Lilliput while he fucks up other people's environments.'

'You are a fine one to talk about that,' replied Jack, 'but I'm telling you, I don't care if he is Chairman of Fuckhead's United, this is one contract I don't want to screw up.'

It was agreed in the end, the last Saturday in May would be set aside for Howard and Jane. Pleased that Phoenix wasn't playing awkward, Jack gave her some space, and the two of them left each other to their own domain. Now Jack owed her a favour, Phoenix felt more confident again about writing to Scarlett without fear of him creeping up on her. He wouldn't want to risk her wrath again.

Dear Scarlett,   **1st May 2001**

When I think back on my past, the sheer bloody miracle that I ever made a right move; terrifies me almost as much, as the mistakes I made.

What if, I had bought into Aunty Phil's mantra of 'no life before death for scuts,' or driven by desperation, I had married some mediocre creep, always at his best, happy to keep me so long as I was grateful.

That could have been my fate.

Jack is a bastard. He cuts me to ribbons with his words, and I've never known a day's security since the hour I met him, because the only way I can hold him, is by keeping the door open wide for him to leave when he chooses.

He must never realise how much I depend on him. The day he does, I'm lost. It's ironic, I've spent almost my entire life despising security and I end up craving it.

Your story Scarlett; was instrumental in me living to fight another day. Perhaps that in itself is pitiable. It read like one long roll call of achieving the impossible. But I have to say it Scarlett, the only part that left me cold, was your infatuation with Ashley. How could you have fancied him?

He was a cowardly two faced shit, who strung you along and betrayed his wife. He did betray Melanie, and in the worst possible way. He did it mentally, and that's worse than physical betrayal, because it has no boundaries; it can occur anytime, anyplace and anywhere.

Being with someone and yet not being with them. That's betrayal, that's what makes men who use pornography so creepy. What runs through their minds, when they are in bed with their chosen woman? Who else is in the bed? Some slut they've just been looking at, photographed with her arse in the air? 'Oh, I do solemnly declare, that I have got my arse in the air' as Jack would say. Sometimes when I'm on a rush hour train, I see men with their 'Look I'm A Man,' mags tucked inside their newspapers, ready to be stuffed between the seats or dropped in the park, spreading all their shite all around. Most of them probably return home hot and sweaty, ready to give a hand with the dinner. New man - but same old wanker.

Does Jack betray me? Who knows? One thing I'm pretty certain of though, is that if he did, it would have to be with flesh and blood. Somehow gawking at a magazine or downloading filth from the net is not Jack's style. There would have to be interaction, flirting and drink.

Anyhow, my first clever move all those years ago; happened when I helped Maria the caterer, with her last function of the Christmas season. It was held in the offices of a building society on Baker Street, on the last working day before Christmas.

I got talking to this bloke who told me he had just moved to London from Devon. He looked a bit out of it. In fact it came as something of a shock when he told me he was the branch manager - he acted more like the caretaker dressed in his best tucker.

Well, he had just been appointed and people called him Mr, but his manner and dress marked him as a country boy in the big city. He was softly spoken and easy going. He told me that his wife and two year old son were moving up to London after Christmas; he had just bought a semi in Acton. He said he could have bought a mansion in Devon for the same price. That's a sure sign of a hick; they are always fretting about what they could buy in the middle of nowhere, if they left London.

I told him that I'd had to turn down the chance of university because I had a sick aunt who needed looking after. But I still needed a proper job, one with prospects. And that is when the miracle happened. He had a vacancy for a trainee clerk, was I interested? I couldn't believe my luck, it never occurred to me, that he might be matching me bullshit for bullshit, but thank God he wasn't.

So thanks to Maria's last party of that Christmas season, I walked from a low paid temporary job, straight into a well paid one with training and prospects.

That Christmas of 1980, wasn't a great deal better than the previous one.

Aunty Phil and I left London on Christmas Eve because Mom wanted me home, and courtesy said that the old dragon had to be invited as well. After all hadn't she done a grand job looking after me so well?

Mom looked tired; Alice was cold, and my brothers disinterested. Alice's husband 'the quack' made several attempts at conversation, but gave up under the glare of her icy stare. Her three children, Sarah, Guy and Tim looked so much bigger. They made me feel as if I'd had been away for an eternity.

It was a strained Christmas Day, everyone wary of saying the wrong thing. It makes me laugh now, though it bloody well didn't back then, but the Christmas number one record was 'There's No one Quite Like Grandma.' Every time I heard it I felt my toes curl. That was distressing enough, but the lowest point of the entire holiday was meeting the ape. Mom and the others had gone to midnight mass, and I had stayed at home preparing the vegetables for Christmas Day dinner.

On Christmas morning, bright and early, I set off for mass. I ran straight up the steps into the church and almost collided bang into the ape. He was in the porch, surrounded by the priest and the parish worthies. Flies around the shit heap was what came to mind when I saw him.

Grace was there, immaculately turned out in red velvet. She hardly recognised me, and for that I was very grateful.

The baby was in the ape's arms and Olga stood by his side looking cool and bored. I wanted to walk backwards, out the door, down the steps and into the sea. But I was trapped. Everyone seemed to be staring at me, even the parish priest fired a look as if to say. 'What the hell are you doing here?'

Olga gave me a cold dismissive look, before turning her back on me. She must have heard rumours about why I have gone away, so consequently I was no longer worthy of acknowledgement. However, since she wasn't in the mad house and the ape wasn't swinging by his balls, she obviously didn't know the real reason. He made as if to walk over to me, but I dived into the church thinking why the fuck hadn't I gone to midnight mass with the others?

Sitting there on that cold morning, watching the ape, baby in one arm, other one draped protectively round Olga's shoulders. I wanted to spit.

The priest prattled on about the light of the world, and as he did, I looked around at the narrow minded judgemental parishioners, all of them thinking they had the winning ticket. I swore to myself that the minute I was free, the minute I had enough money, to get away from my family entirely, I'd never step foot willingly in a church again. The church like trust and hope belonged to the past; from now on I would make my own luck.

Just like you Scarlett, I'm not religious in any real sense, even though I still pray when I need to be bailed out of Shit Street. I can pray about trivial things, but I can't find it in me to ask God for help in the one thing that matters.

When I left the church behind, I never lost my faith in Christ. In fact he became more real, the moment I freed him from the prison that had kept him from me. I was free to know him, not as a member of a community, signing up to endless rules and regulations, living in fear of putting a foot wrong. Unless of course, you are one of the elite, in which case you can do what the hell you want.

Once I extracted him out of the church, I got to know him and I discovered that he wasn't some kind of state accountant, constantly logging all my defects. He was I found out, something of a rebel, always ready to poke the establishment in the eye when it got too sanctimonious. God, he must have been driven mad, by the prescriptive society he lived amongst, with their endless list of does and don'ts. For me Scarlett, the essence of Christ is in the miracle of the water and wine and not just because I'm something of a wino myself. There he is the son of God at a wedding being ordered about by his mother. You can just imagine her saying. 'Jesus, for God's sake help them out, the caterers have muffed it.'

And he does. And he doesn't make a big deal of it. He takes the servants aside, and simply tells them to fill a few jars up with water from the well. Not a bit like the gobshites I know who stand around in bars waving a tenner yelling. 'I'm getting the round in, I'm paying.'

Well that same crowd who hung around street corners watching his every move, less he made someone's day by curing them, were with me on Christmas morning 1980. Honest to God they were, bowing and genuflecting in all the right places, and giving daggers at the scut who had been sent to London - you know, the one whose mother said she had a job, but we all know the real reason don't we?

New Years Eve was celebrated at home. Most of the family came round, and laughed and drank and at midnight Mom tossed her money for luck. In a way though, it was a false, forced joviality. Everyone was still in shock at what the youngest had got up to. There was an air of incredulity; a slut had 'got away with it.' She hadn't been struck with a bolt from the sky.

I cannot explain why I remained silent. Nowadays DNA testing has done away with a lot of denial. But that option wasn't around in the early 80's, even if it had been, I'm not certain that I would have availed of it. Looking back objectively at my family, I really think they had a lot in common with those cultures that practise honour killings.

I remember reading in your book Scarlett about the family; who lynched a Negro accused of raping one of 'their' women folk. It made me go cold, when I read how they would rather kill her than let her testify and advertise her shame. Why must the shame always be the woman's? I reckon my brothers would have fitted into that culture very comfortably. Even if I had come clean about what happened there would still have been shame and revulsion at the idea of an O'Connell being tampered with.

I can almost imagine one of them asking. 'Are you sure you didn't lead him on?' To have led him on might have been more acceptable. What a dilemma for them, what was worse, having a slut or a victim in the family?

As Big Ben chimed in 1981- I made a decision.

The Clash, were dead bloody right, London was calling and I was never coming back. I had nothing in common with my family any more. The chasm between us was too wide. Aunty Phil returned to London a few days before I did. She was anxious to get to the sales, I hadn't the faintest idea why because I don't recall her ever buying anything new.

On my last day at home I packed the final few things I wanted to keep.

I didn't say anything to Mom about never returning, but there was an air of finality about everything we did and said to each other and a distance between us, which burned a hole in my heart, because we had been very close. But the evasion on my part; and the assumption on hers meant we were on opposite sides. She had been too harsh. She hadn't made any attempt to see things from another point of view.

When I was fully packed, I walked into the kitchen and kissed Mom on the cheek and thanked her for the Christmas. She told me to return to study, to be sure and enrol at some evening classes.

As I turned to go I saw a tear roll down her cheek. I felt so wretched and churned up; even thinking about it now Scarlett puts me in mind of a cheerless, black, starless night. I had a sudden urge to throw my arms around her and feel her warm soothing hands on me again. Hers were caring hands that had worked too hard. It was impossible to imagine her fingers had once been long, slender and ringless.

She didn't have to say anything, I knew what she was thinking, had been thinking the entire Christmas. She regretted the adoption. She wanted that baby back where it belonged; with its family.

Throughout the holiday, no one mentioned the baby, it was forbidden territory but its presence was there all the same. Like something out of Dickens's, the ghost of Tiny Tim hovering in the background. After Mom died, Alice found several photos of Joseph hidden in Mom's bag. She must have had them taken in the hospital. She carried them with her, everywhere she went.

Now Scarlett all these years later I finally understand her grief. She sold her soul for me. Having that baby adopted flew in the face of everything Mom believed in. She put my welfare before the baby and was prepared to fight her conscience throughout eternity on it. She figured it was the only way to get my life back for me...

The enormity of the words she had just written paralysed her thoughts and without thinking, she put her pen down and sank her head into her hands.

For the first time, she realized how foolish she had been to think that her mother had arranged the adoption solely out of shame. Now she knew the true motive that had driven her mother.

Why, she asked herself bleakly, why was she was so stupid, so lacking in sensitivity as to how people think, feel and behave? But even in her misery, she knew she hadn't always been like that. There had been a time when she had lived and worked in tune with other people, like when she had looked after Grace and Olga Condon. The ape had employed her purely because she was capable, caring and understanding. But that was all so long ago, she no longer even faintly recognised the person she used to be.

Just beyond the window, the buds on the fuchsia bush slept on obliviously and the quarter moon cloaked by a cloud, camouflaged a hedgehog, as it made its way warily across the garden path. Life was going on all around her, but Phoenix was immune to everything other than the un- rectifiable assumption she had made and moulded into fact.

Like a dimmer switch that gradually floods a room with light, the dawn was just beginning to smudge the night sky with a touch of dusky pink. Sleep was unthinkable, in fact the thought of pursuing it was treacherous; it would be like turning her back on her mother's sacrifice. With no regard to time or thoughts as to what the day ahead might entail, Phoenix picked up her pen and began to write again.

Oh Scarlett, if only I had realised her motive. If only I had had any understanding of her; I could have told her that her worry and concern were all in vain. That child wasn't a part of me; I'd sooner face hell than look him in the face again.

As I opened the door to take my leave that Christmas, Mom spoke and the tone of her voice made me tremble. She said, 'I wanted a different life for you. I didn't ever want to see you scrimp and save the way I've had to. I don't want to think of you as a slave to someone else, cooking and cleaning, when you could have a position in life where others do it for you.'

Now it is too late, all is so very clear.

I told her not to worry; things would turn out fine, if the worst happened and I didn't get to university, well Alice and Eileen had achieved more than enough. She shook her head when I said that. 'They didn't achieve anything,' she said. 'Other than on the backs of others, your achievement if it comes will be your own.'

All the way to London on that rickety noisy train I thought over Mom's words. 'Diddle de di, diddle de da, diddly de,' went the train and I sang in tune to it. 'It's a mistake, I should have said, I shouldn't have gone.'

On that long tedious journey through the drab Kent country-side, I thought I had got the first inkling of my mother as a person in her own right. But knowing what I know now, I see only how utterly crass I was. Her life had been made up of a series of disappointments, a serious case of make do. She had left Ireland not for fun but for the chance to make something of her own; to break out of a community who because it knows your ancestors, dares to think it knows you too - what you should do and what you say.

Mom was intelligent, if only she had been born later - in the era of the Celtic Tiger, she would have ridden it fiercely, but she had been born in the era of the workhorse and she was felled by the first fence. And that Scarlett was meeting and marrying one of her own. His immediate task was to put her back in the box from which she had escaped.

For the rest of her life she was just a very restricted wife and mother and for some that may be fine; but if it's not, it's a caged existence. Forget about a caged robin putting all of heaven in a rage, there is bloody mayhem going on up there on account of all the women in the world forced to live behind closed doors and veils. She lived in fear of one of her children repeating it all again; and on the face of it Scarlett, from what Mom knew, not only wasn't the youngest girl moving forward, she was heading for reverse.

You will understand this Scarlett, because your mother was in the same position. You only saw her as a demure woman always looking for an opportunity to be good and kind just like my friend Magda. You thought she wanted it that way, but of course she didn't. When she lost her chance of marrying the bad egg of her choice, she retreated from life. Her loss was your fathers gain.

God I can feel hate and anger seething through me, because behind every fallen and disgraced woman, there is a man. Why are men such emotional retards? Why does a little power go so extraordinarily quickly to their heads? Take your father, he was dead lucky to get an aristocratic wife, he loved her, he was proud of her, but he still treated her like shite and persuaded himself that she liked it that way. Hadn't she wanted to go to that big fancy bar-be-cue, the one where Ashley announced his engagement, but he left her at home to do the dirty business with the overseer.

He was the owner, but she did all the work.

Why do men constantly have to stand on the heads of others to feel good about themselves? I'm Seriously Angry, Scarlett. I'm going to have to get to heaven, because I've got to sort this out with God. Does He know what His first big mistake was?

Well if He doesn't, then I'll have to tell him.

Quite simply, why did He make men physically stronger than women? That's where and when all the rot started. If there wasn't an in balance between the strength of the sexes, a lot of misery would have been cut out from the start. You wouldn't get wife beating on such a scale. Most gobshites who beat their wives would run a mile if they got a decent trouncing back, and I know what I'm talking about, because if I ever hit Jack again, I know he would thrash me. You wouldn't have countries like Britain passing everything worth having to the first born male. And you wouldn't have vast chunks of the Middle East and China believing that not only should women be kept firmly in their place, but should preferably be detected and exterminated before birth. Men only devised these crazy systems because they have the brute strength to enforce them.

One day when I've got the time and energy I'm going to start my own religion with women in mind. I shall call it Femaleology and I'll publish a basic guide to its underlining principles, a new kind of catechism, something along the lines of…

1) Treat men gently, they are inferior beings locked in superior bodies.
2) Remember, most men suffer from a chronic crick in the neck, which comes about from constantly looking around at what everyone else has.

3) The male is an unclean animal; he suffers from emissions from the armpits, groin, rear and feet. Remember to wash yourself thoroughly should you accidentally pat one on the way to prayers.

4) Men have small minds in need of constant excitement, keep a supply of trinkets for them to dismantle and reassemble. Keep their hands busy for men have naturally prying hands.

5) Be firm with men at all times, they may think they know what they want, they may give a very good impression of being in control. But the male of the species is an unstable creature in constant need of being licked up to. If you understand this you can afford to indulge them from time to time, but be firm and set perimeters. Don't ever let them think they are in control! Situations like that cause all sorts of mayhem, like world wars, dodgy electrical sockets and car accidents.

6) Sex is very important to men. Femalology permits the use of lies in all issues surrounding sex. Do not hesitate if you feel a lie is called for. Men are not sensitive enough to worry even if they know you are lying.

7) In certain primitive countries, males are to be routinely genitally mutilated. This serves no purpose, but it will keep the greater world population of men on their toes, and grateful.

8) Do not educate men beyond their expectations. Teach them all they need to know about how to be good fathers, how to chop wood and keep the home tidy. Do not raise their expectations by offering false hopes of earning money or working in the market place. Their natural inclination to greediness and cheating may place their souls in immortal danger.

9) Femalology permits women up to seven men, one for each mood of the week. The same does not apply to men. A man with seven wives would be guilty of creating social disorder, driving large numbers of women to drink and smoking through repetition and boredom.

10) Paradise for men will be an endless supply of magazines all with a title beginning with 'Which'; Which car, Which

computer etc etc. They will have eternity to make their minds up.

If Jack saw this Scarlett, he'd kick my arse and I'd have to say, 'but you're an exception,' and being a man he'd believe me.

Well anyway, when I returned to London on that train, I looked at things very differently. It was almost dark when I got to Aunty Phil's house. She grumbled about the time when she saw me, almost snapped my head off with, 'Close that door; don't be letting all the heat out.' Did she mean the steam from the kettle? I gave her some pillowcases Mom had bought for her and she said 'I bet they're not Irish linen.' They weren't.

They were Egyptian, just perfect for an old sphinx.

I was back in town. But I knew things were going to be different.

Phoenix.

Chapter Sixteen

Brutal was the only word to describe the weather at the start of May 2001. Staring out of the dining room window, one windy, wet May morning, Phoenix seriously mourned what seemed to be the demise of global warming, and all the Mediterranean weather it was supposed to accrue for England, any at rate.

Anything, she thought would be preferable to the incessant rain and low grey skies that seemed to be a fixed feature of London in recent weeks. She watched gloomily, curtain gathered in one hand as the rain swept against the window pane landing with a slap like water against a sea wall.

But it wasn't just the weather that lacked sparkle in the spring of 2001. There was a general malady at work in the wider world and very little in the media to hint of better days to come. Foot and mouth continued to dominate the news; it had lost much of the drama that had accompanied its earlier reporting, but it still made its dreary way into the daily news bulletin. Drama was briefly installed again when calls were made to cull perfectly healthy cattle on Exmoor in an effort to curtail the spread of disease. This had the effect of uniting both farmers and animal rights protestors, and for a while, a new vibrancy was added to the debate.

Though some people living in the cities viewed the whole problem as one which only affected hillbillies, the summer season was fast approaching, and worried voices from the world of business and tourism became steadily more vocal. If the problem wasn't managed properly, they warned, the whole of the economy would suffer and it would then become everybody's concern.

The government responded by showing just how deeply they feared a rural backlash by calling a general election. A landslide victory was theirs for the taking, even though by any standard they were not handling the foot and mouth outbreak well.

For some, this was taken as proof that the country was on the edge of slipping into the abyss as far as politics were concerned. The people of Britain it seemed had a stark choice, vote for the devils they knew, or for some devils that didn't even know themselves.

There had been a time when Phoenix paid attention to general elections. Though not party political, she was aware and wary of politicians and their promises especially ones concerning tax and red tape.

Jack was delighted when Tony Blair first got elected, he saw the prospect of a reformed Labour party as a breath of fresh air but Phoenix did not share his delight. She disliked the preachy style of the new Prime Minister almost as much as she disliked the slimy way he dispensed sympathy. He was in her opinion, a chancer, someone who could just as easily have been elected leader of the Tory or Green party. He had merely studied the form like a true punter and had weighed up Labour as the odds on favourite. It had nothing to do with policy.

But as for the general election of 2001, Phoenix didn't even have an opinion on it. Her mind was too occupied with the star-tling revelation revealed in her letter to Scarlett. An assumption she had held for over twenty years had been shown to be null and void.

The comfortable assumption that her mother had been moti-vated by shame, no longer held any currency. She now had to live with a new realisation. Love not shame had been the archi-tect of her mother's decision. Love had driven her devoutly Catholic mother to commit an act she must have fundamentally believed to be unforgivable.

That cool September day long ago when Phoenix had handed her newborn baby son over for adoption, had often flashed unsought into her mind, like the odd, unbidden glimpse one catches of themselves in a shop mirror or reflective window. It was an elusive memory, one that refused to be held down and examined, for whenever she attempted to pursue it, her mind simply drew a sudden and insurmountable blank.

But her assumption about the adoption wasn't the only false one she had made. Just as her heroine, Scarlett O'Hara had fooled herself about her mother's life, Phoenix now realised, that she too had been deluded to ever think her own mother had been happy.

In essence, it was said in 'Gone with the Wind,' that Ellen O'Hara, the mother of Scarlett, had only married Gerald O'Hara because marriage to him, was marginally preferable to some of the other options her family had lined up for her. Ellen O'Hara had put her life on hold, until the day she had died, calling out for a lost love. She hadn't been living -she had been, existing

Phoenix had no idea whether or not her own mother had endured a lost love, perhaps she had; perhaps that was the real reason why she had left Ireland. She would never know; but she did know one thing, her mother was willing to do anything, anything, rather than risk her daughter, the one with possibilities, going down the same path to nowhere she herself had trod.

This realisation wasn't liberating. It didn't make Phoenix feel remotely like the articulate self confident women she read about and heard on the radio, who spoke effortlessly about the day they realised their own mothers were people in their own right. It merely presented yet another burden. Her mother had moved heaven and hell to ensure Phoenix was educated, and she in turn, hadn't taken the opportunity.

She was successful, with all the riches and trappings of an educated woman, but she had reached the summit by a different route. Did it count? Could the ends justify the means? If her mother saw her now, would she be proud, or would she feel cheated? Round and round her head her questions chased each other. Did lack of status matter? Was there any chance she could have taken another route, and still ended up with the things she loved, namely Jack and Daisy?

She quizzed Jack one night about the possibility of changing the past.

He was relaxing after dinner, perusing one of the many trade magazines he ordered, yet seldom found the time or inclination to read. She sat opposite him, pretending to be absorbed with the evening paper, but there was nothing in it that could compete with the quest she had in mind. Did he, she wondered, ever regret the route he had taken?

He was surprised by her question. 'What do you mean?' he said. 'The business or us?'

'Oh neither,' she replied with a half stifled yawn, eager to convey the idea that this was just idle chit chat she was indulging in. 'I just mean if you could go back in time, are there many things you would change?'

He thought about it for awhile or at least gave the impression that he was thinking, before replying. 'No. I don't think there is. How can you change one thing without changing everything?' His answer exasperated her; he was missing the point, she didn't want a philosophical discussion about the pointlessness of looking back, she wanted him to be specific, did he have regrets which could be rectified without interfering with the present.

Speaking just a touch more earnestly, she probed deeper. 'But, if you could guarantee the same outcome, would you change certain things, I mean if you could, would you have avoided your marriage to Polly?'

Realising she was onto something and that he would get no peace until he answered her, he replied a little testily. 'Yes in an ideal world I would prefer it hadn't happened, but it is crazy to talk of changing the past, without accepting the present would be different,' and before she could say another word, he picked up his magazine and resumed reading it. A signal that the conversation, as far as he was concerned was at an end. Jack didn't like hypothetical conversations and he didn't like being questioned about the past. Phoenix's sudden desire to hold a post mortem on a dead marriage made him feel decidedly uneasy.

She in turn pretended to read her newspaper; but the words Jack had just spoken resounded uneasily in her mind. The more she thought about them the more aggrieved she felt. She had sought confirmation that the past could be put in its box, but Jack seemed to be saying it went hand in hand with the present, the two were linked and accordingly there could be no separation. He had told her what she already knew, but for once she had wanted to be contradicted. She wanted to believe that she had it wrong - the past and present could exist, as two separate entities.

To find some peace of mind, she had to pin point the time and place where she had been diverted from education and the

exact junction that had placed her on the route she now travelled on.

Dear Scarlett,   **7th May 2001**

Since getting my business together, I have secretly congratulated
myself for being clever and smart, but now I find myself wondering, if all I achieved was a sell out.

Sanctimonious shites Scarlett, say no one can take your -self
respect away, they maintain it is something you give away, but
they are wrong. Condon, not only took my self respect away, he
also robbed me of the respect due from other people, and I had
to get it back.

But did I lose sight of things? Did I settle for less?

Going back to education after Joseph was born was not an
easy option even though my mother insisted at the time, that it
was. After the birth, I felt mentally out of gear; in fact, I felt old
beyond my years. I couldn't bear the idea of hanging around
girls of my own age, all of them bursting with dreams and plans.
Not when I had concrete proof that life can be a serious shithouse. But apart from all that, the baby was born in September,
so that school year was buggered up. I had to wait until the following September to make a new start and the opportunity of
working at the building society was too good to miss. It offered
good pay and the opportunity to save up for college.

I started work there in January 1981 and the night before the
big day, I was so afraid of sleeping in, that I didn't sleep at all. I
set off on my first day feeling like something the cat had dragged
through the bushes and had decided to leave there. When I
arrived at work, Mr Roberts, the man who had offered me the
job at the Christmas party was nowhere to be seen. Instead the
office supervisor, a woman called Sue took charge and introduced me to the people I would be working with.

Life definitely took a turn for the better. Suddenly, I had a
decent wage, and could afford new clothes and I worked with
pleasant people. The only downside of course was still living
with Aunty Phil.

She didn't improve with age, she had more in common with fish, than wine or cheese in that department, but finding a place to rent that was decent and affordable was easier said than done.

Some of the people I worked with invited me to join them on occasional nights out. But I couldn't go, because the old dragon wouldn't give me a key. She was dead put out when I told her that I wanted to go dancing with my friends

'And what sort of pup would you be meeting in a night club?' she barked when I asked one night for dispensation to stay out after midnight. 'I'd have sworn you'd had your fill of strays.'

She really was a nasty person.

Sometimes, very occasionally, I'm inclined to think that perhaps she wasn't that bad, that perhaps it's just that I have a tendency to remember her with shite-tinted spectacles. But when I think about comments like that, I realise she was a thoroughly hairy egg.

The fact is Scarlett; I didn't particularly feel like dancing and frankly I would have taken a hole in the head rather than have sought a boyfriend. I was seriously off men for good. I could handle them on a day to day basis, 'Hello,' 'Goodbye', 'Is the photocopier free?' but as for one of them coming near me in a personal way, well that was enough to make me heave. But in the mind of that gross old woman, dances equalled blokes, and blokes equalled sex.

I just wanted the outward signs of normality, dancing, talking and drinking; my heart wouldn't be in any of them but at least I'd look normal from the outside. Ashley was a bit like that wasn't he? I remember reading how he could shoot and drink and play cards as well as the next fellow, but his heart was never in it, he did it for appearances sake. I think all I wanted was to look and act normal again. I knew I would never be normal again, but it would help if I could look it.

Coming home on the tube I'd listen as people discussed the latest film, or party they'd been to and I wanted to be like them, on the inside of an in crowd, not a permanent bystander.

Walking up the Kilburn High Road, I'd smell the fags and booze seeping out from behind the doors of Biddy Mulligan's, or the Cock Tavern as they got ready for the next session. Normal life was happening all around me, but I felt like a battery hen. It was an existence, but not living like a real seventeen year old girl should be. I'd arrive home, walk up the path, knock on the front door of number 'twenty two' and wait. The old faggot would shuffle slowly along the hallway, (but she could run like bloody Eric Liddle, if they were giving freebies out at Tesco's,) slide the bolt back and call out, 'Is that you Sinead?'

I used to feel like shouting back, 'No it's the mad axe man, but seeing as it's you; it's me that's going to run a bloody mile.'

Once inside, a barrage of complaints and grumbles would ensue. Since the building society had a cheap and good canteen, I didn't eat with her any more. Of course she didn't reduce my digs, but I hadn't expected her to anyway. Do geese drop diamonds? I'd go upstairs put the radio on, read a magazine that I had sneaked in, and eat a Mars Bar, Toffee Crisp or both.

Meanwhile she'd sit downstairs with the telly and her pork pie.

I did my best to reason with her. I washed up for her one night, and gave the kitchen a good clean, and then I pursued her. 'Aunty Phil,' I said. 'It's important that I go out with my friends, I work with them, I'd like to get to know them better; please can I have a key, just for the occasional Saturday night?'

'Why would you want to socialise with people you've been around with all day?'

'Because, they are the only people I know.'

''Tis a fool that mixes business with pleasure.'

'If I go out with them I'll meet others.'

'There's no saying who you'd pick up with, London's full of freaks.'

'Just give me a key for one night.'

'I'll stay up for you until midnight.'

'But the clubs only get going then.'

'In that case you should be home, for God knows the devil reigns after midnight.' Midnight my arse, that bastard stalks around any time of day, usually in a suit, I should know, I've met him.

There was no moving her; she was never going to let me get on with life. With her there was no such thing as redemption. Make a mistake and pay for it, anything else and she would have felt cheated.

There was only one occasion when she attempted something approaching entertainment. I came home from work one cold and windy night to find the fire on in the front room, and a dark haired young man sitting very uneasily on the settee. He'd obviously had the full works from Aunty Phil concerning his age, height and his grandparent's occupation. She had filleted all the details quickly and neatly, leaving the poor guy sitting there, looking gutted.

The most striking thing about him, apart from his unease; was an enormous red, angry looking boil that sat perched on the end of his nose. I was mesmerised by it.

The old dragon ordered me to speak as if I were a five year old. 'Sinead,' she said, 'Talk to Dermot here, he's from Roscommon and he's going to be in the parish for the next month.'

I opened my mouth to speak, but the only word that came out was 'Boil.' He touched his nose, shook his head, and said. 'Actually I'm not from Boyle, I'm from Roscommon town.'

I burst out laughing and poor Dermot sat gaping at me like a fish on a slab. Aunty Phil looked from one to the other of us, not having a clue what the joke was, no surprise really, since her knowledge of Ireland was restricted to the kingdom of Kerry.

Poor Dermot never came round again, I can't be certain if it was the dragon's interrogation, or me putting my foot in it, but he gave the weirdoes at number twenty two a very wide berth.

That stupid remark was typical of me Scarlett. I think I was so un-socialised that the minute I had company, my mind seized up.

Throughout that evening, the more I thought over what I'd said to Dermot, the funnier I found it and in an effort to distract my mind from the blunder, I began rooting out old copies of The Kerryman from the bottom of the tatty wood-wormed wardrobe. I didn't like the laughter, it had a hint of hysteria about it and it frightened me. In one of the papers though, there was an article on the children's page about the Phoenix rising from the ashes. I sat on the bed and read a condensed version of that wonderful story, and I remember feeling as if I'd discovered something magical.

And that's when it occurred to me.

I could be like the Phoenix bird, it was all about control. If I could muster enough determination I could emerge from the ashes of my past and leave all the sordid details behind. I too could rise again and when I did, I'd be known, not as The Phoenix of the Ashes, but as Phoenix Ashton.

Besides wanting to copy a mythical bird, I wanted a secular name, because when I rose from the ashes I didn't want any remnants of the past sticking to my tail. Church and state had to go, Ireland and the Irish would simply remind me of times past when I was setting out to play by new rules.

I didn't start using Phoenix Ashton until I started my business, but once I had decided on a new name, I knew change was on the way.

About a week before my eighteenth birthday a new girl started at the building society, her name was Lesley. She came from a place called Doncaster and was strikingly good looking with long fair hair and green eyes and the impact she had on my life was immeasurable. She was small and angelic looking with delicate white skin, and dainty hands and feet, but looks can be deceiving. She swore like a seriously linguistically challenged trooper. I've never heard the likes of her before or since; she could certainly teach Jack's gang a word or two.

When she first started at the building society she lived in a hostel, a short-term measure while she looked for a flat or a house share. In another life I would have avoided her like the plague, but since I was as desperate as her for a new place to live, I found myself suggesting one day that we might go flat hunting together.

'Where should we start, North or South London?' I asked

'It's got to be the fucking north, the south is always full of twats,' she replied, very decisively.

'But you're in the south.'

'Don't I fucking know it,' she replied. I had never heard a mouth like it before. But it wasn't just the swearing, it was her sharp tongue as well. You could ask the most mundane thing of her and you never knew what she'd say in reply. Everyone was dead wary of her.

Sue the supervisor would say something like, 'Lesley will you take a look at these figures,' and she'd say.

'Yeah sure beats looking at that ugly mush of yours.'

But she had a way of saying offensive things in a light-hearted way, so that if you took offence, you'd be the one to end up looking churlish. She did it to everyone. From the moment she appeared I made doubly certain to brush my teeth and check the mirror, because no personal insult was beyond her. As well as doing some auditing of passbooks, she did audio typing for Mr Roberts. He'd call her into his office and she'd turn round to the rest of us, and say, 'Just off for a bit of dic.' Mr Roberts would blush the colour of a beetroot and retreat hurriedly back into his office. He definitely developed a bit of a stammer from the moment Lesley arrived. Sue said it was the stress of working with Lesley, but Jilly said she suspected it was the sign of an old engine clanking back into life. Perhaps we had all misjudged Mr Roberts? He tut tutted Lesley and looked shocked, but he didn't cut back on his dictation.

Everyone, except me, soon copped on that Lesley was just a big mouth and took her in their stride. But she made me feel uneasy. I felt her directness and hard stares had the potential to weed more out of me than I wanted to give. I could imagine her saying things that were nearer the truth than she realised, things that might cause me to panic and force me to whip out my past to protect myself by saying something like. 'Oh please stop, you don't know what I've been through.'

She was like a pig snuffling for truffles when it came to secrets, nothing ever deterred her from finding out all the gory details. The only way I could keep her at bay, was by fighting dirty, matching her insult for insult, and I suppose in a way that marked the start of the new me.

I had to make her wary, so when she said things like 'Move your arse Sinead, I know that's a big request,' instead of laughing it off or saying, 'Oi watch it cheeky,' like Jilly would have said, I matched her.

I'd wait until someone like Mr Roberts was present before asking her things like, 'Is it true you've only been employed here to keep the flies out of the canteen?'

She fought fire with fire and the attrition went on for weeks. I also enquired of her in a helpful way, if since she was from the north, had she managed to work out what the big white thing in the bathroom with taps was actually for? The others were shocked with me, I had always been the quiet, well-spoken rather sweet girl from the garden of England who looked after the sick aunt and for no reason it seemed I had become a shit. I knew instinctively that I had to keep her at bay.

Mind you inferences about teeth and skunks weren't half as effective as calling her Les, she really didn't like that. You'd think given the level of cross fire between us that we'd have been the last people on earth to set up home together, but it happened because we were as desperate as each other.

She taught me a lot of things, and the main one was that words are weapons, she was rude, crude and vulgar, but she took no shit mainly because everyone was too wary to give her any.

Poor Simon, a guy from South Africa, descended into hell the day she arrived. She had him sussed as a gawk within seconds. He was someone to take the piss out of when she was bored or felt vicious. Everyone recognised Simon for what he was, a mummy coddled little boy who wore a string vest even in summer because his mother had warned him about the wicked English weather. Lesley extracted from him every intimate detail of his life. It soon became common knowledge that he wore tiger print pyjamas, he never left his bedroom without his dressing gown, he drank milky drinks last thing at night, and had never slept with a girl or another man.

He also kept a bolt and chain on his front door, and his nick name at school was 'Turkey,' but even Simon wouldn't tell Lesley how that one came about. He made the fatal mistake of trying to lick up to her, laughing at her insults and glancing round at the rest of us as if to say 'didn't hurt, I can take it.'

The hostel where Lesley lived was a single sex one. She started grousing about it one day. She said, 'It's bloody disgusting, banged up with all those dykes.' That's when I piped up and suggested we find a place together.

Sue the supervisor was immediately surprised 'What about your poor old aunt?' she asked

And I said. 'What about her?'

Liars need good memories; I'd momentarily forgotten that I had told everyone that I was looking after a sick old aunt. I said my aunt was going into a home.

Sue, like Leslie was from Yorkshire and even though they are meant to be very clannish up there she took me aside one day and said. 'I'm really worried about you sharing a home with the likes of Lesley; she's really not the sort of person Sinead, you should associate with, why don't you wait and see if somebody a little more decent turns up?'

Sue made the mistake of judging by outward appearances. She saw me as the quietly spoken young girl being led astray by the loud foul mouthed one, but the things I thought in the secrecy of my mind were worse than anything Lesley ever said. Back in the days when I was a young teenager in Kent I would have found it impossible to believe girls like Lesley even existed, but I wasn't in Kent anymore.

I could imagine Mom describing her as belonging to the gutters. 'Lie down with dogs and you'll rise with fleas,' and 'you'll always be judged by the company you keep.' They were Mom's gold standards, but the fact is they didn't stand up to the test, because on the face of it, Jerh Condon, was the man to be seen with. If you were one of his mates, his associates you were okay. But the truth was, he was a complete and utter dog, and I came away with more than a few fleas from my association with him.

I wanted a clean slate and a chance to start again, and sharing a home with Lesley was a start. She was true working class English. Mum a cook, Dad and brother both miners. She had never willingly been in a church in her life. She hated 'fucking foreigners,' but loved curry and taking the piss out of the knobs - that is, anyone who spoke with a southern accent.

After work we would buy the Evening Standard, and traipse round London, looking at flats. We saw some absolute doss houses and potential flat mates from hell and Mars, but eventually we found a house in East Acton. Two students were currently renting it and they were offering a double room suitable for two sharers. It was on the circle line, it was cheap and allowed smokers so we took it. Later that same night I phoned Mom to tell her that I was moving. She didn't take the news well, she cried. I tried to explain tactfully that Aunty Phil was not an easy person to live with, but she kept saying 'she has your interests at heart.'

I declined the opportunity to tell my mother that Aunty Phil didn't have anyone's interests at heart apart from her own, that in fact she was a cold and unforgiving woman. I didn't tell my mother because I felt she had been through enough without me grousing at the other end of the phone, but I was adamant that I was moving on.

'You will regret it,' Mom said, I told her that I was willing to take a chance on that and Mom replied, 'If you leave Phil's place and end up in trouble again, mark my words I will not stand by you, I won't be there to pick the pieces up again.'

Then I said it Scarlett, the words I regretted instantly and still regret to this day, I said 'You didn't pick them up last time Mom.' They came out without thinking, like the comment about his boil to the trainee priest. I didn't know what to say, so I put the phone down.

I felt bleak, overwhelmed by the same feeling of blackness and despair that used to sweep over me when all the madness first started. I had to break with the past because the people in it were tying me up, I know they didn't intend to but they could only see me in terms of the mistake they all thought I had made. If I went to the dogs it would be because of that business, if I flourished it would be a case of 'she doesn't deserve to.'

I was in a classic no win situation. There was no honesty, no calling a spade a fucking spade and being done with it. So much shite is written about putting the past in the past and time being a great healer, but all of it is false. I discovered back then, that the only way to get rid of the past is to deny it, tell no one, forget it, present the picture of yourself that you want and be judged on that.

The denial worked, it really did, until one day the past began to start showing its ugly face again in flashbacks and uncountable anxiety attacks. That's why I'm sitting here now, dredging it all out again.

Now Scarlett, now that I finally understand Mom's motives behind the adoption, I feel again the cruelty of my words. I am so sorry for them. I never intended to hurt. I truly thought protecting the family name, was her only concern. Telling Mom I was moving on was bad, but telling Aunty Phil was deadly. She was scathing. She said I couldn't wait to walk the streets again, and I don't think she had promenading in mind when she said that.

Apart from her fear of having no one to bark at, I think it was her tightness that made her so angry with me for leaving. I paid her the going rate, yet I didn't eat anything in her place, use any heat or ask any favours. Yes, she was sorry to see me go. I did thank her for putting me up, and accompanying me to the CAA and the hospital. She had done none of those things gracefully, but she had done them all the same and I owe her for that.

Lesley offered to come and help me pack, but there was no way I could let Aunty Phil clap eyes on her. She'd class Lesley as a street walker - in fact she would think we'd make a great team. I didn't have much to pack, most of my stuff was old anyway and I wanted to leave it with the past. I knew the old dragon would rummage through my things the moment I left. She could keep them as far as I was concerned.

I left the jacket I had bought with the ape's money behind in the wardrobe. But I did take your book Scarlett. I don't think Aunty Phil even knew it was there. But I left John O'Brien's Faith of Millions behind.

One of those millions had now defected.

A week after we moved into the house in Acton, it was Lesley's eighteenth birthday. The two other sharers, Sally and

Fiona were both training to be teachers, and they invited us to a disco up at their college to celebrate Lesley's birthday.

Sally was from Essex and proud of it, after all somebody has to be. Fiona was from Hong Kong originally but had been brought up in Hertfordshire. We were all wary of each other to begin with, unnaturally polite and considerate. The night of the disco, we went on the bus up to the college and I drank Bacardi and coke, and danced like the girl with the red shoes. I was intoxicated with freedom and it felt good.

We had to walk home because the late bus never turned up. The two students walked ahead and Lesley and I walked, well staggered arm in arm. She sang 'Gimme Gimme A Man After Midnight,' at the top of her voice. Yuck, I'd have preferred a take away. We weaved and stumbled but as the night air began to sober me up I felt an overwhelming need to get Lesley home. She was wolf- whistling everything in trousers, even a couple of Muslim girls.

'Are you thinking of converting Lesley?' I asked.

And she replied, as uncouthly as ever. 'No fucking chance, I'd miss bacon sarnies too much and besides I wouldn't want to spend the rest of my life walking in the slip stream of my husband's fart.'

At one point she said 'stop, be back in a tick,' and disappeared up a little alley. I turned and walked straight bang into a cop.

'Looking for someone or something missy?' he asked.

I said I was waiting for my friend to catch up; she was getting a stone out of her shoe, but as I spoke I saw out of the corner of my eye, a river of piss scurrying towards the cop's feet. I begged God, not to let Lesley come wandering out of the alley with her knickers round her ankles. She didn't. She emerged with them on her head.

'Evening constable,' she said. 'Aren't I the lucky one, I've just spent a penny and now I've found a copper.' And with that she took my arm, and we marched off down the street to a real home, with friends in it and food and heat. Sounds almost like the Little House on the Prairie doesn't it? Even if I do look back on certain things and people with shite tinted spectacles Scarlett,

I don't want you to think that I have now reverted to the traditional rose coloured ones, but those days were so good.

At the time, I thought that boring little semi in Acton was nothing more than a safe haven after the escape from family, and a miserable past. But it wasn't. It was a launch pad. I'm not saying everything was wonderful, that there were never any arguments or raised voices, but even the worst days couldn't compare to the hell I'd left behind.

The people in it and the ones I met while there shaped my future so drastically that I can't really believe it was all just chance. First there was Lesley - on the face of it we had nothing in common, different backgrounds, not just in culture and religion, but in every possible way. She never changed; she remained the loud crude girl she had always been, but in a way I'm wrong to say that, because I don't think she had always been as aggressively in your face as she made out. In fact all that piss taking and lashing out with her tongue was something of a front, because Lesley had her secrets.

I awoke one night to find her sitting up in her bed just staring out the window; I think she must have knocked a cup or something off the ledge and that's what had woken me. I sat up, switched on the lamp beside my bed and asked her what was going on. She didn't tell me to fuck off, so I knew instantly, something was wrong. I climbed out of bed and sat beside her. She asked me for a fag, and I asked her again, what was wrong. She said she wanted to tell me about something that had happened when she was sixteen. I felt as wary as sin when she said that and as I sat, listening to her story un-fold, I truly thought I was going to pass out.

She had passed seven O'levels all of them straight A's. Her parents were dead pleased, because she was the first person in the family to have sat an exam successfully, so it was something worth celebrating. Her father insisted on taking Lesley and her mother out for a slap up meal.

I said 'Did that mean he was going to treat you to gravy with your chips?' It was a running joke between us. I was certain northerners had gravy with everything. Instantly I knew that I had made a gaffe; she wasn't telling a funny story.

As they were getting ready to go, Lesley's older sister Jean came back from work, (this came as a bit of a surprise to me because I thought Lesley only had a brother.) Anyway, when Lesley's dad saw Jean he turned on her. He said, 'what does it feel like having a sister that can do something positive, like pass an exam, when all you can boast off, is more pricks than a second hand dart board?'

The crudity and harshness of his words made me shiver, (no wonder he never passed English language at O'level.) It turned out that Jean had had a baby when she was sixteen, it had been a still birth, and now she was nineteen and pregnant again. I thought I was going to faint, I wanted to scream 'Stop, Stop this minute.' I must have been pretty paranoid, because I remember thinking 'Lesley knows all about me, she's just going round the houses, but she knows all the same.' But of course she didn't. It wouldn't have made any difference even if I had shouted 'stop' because Lesley was talking as if I wasn't there. Jean started crying, the mother wept and the older brother turned on the Dad and the perfect evening turned into something of a punch up and a verbal free for all.

Two days later, Lesley returned home from a friend's house and found her sister dead on the bed. She had overdosed with Paracetamol

I didn't even know that was possible. I was used to eating a packet of them at a time and still having a crashing head. When she eventually stopped speaking, I felt cold and numb. I wished Lesley hadn't told me; I preferred the illusion of the naturally loud and flamboyant girl who had come south merely to shake the southerners up.

She had come to London to punish her parents, she was very bitter towards them, especially her father. They were no longer on speaking terms, but they both blamed each other and I remember thinking, that's a really smart way of making sure nobody takes the blame.

Lesley said she didn't often think about her sister, but some-times she felt overwhelmed with guilt for not being there for her. She didn't say what do you think, or what would you have done. She just told it as it was. She shared a personal part of her life with me and I should have done the same, it would have sealed a bond. But I didn't, because I didn't want a bond with anybody and apart from that I just couldn't do it. I had put my nightmare, so far back in my mind that a part of me was already beginning to think that it had never happened.

In the morning, the old Lesley was back, it was as if a light bulb had been switched off, switched on. There was no sign of the fear or tremor of the night before. She walked over to my bed pulled the covers off and said 'Get up you shagger, you're going to be late.'

She never mentioned her sister again and neither did I, but I spent a lot of time thinking about what Lesley had told me. I began to understand why she was so brusque and crude. It was her way of keeping the world at bay, of dealing with it on her own terms. If people like you, they'll accept you as you are and if they don't, they will keep away.

As I said already, I learnt a lot from Lesley, including how to talk like a trooper, like they say, if you want to learn a foreign language, live amongst the natives. I can swear Jack under the table with no hassle, but I never copied Lesley's crude talk, she really was obscene. It was impossible to mention certain foods without starting her off on a series of innuendo, words like stuffing, cucumber, sausages, boiled eggs all took on completely different meanings. And oh God I still can't believe the joke she told me about rhubarb, I seriously think I'd eat a bowl of snot before I'd ever dream of eating that disgusting muck.

And she wasn't all talk either. She was promiscuous in the extreme. Long before AIDS hit the billboards and frightened the shite out of everybody, Lesley carried condoms with her. Her favourite saying was 'I am a boy scout and I always come prepared.' She didn't want a relationship, just lots of experience. In lots of ways I remained my mother's daughter. I never sat down on the toilet after she used it, and I took to putting baby oil in the bath as a way of developing a protective film round it. I lived in fear of catching something red and angry looking from her. One night though, I forgot to wash and rinse the bath out after using it, and when I was tucked up cosily in bed with a coffee, the TV and a book, I heard an enormous splash, followed by 'What fucking bitch has left this bath like an ice rink?' I pretended to be asleep, when she limped back into the bedroom that she had skipped so merrily out of only minutes before. Still her sprained ankle got her four days off work.

Sally and Fiona were both wary of Lesley for even though they wanted to appear cosmopolitan, 'anything goes,' city girls, she sometimes she bit deep into their suburban roots. Sally refused to speak to her for a week after her granny phoned up, and Lesley answered her with 'Hello, Battersea Dog's Home here, which bitch do you want?'

She was unique to me, perhaps I was a naive fool and people like her are two a penny in Doncaster. Perhaps up there it's the only way to behave. She might even be refined by Doncaster standards, but to me she was a breath of fresh air.

As for Fiona and Sally with their books and duffle coats, jeans and folders they jabbed at my conscience. They discussed and exchanged notes with each other and groaned about T.P (teaching practice.) It wasn't that I wanted to be a teacher, but I was still determined to go back to education. Lesley had absolutely no interest in study, in her own words she wanted to sleep her way round London, earn some money then return north as a clerk from the 'Big Shitty.'

Fiona and especially Sally were envious of our cash, and were always talking about how tough life was on a student grant. They discussed endlessly the possibility of getting part time jobs, but neither had the gumption to do anything about it. I thought they were mad. It seemed to me they had the best of all possible worlds, casual dressing, sleeping in when they felt like it, loads of friends with the same interests, always something to do and somewhere to go.

There always seemed to be a disco or a union meeting, or a boycott to get worked up about. Sally and Fiona seethed every time I opened my Barclays chequebook, or when Lesley bought home Cape grapes. They decorated the living room with placards proclaiming 'Free Nelson Mandela.' 'With what?' Lesley asked. And when challenged about the fruit she was eating; Lesley always replied, 'Fuck the cause I've no time for fuckery duckery.'

I don't expect you'd have a lot of time for Sally and Fiona's principles either Scarlett, since you kept a fairly big parcel of slaves yourself, but I think you might have expressed yourself more elegantly.

I was bothered by apartheid, but I didn't see how not eating grapes was going to help. Sally and Fiona were obsessed with South Africa, but for all their passion and education, they were pitifully narrow-minded. They loved hearing how Lesley took the piss out of poor Simon the South African at work. They goaded her into being even crueller and more hurtful to him, as if by putting the boot into one member of the hated race, they were doing something positive to end the evil empire. But it was wrong because the likes of Simon had left it all behind, in fact I think he had a secret fancy for West Indian Jenny, but was too stupid to do anything about it.

To me the life of a student was definitely better to that of a worker. Work was easy and the money attractive, but it was all so rigid, breaking your arse to be there on time, rushing to leave on the dot. Watching the two students and egged on by Mom's letters, I became determined that one way or another I'd go back to college. I'd get my 'A' levels and I would become a barrister; a specialist in family law.

I told Sally one day, when I was feeling really pissed off with her, that I had ten O'levels. All of them straight A's! I rarely mentioned anything in the past tense, but sometimes Sally's teachery voice and need to control everyone got to me. She was shocked; she had scraped into teacher training college with just five O' Levels. She was just a trainee but she spoke like a tired out old Careers teacher, she said 'Yes, but you don't need 'A' levels do you? I mean someone like you could easily work your way up in the building society.'

She was right, I could take internal exams and become an assistant branch manager, even a manager, but it wasn't what I wanted. People in education are multi tasked; they do two things very well, they talk it down, and they try to keep outsiders out. It's an exclusive club. Educationalists love to prattle on about 'the real world, they say things like 'you don't need exams and degrees in the real world,' but how do they know? They are the ones tucked up in fairyland. You can mock a degree, if you have one- dismiss it as bog roll if it's in media studies. But nobody can take it away from you.

I was out to prove myself, not to anyone other than me and I knew education was the key. So I enrolled at the local further education college on a part time evening course, I signed up for 'A' level, English, Economics and Law.

Lesley thought I was sad. Fiona and Sally smiled sweetly, as if to say 'Poor girl, she's desperate to be as good as us.'

I smiled and gave them all the fingers, metaphorically speaking of course.

Phoenix.

Chapter Seventeen

As far as business was concerned, Jack Keane had developed something of the Midas touch. The overwhelming success of his venture into the restoration of old and historic houses had taken him by surprise; what had started off as a side-line was promising to become the central core of his entire business. His enterprise now stretched well beyond the borders of south London, into deepest Kent, Surrey and Sussex and hardly a day passed by without an enquiry from somewhere near or far.

So when he received an email one Tuesday morning, from a government agency regarding a project in the provinces that was seriously behind schedule, he didn't regard it with anything other than nosey interest.

The project concerned the urgent renovation of a listed building into a leisure complex; the coming election obviously had something to do with the urgency of the situation. A shortage of skilled labour in the region necessitated the hiring of outside skills and all kinds of tradesmen were being sought, including electricians and plasterers. Could he supply a gang of labourers? He was about to press delete, when something caught his eye. The job in question was in Boston. Boston!

He sat up and read the statement again and soon discovered that the Boston in question was not the one across the Atlantic, but Boston, Lincolnshire. The brief confusion made him smile, he hadn't even been aware there was a Boston in the UK. His sister Mary lived in Boston Massachusetts and although he didn't know what that had to do with it, it had the effect of increasing his curiosity.

Later that same day while out on site, he casually mentioned the email to his foreman Sam. It didn't surprise Sam in the least to hear that Boston was in Lincolnshire, he had a brother in law from Lincoln and he turned to Jack with something of a smirk on his face.

'It's some class of a shit hole Jack,' he said pushing back his hard hat in order to scratch his head, 'and the people there are as odd as two fucking left shoes, but if you've got a bob or two to spare it's probably worth investing in.'

'Is it cheap then?' Jack enquired.

'Cheap? Dirt cheap is more like it,' Sam replied, 'and apparently it's set to see a massive flood of EU immigrants, and that's bound to boost the local economy.' He paused a moment and pulled his hat forward, 'mark my words,' he said 'it's going to be the next boom area.'

It was that latter piece of information that heightened Jack's interest. The London housing market which he had invested widely in was steadily rising, and his attention was now focused on other areas, ones which would benefit from the ripple effect of the Capital city. He emailed the agency back and sought more details. Plasterers with a good working knowledge of listed building consent were required as a matter of urgency. The work was scheduled to last a maximum of five days, with a decent bonus being paid out if the job was completed ahead of schedule.

He sat and stared at the screen in front of him, tapping the desk with his forefinger as he did so. One hundred and twenty miles, wasn't so far away; he could always return south if he had to. He thought over Sam's words, ignoring the reference to odd feet and finally came to the conclusion, that if nothing else; it would do his portfolio no harm.

He would want Phoenix to come though, if it was half as promising as Sam reckoned, then the two of them should invest in it. But would she come? Yes, he told himself, as he pressed the print button, she would if he handled it properly. He wouldn't make the mistake of presenting it as a fait accompli like he had done with Ireland. More sensitivity was called for this time.

He wanted a strong team pulled together as soon as possible, so he asked Tosh to accompany him home that night with the intention of setting his ganger to work immediately, on the task of sourcing some reliable workers. But as he watched Tosh walk jauntily ahead of him towards the front door he felt a faint murmur of misgiving, perhaps having Tosh around when he wanted a favour from Phoenix was not such a good idea. He left his ganger in the kitchen with strict instructions not to go rooting, and went in search of his wife.

She was in the process of putting a very lively Daisy to bed. Instantly upon seeing him, Daisy leapt out of the bed she had just been cajoled into and landed straight in his arms.

'Thank you Jack,' Phoenix said in exasperation, 'It's taken me over two hours to get her upstairs, so you just make sure she stays here.'

'Of course I will,' he said, 'but before that, I've got something to ask you.'

'Oh yes?' she snapped. 'What do you want now?'

'I want to ask you a favour.'

'Like what?'

Jack hesitated, one full look into her face confirmed she wasn't in the form for dishing out favours, but he decided to fire ahead anyway. 'I want you to come to Boston with me.'

'Boston!' Phoenix repeated in a whisper. She was stunned. Years ago when she had been ready for anything, she had nagged him to take her to America, but each time he had declined outright. She had always suspected he was jealous of his sister Mary, who apart from being married to an attorney, had her own PR agency in the heart of Boston.

America was the only place in the world Phoenix had ever wanted to visit. Her affinity for all things American had been caught from her mother; for Bridget O'Connell had viewed the United States of America as the 'promised land.' It was according to her, the Americans who had taught the world to sing and dance, and America who had won the war. The story she told of the fleeing Irish finding a safe haven in America had made more impact on her young daughter than any biblical tale of seas being parted to accommodate fleeing Israelites.

Immediately upon listening to her mother, Phoenix had sworn that one day, she would go to America and she would see Boston and New York for herself. Years ago when she'd had the time she hadn't the money, but now it was the other way round.

Now Jack was taking her - he was putting aside his natural resistance just for her! She couldn't rebuff him, not when he was putting his hand out to her, but this was the wrong time, she couldn't go, not in the confused state she was now in. She turned to him and said, very hesitantly.

'Are you really asking me to go to America Jack?'

It was Jack's turn to be shocked. 'What?' he replied, and was about to clarify the situation when he realised, that she was making the same mistake he had made when he had first seen the email. The opportunity for a joke proved irresistible, and his determination to be honest and sensitive crumbled in the face of the overwhelming temptation for a laugh. He struggled to keep his face straight, before saying. 'What do you think then?'

'Just you, me and Daisy?' she said, a little warily.

'Well yes,' he said, 'and Tosh.'

She stared at him, her face incredulous for a moment, until rage submerged all feelings of sentimentality and surprise; she lashed out with her foot, sending a headless, naked Barbie scurrying across the lacquered wooden floor.

'Well in that case,' she shouted, 'you can poke America up your rat infested arse, it's bad enough that he practically lives with us as it is, without dragging him on holiday.'

He put a finger to his mouth and urged her to quieten down. 'Sh sh,' he said. 'He's downstairs, he'll hear you.'

'Piss off Jack,' she exclaimed impatiently, 'you have to have sense to have feelings and Tosh hasn't got any; and no, I will not quieten down in my own house.'

She was furious. Relief and bitter disappointment tormented each other. For a moment she had really believed Jack was being sensitive, taking her to America to show care and consideration, but as usual she had it wrong. Her reaction took Jack by surprise; he hadn't banked on her taking him so seriously, and he was now faced with the problem of extricating himself from his own backfired joke, without losing all good will on her part. He weighed the situation up, and decided against trying to soothe her extremely ruffled feathers. He would let it run its course and with luck regain control a little later on.

'Listen,' he said stepping forward with Daisy in his arms. 'I should have explained, it's not really a break, it's to do with work, come downstairs and we'll talk about it properly.'

She followed him down to the kitchen, determined he should know the full extent of her aggravation, but her plans were forestalled when she saw Tosh ready and waiting for her. He had made himself well and truly at home; the television was on and he sat contentedly, with a bottle of beer in one hand and a ham sandwich in the other. As they entered the room he flashed a smile of welcome and gestured at them to pull up some empty chairs, as if they were the visitors.

Phoenix glared at him. He was like a bad smell, she thought, clearly identifiable, but impossible to get rid of. She sat down on an easy chair, away from the table, and Jack plonked Daisy on her knee and walked over to the fridge. A drink would help things. He took out two bottles of beer which he opened, before handing one to Phoenix and sat down at the table opposite Tosh. Daisy immediately scuttled back to her father.

'So,' she said. 'What kind of work is taking you to America?'

The baton of the shocked face was now passed to Tosh. He coughed into his bottle and stared enquiringly at Jack, a look of hurt spreading rapidly across his face, as he realised Jack had not made him privy to this startling piece of news.

Jack raised his bottle to his mouth and taking full advantage of the cover it offered, he winked at Tosh. 'Phoenix is amazed at me being offered work in *Boston* Tosh' he said matter of factly.

Tosh quickly caught onto the idea that Jack was up to no good and happily joined the fray without fully understanding where it was leading. He threw Phoenix a contemptuous look and said in utter seriousness. 'I don't see why she should be after all it was put out to tender and you won fair and square, someone had to get it.'

'But I don't understand,' Phoenix said falteringly. 'I mean America doesn't have a shortage of builders does it, and it must have fairly strict regulations as well.'

'I'm sure it has,' Jack replied, 'but there is always a market for consultants, and now I'm an expert on old wrecks and conservation in general, I'm sought after. Isn't that true Daisy?' he asked his daughter who sat on his knee as if she were the rightful owner of it. She nodded her head vigorously in agreement.

Phoenix was perplexed; it sounded plausible, but something still didn't feel right, and she didn't like the nasty little gleam in Tosh's eye. Pain in the arse she thought, sitting there like he was

Jack's very own Brian Epstein. He was definitely up to some-thing. 'You are having me on Jack, aren't you?' she said lightly, hoping he would take the hint and come clean if it was all a big joke. 'Swear to God, you've been offered work in Boston.'

He looked her in the eye and said slowly 'I swear to God, I've been offered a job in Boston.'

Now she didn't know what to think, he wasn't lying, of that she was certain. A tiny stab of panic began to jab her as she feared the possibility that he was telling the truth. How could she go to America when distinguishing one day from another was already a problem, and that was without jet lag? How could she get out of this?

She looked up to see Tosh's shoulders heaving. He was laughing. 'What's your problem?' she asked.

'Oh nothing,' he replied. 'It's just seeing you there, with your mouth open, reminds me of the three old dolls who saw a streaker, the first two had a stroke, but the third one didn't quite reach.'

She jumped in alarm as Jack snorted and began choking on his beer. He evidently found Tosh's joke funny. Now she was more than annoyed, how dare Jack laugh at her in front of an undernourished maggot like Tosh? She turned on the ganger, wagging her finger at him, 'If you are going to act like a turd, go out and find a shoe to stick to.'

She then addressed herself to Jack, ignoring the snorting and laughing that came from the ginger haired imp at the table 'When are you due to go to America?'

Jack looked up and pointing his finger at his chest he said in a surprised voice. 'Who said anything about America, it's Boston Lincolnshire where I'm going.'

That was the firing gun for both Tosh and Jack to laugh freely, even Daisy who didn't have a clue what the joke was about laughed, and clapped her hands with excitement.

Phoenix looked at Tosh bending and straightening by turns as laughter consumed him. How she disliked him. He was such a key ring monkey - she wouldn't give him the satisfaction of appearing annoyed.

'Well,' she said, taking a swig from her beer. 'Aren't you funny, as if for one minute, I believed America would allow the likes of you in.'

When the laughter died down, Tosh asked if anyone, in the name of God had the faintest idea where Lincolnshire was anyway and Jack said he didn't know exactly, but he thought it was somewhere in the East Midlands. Phoenix walked over to the book case and pulled out a motoring map of Britain, which she casually handed to Tosh, determined to show that she was unperturbed by the big joke. He looked at it studiously before pronouncing in surprise. 'It's in Cornwall, Boston is.'

Jack snatched the map off him and carefully searched through the index. 'You great tick,' he said, 'You've looked up Boscastle; Lincolnshire is on the East coast, just above East Anglia.'

'Well,' he said looking across at Phoenix. 'Will you come?'

She in turn glanced across at Tosh; he was sitting back in his chair, joyful anticipation of an argument written all over his face. And because she didn't want to give Tosh an inch of satisfaction, she replied to Jack's immense surprise. 'Yes, Jack, I will.'

Those words uttered in haste, were soon regretted. She didn't want to visit the back of beyond even for a day, never mind a week for she was too confused to face anything out of the ordinary. For years, she had silently licked the wounds of being the victim of a shamefaced mother who had arranged adoption purely to save face. Now she was beginning to understand, that her mother was also a victim. One who had taken the road to hell in order to give her daughter the chance of life lived to the full. It was proving to be an impossible burden.

But if life for Phoenix was proving tough, things for Tosh were looking spectacularly good. He had managed to pull together, at very short notice, a team of eight highly experienced plasterers for the Boston job. Most of them had worked on similar projects, and Jack was delighted with their credentials. Tosh had once again proved that he was indispensable and worth every penny of the sizeable bonus Jack duly paid him.

Busy with the logistics of his new venture into untried territory, Jack left it to his secretary Rita, to arrange accommodation for his newly formed team and this she efficiently did, finding a reasonable guest house in a little village just north of Boston called Swineshead.

She informed Jack about the booking one night, as she put her coat on ready to go home. 'It sounds good Jack,' she said. 'It's not too far out, and one or two rooms have even got their own toilet.' She paused for a moment and gave a little laugh, and Jack who had hardly been listening to her looked up, wondering what the joke was. She smiled across at him, and started laughing again.

'Come on then,' said Jack, 'share the joke.'

She shook her head. 'Oh it's no joke really Jack, it's just talking of shit houses, reminds me of the time I went to Boston.'

'You've been there?' he said in surprise. 'You never said before, Sam's got relatives there you know, I never even knew the place existed until the other day, now it feels like a hot spot; what did you think on it?'

'Well it was about five years ago,' she said. 'I took Bill as a treat for our tenth wedding anniversary and he still hasn't forgiven me.'

Jack was now thoroughly intrigued 'Go on,' he said. 'Tell me about it.'

She looked at him half teasingly and sensing that he was both wary as well as interested in what she had to say, she toned her reply down. 'There's not much to tell really Jack,' she said. 'Bill has always fancied himself as a bit of a bird fancier so I booked a cottage in Boston because the Wash is the big deal as far as birds are concerned.'

She stopped for a moment to search in her pocket for her house key and finding it safe and sound, she patted it comfortingly and continued her tale.

'To cut a long story short, Jack, it was bloody awful; we booked a week and left after two days.'

'What was wrong?' he asked, now seriously interested.

'Do you want a list?' she replied laughing at his discomfiture, 'because to be perfectly frank it would be easier to tell you what was right. *Absolutely nothing*, it was cold, wet and ugly and the locals were hideous, they seemed to think there was something wrong with us because we lacked the obligatory two heads and six fingers.'

She reached across and touched his arm lightly, 'Don't look so concerned Jack,' she said, 'after all it's business not pleasure you are chasing,' and with that she was gone.

Rita's revelations about Boston made Jack feel decidedly uncomfortable. They seemed to back up what Sam his foreman had said about the place and he couldn't dismiss her story out of hand either, because Rita was a tough cookie. By knocking her off her stride, Boston had achieved something no labourer had ever managed.

Later that night when he arrived home, he told Phoenix about the accommodation booked in Swineshead and she laughed and said it sounded just perfect for Tosh, but he didn't mention Rita's holiday cottage. Who, he asked himself as he sat down to dinner, would take heed of a bird watcher, weren't they all freaks anyway?

The following day, he declined Rita's offer to book his personal accommodation, (perhaps fearing she was jinxed,) and took the task upon himself. What he was after was something safe and straight forward like a Post House, or Holiday Inn, preferably with a swimming pool, but a thorough search on the net, confirmed that there was no such place within a thirty mile radius of Boston.

As his choice of hotels shrunk, his sense of unease grew, he had no idea what to expect from provincial England for he had never been there. With the exception of recent work in wealthy mid Sussex, he had never gone beyond metropolitan Kent. There were no motorways near Boston, no airports and no chain hotels. So it was pretty certain it wasn't aping its American namesake.

Eventually he hit upon a website for a hotel in the town centre. It looked chintzy and attractive to a point, a little old fashioned, but perhaps that was its hidden charm. It wasn't exactly what he wanted, but it would have to do. The whole booking procedure reminded him of a Christmas party he had once taken Daisy to, where the penalty for pinning a tail on a donkey in the wrong place, was being forced to sit on a balloon until it burst. Get this one wrong, he told himself and there would be more than gas flying.

The venture which had initially got off to a smooth start thanks to the easy acquisition of skilled staff, turned very taxing, with a lot of pernickety changes cropping up at the last minute. Jack was so taken up with minutiae that he failed to notice how stressed Phoenix was becoming. He dismissed her anxious face as nothing more than typical of her hatred of leaving her work in someone else's capable hands, and sailed forth with many plans in mind.

He was determined, that no matter the vibes; this was going to be a successful enterprise and he even surprised himself, by calling into a tourist office and bringing home leaflets about Boston and its surrounding area. He didn't look at them, but Phoenix did and her heart sank even further.

It was not an inspiring place. It had a windmill, England's biggest parish church 'known affectionately by the locals as 'the Stump,' and she thought, piss all else. She didn't say anything to Jack, but from what she'd seen, she reckoned Sam the foreman, had summed it up succinctly, it was a shit hole in waiting.

One week later, on a bright and sunny Monday afternoon, the London plasterers set off to a less than auspicious beginning. Jack had given the two drivers instructions for an early start, but they were delayed by the late arrival of two vans from Croydon, an accident had caused a massive diversion. The entire gang set off over an hour behind schedule, enough to put Jack in bad form, because in spite of his apparently easy going existence, Jack was a man who hated disorder.

He drove fast and furious shouting instructions into his mobile phone, causing Daisy to retreat into the safety of a book, and Phoenix to stare stonily out of her window.

She felt irritated with his constant cursing. How dare he act annoyed, this foolish time -wasting trip was all his doing! She did her best to ignore him but when he got stuck behind a woman in a Ford Ka she was forced to intervene. She had to admit the woman was incompetent, touching her brakes for no good reason, and consistently blocking two lines of traffic. But even so, Jack's reaction was excessive.

'For God's sake Jack,' she pleaded, when he started thumping the steering wheel, 'calm down, the bloody woman will turn off soon.' But all he could reiterate with increasing vehemence was 'Move over you fucking fart,' and when the woman dawdled up to a set of traffic lights with what seemed perfect timing to just about miss them, she almost had to restrain Jack from jumping out of the car and performing an act of raw car rage.

'Take a look at it for God's sake,' he shouted. 'One fucking look at that back window tells you everything.' The back window in question belonged to the blue Ford Ka. It was plastered with 'I love Poodles' stickers and the perennial 'A dog is for life not for Christmas.' Little heart shaped stickers proclaiming undying love for all things canine festooned the little car, but they didn't touch Jack's heart.

'I'll give her more than a fucking dog for Christmas if she misses another set of lights,' he threatened. When the woman eventually began indicating and pulled off a mile later at the Ware signpost, Jack said, 'That's appropriate, she hasn't got a fucking clue where she is going.'

Phoenix said nothing other than a silent prayer of thanks. Jack's shouting was giving her a headache, and disturbing her train of thought.

They drifted off a crowded M25 and onto a calmer A1 and the journey north began in earnest. The sun at least kept shining, and anyone looking at them might have imagined they were just a happy family out for an afternoon drive, albeit a very fast one.

As Phoenix stared out of the window, it occurred to her that she knew very little about England. There were so few places she had ever bothered visiting. Certainly the north was unknown territory. She had been to two exhibitions at the Birmingham NEC, both times by train and had hardly raised her head from a book on either occasion.

Jack continued to talk into his mobile, giving instructions and telling his gang how he wanted to play things. She was glad he didn't particularly want to talk to her; she had nothing to say but plenty to think about. Glancing into the back of the car she saw that Daisy was well sorted with her toys and picnic and feeling free to day dream she turned her attention back to her window and the views beyond it.

The unfamiliar names of places she didn't even know existed filled her with a slight sense of confusion. How strange it was that communities existed in isolation from each other. Here were towns and villages with short cuts and nick names known exclusively to their residents and here she was, passing through unseen and unnoticed. All the things that were so dear and familiar to the inhabitants were insignificant and inconsequential to her.

Cambridge appeared on the signpost and her heart gave a little start. Just how different would life have been if she had achieved her dream? If she was now a respected barrister, making and shaping peoples lives by the sheer genius of her perception.

She turned to Jack and said half dreamily, 'Shall we stop in Cambridge on the way back and take a look at the colleges and the river?'

He laughed without even moving his head sideways. 'Sure thing,' he replied. 'I can't wait to see what a city stuffed to bursting point with clever dicks looks like.'

She turned away, irritated as the feeling of confusion that had swamped her earlier returned, there it was again. What was it, arbitrariness or a lack of empathy? She didn't know how to describe it, all she knew was that two people, who supposedly knew each other, looked at the same signpost and one mourned lost dreams, while the other dismissed it out of hand as a place to ridicule.

Abruptly, she turned her mind to Boston, she didn't want to think of 'what ifs' not when she was trapped in a car with nowhere to run to, lest panic overwhelm her. What she wondered, would Boston be like, was it a quaint but interesting backwater, would she notice any discernible difference in the people there? Her questions echoed artificially in her ear. She didn't give a meercat's piss what Boston was like; all she wanted right now was distraction.

Perhaps a change of scene might do her good. Jack would be working most of the time and she could take Daisy out into the country and live a make belief life for a few days. Sip afternoon tea in thatched cottage teahouses, even wear a green anorak and fake an interest in wildlife and architecture.

She shuddered slightly at the thought of life in the back of beyond. She didn't hold with the view that small towns fostered more harmony. Her experience had been that small towns harboured small 'lives'. People obsessed by other people's business. Living their triumphs and wallowing in their misfortunes. At least with a city there was vibrancy. It was in her opinion a lot of cod that community spirit was more evident in back water places. The same argument she reckoned was used in campaigns to save corner shops. Why go to Tesco's and buy something fresher and cheaper went the argument, when you could wander down to the corner shop, and be ripped off by a miserable old git who sells you out of date goods, and kicks up a stink when you haven't got the odd penny.

Her thoughts drifted back to her own little seaside town. That was a prime example of her small town, small life philosophy, not one person there had stood up to be counted as a friend. She knew that all her school friends had known about the baby. She remembered Madga phoning her up. It had been a short stunted conversation. A call to say goodbye really. She never mentioned anything about a baby.

Then there had been that letter from her friend Clare, the girl she'd gone to the school disco with. Now she had mentioned the baby. She had called Sinead 'a dark horse,' and from that moment on Sinead had wanted nothing more to do with her. 'Join the list of the great assumers,' she had thought as she screwed the letter up.

No one had questioned how it was that Sinead O'Connell who didn't even have a boyfriend had managed to have a baby. Most friends had simply treated her like someone with a contagious condition.

The more she thought about it the more convinced she was that there is more sense of community in Oxford Street's McDonalds on a Saturday afternoon, than in any small town where those with half a brain are bursting to get out and the other half, the brainless brigade remain like stagnant pond life.

As they neared Peterborough Jack became more talkative. He told Phoenix that he had asked Rita to chase up property prices in Lincolnshire, they were he declared 'unbelievable'. Terraced houses near a college, were selling for less than twenty grand, they could buy them up and let them out to students.

'Wow,' she thought scornfully, 'Lets go up and buy our very own Coronation Street!'

'You never know,' he said jokingly, 'you might like it so much we'll end up relocating.'

'Piss off Jack,' she replied irritably. 'I've only just accepted we are not going to the USA, so don't push your luck.'

Peterborough flew past and the uneventful journey turned tedious. Daisy had long abandoned her toys and began to repeatedly ask 'Are we there yet?' and since neither Phoenix nor Jack knew anything about the area they were not in a position to reassure her. Jack had assumed that even though no motorway went to Boston, the roads would at least be dual carriageways, but for the most part they were single track roads that sliced through never ending fields, and there was nothing for it, but to move slowly, ever onward.

It seemed as if the traffic had suddenly increased, but it hadn't. It had merely changed in nature. Now it consisted mainly of huge vegetable laden articulated Lorries from Murcia snaking behind ponderous mud caked tractors. The landscape itself had also changed, there were no longer any hedgerows or meadows dotted with drowsy sheep to be seen, instead vast, flat brown derelict looking fields stretched on for eternity. The sight filled Phoenix with some alarm and turning to Jack she asked hesitantly 'Is this what they mean when they talk about brown field sites?'

Jack however, was not feeling a great deal more confident himself; the whole area wasn't looking at all how he imagined it to be. 'I've no idea,' he replied shortly, 'but it looks to me as if the area is still recovering from the last war.'

His answer did not pacify Phoenix in the slightest. The never ending wasteland, interrupted by the occasional string of pylons filled her with a growing unease. She felt the distinct possibility that the earth was flat after all and that at any moment they might go skidding off the edge of it. Turning her face from the window, she searched in her handbag and pulled out a small bottle of Bells. That whiskey was going to be called upon to see her through this journey had been so obvious to her, that she hadn't even bothered trying to disguise it, she certainly had no intention of letting Jack know the truth about the contents of her perfume bottle. In seconds she deftly unscrewed the cap and held the bottle to her mouth.

It didn't take long for the smell to drift across to Jack. He looked across at her and raised his eyebrows. 'Put that away,' he said. 'You can't be that desperate.'

'I'm not,' she lied, 'but I am that bored.'

She spoke lightly for the worst possible thing would be to let him know how anxious she really was; he would fuss, tease and cajole her and that would only make her feel fifty times worse. She hated drinking in front of him like an old soak, all it would take now to complete the picture of bag lady extraordinaire, would be for her to emit a loud belch and start a fight. The effects of the valium she had taken at the start of the journey were beginning to wear off and whiskey was all she had left to rely on.

The fact that the traffic had slowed down to crawling pace heightened her anxiety. She couldn't bear dawdling at the best of times, and now trapped behind endless tractors in an alien land-scape, panic began its ugly rise. She looked about her desperate for distraction; even Daisy had drifted off to sleep.

But there were plenty of tractors to look at, some were busily engaged in working the land, some sat despondent by the roadside, while others still, were out to frustrate the life out of Jack.

'For God's sake,' he shouted, as one enormous tractor, slightly ahead of the car in front, flashed yet another one out of a field to join what felt like a funeral crawl into Boston. 'What the fuck are bloody tractors doing on roads like these? Look at the jam they are creating.'

Phoenix looked across at him and began murmuring. 'Ah, Cynddylan on a tractor...'- her voice petered out as the words eluded her and rose again as they flicked back into her memory. 'The clutch curses but the gears obey..."

Jack glared across at her but before he could say anything she said, 'It's okay Jack. I'm not commenting on your driving it's just all these tractors remind me of a poem I learnt at school, Cynddylan on a Tractor, by R.S.Thomas.'

'Never mind bloody Cynddylan on the tractor,' he retorted poking his head out of his window like an engine driver, 'It's more a case of twat on a tractor round here.'

They continued the slow crawl all the way into town and arrived to find a quiet and deserted looking Boston awaiting them. A feeling of the 'hour before midnight' permeated the entire place for although it had only just gone six o clock there was no sign of any human activity.

'Well,' said Jack as he pulled to a halt near the market square, 'this is it; don't be getting too excited by it all.'

'Where is everybody?' asked Daisy.

'I've no idea,' replied Jack, 'perhaps they are in bed; they might not come out until after dark.'

The stillness of the place unnerved Phoenix and Jack's flippancy aggravated her. He had been in foul form for most of the way, and now they had arrived it was all cheery, cheery, but from what she could see there was nothing to cheer about.

She stared around at the forlorn looking market square. It was wide and vacant looking, and nothing other than the occasional piece of litter moved in the cool evening air.

'Do you have any idea where this hotel of ours is supposed to be?' she asked, 'there's no sign of anyone to ask.'

Sitting aimlessly in the car was irritating her as was Daisy's interactive book which constantly called out 'you are wrong, try again'. She was about to tell Daisy to throw the book away when Jack nudged her arm

'Not quite true,' he said and she looked up to see a youth pushing a bicycle towards them. He wore a cap that was clearly too small for his very large head and oversized trousers that flapped like the sails of a ship confronting the wind. More intriguing than his attire however, was the loud and aggressive argument he seemed to be having with the saddle bag on his bike.

'Are you going to risk it?' Jack asked.

Phoenix took a look at the deserted street and replied. 'I'm going to have to, I don't fancy sitting in the car for the rest of the night, do you?' She wound down the window and called out.' Do you have any idea where the Old Bear Hotel is?'

'Fuck off' he said without even looking up. 'You're not from round here'.

'Thank the good Christ for that,' Phoenix retorted furiously, but the youth had moved on, his attention once again focused on his errant saddle bag.

'Close the window,' ordered Jack, 'his condition could be airborne.'

For a moment the three of them sat silently in the car, Jack drumming his fingers on the gear stick, Phoenix staring into the wing mirror at the retreating flabby backside of the yob she had just questioned, and Daisy fiddling with her book. Eventually Jack opened his door with obvious reluctance, and climbed out of the car. He then leaned through the open window and said 'I'm going in Trinity,' and when Phoenix merely stared at him blankly, he said, 'You are meant to say, I forbid you Neo and that is an order,' and he walked off pretending to tiptoe as if he was walking through a mine field.

Fool she thought irritably, this is worst than the bloody Matrix at least that wasn't real. The sight of a clearly reluctant Jack disappearing down the forlorn street, proved too much for Daisy and she immediately began to wail for she was bored and hungry and tired of the tense atmosphere. Phoenix turned round and fiercely told her to hush up. She spoke more sharply to the little girl than she intended and was immediately contrite. Intuitively she just knew that they were engaged in a wild goose chase, and the thought made her feel exasperated and trapped.

It didn't take Jack long to find the hotel and when he reappeared, she instantly detected a sheepish feel off him. 'Go on,' she said 'Spit it out, it's a heap isn't it?'

'Well,' he said turning his head away from her, 'It isn't the Ritz, but on the plus side it is only a short walk away.'

Only a few days previously, Phoenix had rather liked Jack's description of the hotel he had booked; he had described it as being like an old fashioned coaching inn. In fact he had painted a picture that had reminded her of the sort of hostelry featured in the Herriot novels, good substantial home cooking, old but comfortable furnishings with the gentle whiff of beeswax polish in the air. In short the sort of place where the emphasis is on comfort and service rather than on delusions of grandeur.

One glance however at The Old Bear hotel immediately informed Phoenix that neither service nor grandeur was its speciality. The reception area that had appeared warm and cosy on the net, turned out to be dark and narrow to the point of pokiness, with a faint smell of unappetising food thrown in for good measure. She looked around at the furniture, it was handsome, cheap reproduction, designed like many TV stars to photograph well and look good from a distance. Instinctively she ran her hand along one of the fake dark wood tables and silently came to the conclusion, that no one had ever lovingly tended them with liberal helpings of beeswax polish. It was, she decided, Jack's business and he could get on with it, she couldn't even guess as to what had possessed him to book such a place. She folded her arms in a gesture of metaphorical hand washing and walked towards the window, leaving him to do the signing in.

Jack also felt like passing the buck on the whole situation, this dreary jumped up boarding house had nothing in common with the quaint hotel he had booked just a few days ago. He stood by the reception desk feeling increasingly frustrated, with Daisy clinging protectively to his left leg, waiting for the bell he had rang a few minutes previously to be answered. Just as he was about to walk over to Phoenix and suggest finding somewhere else to stay, a rather sullen looking girl approached him from behind. She flashed him a look of pure winter sunshine, all glare and no warmth, and made her way to the other side of the desk.

'Have you got a reservation' she asked, in a querulous tone.

For a moment Jack was perplexed, torn between turning on his heel and walking out the door or launching a fully fledged

verbal assault on the unattractive teenager. In the end, since he
didn't fancy traipsing around the deserted looking town, or risk
winding Phoenix up, he settled for sarcasm and replied curtly.
'Now you mention it, I've got plenty'.

She stared boldly straight back at him, unaware that he was
being facetious. He returned the stare, noting that although her
face was thick with make up; her hands were unkempt and
almost grubby looking. She looked like a land worker. Feeling
deeply uneasy, he decided against spinning the line any further
and hurriedly got on with signing the register, keen to be out of
the tense surreal atmosphere.

The receptionist motioned rather than asked him to follow
her and he in turn beckoned to Phoenix to join him. As they
walked silently up the narrow stairs Jack fervently prayed for a
hidden gem to be awaiting them. Perhaps this was a passion
fruit scenario; they were delving through an ugly exterior to get
to a heart of sweetness. But he prayed in vain.

In stark contrast to the rest of the building, the bedroom
which was situated to the rear of the hotel, turned out to be a
pine room. A gaudily furnished one that smelt faintly of saw
dust, probably due to the fact that it had recently been refurbished.

As befitting of a hostelry in England's premier horticultural
region, flowers featured heavily in its décor, there was an abundance of them - silk ones all the way from Hong Kong. They sat
in bunches on every surface, many of them still bearing a price
tag. The floral theme was continued further in the various
Monet prints which adorned the walls, all clad in cheap pine
frames and securely nailed down to safeguard from trash thieves.

Phoenix, bristling with hostility, glared as the sullen girl concluded her duty stint by rattling off in record quick time the
restaurant's opening hours. 'Go on' she thought viciously,
'scuttle back like a rat to your hidey hole under the stairs while
you still can'. When the door clicked shut, an eerie ominous
silence filled the room. It was broken by Phoenix, who could
hardly contain her anger.

'For God's sake Jack,' she said through clenched teeth, 'Tell
her to come back here at once.'

'What for?' he asked.

'What for?' she demanded. 'Did you know you booked this?'

'Of course I didn't,' he said. 'I swear to God it looked nothing like this on the web, they must have bribed David Bailey to take the photos, or else they nicked them from somewhere else.'

He walked towards the window one hand held to the back of his head, tired with the tedious situation; the whole venture was beginning to feel farcical. A ramshackle spread of rooftops greeted his gaze, what lived beneath them, more monsters like the one he had just met downstairs?

'For fucks sake,' he said turning round to face Phoenix. 'I didn't want the fucking Ritz, just somewhere normal like a Holiday Inn or a Marriot, somewhere with a leisure centre for you and Daisy, but there isn't anything like that for miles.'

Phoenix, pacified that at least he wasn't trying to pass the debacle off as a joke, sat on the bed and sighed. Daisy meanwhile found a wardrobe with a squeaky door, just the thing to get attention with. She sawed it back and forth, and both Phoenix and Jack shouted at her in unison to shut up.

'Look,' Jack said throwing his hands in the air in defeat, 'Let's stay tonight, have a bloody good drink and tomorrow we will find somewhere else.' And Phoenix, suddenly conscious that a search through a town that she already despised, might only unearth somewhere worse, declined to suggest anything else.

Though Phoenix and Jack were not happy with the hotel, their discontent was not shared by Daisy. It was she thought far more entertaining than her interactive book, that only squeaked 'Wrong Answer,' or 'Well Done,' but this hotel had doors that squeaked, floorboards that creaked, and a tap in the bathroom that whistled just like the kettle in her Enid Blyton story.

While Phoenix showered, Jack contacted his gang on his mobile; they had arrived and were already in a bar and in exceptionally high spirits, which only served to heighten Jack's sense of frustration at his own predicament. He certainly didn't feel like exploring the town for a restaurant, and neither thankfully did Phoenix, the hotel one would have to make do.

'Come on,' Jack said coaxingly when Phoenix emerged from the bathroom, 'let's see if the place excels itself in the dining room, after all, they say some of the best restaurants in France have the shittiest exteriors.'

'True,' replied Phoenix fishing in her bag for her lipstick, 'but this isn't France.'

They entered the dimly lit restaurant to find it virtually empty, all the same a tall gangly waiter; told them to wait while he checked to see if there was availability. He returned within minutes and showed them to their table which to Phoenix's relief was situated near the window. He then presented them each with a menu; took an order for drinks and that was where normality ended.

The aura of farce Jack had sensed earlier on returned with a vengeance, in fact as he later recalled, it was a night of pure entertainment, like being in a cabaret show, a comedy one with the artistes performing amongst the diners.

The first casualty was the drinks order. The bottle of Merlot and glass of orange juice were nowhere to be seen; instead the waiter offered Jack a pint of mild, and Phoenix a glass of cider and seemed genuinely baffled when they declined them. It only took two more attempts before they got what they ordered, but the bumbling confusion made them the focus of the few other diners, and both Jack and Phoenix were well aware, that since they were the outsiders they were deemed to be at fault.

Jack fleetingly remembered what Rita his secretary had said about being stared at all the time when she had visited Boston. Hadn't she put it down to being without the obligatory two heads and six fingers? The recollection made him feel slightly queasy. He pushed his menu away, and sat back while Phoenix helped Daisy to choose her meal.

It was a simple order, Phoenix told the insipid looking waiter, chicken fillet with fries, for the child, and sirloin steak twice for the adults. He wrote it down laboriously, as if taking minutes at a U.N meeting, and jumped nervously when Jack interrupted his flow by saying, 'Actually just make that the one steak, I think I'll go for the vegetarian dish of the day.'

'Mushroom Stroganoff,' exclaimed Phoenix incredulously. 'I don't believe you Jack, you'll never eat that.'

'Well don't say I never surprise you,' he replied shaking his head, and turning to the waiter who was looking slightly confused, he said, 'See, you can take a woman out of the bog, but you can't take the bog out of a woman.'

The waiter, not sure if Jack was being insulting and if he was, just who the butt of the insult was, fumbled for a moment with his pencil. But luckily the penny eventually dropped and as he leaned forward to take the menus away, he said very confidentially to Jack, 'Actually, the ladies are just outside, to the right.'

Jack ignored the clumsy comment as befitting of the inarticulate youth who had hardly strung two coherent words together since they had entered the restaurant. Phoenix however, had watched the interaction carefully and she knew that the young fellow hadn't a clue what Jack's talk of bogs and women had actually meant. She laughed so much that tears streamed down her face and every time she thought she had regained control of herself, one look at Jack's bewildered face set her off again. When she had fully exhausted the joke, she looked at Jack and said. 'Well after a slow start, you're in some form, but whatever possessed you to order vegetarian, are you sick or just dying?'

Jack took a long sip of wine from his glass, glanced furtively around as if to make sure no one was listening and then leaned forward very conspiratorially. 'Do you know something?' he said very quietly, 'All that stuff in the news recently about foot and mouth and Mad Cows, well it has made me think.'

She looked at him disbelievingly 'But you always eat meat, you even ate bacon this morning, if you didn't fancy the steak, why didn't you have fish?'

'No chance,' he whispered. 'What's the betting that round here if you ordered a plain fillet, you'd more than likely be presented with a leg of finest Lincolnshire cod, I think I might play safe and stick with booze.'

It only took the waiter three attempts to get the drinks order right, but when it came to the food, he wasn't so sharp. Four times, he bought the wrong food, sausages twice for Daisy and a steak for Jack, followed by a rack of ribs. Each time, rather than acknowledge his mistake, he simply stood waiting for Jack or Phoenix to do the decent thing and just accept what he offered.

Even the second bottle of wine (which took an inordinate amount of time in arriving) turned into a saga. It was corked, and Jack who was beginning to feel he'd known the young waiter for most of his life, called him across and informed him of the wine's condition.

'It is corked,' he said, holding up the bottle.

The waiter nodded his head 'I know,' he replied. 'I corked it myself.'

'I'm sure you did,' Jack said, 'but please believe me, it is off.'

'Yes,' replied the waiter, baffled by this customer who seemed to like reiterating the obvious. 'I took it off behind the bar.'

Jack looked across at Phoenix 'Tell me girl,' he asked, 'am I speaking clearly or have I lapsed into ancient Dutch again?' but Phoenix, who had been simmering with laughter ever since the waiter's literal interpretation of Jack's scenario concerning taking women out of bogs, was too choked to reply. All she could do was wave her hand frantically in a bid to silence Jack for she now had an aching stitch in her side. She didn't want to hear anything that would cause the laughter already consuming her to bubble up and overflow completely. Giving her up as a useless ally, Jack tried again.

'Can you forget the cork for a moment?' he said. 'I'm talking about the wine, it's off, rotten, sour, here take a sniff, it stinks.'

He held the bottle up to the waiter, who backed away as if Jack was holding a gun. 'Oh I don't drink wine,' he said, 'but I'll tell the boss you don't like it.' And he walked away with a look of abject confusion all over his pale sun deprived face.

The idea of complaining was preposterous. To have done so would have felt akin to heckling a first class comedian, causing him to falter on his long awaited punch line. It did occur fleetingly to Jack; that they were being set up for some kind of hidden camera programme, but he assured himself, 'No actors could be as convincing as these guys.

Following in a long line of comic tradition, the waiter turned out to be part of a duo; his side kick being a tubby barman, who for most of the evening played the straight guy, until he deviated from his role by serving Phoenix cognac in a champagne flute. Like true professionals neither Fatty nor Skinny let anything ruffle them. They just stoically continued with their duties, heads down and feet shuffling in perfect harmony.

Daisy enjoyed herself as well. True, her chicken was too tough to eat and she noticed that neither of her parents ate their dinner, but she had never heard the pair of them laugh so much. Certainly she couldn't remember the last time she had seen wine spray out of her mother's mouth, or trickle down her father's nose.

When the meal was over and the waiter had gone to double check and check again that they were residents and not black-guards who had dined in luxury prior to absconding without payment, Phoenix raised her glass.

'I want to propose a toast to you Jack,' she said, speaking just a little slurred, 'With no hard feelings whatsoever, regarding your lousy little trick, delivered in front of Tosh, about taking me to America.' She paused for a moment, took a sip from her glass and continued, 'But as I look around me here, I know two things, one, you're going to love it and secondly God definitely exists,' and with that she finished, the last of her brandy.

Jack sighed and glanced around the room. 'Well all I can say,' he said, 'is that if God exists, He has a shite sense of humour.' When the waiter finally established that they were residents, and not set to do a runner, they wandered into the hotel bar and just as Jack was ordering a round, Tosh came in bouncing with life and enthusiasm.

The barmaid, an old woman in her early thirties with a sour begrudging kind of face fired a look at Tosh that told him he was as welcome as weeds in June. The look didn't go unnoticed by Jack. He had laughed in the restaurant because the whole experience had been too bizarre to do anything else, but he was out of the theatre now and something about the hushed subdued atmosphere in the bar inexplicably touched a raw nerve within him. This raw nerve was further tweaked, when the barmaid rudely thumped his change down on the counter with a curt 'Take your change duck.'

As she turned to walk away, he raised his hand to attract her attention. 'Tell me something' he said. 'Is there by any chance a local bylaw that makes the wearing of caps compulsory in Boston?'

'You what, duck?' she asked, looking bewildered.

Jack glanced at the ceiling before replying. 'Why what's coming?'

Not understanding his meaning, she just shrugged her shoulders and moved away to serve another customer. Jack picked up his drinks and walked back to an astonished Tosh and Phoenix.

'What on earth was that all about?' asked Tosh, who had been listening to the entire exchange with interest.

'Why the hell does everyone round here say duck? Duck for what? A low ceiling?' asked Jack sharply.

'Oh come on,' replied Tosh, 'it is obviously a local habit.'

'Well it is one I can do without,' said Jack. He took a drink of his beer and leaned forward. 'I'll tell you another thing, if most blokes wear a beard to hide a dodgy chin, what the fuck are these lot hiding under those caps?'

Jack was not impressed and for once, Tosh acted like an adult and said that as far as he could make out, they were just country people with simple ways and sayings and that in some respects, the place reminded him of Ireland.

'Fuck off,' said Jack seriously nettled, 'it's either been far too long since you were home Tosh, or else you've been at the beef.'

Feeling as if he were a lone voice in the wilderness, Jack placed his glass on the table with the intention of turning his attention to look at some leaflets on a rack behind his head, but he was forestalled in his plans by Daisy. She was tired and bored with the subdued atmosphere that contrasted so vastly with the manic comic one that had existed earlier in the restaurant, what she wanted now was to go to sleep in the crook of her father's arm. Phoenix watched on as Tosh, in a conciliatory gesture edged his stool closer to where Jack sat. She knew that he didn't have a clue as to what was irritating Jack, so he would be bound to steer the conversation around to safe territory, like work or horses. She was right and when she heard Tosh's opening gambit, she turned and stared around the room, not wanting to be a part of it.

The bar wasn't busy, just a few local stragglers with the regulation caps stood around talking about the town football team. She glanced out of the window into the lonely town square, the emptiness was almost palpable. Sitting there, in that deserted hotel lounge she felt as if she was back in the Kent of her childhood. The place stank of the routine familiar to all small town life. Monday nights she concluded, were obviously recuperation nights after the weekend exertion of pissing wages up the wall.

It's not the same in cities she thought to herself, this sense of routine and allocating different days for different things, like the nursery rhyme that says, Monday is washing day, Tuesday is for ironing. Busy lives can't be structured like that, there has to be flexibility.

She gazed up at some faded photographs which adorned the walls of the hotel, photos that celebrated Boston's past, and thought that they displayed a striking resemblance to its present. It was as if she had taken a step back in time. Like Jack, she noted the barmaid's ease with locals and her palpable unease with strangers. It's a different world compared to the one I'm used to, she thought, yet I've been here before. The feeling of confusion regarding time and place that she had experienced on the journey washed over her again; how strange it was to think of communities big and small living out their lives, it was pure luck of the draw as to where anyone was born.

And as she sat, adrift from those closest to her, a feeling of inevitability almost suffocated her. What if there was no way out, what if it was all pre-ordained and life simply had to be lived the way it had been mapped out?

If, she pondered to herself, if I hadn't left my community so abruptly, where and what would I be doing now? Would I have returned to Kent after university, or would I have been grabbed by the freedom of the city and be hooked up in some little penthouse over in Docklands.

Mentally she shrugged her shoulders. The only thing she felt with any certainty; was that if she had become a lawyer, she wouldn't be sitting in a hovel in the Midlands of England, with a gang of plasterers on a mild May evening in the early stages of the new millennium.

Tosh was the only truly relaxed one amongst them. Phoenix watched as he tried to tease a smile out of the barmaid, helping himself to fistfuls of complimentary peanuts from the dish on the bar, telling her that they would come out a Treat in the morning. He remained undeterred by her hard puritanical face and Phoenix reckoned he had more chance of extracting a laugh from the poker beside the fire than out of her. He didn't seem to notice that all his jokes fell as flat as the surrounding landscape or that the barmaid was irritated with him. She so obviously wanted to be left to talk to her regulars, well talk was an exaggeration, she wanted to stand there and throw in the occasional 'Yeah' or 'Dunno'.

Several times she glanced over at the sleeping Daisy on Jack's knee, and both Phoenix and Jack could tell she was itching to say something like 'that child's very tired,' so that the hint would be taken and they'd leave and let her get on with her routine.

Jack sat listening to Tosh ramble on, Guinness in one hand the other wrapped around his child. He gave the impression of listening but his mind was elsewhere. Even so he still managed to feign interest in what Tosh said, for he was a good manager. He knew workers have to feel listened to; and that the feeling is often more important than the reality.

Phoenix glanced across at him. She could tell he was barely listening to Tosh. She wondered what he was thinking about, was he as she suspected, regretting the whole trip already? Jack though, she reminded herself wasn't given to regrets. She couldn't help looking at him with a question in her own heart. Just how satisfied was he really? How much would he do differently if he had the chance again?

Watching him, lean back, nod an agreement, smile a refusal, she couldn't see that he had that much to regret, nothing except perhaps that first brief marriage.

But nothing can be taken on face value, she told herself because Jack could look at her and think, now that woman has had a charmed life. She came from a little terrace in the back of beyond, started her business, had a child and didn't piss about with a crap marriage. She's achieved more than she could have dreamt possible. She is living proof that you can have it all.

This was his illusion and the thought of it being shattered was more than she could bear. It was a fairytale that she didn't want to end, but she knew instinctively that as sure as the moon shone and disappeared no matter how grimly the stars fought to tack it to the night sky, that Jack was going to find out the truth about her. A great wash of sadness swept over her as she realised her mistake in not having told him the truth, a long time ago.

If only that baby had been the result of a five minute affair, or a schoolgirl crush she could have told Jack. She could even have used it to her advantage, look what I did and still went on to do. A baby conceived like that would be would have reflected the fact that somebody had wanted her and not used her.

But, it was stupid to think that telling Jack about the baby would have been a different proposition if it had been a wanted one, because if it had been she would never have let it go, would she? She wouldn't have worked in the building society, shared a flat with Lesley or started a business or even met Jack at all. Life was like a house of cards, each one relying on the previous one being in place.

She turned her head as Jack's voice cut like an axe through her thoughts. He was becoming more animated, more like himself, telling Tosh in highly exaggerated language, how the deputy Prime Minister, after getting pelted by an egg had given his attacker a smack in the mouth. Jack was full of admiration for him, but Tosh was adamant that 'two jags Prescott' had it coming.

'If I was there I'd have thrown a bucket of shit at him, payback for all the shite he talks.'

If, Phoenix repeated to herself, always if; how Tosh loved that word. If he won the lottery, if he had backed that horse, how different life would be but for if!

Life was so complicated yet it hinged around one little word. A little splinter of a word, that slipped in and out uninvited and cause untold mayhem. If!

Jack was right; she declared to herself, the English were a queer race. They set such store about silly things, even electing a stupid poem in honour of the runt word as the nation's favourite poem when basically, it was nothing more than an instruction manual. Telling men what they had to do if they wanted to be real men. Kipling, she thought dismissively, ought to stick to baking cakes.

She decided with finality that 'if' was for losers. It could be used shamelessly to excuse almost anything. There was no point whatsoever in her saying, 'if I didn't have Jack, if I didn't have Daisy.'

They were her reality.

She was shaken out of her thoughts again, this time by Jack, tapping her knee with the toe of his shoe. He was now speaking directly to her. 'What do you think?' he was asking.

'About what?' she asked.

'Two jags getting an omelette in the face.'

'Waste of a good egg,' she replied disinterestedly. She listened for a moment to the conversation Jack and Tosh were engaged in, they were discussing the coming election, Jack was rooting for Blair, and Tosh who had declared on many an occasion that he couldn't give a ferret's fart who governed the country, played devils advocate.

'Blair,' he declared, 'Is a slimy chancer,' and Phoenix even though she hated sharing anything with Tosh even a dislike, silently concurred with his opinion.

Jack though would have none of it. Blair he reiterated; had moved things forward and he had buried old Labour. There was nothing to fear from the left anymore.

'He is greasy and sly and on top of that...' said Tosh searching for a finale, 'he is a stupid bastard,' and as Jack made to interrupt Tosh added 'and they are just his good points.'

Jack shook his head. 'He might be greasy but he certainly isn't stupid. Isn't he a QC?' he asked Phoenix.

But before Phoenix could answer Tosh had decided to play contrary again. He shook his head emphatically. 'No,' he said, 'You are wrong about that last bit Jack. He's married with kids isn't he?'

Since neither Jack nor Phoenix could top that as a conversation stopper, talk about the election gave way to other topics.

And chief amongst them was the freakiness of the other customers who consistently threw unfriendly glares in their direction.

The next few days in Boston, saw Jack admitting for the first time ever, that purgatory might exist. Something about the place bit deeply into his psyche, for his fundamental stance on life was that people are good, and that given half a chance most people want to like and be liked. But Boston was challenging his long held belief.

As for Phoenix she didn't discover any winding country lanes with overhead trees, meeting to form dark and mysterious tunnels, or any cosy teahouses complete with thatched roofs. All she came across were roads cutting through massive slabs of land, huge fields with churned up black soil, and the occasional vast expanse growing spuds and cabbages like there was no tomorrow.

She thought often of her red book, locked safely in the drawer back home. How much it contained about her life and how dreadful it would be, if she met her death in this foul backwater and for her secret to come tumbling out posthumously.

The sight of tractors, with row upon row of seats on the back of them filled with people planting or trimming, awakened a curious pity within her, it looked like a scene from a textbook about somewhere in Eastern Europe. The toil looked immense. No wonder the entire population wears hats she thought to herself, they must all have to take a spin at digging and planting, whatever the weather.

Jack on the other hand, wasn't at all sorry or philosophical about what he saw. The locals he was working with were not happy with outsiders being bought in for the job and he in turn swore that he had never met such a bunch of cantankerous humourless langers in his entire life. He found them closed, suspicious and resentful, with a habit of muttering under their breath. Jack had no sympathy for them - working with them he said, made him feel like Dr Doolittle, 'talking to the fucking animals'. They were unreliable fat arses on the make.

The entire experience placed Jack on a steeper learning curve than the one he had grappled with upon his first arrival in

England. He had never met people like these before. There was as far as he could make out, no delineation between the plebs and the bosses. Even the architect in charge of the project was in his opinion, shit thick.

'Jesus,' he said to Phoenix, 'But for the fact he also wears a cap I wouldn't know if it was his head or his arse I was speaking to, he's designed the ultimate in crap and they are applauding the fucker as if he is a genius.'

Phoenix didn't like the place any more than Jack did, but at least she had read up on it, and was more able to put what she saw into context. As she watched the land-workers congregate on the streets of Boston having been dropped off by their gangers, she had a curious feeling that this was the British equivalent of serfdom in Russia; the many working for the few, the reality behind the romantic notion of a corner of England given over to arable farming.

No one, she thought, with a taste for beauty or the finer things of life could bear to live in such a place. For all that historians might beg to differ; Puritanism was alive and kicking in Boston. It was apparent everywhere, from the unsightly no frills food served to the ridiculous pragmatic names of places and things. There was nothing pretty or surplus to requirement about the entire place. The waterways that drained the land didn't have evocative names like Badgers Flow or Lily Stream. In Boston they evidently believed in calling a dyke, a dyke.

When she commented on this to Jack, Tosh intervened defensively. 'Well perhaps they ran out of names,' he said, 'After all Lincolnshire has more dykes than anywhere else in England.'

'I can certainly believe that,' replied Jack, 'because it's the queerest fucking place I've ever been to.'

Jack kept true to his word and on their second day in Boston, they left the comedy of errors that masqueraded as a hotel. Before doing so, Jack asked Phoenix in all seriousness, if she wanted to return home but she declined. She had already mentally resigned herself to being there for the best part of a week and she had also discovered, that Jack was telling the truth about the type of hotels available in the area. They ended up staying in a motel on the edge of town, a solution they both preferred to the other option of travelling to and from Boston every day from Peterborough or Lincoln.

For the remainder of the week they ate out in country pubs where they discovered just how truly awful Lincolnshire food can be when it puts its mind to it. A waitress seeing the look on Jack's face as she slapped down three mountainous looking plates of overcooked vegetables said, 'we pile it high and sell it cheap in Lincolnshire, duck.'

'That's a fine philosophy,' agreed Jack, 'Provided its horse manure you are flogging.'

At this, the waitress folded her arms and shook her head. 'Oh but we don't, duck,' she said apologetically, 'But there's a farm up the road that does.'

Jack winked across at Phoenix, whose urge to put the woman straight was causing her nose to quiver. 'Do you know?' he said to her, 'Telling jokes or making quips round here is like listening to the thud of earth on a coffin.'

On the Wednesday the town held a market, complete with an auction of bikes and flowers, it looked a bright and colourful affair and Phoenix asked Jack to accompany her and Daisy to it.

Not only did he have no desire to see the sights of Boston, he was also extremely wary of leaving his gang. The previous day a furious argument had broken out between them and some of the locals working on the same job. It was clear Jack was not the only one who intensely disliked the area. Several Londoners who had come with romantic visions of downsizing to the country had been cured of their dreams. One of them said coming to Boston was like watching evolution in reverse!

It took a lot of persuasion, but in the end Jack agreed to accompany his wife and daughter. Together the three of them set off for the market, where they found a hustle and bustle that is peculiar to country folk, excited by a big day out. For the first time in years Phoenix actually saw women with shopping bags, in fact the people reminded her of characters from the world of Enid Blyton with their big red faces and wicker baskets. She pointed out the occasional one to Jack, but he refused to be impressed.

He said it was how he imagined Lourdes to be, except the people there wanted to be cured. These people looked as if they were all related. The whole town was busier than either expected it to be, and when Jack eventually found a space to park the car a small crowd gathered round to watch him reverse into a tight space.

An old man who had almost certainly never driven a car in his life began making furious circling movements with his arm telling Jack how to turn the wheel. Within seconds a crowd of spectators had gathered and their heads moved in unison, every time the car moved forwards and backwards like a Wimbledon crowd.

'What the fuck is the attraction?' asked Jack and Phoenix mimicking Tosh said they were just country people looking for the excitement of a scrape. Jack replied that he didn't care what they were, but if the old fucker didn't get out of his way, he'd get more excitement than he bargained for.

Once the car was safely parked, the crowd melted away with an air of anti-climax and Phoenix found herself feeling unaccountably sorry for Jack. He was out of his depth, she thought because this was a place where charm didn't work. He was obviously suffering from a very nasty cultural shock.

She was not wrong in her estimation of how Jack felt. He had indeed breezed in telling the indigenous workers, that he'd heard marvellous things about them all. And instead of recognising it as blarney, oil to make the wheels of work turn smoothly they had responded by asking themselves and each other 'What does he want, what's he after?'

Not being an analytical man, the constant suspicion and animosity merely exasperated him. He had no time for people who simply couldn't get on with the job and keep their mouths shut. In Jack's opinion, gossip and intrigue belonged firmly in the pub; work was about making a living.

After visiting the market, they drove at the instigation of Phoenix to a village on the outskirts of Boston, called Fishtoft. She had read about it in a pamphlet Jack had collected from the tourism office in London. It had a tourist attraction known as the Pilgrim Memorial, a monument to the Pilgrim Fathers who had attempted to leave Boston back in 1707 for a new life in Boston, Massachusetts and instantly Phoenix had thought of Jack's sister Mary across the sea.

'Why don't we pay a visit,' she asked Jack, 'We could send a photo to Mary in Boston and let her know a thing or two about the ancestry of some of her neighbours.'

As Phoenix drove, Jack flicked through some property details he had collected from estate agents in the town. He emitted several loud exclamations as he did so and Phoenix deliberately ignored him.

Finally in a gesture of exasperation he threw them down on the dashboard. 'For shit's sake,' he said. 'I've never seen houses so cheap, it's like Monopoly, only you'd have to be pissed or mad to play this game.' He turned and looked out the window at vast acres of dead cabbages that had been left to rot. 'Look,' he said to Daisy, 'look at the sheep.'

Amid the rotting vegetation a flock of sheep munched dejectedly at the decaying yellow leaves and stalks. 'My God,' he said to Phoenix. 'I wouldn't fancy being anywhere near them tonight.'

'I'd be surprised if you did,' she replied, 'but just out of interest, did you know there isn't a single case of foot and mouth in Lincolnshire?'

'Well what do you know,' he replied staring around at the shambolic farmland, 'An intelligent disease.'

As they approached the village, at least two imbeciles on bicycles peered into the car, and upon spying strangers appeared to be overcome with an urge to give the fingers. Jack was incredulous. 'For God's sake,' he asked. 'Just what is wrong with the place?'

'Still fancy buying some property Jack?' enquired Phoenix, 'After all you were rather keen not that long ago.'

He grimaced at her 'Don't even mention it,' he said. 'I'd throw money down a rat hole first, but I have had one good idea.'

She turned her head away and laughed. 'I'm not sure I want to hear your good ideas any -more.'

'But you will like this one,' he said. 'I think we may have found the ideal place for Shitlegs O'Carolan to relocate to.'

'Now that's just plain nasty,' she replied peering about her perplexedly, 'but anyway, balls to him, where is this wretched monument, I can't see any more signposts.'

'I've no idea,' Jack said looking with disinterest at the village church as it whizzed by. He told Phoenix, to pull in and he'd find someone to ask and she pulled up outside the driveway of a manor house.

They were in luck, for a man was busily engaged in trimming the bordering hedge. He looked up and smiled across at them as did the young blonde haired girl who accompanied him. 'Shall I risk it?' asked Jack.

He took the risk and jumped out of the car and despite her mother's order to the contrary, Daisy followed, slipping out like an eel. Luckily for Jack, the man was not from the area and he welcomed the opportunity for a break. Jack commented on the size of the job at hand and the man laughed. He said he had been sent by his wife to do it. They were selling up.

Jack made a vague, investigative comment about the area being unusual.

That made the man laugh loudly. He said that wasn't the word his wife used to describe it; she had gone to Ireland, to Cork in fact, to have a baby rather than risk it being born in the locality. At that point, the young blonde girl who had been making a fuss of Daisy chipped into the conversation. A boy at her school she said, had been born with six fingers and what was more, the parents had taken a family photograph of it.

As Jack chatted, Phoenix watched him and his companion being watched. A hefty woman dressed in men's shorts with a ludicrous looking sun visor clipped to her head stared at the pair of them, hostility bristling off her. She had been in the process of washing her already immaculately clean car, but seeing her neighbour talking to strangers was obviously far more interesting.

The woman looked crazy and a frisson of fear ran through Phoenix as the thought occurred to her; that madness comes in many forms. This woman looked mad and anywhere else she would probably be deemed to be mad. But here she was apparently normal.

Jack came back to the car and Daisy thrust a bunch of conciliatory daisies onto Phoenix's lap. 'That,' he said, 'was the first normal guy I've met since we left London.' He then proceeded to tell her some of the horror stories the man and his daughter had told him about the area. Talking with the stranger had confirmed his opinion on the place. It wasn't a case of being all in the mind; and Jack felt marginally uplifted.

The monument they were seeking; was actually just over a mile away, on the banks of the Wash. It was a bleak and desolate place. On one side, broccoli was growing as far as the eye could see, while on the side near to the Wash, cattle grazed on marshy looking ground. There were notices pinned at intervals along a timber fence warning of the necessity of keeping Lincolnshire free from Foot and Mouth.

As Phoenix stared at the sullen stretch of water with just the occasional call of the crows to break the eerie silence, she found it all too easy to imagine a boat trying to sneak its way out of this forbidding area with hidden cargo. She shivered as a brief recollection of 'The Heart Of Darkness' washed over her. She had expected to see a thriving tourist venue with kiosks and film shows, but the monument turned out to be a grey tomb stone, with a faded inscription to the men in black who had tried to flee Boston many years ago, only to be shopped by the captain at the last minute.

'You can feel for the poor fuckers,' Jack said as he read the inscription, 'I'd personally take emigration to Bosnia rather than stay here.'

He stopped and sniffed the air for a moment, like a blood hound on the scent of something exciting. 'If I didn't know better,' he said. 'I'd say Tosh was about, what is that terrible smell?'

Phoenix pointed downstream 'I saw a signpost for a sewage works on the way here,' she said. 'It's probably that.'

'Oh yes,' he said, 'A sewage near a monument, very likely, you old liar.'

'I'm not,' she insisted. 'I saw a sign for one just down there.'

He placed his hands on the monument and began to laugh.
'What's so funny?' asked Phoenix.

'Just think,' he said, 'All those years ago in Ireland, they
merely threw a wake for departing emigrants and here they built
a bloody sewage. A reminder to one and all, of the shit hole, left
behind.'

'Well,' said Phoenix, 'at least you've got to give them top
marks for literal thinking.'

The last day arrived and Battersea Plasterers, made a short
but grateful convoy out of Boston. Socially the trip had been a
disaster, but the job was completed to perfection and all the
workers had received a bonus for early completion which went
some way to lifting their spirits.

On the road out of town, Phoenix pulled out her mobile
phone to tell Carolyn she would be calling in later that afternoon.

'Yes,' she told Carolyn glancing across at Jack, 'We had a
wonderful time, Jack particularly loved it, doesn't want to leave
in fact.' He shot a glaring look at her and let out an expletive as
a white van pulled out in front of him.

'Be honest Jack,' she teased, as she packed her phone away,
'You know you loved it really.'

'I'm incredulous,' he said. 'It was like being on the set of
Monsters Inc; I can't believe I haven't dreamt this week.'

Only Daisy was sad at the thought of going home. It had
been a week of treats and attention with plenty of laughter and
she wanted it to last forever. They paused at a set of traffic lights
and Phoenix took the opportunity to settle her daughter, arranging a collection of books and toys to keep her occupied and
happy.

'Look at that,' Jack said, with real awe in his voice,
'Wherever have you seen the likes of that before?' He was
pointing to the back of the white van that had pulled out in
front of them only moments earlier; someone had etched on its
dirty back door 'I fuck goats.'

'You find foul graffiti in London as well Jack,' Phoenix said
pushing back her head rest.

'Yes you do,' he agreed, 'But not stuff like that! That is pure country,' he insisted. 'Do you think the driver knows it's there?'

Phoenix shrugged her shoulders, bored with Jack's apparent sudden fascination with imbeciles, 'Who knows,' she replied dismissively 'Perhaps one of his kids did it.'

She put her head back ready to attempt relaxation, but the aptness of her words struck her at the same time as they hit Jack and they laughed their way out of Boston.

PART TWO

The one charm of the past – is that it is the past.
Oscar Wilde

Chapter Eighteen

Dear Scarlett,   23rd May 2001

Shelby the shrink thinks anxiety can be controlled by diversion
or breathing techniques. If you inhale, deep and slowly through
the nose and exhale long and laboriously through the mouth,
anxiety, she says, will disappear just like that. Frankly I think
she is talking rubbish, it never works, it just makes me sound
like a steam train puffing in from Fishguard, laden down with
Guinness.

Anyway, breathing is physical and panic is mental and I don't
see the relationship between the two. I think she might be right
though about the diversion premise, because accompanying Jack
on his crazy batter to Boston certainly diverted my mind from
dwelling too darkly on the imminent and un-faceable.

Since arriving back in London, Jack hasn't been himself at
all. He's even taken to waking up during the night and that has
seriously hampered my attempts to write to you. I'm both sorry
and contemptuous of him, because he had no business going to
Boston in the first place. If he had done even the slightest
research, he would have avoided the place like the plague.

But right now Scarlett, Jack is not my main priority. In the
same way birds feel the urge to gather on a washing line when
they perceive a storm in the air, my mind seems to be preparing
for catastrophe, I have no faith in anyone or anything other than
premonitions.

Perhaps it's in the blood, because two days before my father
was killed, knocked down by a motorist, - a retired man driving
on his way to a new life on the continent, my mother had a premonition. It was so realistic, that when the police came to the
door, she told them. 'It's Frank,' she said, 'you've come to tell
me he's dead.'

Poor buggers, I bet they were spooked, but she was dead
right, daddy was dead.

My mother occupies my mind all the time now, she slips into
my thoughts and drifts as effortlessly as a ghost through my

dreams, there is no obstacle she cannot surmount in her quest to accompany me. I feel riddled with guilt for not achieving the things she so badly wanted for me and somehow all the money I've accumulated just don't compensate for no degree, no letters after my name and no respectability.

Guilt was the main ingredient of my mother's life and her recipe for living has been handed down to me. After Daddy died, she struggled from the guilt of not having told him about her dream. If only she had warned him, if, if, if.

She missed the point though - premonitions foretell what is going to happen; they don't exist to give warnings. People who escape disasters, like say a train crash, due to a traffic jam or whatever, aren't touched by the supernatural, just by plain good luck.

I'm frightened Scarlett, because I know something terrible is going to happen and I'm powerless to do anything about it. All I can think about are the consequences when Jack finds out. Fear and guilt are mopping up every drop of joy. I wish to God I'd never set eyes on him and given him Daisy, if the payback is to be total humiliation.

On the 11th September 2001, that boy, my son Joseph, will be twenty-one and I know Scarlett he will come looking for me, he will come searching for his identity and in the process will wreck mine.

What kind of life has he had? Was it formed in some cosy little homestead in the West of England? They are all dairy farmers down there and if he's anything like his father, he will probably be a monstrous looking cow hand with enormous hairy feet and hands. He will also be unashamedly traditional and will insist on waiting for his 21st birthday before looking for his birth mother.

And what if anything, have his adoptive parents told him? Did the woman from the CAA ever tell them about my outburst and if she did, have the parents told him? Does he think he is the product of a mother who ran off after discovering she couldn't handle the result of her fun? When he comes looking, will it be with a heart riddled with hate and loathing, or is he one of those people you hear about, who spend their entire childhood obsessed with the mother who gave them up? These are questions whose answers I do not want to know. I don't ever want to see my son again; just looking into his face would tear my soul apart.

I hope he is happy and that his adoptive parents have found joy with him, but I don't want him tracking me down. I don't want the responsibility for breaking his dreams just as surely as he will shatter mine, because if he finds me, I will have no control. If he insists on searching for the mother who does not want to be found, he will find the father and the truth about his conception, because I have paid the price long enough for hiding the ape. The pretence will end with his son. In finding me Scarlett, he will find a truth that he will regret forever. If only there was some telepathic way I could warn him to leave well alone.

Life in the 21st century is hard Scarlett, especially for women even though we are constantly being told that we have it all. You didn't live to see it and I know you wouldn't have given a shit, but we got the vote and the right to divorce and to even enter the professions.

Even equal pay for equal work arrived eventually, (well in theory anyway) and in exchange for equality, all women had to do was surrender their entire peace of mind forever. It seems to me that we can't win. Women who stay at home get called lazy parasites; even though cooking and feeding, never mind scraping shit off backsides, curtains and carpets makes up the best part of their day. On the other hand women who go out to work are heartless home wreckers, rearing broods of potential vandals and muggers.

Right now girls are taking the boys on at their own game and are thrashing them; but their good grades aren't seen as self advancement, they are viewed as an attempt to crush boy's egos and nick their jobs. According to all the right wing rags, girls working hard at school are driving boys to distraction, causing them to seek refuge in gross behaviour, like duffing their teachers up and pissing in telephone boxes.

And on top of all this Scarlett, the biggest crime women of the 21st century can commit is to break the new number one commandment, 'Thou shalt not grow old.' Fat guts, backsides and thighs are signs of the new infidel. Woe to the woman who turns her cheek to the face-lift, bum lift and all gravity defying lifts in general.

This Scarlett is the climate of the new millennium. When Georgia fell and the Yankee troops took over the Old South, a new civilization arrived as the old one disappeared with the wind. Sometimes, it feels to me as if the Western world is going through some kind of reconstruction. The old ways are dying and good riddance to most of them, but nobody knows what is coming in their place.

There are times when I'd like to put my head on Jack's knee and ask him to take over, but I can't; I can't be seen to be dependent, to shelve responsibility. Men have always got on because they are prepared to fight dirty, but the difference is, they are usually admired for it.

Jack worked hard and still works hard at his business, from the start he was determined to be successful. It wasn't just luck. He knew from the very day he set foot in London, that he would never end his days in a piss stained hostel taking shit from a navvy. He worked hard and cheated like all builders do, but he never lost sight of himself. Jack can, and frequently does walk into bars all over south London and is greeted like a friend by the very people he diddled and cheated on. Few people have a bad word to say for him. They know all his tricks, but they also know that if they were in his position they would have done the same. Jack knows the unwritten rules of the building trade by heart and he has never broken them, never tried an honest quote when a bent one was called for. He has played by the rules because they are flexible ones made to be bent and broken and he has emerged a respected man, admired for his good business sense, and the fact that he is a family man with a wife and child and a smile for everyone.

Such an option was never open to me. I was every bit as determined as Jack, I knew right back when I was eighteen, that success would be the only thing to redeem me from myself, but when you're fighting against the odds you have to play dirty. Smiles and charm do not work in the same way for women.

Men see you as a push over and other women see you for what you are, a wolf in stiletto's.

Writing all this stuff is very sickening Scarlett, because it was the same for you, proof that the world hasn't really changed so much. After all, when you took over old Frank's business after the war and set about calling in all the debts owed, you became a hated woman, but if Frank had had half the gumption to do what you did, people would have said. 'Now that's what I call a man, you've got to hand it to him, he knows what he wants and he goes for it.'

All those years ago when I lived with Lesley, Fiona and Sally, I too was fired with determination, I went to college to fetch three decent A' Levels, all with the aim of becoming a barrister and specialising in family law. And it wasn't easy! Travelling every day on a tube too overcrowded to study on and going on to college three evenings a week after a full day at work. But the cherry on the dunghill was trying to contend with Lesley. She was furious when I started studying and declined to frequent the pub with her. She used to say, 'You're a fucking sad twat Sinead, you're gonna end up with square eyes and varicose veins in your arse with all this sitting about reading and squinting.'

I didn't care about her insults, but I found her constant prattling on irritating, when all I wanted to do was read or simply think. At the beginning, I found the English classes at college tedious, because although I loved the books, I couldn't stand all the discussions and post mortems accompanying them. It's hard to explain it, but I felt too experienced, too jaded to be surprised by anything, and the sickening optimism of the other students, made me cringe.

Mr Rigby was the main lecturer; he was old and highly excitable. I used to sit at the front of the class and on more than one occasion I had to wipe a shower of spit off my nose and out of my eyes, the result of his excitement as he said things like, 'At this point, can't you just feel Shakespeare reeling from shock at Othello's reaction?' I would be sat there thinking, 'Hang on a moment, Shakespeare wrote the bloody story, so how the hell can he be surprised or shocked by anything your man does?'

Looking around the class, most people's faces looked bright with interest, (or in the case of a few Thai's, just plain bloody perplexed.) It was only me who had such a nasty, dogmatic view. In a way Scarlett, I think the irritation was similar to the one you felt when you finally snapped with Ashley, when he referred to Melanie as a dream and you said, 'always dreams never common sense.'

Mr Rigby was ill one night and we had a supply lecturer in his place - a foul specimen of a man. He wasn't in the classroom five minutes before he told a story about some Irish writer who had slated his Cambridge college. 'I was most put out,' he said in a really smarmy voice. 'Nobody likes to hear their college being trashed, do they?' I had my head down and I remember thinking, what a long winded way to go about letting us know he is a Cambridge man. As I raised my head, I caught his eye, and I knew he knew what I was thinking, and both of us flushed red.

He got his own back though, he asked for some examples of heroines in twentieth century literature. I volunteered you, Scarlett, and do you know what that greasy gorm did? He laughed at me. He said 'Well I can see why you've had to return to college, Gone with the Wind isn't literature, it can't be it's American.' That got a ripple of laughter from the class and encouraged the pompous piss to strike again, 'Anyway,' he said. 'I can't think there are many women who would want to be like Scarlett O'Hara, didn't her husband ditch her in the end?'

I couldn't bear the way he dismissed you Scarlett, it struck at my heart. I wanted to leap up and call him an obscenity. I didn't though, because back then, I might have been nice, but I was also mighty gormless. However, I didn't let him get away with it entirely. I said 'Well I may be wrong but it seems to me Scarlett O'Hara had everything she wanted, money, a waistline and independence, so why should she need a husband?'

This time the class were with me, especially two seriously hefty girls who sat suspiciously close together in the back row.

I loved all the books we covered, so did Lesley; in fact I reckon she got more fun out of them than I did. She was forever picking my books up and flicking through them, taking the piss and quoting Othello in a heavy northern accent calling him lad, and saying things like 'Now then Othello lad, stop acting like a twat and look after tha tart of thous.'

Looking back, I realise now what good days they were at Acton College. It was hard work but a lot of fun - God I sound like Granny Grunt, reminiscing about how marvellous it was to starve during the war. But I do remember happy times there,- old Mr Duffy who taught criminal law, yet didn't look capable of parking on a yellow line, and Miss Hobbs, the economics lecturer, dry as a bone and not half as meaty. Supply and demand and market forces were her mantras. Of all the lectures I attended, it was the dully delivered economics ones that made the most impact on me. When some people take their first sip of alcohol they remember it as 'the day I arrived home.' Well when Miss Hobbs droned on about division of labour, the going rate, half the class yawned and the rest wrote letters home, but me - I felt like the alcoholic- I had truly arrived home.

I listened avidly to her every word and as she spoke, the society we lived in, the society that was the early 80's began to take shape before my eyes. I was no longer just an unthinking clerk in a building society, totting figures up, waiting for pay day. Suddenly I began to understand what all those cash books represented, the necessity of interest rates; the role of borrowers and lenders and cash reserves. For the first time in my life I looked at the bigger picture, the monetary needs of a country, the meaning of a manufacturing base, making to sell, the point of fresh money in the system, as against the tired old money, pedalled round by the service industries. Things suddenly had a purpose to them.

I suspect Miss Hobbs was probably Hitler's au pair in terms of being to the right, but she really saw what was coming and taught us, her students to dance in tune.

You see Scarlett by the 1980's we didn't just have the vote. We had a woman Prime Minister. Mrs Thatcher, the milk snatcher, and unlike every male minister before her Mrs Thatcher didn't agree with taking the bull by the horns, she took it by the balls and actually milked it so to speak.

'Face the facts dears,' Miss Hobbs announced one night. 'Collective bargaining and restricted markets are out, the free market economy has arrived and it's here to stay.' One or two guys whose dads 'have always voted labour', tried to shout her down, quoted all sorts of shite about workers unite, but she told them they were spitting in the wind, they were to go home and look up a new word for homework, - 'reality.'

I didn't and still don't know much about Marx, Trotsky or any of that gang, and I didn't know much about Thatcher either other than the fact she had an exceptionally irritating voice, but Miss Hobbs's description, of what she perceived to be the Thatcherite way rang a bell with me. Perhaps it was my lack of lateral thinking, but supply and demand, and the freedom to run your own business the way you see fit, struck me as plain common sense and totally linked.

I tried to raise some of the points we covered in class with Lesley, but talk about a closed shop. She wouldn't hear a good word about Thatcher, said the woman was mad, creating chaos up North, 'Calls herself a fucking Prime Minister, prime arsehole is more like it, do you have any idea what she's doing to the miners and steel workers?'

And I replied all primly, 'Yes, but if the mines and the steel works aren't productive, what is the point in keeping them open?'

That got Lesley really mad, she said, 'The bloody point of keeping them open, is so that people have jobs, if a pit shuts down, where do, the miners go?'

And oh God, I can't believe it now, but I said, 'They can move, go South; get a job elsewhere.'

Lesley went ballistic, she practically danced with anger, 'Are you a fucking moron O'Connell, how do you suppose a Yorkshire miner could ever afford a house down South, and just what job have you got lined up for him, apart from dishing out shite in a bucket in some crappy takeaway. You're a typical fucking southerner with your head packed straight up your arse.'

Well I got the message; Lesley was not Mrs T's biggest fan.

Actually Sally and Fiona didn't like her either, but the truth is I did. I liked the way she took a hard edged broom and cleared out all the old corners of Britain so thoroughly. To me, she was saying, 'If you want to get somewhere, get up off your arse and make the move,' to my friends she was saying, 'You can exploit who you want just so long as you are smart enough to get away with it.'

The truth is Scarlett, they were concerned for others, and I was concerned for me. I took Thatcher's words to mean 'no matter how you do it, if you are successful, the ends will always justify the means.'

'The ends will always justify the means'. The words floated off the page and danced in front of Phoenix's eyes. She put her pen down and slowly read again the paragraph she had just written. The words were self explanatory; she had searched and she had truly found. There had never been any distinction in her mind between money and success, money meant success and success meant money, the two justified each other, it was as simple as that. It was almost too much to take. Leaning forward she cupped her chin in her hand and closed her eyes, picturing herself back in the old fashioned college, with its concrete floors and tiled walls and faint smell of disinfectant.

She felt her eyelashes flutter slightly, as she screwed her eyes tighter, in a bid to summon to her memory, pictures of her fellow students. One by one they reappeared, some she could put a name to; others remained what they had been all those years ago, just faces. In the midst of her past acquaintances, she caught a brief fluttering image of her youthful self laden down with books and excitement.

Yes, the return to education had been exhilarating, but the facts were; something had persuaded her, that there was another, better route, to take. She hadn't drifted aimlessly into business, something more than a nerve had been touched, the moment she had started studying economics, commerce in some form or other, was her calling. The pulse of the Kerry publican lurked beneath her skin and circumstances might have kept it at bay, but the moment a fitting chance arose, all prospects of being a smart demure Kentish lawyer were buried forever.

She debated for a moment whether to continue with the letter. Night was sliding into day and she knew that she would feel wrecked later; but this was a letter that had to be finished while the memory of those far off times were stirred and ready to be pinned to paper. She picked up her pen and continued to write.

Opportunity is like knock down ginger. The game kids play when they knock on doors and tear away before someone answers, it doesn't hang round for an answer, you have to be there waiting for it.

And you of all people Scarlett know exactly what I mean by opportunity. You took the opportunity to steal your sister's fiancé because you had to and you had to do it quickly, or the chance would have melted before your eyes. By acting smart you saved your home and integrity and into the bargain you won Rhett - mind you as I read your story now, I'm not so certain Rhett was a bargain!

I saw an opportunity and I went for it and I didn't waste time questioning or fretting about how I'd have to spend the rest of my life, excusing myself. Half way through lectures, there used to be a fifteen minute break and most students congregated in the small scruffy canteen that sold warm tea and out of date donuts. I used to sit with a mixed group of people, some from Hong Kong, an Irish girl called Maggie and a couple of locals. Sometimes Poppy, a tiny Filipino woman who was one of the college cleaners, would rest her broom and chat with us to practise her English. She was only in her twenties, but she looked worn out, pushing a rickety old trolley laden down with brushes and cleaning stuff, like a bag lady on the lookout for a sandwich. Her colleague was an old doll from Clare called Patsy.

Although Poppy looked jaded she was actually incredibly upbeat and positive. She loved the cinema and must have spent every penny she earned watching film after film. She enjoyed them all; I don't recall her ever seeing a 'turkey,' but that was typical of her to see credit in everything and everyone. She loved London even though she had a crap job, worked like a dog and lived like a pauper. I don't know what her real name was, or how she got to be called Poppy but it was a marvellous name for her because she was bright and vibrant just like the poppies that pop up in a field or along the roadside and dazzle and amaze with their colour and energy.

Patsy also looked knackered but in a different kind of way. Poppy's tiredness was from sheer overwork; Patsy's was to do with attitude. She was thoroughly pissed off with life, always moaning about 'the old bastard' at home. The old bastard was her husband Con, who had had a stroke some months previously, which had left him virtually incapacitated. She had no sympathy for him which made me suspect that Con may have been a brute in his mobile days. Patsy must have felt he was getting his payback.

'Hello Patsy,' I'd say. 'How's Con doing?' and she'd reply.

'I left the pooka in his bed moaning; I've spent the entire day fetching and carrying for him, he makes no effort at all, you know, there are others who've had strokes and don't carry on so.'

She sounded tough and harsh but she wasn't, just defeated and dejected. A few months after I started college I came in one evening and there was no Patsy, Con had died in his sleep. When she did return, she was sad and red eyed. 'Poor old divil,' she said. 'He wasn't so bad.'

What a thorough whitewash job death does. Why speak no ill of the dead if they were evil in life? If I heard that the ape had died, I'd do the Can - Can on his grave.

Poor Patsy, she spent a lifetime dominated by a bad egg and when he died, guilt stopped her from jumping for joy. She continued in the job and gave up complaining about Con, and took to talking about her guts instead. She'd poke the broom under the table as if seeing a rat off, rattle it about bruising our ankles, then lean against the wall tired out by her exertions, and say something like 'God, I've terrible guts, it must be the apples I ate earlier.'

One February night as Patsy discussed her guts; Poppy joined us. She said the firm that employed her were extremely short staffed, and she'd been doing extra hours all over the place, in fact they were in danger of folding, because there was too much work, and not enough staff.

And do you know what I did? I told her I wouldn't mind doing a few hours here and there. I don't why I said it and looking back now, I still don't have a clue what prompted me.

Poppy was shocked, 'But you a student,' she said.

I said 'Yes but I also need extra money.'

Poppy was incredulous, 'But you get job anywhere,' she replied totally confused at what I was suggesting.

I'm surprised she didn't add 'Miss Sinead'. She seriously thought all students were superior to her, not in a chip on the shoulder sort of way, just as a matter of fact. My big venture almost never got started because my biggest obstacle was convincing Poppy that I wasn't pissing about. In the end I convinced her, and she said she would give my name and number to her boss.

I don't know why I pursued Poppy because as she said there were plenty of jobs I could have got, shop jobs, theatre bar assistants, all much easier and more glamorous than cleaning, but something just seemed to push me forward. I certainly wasn't being helpful. It must have been some kind of intuition. I needed money; that was a serious factor. I knew whatever I ended up doing, money would be critically important because when all the crap is cut from the stalk, the fact remains money alone buys self-respect. I hate people who say 'Money can't buy love,' of course it bloody well can't, but it can buy some pretty good imitations of it, just ask Hugh Grant.

And equally I hate people who say 'I'd rather be poor and happy than rich and miserable,' as if the two were mutually exclusive. They point to people like Marilyn Monroe and say 'Look, she had it all, looks and money, but it didn't make her happy,' but they forget the millions of ugly bastards just as depressed and despairing who have to cope with the added crap of poverty. Whenever Lesley was down she used to say 'Life is a shit sandwich, the more bread you get the less shit you have to swallow,' and I knew she was right. I was determined to get as much dough as I could. I can only describe my need for money being akin to a raging thirst. It had to be satisfied.

Lesley, Sally and Fiona pissed themselves laughing when they heard I was cleaning, Sally used to call out as I was leaving the house, 'Get your baggy stockings on Sinead, you must look the part.'

And Lesley would comment as I flopped into bed, 'Oi, Miss Mopp, you've forgotten your fucking curlers.' Oh they were so funny; I would have split my sides laughing if I didn't have a sense of humour. I did two evenings a week up at the college, plus Saturday mornings at an industrial estate, cleaning the offices of a fabric wholesaler.

At the college I was given the Science and Technology rooms, wiping surfaces, sweeping floors and brushing up wood shavings and saw dust. It used to astound me when I saw all the mess made by the creation of some little boxes and key rings in Technology. One look convinced me that the students would have been better off cutting out the middle man and buying some kit out of Woolworth's.

Cleaning those rooms really hardened my attitude, picking up the snotty tissues and gum left behind by fat lazy arses. Talking of snot, a frizzy haired girl at the college threw her plastic cup on the floor right in front of me one day, just tossed it down, like she was the Queen of Sheba and not her dog. Her friend looked dead embarrassed and said 'You didn't have to do that, right in front of that poor girl,' and do you know what frizzy knob said?

'If there wasn't crap on the floor, the likes of her wouldn't have a job.'

It's taken as read doctors speak to you as if you're not there, but at least they have earned a white coat. The sight of that heap bursting out of her denims trying to be as good infuriated me, I considered for a moment letting Poppy down and rearranging frizzy's face with my broom.

It was odd but students at the college and workers in the fabric factory both seemed strangely put out at the sight of a young girl being a cleaner. W.C. Fields apparently said that he forgot to thank the woman who drove him to drink, and likewise I've never thanked the factory workers, the students, or Lesley, all of whom drove me to success. All their nasty comments went straight into my memory bank, and unknowingly, those begrudgers shaped my future business more than they could have dreamt possible. When I eventually started out on my own I knew that to make it big. I had to break the stereotype associated with cleaners and cleaning. I had to break the mould, in fact to use modern jargon I had to make cleaning sexy.

Why not, everything else is, even the BBC describes certain wars as 'sexy' so imagine what you can do with a business that involves rubber gloves and lots of beating.

Initially I was paid strictly by the book, but as the hours increased and the jobs became more chaotic in terms of location I began to get paid in hand. Thatcher had opened up all the catering and cleaning contracts in the health and education services, and the competition for the work became something of a free for all. The cleaning services at the college in Acton were operated by a small firm and once a week on a Saturday afternoon, I use to call in at a grubby little office in a back street near Shepherds Bush market to collect my wages and it made me smile to see a cleaning company being run from such dirty premises. The owner was a bloke called Nick Grainger, who fancied himself so much, that he chased all possible competition well away. He ran the business with the aid of a telephone, a big black diary and a couple of school exercise books. Sometimes he'd be jabbering away on the phone and I'd hear him say 'Just hang on a mo, I'm getting your details up on the computer now,' and he would wink at me, make a gagging gesture with his hand around his throat, then open his tatty black diary up and say, 'Ah yeah, here we are, your details are just coming up as we speak.'

One Saturday afternoon, he asked me if I would be 'an absolute doll,' and hang around for a short time. 'I've got to see this geezer Sinead about a booking' he said, 'Would you mind holding on a few minutes in case someone calls in? Oh and if anyone phones just say I'm on the other line.' (What other line, the whirly gig?).

I knew bloody well his appointment was with the bookies and the pub. He was the new breed of entrepreneur that was spreading like a nasty form of herpes in the early 80's. He was clever enough to see that de - regulation meant money but not astute enough to realise slick talk and promises have to be backed up. Another giveaway about his definite demise was that although he dressed like a typical 80's man with his pin striped shirt and braces, he was a seventies slob at heart. It shone through in his estimation of women. He left that office thinking he'd impressed the little bit of skirt with his talk of other lines and bookings, and left behind his diary and entire rota system for me to peruse.

What a mess. I couldn't believe he was running a business from the crazy system he had in place. Tacky bits of paper stuck here and there, memos to find missing names and addresses. In his appointment diary there were several cases of names without addresses and vice versa, they sprang out of the page because of the big panicky question marks accompanying them. He was getting work through pure fluke and probably losing more through sheer disorganisation. As I looked round the tatty office with its out of date calendars, dust and heaps of paper, single line phone and diary, I realised I could run the show a thousand times better. I felt like you did Scarlett, the first time you set eyes on Frank Kennedy's book keeping, and realized there was a hole in his business skills bigger than the black one in Calcutta.

At the back of the office was a musty little store room stacked full with boxes of cleaning materials and hired equipment. The idea that I could run a business made me tingle, it seemed too enormous to be true, and it might have galloped straight through my mind and out the other side had the phone not rung.

It was a nursing home, all the way from Clapham. They wanted someone round for a quote as a matter of urgency because they had exhausted Yellow Pages south of the river, and were now trawling the north in the hope of finding a company cheap enough and available.

'No problem,' I said. 'Tuesday morning is not possible as we are rather busy but I can squeeze you in on Wednesday afternoon.' I wrote the name and address carefully on the back of my cheque book, and told the woman on the other end of the line that Phoenix Ashton would be coming at 2.45 pm sharp.

When I put the receiver down my hands were shaking, I couldn't believe what I had just done. I realised instantly that I would have no idea what to quote, so I searched old Nicks desk and eventually in one of his grubby school exercise books I found a kind of schedule with rough estimates of prices and staff allocation.. I cursed him for not having a photocopier, tore a couple of centre pages out of one of his exercise books and began copying at speed.

When he came back, he asked if there had been any calls, I said 'Oh, just one wrong number'. He was flushed and sentimental from the drink and over profuse with his thanks. More importantly, he told me not to hesitate if I wanted more work. In return I told him that I'd be more than happy to man his phone any Saturday.

After he gave me my wages, I set off immediately for Oxford Street to find something cool and business like for Phoenix Ashton to wear for her business appointment on Wednesday. So, in a nutshell Scarlett, apart from a few near nervous breakdowns that is how it all started. In effect, Nick Grainger's office practically doubled as mine for the first few weeks. He advertised, paid the rates and the rent and I diverted his calls and took his custom.

When I got home later that Saturday night, I told Lesley I had a terrible headache and wouldn't be going up West with her. Instead I stayed at home and tried to decipher the notes I had made earlier that afternoon. The only way I would be able to get the contract would be by seriously undercutting the likes of Grainger. I would have to operate to begin with on 'loss leaders.' Miss Hobbs at the college would have been proud of me. I knew I could do it, it's hard to explain but there was just a definite belief that I was on to something good.

During my lunch hour on Monday I went to a printer and ordered a set of business cards before going into Smith's and buying my first ever diary, a desk one for appointments.

I didn't say a word to Lesley or the others, telling anyone about a big idea before its time, is the surest way of nipping it in the bud - besides, I didn't trust Lesley. She had already told people at work that I was cleaning; you should have seen the looks I got; you would have thought she had told them I was on the game. Sue the supervisor was very concerned, she took me aside confidentially and said that if I was struggling financially I ought to have a word with Mr Roberts, my work was good and she knew he would be sympathetic to a pay rise for a good worker like me. I assured Sue that this cleaning lark was just to help out a woman I'd got to know at college, and she seemed a little more comfortable with the idea. Nevertheless I took her advice, saw Mr Roberts, put up a good case and got a raise. I needed every penny I could get hold off, for as the conscientious little boy said as he peed in the ocean 'Every drop really does count.'

On the big day of my interview, I woke up to a cheerful sun filled morning; the omens certainly looked good. I felt in top form but I had to feign a downbeat pained expression as I told Lesley that I had bad guts, and wouldn't be going into work. She gave me a dead suspicious look and I knew I was right not to trust her. She had already spotted my new suit, the one I had got from C&A on Saturday and she had been on it in a flash,

'Got an interview coming up have you Miss Mop?'

I told her, I was going to a cousins wedding in a few weeks time and she said, 'you'll look like the bloody registrar in that get up.' The 80's were the era Scarlett for power dressing; it was suddenly the 'in' thing for women to sport shoulder pads, wear suits and walk as if they had a pair of bollocks to contend with. I chose a pin stripe one, because the formality of it aged me. I could pass for someone in her mid twenties, not as the twenty year old; with a three year old child somewhere that I knew I really was.

Sneaking out to the printers to collect my business cards, I felt certain I'd bump into Sue or Mr Roberts, lose my job, flop my interview and end up like the drunk who stood beside his broken down car with the placard 'Pis'ton broke.' The printer showed me the specimen and my heart nearly burst with excitement and fear when I read the words, 'Phoenix Ashton, Cleaning Enterprises, Commercial, Industrial and Domestic, Phone or Fax for a free quote.'

The woman who interviewed me was pure management; Celia Smith was her name. She gave the impression that she had been in situ for donkey's years, but I found out she'd only been in the job for a matter of weeks. She was history as well by the time my contract came into effect. For some reason I'd been expecting a matron, a stout old woman like Aunty Phil in a uniform, so it threw me, when I saw she was young and dressed in a suit rather like the one I was wearing.

She was very business -like, concerned purely with money, hours and insurance. She didn't ask once about quality of work. I think I must have thrown her too, perhaps she'd been expecting Ena Sharples. She was impressed with the quote I gave and when she asked me where some of my current contracts were based; I reeled off Nick Grainger's client list. I asked her how many references she would like, and the fact I bought up the subject, seemed to be enough for her to dismiss it. It is a fact; nothing hides a lie like the truth or something that at least sounds candid.

I had already taken the precaution of writing two testimonials on headed paper from both the college and the fabric factory. That was easy, because cleaners always have a viable excuse to be somewhere where they shouldn't be. Most employers put it down to conscientiousness, usually its plain nosiness. I got the contract; and a warning. She told me she had been forced to terminate the contract of her current cleaning company after she discovered some of their techniques. They used coloured water in place of bleach and disinfectant; and rather than apply polish to furniture they sprayed it in the air. And what was more; on three occasions they had left the lavatories like skating rinks, causing several of the elderly residents to do a Torvill and Dean routine; before suing the management when the applause had died down.

I shook my head in disgust and made a mental note to go easy with the dilution. The secret was obviously not to be too greedy. I got the contract, with three weeks to spare before it came into effect. As I left I gave Celia my card and told her that Phoenix Enterprises would shortly be opening an office south of the river.

I walked slowly and sedately down the drive, but as soon as I cleared the hedge I punched the air and shouted, 'I've done it,' and just missed colliding with two elderly women who were approaching the driveway with the aid of Zimmer frames, like snails returning home. They looked at each other in shock; then one of them pointed at me and said 'You're not the only one; we're not all going to die wondering.'

I was *very* shocked.

A sense of urgency nearing panic seized me in the following days. I needed a loan Scarlett and nobody knows better than you just how stressful that job is! But there was no Rhett Butler to ask and no pathetic Ashley Wilkes to shake his head sympathetically. Mom didn't have any money and frankly it would have been easier to teach a horse how to break dance, than get money out of my brothers or sisters. If there had been the remotest possibility that one of them would have lent me the money, I would have taken all the crap they wanted to dish out, but although I was pretty certain of getting a lecture, I was absolutely certain that I'd never get the money. They were not up to chances.

There was nothing for it but to go to the bank.

So much rubbish Scarlett is talked about pure hard graft being the sole reason for success in business. But you can work until your legs drop off, but without a tiny splash of luck you'll have piss all to show for it, other than a limp. I've worked hard Scarlett for my success, but I'd never have got started if luck hadn't turned up. And the first place it made its appearance was on Acton High Street. The minute I set foot in the bank all my confidence deserted me.

I expected a grey haired old man to pat me on the head and say 'Come back when you've grown up,' or 'Bring your Dad and I'll explain the tricky bits to him.'

Mr Stubbs was slightly grey but he wasn't old. He listened carefully, made suggestions but more importantly, he gave me the money! And he didn't compile a list a mile long of does and don'ts, agree to it reluctantly, or warn me of the consequences if I ballsed it all up. He just inspired me; he said 'I'm going to see that you get this loan because you've got the confidence to ask for what you need. Only a fool thinks success comes cheap.'

So with the loan, I bought the most basic equipment, the big stuff like vacuum cleaners I could hire and I didn't bother with detergents because I reckoned I could use Grainger's for the time being. I booked a 'crash' driving test which I passed on my first attempt, even though I put the windscreen wipers on every time I meant to indicate and that of course lead to my biggest expenditure. An old yellow variant estate car. I needed the car Scarlett because of the equipment I'd have to hurl to Clapham. I remember reading how you were so desperate for transport you even hired that wife killer Archie to take you to your mills. I didn't know many wife killers round Acton, I sort of knew a few guys who fancied themselves as lady-killers, but I don't think running a cache of mops and buckets round London would have done much for their image.

I was so caught up with everything that I left it months before phoning Mom. She sounded very down. Looking back now, I realise that she must have been lonely because at this point she lived alone, James (my brother) had finally married his long-standing girlfriend.

In spite of all my protestations about never going home again I did return briefly for the Christmas of 1982. Alice still dished out the leper treatment and Eileen was home by this point from South Africa. She was of course informed about my atrocity and meted out a second helping of Alice's recommended treatment. Sitting at the dinner table on Christmas day, I caught her giving me several appraising looks. I remember looking at her head and thinking how hugely reminiscent of a chicken, she was. You know the way a hens puts its head to one side and no matter how inquisitive it tries to look; there is no escaping, it's as daft as a brush. She had exploited the blacks but still felt up to judging me. But then she was born with a talent I am actually very envious off. She can change her mind on a whim and things she once condemned, become not just acceptable but almost mandatory, once she, Eileen O'Connell establishes a desire for them.

Her husband Harry though, was nothing to be envious of. He was an ignorant, sanctimonious, moralising twerp of a man, akin to something you'd expect to creep out of an orange. In the same way dog owners seem drawn against their will, to stare at their pooch as it defecates; well Harry had that effect on me. He was unbearable but I just had to look at him and enjoy my disgust. He saw himself as Kent's answer to Einstein and nothing gave him more pleasure than the Christmas quiz shows, he was first off the block every time with the wrong answer.

His general knowledge or lack of it might have been amusing, but his politics weren't. He only had to open his trap and instantly you found yourself thinking Alf Garnett was a fairly reasonable kind of guy after all. They had a young child, a boy called Julian; the reason for their return to Britain and for that Christmas at least, they still had slaves, Mom and me. Aunty Phil had been invited as well, but thank God she was torturing the natives in Lourdes instead and so was unable to come.

The Christmas hit that year was 'A Winters Tale sang by David Essex, a guy my best friend Clare had set her cap on, a few years previously. It made me go cold every time I heard it.

It tells a truth no one likes to acknowledge - no matter how much the Mother Teresa's of this world, stress the importance and dignity of the individual, each of us is inconsequential when set against the enormity of the world and its affairs.

It's a fact, you can be sitting drinking a cup of tea, or arranging a vase of flowers and in that instant; somebody's world is being ripped apart, through death, betrayal or disease. In world terms, what with wars and starvation, what the ape did to me was inconsequential, but for me it was the ultimate, yet nobody was going to go banging on the doors of the U.N on my account.

You know for all its hype and crass goodwill, it strikes me that Christmas dishes out more than its fair share of tragedy and stress. It's the human equivalent of tying a number of Siamese cats and Rottweiler dogs together, and saying 'get on with it.' Everybody is shocked at the blood and guts spluttered everywhere and yet they have no right to be. What do they expect, after putting together those who should be kept well apart?

I couldn't wait to return to London. Thankfully I had signed up for work on New Year's Eve. Lesley had also returned early as well and we spent the day at work stuffing ourselves with chocolate, totting up a few passbooks and passing and receiving obscene notes around the office. Later that night we went down to Trafalgar Square to listen to Big Ben chime in the new year of 1983. I shivered as I listened and each 'bong' struck at my heart. I told myself that this would be the year things really changed.

Now, when I think of Mom alone in that house, it tears at my heart, but back in 1983, it never occurred to me she might be lonely. She asked if I was still going to college and I said 'Yes,' but the truth was I had packed the lectures in. I now went purely as a cleaner. I couldn't tell Mom that of course, it would have confirmed her worst nightmare and destroyed her. I intended to keep my business a secret until it was so established that its sheer success; would compensate for its lack of respectability.

I couldn't keep it a secret though from Fiona, Sally and Lesley. I had to explain why I wanted the telephone answering cum fax machine I had just bought, plugged in instead of the little plastic post war cream one we were all used to. They were shocked when I told them my big idea.

Sally said 'Oh Sinead, don't you think your aiming low, I mean you've got really good O'levels,' and Fiona chipped in with.

'My family would be furious, if I did menial work, they didn't even want me in the family restaurant, that's why they sent me to London.' They took it so seriously; they were like parents, working class ones at that, all they could think about was security and stability.

Sally was the worst, 'But what if it all fails,' she whined, 'Imagine how awful that would be and you'd be hard pressed to get another job as good as the one you've got now.'

I tried to explain a new era was upon us, an era of enterprise, a chance for women to be bosses and not bossed about, but it kept coming full circle round to, 'Yes but cleaning is women's work.'

They couldn't see beyond it, they couldn't grasp cleaning was merely the vehicle. Of course Lesley as usual came skidding succinctly to the point, she stood there, arms folded and said. 'Shut it, you lot, Sinead's going to make her fortune shovelling shit, so make space.' They all spoke shite, and since I'd started the cleaning routine I'd got pretty good at recognising it, so it didn't bother me.

But their reaction to my enterprise was nothing compared to their shock, horror and fury when I asked them to give me a hand, just for a few weeks until I got staff sorted out properly.

Lesley was adamant, 'I'm not cleaning up anyone's crap,' she said, 'and that's definite.'

Sally on the other hand was mortified, in fact she almost wept. But Fiona, perhaps because she was sorry for me eventually said, 'I don't mind helping for a week or so.' Of course what she really meant was, 'I'll help for the short time it takes Sinead to realise she's making a complete arse of herself.'

Eventually, the others softened under her influence, and my wheedling and the three of them helped me to distribute flyers all over Acton and beyond. Newsagents, pubs, nursing homes, schools even churches, all got a mail shot telling them about 'Phoenix Ashton Enterprises.'

If they had all responded I would have died on my feet, but they didn't. Some did though, and eventually against all good advice and common sense, I gave in my notice at the building society. I turned pro with my three live in helpers, plus Poppy and Patsy and my yellow Variant Estate. 'Sink or swim and all that jazz,' was my motto.

But I didn't sink. I learnt to swim like a fish. In fact I took on board all the attributes of a great white shark. I was fearless.

Love Phoenix

Chapter Nineteen

Not once in the weeks following the bizarre visit to provincial England, did Phoenix raise the subject of Boston. She neither teased, questioned or reproached Jack about it but disinterest rather than empathy lay behind such an uncharacteristic show of benevolence.

From the moment she arrived back in London, only one thing obsessed her, and that was finding the opportunity to write to Scarlett. She only became aware of all not being well around her after she had finally put pen to paper.

Boston had been no tea party for Jack, since going there, something had changed and he was at a lost to explain what it was. Rationally he could count himself lucky, not only had he boosted his portfolio and attracted further offers of work, he had also made serious money. Neither gave him any satisfaction.

He found himself in the unique position of analysing what had passed, questioning things he had said and done. Unlike his father who had treasured all things historic, Jack belonged to the progressive school of thought. His mantra was 'Live today and to hell with what's gone,' therefore this new tendency disturbed him, though not half as much as Daisy's request to go back to that 'funny place.'

Jack Keane was no child psychologist, but even he had to question, why his daughter had been happier without her toys and decent food in a dreary backwater, than she was in her own warm and comfortable home.

When Phoenix finally got around to noticing Jack's more subdued demeanour, she put it down to him feeling shamefaced at having orchestrated such a debacle of a business trip. At first his discomfiture gave her some satisfaction. It was good she thought, to see that egg had replaced the usual shit eating grin on his face. But as the days passed, irritation replaced satisfaction and she questioned his right to such a personality change. Why, she asked herself, does he have to be such a perfectionist? Why couldn't he just accept he'd made a duff call and get on with it?

She certainly wasn't going to run after him and pamper his ego. He had Bleasdale coming to dinner in less than a week, and if he wanted her co-operation he had better get his act together. She certainly wasn't going to chase him.

But Bleasdale didn't come to dinner, because two nights before the event Jack was awakened by a telephone call in the early hours. Danny was dead. He had returned to the house after milking and had died instantly. A massive heart attack. Jack broke the news to Phoenix with his back turned to her. Before he uttered a word, she knew the news was bad and she begged God to prove her wrong. But He didn't.

Jack's words echoed in her ears and a sheer wave of grief and shock flooded through her as she came to terms with the fact that a good and kind ally was gone. She put her hand out to Jack, but he ignored it; instead he made straight for the wardrobe, which he opened, taking out a sports holdall.

'I will fly out this morning,' he said.

Instantly she ran to him. 'All of us Jack,' she said. 'All of us will go, I'll phone Carolyn; she can manage for a few days.'

He didn't even look at her; he just continued folding clothes into the bag. She pulled his arm and repeated 'We will all go.'

He pulled the zip shut and finally faced her, albeit only for a moment. 'No,' he said, 'there is no need for that; I'd prefer you to stay here and look after Daisy.'

She pulled his arm again more urgently until he had no option but to turn around and face her again. 'Are you mad?' she said. 'How could I stay here while Danny is being buried, you know how I loved him.'

He picked the bag up and looked at her with a face completely devoid of emotion. 'No,' he said. 'I can't say that I do, as I recall, every time we visited him, I had to drag you kicking and screaming.'

His coolness baffled her and it took a moment for her to realise he wasn't teasing. In fact, he was deadly serious. She ran ahead of him blocking the bedroom doorway. 'But you are wrong Jack,' she said. 'I loved Danny, it was never him I didn't want to see; you always chose my busiest times to go to Ireland.'

'Well,' he said. 'Don't worry about it, you can now attend to work uninterrupted, I'll only be gone a few days.'

She felt sick and very confused. Jack was being a bastard, he knew she loved Danny, but he seemed intent on punishing her. But she couldn't leave it, she had to go. 'Jack,' she said, 'Stop doing this to me; I want to come, please believe me.'

He put his bag down and walked across to her and for the first time he made a gesture of being comforting. He put an arm around her shoulder but she was aware that it was a calculated action rather than a natural one. 'I'm not doing anything to you, but I really want you to stay here to look after Daisy and to take care of a few things for me.'

'What sort of things?' she asked slightly mollified that he needed her help.

'Well O'Carolan for one thing, he will need pacifying that I will step in now that his latest buyer has pulled out and Bleasdale. I want you to smooth that old fucker.' She nodded her head, disappointed that the only help he wanted from her was to do with work, and walked off to awaken Daisy.

Although he insisted the tube would be quicker and more convenient she was equally adamant that she would drive him to Heathrow. He sat beside her as she drove through the early morning traffic, making the odd comment here and there. She didn't listen to him. He was talking because he thought he ought to and she detested duty.

On arrival at Heathrow, he told her to head for set down rather than short term parking and she did so, without question. She turned the engine off and he leant across and kissed her on the cheek, a dry cool kiss; the type she would inflict on someone like Aunty Phil. Jack really was over playing the duty card. He then turned to the back seat and kissed a pyjama clad Daisy who instructed him to bring back an Irish doll and one of Aunty Eileen's piglets.

'See you soon,' he said and was gone.

She watched him cross the road and enter the terminal building. Not once did he look back. That, she told herself was Jack. When he discovered her secret, he would walk away just as briskly.

She sat watching the space Jack had recently occupied, unaware of Daisy's growing restlessness. The child was tired, bored and somewhat confused. 'Why is Daddy going away?' she asked and Phoenix unwilling to talk death, made up some excuse about Jack having to see his family. She would explain it all when Jack came back. Daisy still wasn't pacified, but even her natural enthusiasm for chatter waived under Phoenix's obvious disinterest, and eventually she abandoned her questioning and took to staring out the window instead.

Phoenix looked around her at the people scurrying about. Some were obviously on business; others were there purely for leisure. They had a purpose, but she didn't. She had just driven across London in an effort to make herself feel good, and suddenly it seemed ridiculous. She should have let Jack take the tube.

She picked her bag up from the floor, opened it and took out a bottle of Coco Chanel. What she needed right now was a drink, just a small one. She was just about to put the bottle to her mouth when she heard Daisy say 'Who is that man Mommy?'

Phoenix looked up and saw a police woman standing by the wing of the car, a radio clutched to her mouth.

'Oh fuck,' she cried and quickly screwed the cap back on the bottle before flinging it to the floor. She would have driven away but her path was blocked, there was no option but to calmly open the window. The policewoman walked over and leaned down, until she was almost face to face with Phoenix.

'Aren't you aware that this is for set down only?' asked the officer aggressively, 'You've been here over fifteen minutes, you could be arrested.'

'I'm just going,' Phoenix replied defiantly and made to do up the window, but as she did so, the policewoman put her hand on it.

'Have you been drinking?' she asked suspiciously. The shocked look Phoenix returned her was genuine. In an instant she saw how close she had come to public humiliation. She looked more closely at the officer and noted the coarse, unmade up complexion and straw textured hair peeping out from under her hat. This woman would not buy any excuses; this tough Sweeney looking cop would exercise full earth mother outrage at finding a woman with a child under the influence of alcohol. Phoenix knew she had to be definite.

'How dare you make such an insinuation?' she replied, as if mortally wounded by such a suggestion. 'Can't you see I have a child with me?'

'When you opened your window madam,' the officer said dryly, 'a distinct smell of alcohol came out of your car.'

'That,' said Phoenix, dropping her eyes and looking embarrassed, 'Was most likely from my husband, whom I've just dropped off. If you don't believe me, by all means breathalyse me now.'

The officer leaned further into the car, looked at Daisy safely belted up in the back and stared directly at Phoenix. Certainly no smell could be detected from the red headed woman's face. 'Got a bit of a problem has he?'

'No,' replied Phoenix, 'Just reaction to a bit of bad news.'

'Well,' said the officer straightening up, 'You'll be getting bad news if you over stay your welcome here again,' and she indicated with her arm permission to drive away.

Phoenix felt her hands tremble as she steered the car forward. Not once on the entire journey home, did she exceed the speed limit or break a set of lights, so convinced was she that the self righteous little policewoman had merely motioned her away to be trapped in a lair further along the road.

She headed straight home hot and bothered, mortified at the prospect of almost being caught red handed, but not in the least perturbed at having trashed Jack's character. 'Bollocks to school today and to work for that matter' she told herself as she fumbled with the front door key. But miraculously the door swung open; Helen was there, polishing the hallway. Phoenix felt her heart drop; she didn't feel any need for company especially not that of a sanctimonious shite.

'I wondered where you all were,' Helen said as she closed the door. 'Is Daisy not feeling so good?'

'No, I mean yes, she is fine' replied Phoenix, 'but it's a teacher's day today.'

'Really,' replied Helen 'I could have sworn I saw some children in Yew Wood uniform, are you sure?'

'Yes, yes. Definitely.' Phoenix replied irritably and walked up the stairs desperate to get away from her housekeeper. Why didn't Helen know when to fuck off? She found herself at the top of the stairs with no reason to be there and she looked back down them feeling rattled and confused. She could hear the murmur of Daisy's voice as she chatted to Helen. No doubt she was informing the woman about the airport, and Jack flying off and the police giving Mommy a going over.

She didn't want to talk to Helen; in fact she didn't want to talk to anyone. Calm, kind hearted Danny was dead, Jack was in Ireland, and she was somewhere, twenty years away. The news about Danny hovered on the fringes of her consciousness and even though she refused to acknowledge it for fear of stirring up something too unpleasant to contemplate, there was no denying the familiarity of the mixture of grief and emptiness she was now feeling.

She walked back down the stairs and found Helen in the kitchen where she was occupied with pouring Daisy a bowl of cereal and commiserating with her on her hungriness. What bastards children are; Phoenix thought viciously to herself, now Helen would gloat and go home feeling superior, thinking 'That Phoenix frankly can't look after a cat, never mind a child.'

'Helen,' she said. 'I'm afraid we got bad news today, Jack's brother D I E D last night and Jack, has gone to Ireland.'

Daisy looked from woman to woman, trying to gauge how serious it all was. She hadn't been told about Uncle Danny, but she knew from the atmosphere that Jack hadn't gone on any holiday, only fear kept her from asking too many questions.

'Oh I'm sorry to hear that,' said Helen, instantly feeling guilty for her recent thoughts regarding Phoenix's mothering skills. 'Was he ill or did it happen out of the blue?'

'It was sudden,' Phoenix answered curtly, 'and you know who does not know about it yet.'

'Oh,' Helen replied, nodding her head to indicate she knew Phoenix was talking about Daisy. 'Is there anything I can do?'

'As a matter of fact there is,' Phoenix said, noting the look of trepidation that instantly flicked across Helen's face. She evidently hadn't calculated on her offer being taken up. 'Would you mind taking Daisy out for a few hours, to the park or the shops, I have a few things I must get on with.'

'Well, no I don't mind,' Helen said hesitantly, 'Only I shan't be able to do the house as well.'

'Never mind the house,' Phoenix replied brusquely. 'I just need five minutes to myself.'

She turned and left the kitchen, feeling if she remained there one second longer, she would slap the woman. Why do the stupid never grasp the concept of 'either/ or?' she asked herself.

She went upstairs to her bedroom and waited until she heard the click of the front door before making her way to the balcony window from where she watched Daisy, trotting beside Helen. She watched until they were out of sight before walking briskly out of the room and heading for the telephone in the kitchen.

There she held a smooth conversation with Bleasdale, cancelling the dinner and sounding genuinely disappointed. He told her she was sweet and that she wasn't to worry at all, he also sent his condolences to Jack. It was just as well really he said; there had been a break in on his estate in Scotland and he might have to go up there. 'Stupid old bastard', she thought as she replaced the receiver, 'how crass to imply Danny's death has an upside to it.'

She then contacted O'Carolan. He was worried sick. His conversation was in stark contrast to the rather silky one she had just had with Bleasdale. It was punctuated with obscenities as he told Phoenix how some Irish bastard had pulled a fast one on him, making an offer through a solicitor, pissing him around by asking for countless details and then pulling out for no good reason.

Phoenix told him Jack had expressed a vague interest in the garages himself, but personally, given the contrariness of the property market, she was opposed to it. Such a declaration met with exactly the response she was hoping for, he wheedled and pleaded his cause. He needed a sale he told her, for debtors were on to him, and his wife had left and Jack was the only friend he now had in the world. That will be news to Jack, she thought as she listened to his pathetic whining. She reassured O'Carolan she would think it over, and put the phone down.

With Jack's business sorted out, she turned her attention to her own. She had already left a brief message on the answer - phone for Carolyn saying she would not be in until later. She hadn't gone into detail, but now she knew she wouldn't be going in at all, she phoned Carolyn and told her about Danny.

Carolyn reacted just as Phoenix knew she would. She sympathised and reassured Phoenix all was well and that she was happy to take control for as long as required. Phoenix found this conversation the most difficult one of all. She didn't want condolence, sympathy was something she never expressed or personally desired. Life went on.

Having done her duty, she headed straight to the kitchen cupboard and poured herself the long cherished drink; that had been on her mind since the airport. Though the whiskey doused some of the flames of anxiety raging in her heart; it did nothing to soothe her fear.

With confidence inspired by the whiskey, she allowed herself to think about Danny and found his face frighteningly easy to recall. Along with his picture came memories of his many kindnesses, and although she felt a terrible grief, tears refused to come.

Could it be, she really was mad? Was it true that an inability to show emotions was a sign of insanity? She wanted to cry, tears would surely relieve some of the agony she felt inside, but hardness had descended on her heart and the tears refused to fall.

This feeling of being adrift from others wasn't a new one. There had been another occasion when she had felt every bit as lonely and fearful as she did now, when the central rock of her life had been removed suddenly leaving her without any visible means of support. She refilled her glass and headed for the study and ignoring her resolve never to write alone, she took out her red book.

Dear Scarlett,

There might be a fate worse than death, but nothing beats news of it for sheer shock and terror. Poor Danny is dead. Decent God fearing Danny who wore his pioneer badge and lived decently and sedately has succumbed to the type of death usually reserved for drunken, cholesterol sodden smokers.

How Jack will cope? He relied on Danny far more than he probably realises. It was Danny who gave Jack the money to come to England in the first place, and who fixed up a trusted supply of local labour ready to go to London when Jack called. More importantly, it was always Danny Jack turned to for advice when the going got tough.

Jack said that when he told Danny about Polly and the divorce, Danny had looked so ashen that he had panicked for him. Divorce struck against his ideals of loyalty and trust. It was according to him something that belonged to England. He said the English had the temperament to cope with it having neither religion nor love of family to contend with, so Jack must have turned, in more than one way.

I thought they were damming words but they simply rolled off Jack's back. By telling Danny, he relieved himself, and placed an enormous burden on his brother's back. Even so, Danny stood by Jack. He was a good man and it's not often you'll hear me say those words Scarlett. In a way he was like Melanie, because although he was virtuous and principled, he could still get along with people who weren't, in fact he went out of his way to make me feel welcome. He didn't want me to feel threatened by the closeness between him and Jack. It was him who saw to Daisy getting baptised, because neither Jack nor I bother with church anymore. Jack because he doesn't believe any of it anyway and me; because of the way the church let me down, when that parish priest all those years ago, just assumed I had done a wrong..

Danny knew a priest in a parish just beyond Skibbereen and Daisy was baptised with Danny as Godfather, and Jack's sister as Godmother. The priest, Father Brendan went about it solely as Daisy's Baptism. Not Sinead and Jack's interrogation, which is what I had feared, would happen.

Danny was always there in the background helping and advising long before I was on the scene. Even at Easter when Jack's snotty sister stared at my shoes and inferred that I was washed up and out, he shielded me. How I wish I hadn't kicked up about going to Ireland for those few days.

Without Jack the house feels cold and lonesome even though the sun is shining and the world is looking its best. With the knowledge that Danny is dead, I have such a feeling of emptiness; an era has come to an end and that is always hard to take.

In 1986, just as my business showed its first real signs of growth, Mom died. She died on the seventeenth of December, still believing that I was at the building society.

Business was booming, but it still hadn't hit the big time that I knew it was destined for. When that day came, I would reveal all to her and every luxury she wanted would be hers. The first thing I planned to do was take her to America. She wanted to go there more than anywhere else on earth.

She never got there because on the fifteenth of December 1986, she woke up with a crushing headache, so bad that she phoned Alice and cancelled a Christmas shopping trip to Canterbury.

Later that afternoon Gerry called round and found her unconscious. After contacting the family nearby, Alice phoned the building society, the one on Baker Street where I use to work. They didn't have a clue what she was talking about. I had left it almost three years earlier. Eventually that night, Alice phoned me at home. She was very stiff; she asked me what sort of game was it that I was playing.

When I got to the hospital Mom was sinking in and out of consciousness. Scarlett, in some ways you got the better deal coming home to find your mother dead, at least her agony was over and you didn't have to witness it. Mom reached frantically for my hair and fought so desperately to say something, but the words couldn't be formed.

A nurse standing nearby took a pencil out of her pocket and said, 'Give it a try, perhaps she might be able to write something down.' But it was useless, whatever Mom wanted to say remained unspoken, and the next day she died, holding my hand.

Joe's wife said, 'That's how it should be at the end, the first and last.' That didn't endear her or me, to Alice and Eileen. The pair of them looked at me as if I was something you mind find on the sole of your shoe.

Later that night, Alice gave me four photos of Joseph, tiny passport ones. She said Mom had carried them everywhere with her, in her purse. The photos must have been taken at the hospital, probably the day after he was born. She never got over losing that baby, I see that so clearly now. Alice gave me the photos, but I didn't want them. I didn't even look at them properly. Scarlett I feel so hard hearted, that it frightens me, but it was just too terrible. I felt burdened with them. I didn't know what to do, I couldn't burn them, I'm too superstitious for that; so I left them on a table in a café.

Mom dying peacefully, hand in hand with me was more than I could ask for, but the next day when I visited her in the hospital mortuary with Eileen and Alice, her face didn't look peaceful anymore. It looked resigned, as if to say 'Thank God that's all over,' and I compounded my feelings of misery by leaning over and kissing her. The coldness of her skin startled me and I became hysterical. Alice and Eileen were shocked. They probably thought guilt had finally caught up with me. That feeling of coldness beyond eternity has never left me; its only function was to drive out the warmth of that final moment with her alive.

After Mom died it was the end of an era. I was twenty-three and with no parents; the family circle was destroyed forever. Her funeral was also the last time that I saw the ape. He came with Olga in tow and I half expected to see Grace being exhibited in dark velvet. Olga was dead cool towards me, but grave and sympathetic towards Alice and Eileen. He had hardly changed, but Olga had clearly aged. I think with Mom dead, he recognised that he was more vulnerable than he'd ever been before. He oozed slime and concern with the entire family, and they acknowledged him politely and gravely. All of them recognising the necessity of grease from an oil slick.

But when he came up to me, I couldn't keep a lid on my anger or revulsion. It was hardly believable that he would dare to approach me under the protection of my mother's funeral.

'I'm very sorry Sinead,' he said. 'She was a good woman.' To hear him, the ape compliment my mother was too much, it sounded as genuine as a wee free calling for three cheers for the Pope.

I was standing in the function room of the Hillden Hotel, when he spoke to me. Alice had seen to the funeral arrangements. She felt a grand send off for Mom was in order and although Mom herself had never so much as eaten a sandwich in its hushed restaurant her funeral tea was stuffed full with those who had. When the ape approached me I was standing by an arched window that looked out on the English Channel. I had been thinking about the requiem mass, most of it had gone over my head.

The priest was a young fellow I'd never seen before. He spoke of Mom's devotion to her children, her faith and loyalty and I felt the same old twinge of irritation at the way the church indulges in platitudes. To condense Mom's life down; to children and faith; seemed demeaning and to miss the point. What did this little guy know about Mom's life? What does anybody really know about another person's life? Did that priest have any idea of the young girl who grew up in the 1920's who ran bare foot through the wilds of Kerry? Did he know what drove her to England or into the marriage that trapped her more securely and viciously than any gin trap that cranks make such a song and dance about? Did he have any idea of her hopes and dreams, or how she saw her children fulfilling them? Of course he didn't.

He was a fool who liked to think she had chosen a downtrodden life, the cannon fodder of the Catholic Church, the ordinary decent woman who leaves the luscious sins to wealthier members who can buy their way out. I watched my brothers and sisters as the priest spoke; they seemed to take the adjectives of humility, faithfulness and meekness as fitting. I saw Alice's head nod in agreement while Eileen sniffled. Directly in front of me was a huge statue of St Joseph, in fact his feet were about three inches from my nose. I felt nothing other than complete coldness.

I deliberately turned my thoughts away from the drivel that was dribbling out because Mom deserved better than sanctimonious, pious tripe. I remember looking around the church to see how many faces I could recognise. Lots of the old crones Mom would move hell and high water to avoid when out shopping were there. So was my old school friend Magda. She was dressed in a dowdy raincoat and I couldn't help noticing how staid and old she looked. Instead of thinking how kind of her to come, I merely thought, 'all things considered, I hadn't done too bad for myself'. You did the same thing Scarlett at your Pa's funeral, when you saw your old friend Cathleen looking dirty and dingy and compared her fate to yours. Sometimes you have to pat your own back. Perhaps that's why God sent the ape to see me, payback for my smugness. I couldn't grasp his audacity. I looked beyond him for a moment and noticed Olga sitting beside Alice; both wore grave faces, but there was no doubt about it, someone was getting a verbal thrashing.

'Sorry,' I said to the ape. 'You are telling me you are sorry?'

He looked dead shifty; he must have known something was coming. He leaned over and said 'Well of...' But do you know something Scarlett? I didn't give him a chance.

I said 'You aren't half as sorry as you're going to be when your son seeks you out.' The relief I felt in delivering those words was indescribable. Now he knew for sure, that there was a baby, and he too would have to live with uncertainty, for the hour and the day, when his particular chicken came home to roost.

But do you know what he did? He glanced coolly over his shoulder to where his wife was sitting, then turned towards me and said 'Prove it. Just try and prove it and I'll see to it that everyone recognises you for the whore you are, because that's the way I'll play it, the school girl who came round for it on a Saturday night, for money of course, in the car, against a tree, she wasn't fussy but she was fucking awful. Just try it Sinead.'

He walked off, stopping briefly to lift a glass of red wine from a tray and anyone looking on would have sworn that he had just passed a few words of condolence with me. Every bit of fire within me died at that moment and coldness like snow drifted through me. I just stood there like a fool. With my mother dead I saw in that instant that there was no longer any need for the pretence of making a life. Who did I need to impress?

I just had an overwhelming desire for it to all be over. I walked out of the hotel and down a little lane that lead to the sea. It was bitterly cold and there was hardly any wind but the tide was in and the dirty snot coloured sea was heaving and lapping against the wall. I wanted so much to jump in. I could picture myself, falling slowly deeper and deeper, to the bottom of the sea, and in my imagination, it wouldn't be cold at all, just warm and silent. I held on to the railings but I just couldn't let go.

There was nothing for it but to go back to the hotel, collect my bag and say my goodbyes. Aunty Phil was there, filling up on brandy and bemoaning the fact that I never visited her, which was almost true. I did visit her at Easter and Christmas; taking brandy, chocolates and flowers with me.

Visiting Aunty Phil was a remnant of a Catholic upbringing, a combination of guilt and fulfilment of Christmas and Easter duties. She continued to treat me like dirt. It would have been more simple and painless to have simply gone to Mass twice a year instead. But visiting her, albeit infrequently, robbed her of the chance to tell the world that after all her kindness, Bridget O'Connell's daughter had forgotten her.

Not a bit of it Aunty Phil, I'll never forget you.

Actually she died a couple of years ago. I didn't go to her funeral, but I sent flowers and a hopelessly inappropriate card. It was the only one the gormless newsagent had, a silky and sentimental one, with ridiculous words about meeting up again in 'that sunny far off land.'

I thought, 'if we do, we've both landed up in hell.'

As I left, Alice and Eileen accompanied me to my car; a red convertible BMW and they gasped when they saw it, which was a ridiculous thing to do since both of them drove far more expensive models. They thought it wild and excessive because it wasn't a Ford, and there wasn't a tartan travel rug in sight.

Alice said 'Good God, who lent you that, or did you steal it?' and Eileen walked around it, like a cop checking for an expired tax disc.

'You've even got a personal number plate,' she said. But it wasn't a personal one at all; it was a northern Irish one. That was Lesley's idea, she said it suited me because the first three letters were FIB and fibbing was something I had become pretty good at.

Both of my sisters bombarded me with questions; the gist of all of them being, 'How can you afford a car like that?' It really pained them that I patently wasn't on my knees. The truth was Scarlett; I could hardly afford the car at all. It wasn't as new as it looked, and the 'personal number plate,' apart from being fun, disguised its age, but my business was developing to a stage where I needed to impress people. Getting a loan is much easier when you look as if you don't need it.

I told them briefly that I had started a business; I couldn't bring myself to say it was a cleaning one. I described it as a housekeeping agency. Alice said, 'Well it looks like you're never going to become a lawyer then.' I could have said, one barrack room lawyer is enough in any family, but I didn't. I was tired and just so very pissed off.

Instead I replied, 'No, so it looks as if you can sleep easy now Alice.'

That immediately stirred Eileen off her perch. She turned on me and said 'Nobody wanted to deny you university, so it really is time you dropped your persecution complex.' I can still hear her voice; it was silky and preachy, like you'd expect Billy Graham to sound like.

Encouraged by Eileen's deft footwork, Alice put the boot in again. 'Genuinely Sinead,' she said, 'You have never acknowledged how much you hurt Mom; you broke her heart, when you slunk away to London. It wasn't a brain haemorrhage that killed Mom, it was a broken heart.'

She sounded like a politician or a bum historian with her rewriting of the past. 'Slunk away to London,' that's not how I remembered it. The pair of them dressed from head to toe in black, looked like something out of Cromwell's army. The assumption was obviously alive and well. They still believed against all the odds; that their sister who had received the same upbringing as themselves had chanced it, got caught and had gone on to live the high life in London.

I looked at Alice and the sight of her blonde hair tinged with grey and her once slim figure turning stout chilled my heart. Eileen stood there, tall and defiant, arms folded, her dark hair well cut, acting as Alice's personal bouncer, ready to move in with the killer blow. They were my sisters. There had been a time when we were friends. I had been a bridesmaid at both of their weddings. There were days when Alice would return from her shift at the hospital with sweets for me, and I'd go to her house for the weekend as a treat, watch her big telly and play records on a fashionable stereo. But three, is an awkward number; three is a crowd, three in a marriage as the wise woman said, makes it overcrowded. It was two against one, if life had run its natural course it would probably have been Alice and me against Eileen, for the way she had expressed a vague interest in South Africa, and then left less than six weeks later to live there. But she came back and the two older sisters united against the common enemy, the youngest sister who disgraced the family.

Looking at the pair of them, I felt a twinge of pity, because on the face of it I had done the dirty, and they saw themselves as Mom's guardians. But even so, it wasn't enough to excuse them. Even if their assumptions about me had been correct, it still would never have justified their out pouring of bitterness and frustration, because that is what it was. They were two women, one middle -aged, the other fast approaching it, and both of them were stuck in a time warp. Mom for all her faith and belief had momentarily considered abortion as a way out, but it was the religious police in the form of Alice who had cordoned off that escape route.

Mom who had lived through tough times was capable of thinking the unthinkable, but poor Alice and Eileen bought up in security and safety had only one vision of morality. Eileen could travel the world all the way to South Africa and condemn

wholeheartedly the permissive behaviour of the indigenous population, without even raising an eyebrow about apartheid.

I seriously debated for one moment whether to tell them the
truth, but looking at them I decided it would be pointless, about
as satisfying as catching a fart in a colander. Mom had been
owed the truth, not them. So I said 'If it makes you feel better to
think that I caused Moms death that she didn't die of natural
causes, then think it. I'm all in favour of therapy no matter how
delusive it might be, but the truth is neither of you know the real
story, and I can't be bothered to even begin telling it to you.'

Driving back to London that dull cold foggy night I begged
God to send a juggernaut across the central reservation. I had
already proved that I was too superstitious, too cowardly to take
my life in my own hands. The days that followed were black
ones. I didn't live with Lesley and co anymore, I had my own
place in Clapham; I got it after approaching the local council as
a key worker. I told them I was a cleaner at a nursing home. I
didn't tell them of course that I owned the firm, because at that
time in the 1980's, Lambeth was a mini Russian republic, up
with the workers and pink and blue zebra crossings. The
moment I got the contract for 'The Balmy Evenings' nursing
home, more and more work south of the river came my way and
I had to move.

The woman in the housing office was kind to me; she was
shocked when she heard I was a cleaner. 'But you're too young
and pretty to be cleaning up after old biddies,' she said every
time she saw me. I told her that since I was not bright enough to
become a nurse, cleaning was the closest I could get to the caring
profession.

Mind you, I didn't tell her that while some nurses might
indeed be angels the ones I met at 'The Balmy Evenings' certainly flew low. Old Miss Copper and Mrs Dickens might well insist
on being addressed by their full surnames in public, but in the
staff room they were best known as 'The Old Fucker' and 'The
Mouldy Faggot.'

Of course I never told that to the kind lady in the housing
office. The housing interviewers as they were called; went to
great lengths to explain that the allocation of housing was

nothing to do with them. It was all to do with points, if you had a dodgy chest, a couple of bastards and no fear of heights you were quids in.

On the other hand, if you were a healthy young girl or bloke with an aversion to piss stained lifts you'd stand more chance of finding digs at Buckingham Palace, than getting your own flat. Most of the housing staff lived in fear of reprisals from those offered shit flats on skid row, that's why they always made it very clear 'Allocation is nothing to do with us.' But even so, I'm pretty certain that the woman who interviewed me had a hand in getting me a lovely maisonette in the better part of Clapham, and then Mrs Thatcher obliged with her right to buy scheme for council tenants and set me on my way.

Christmas 1986, was a dismal affair. I didn't spend it entirely on my own; I had the company of ghosts from so many Christmas's long past. With Mom dead, an era had come to an end and her passing bought so many memories to mind, but it was the happy ones that were the hardest to bear. Christmas long ago when as the baby of the family my older brothers and sisters had given me money to buy presents with, pressing ten shilling notes and even pound notes into my hand.

Then there was the decorating of the tree and the last minute dash on Christmas Eve to tinsel clad shops, and the big family dinners and treks through the snow to Midnight Mass, hurrying back fearful in case we met Father Christmas and caused him to boycott our house. It was a well-known fact my mother always told me, that Santa hates to be seen in his working clothes.

Now it was over. I felt old and my heart physically pained me, I had such a hurt in my chest that I could hardly breathe. From my bedroom window I could hear the rowdy out of tune singing, and shouting matches between drunks as they stumbled home, while my flat felt as cold and cheerless as a pub after throwing out time.

Two things saved me though, work and hate. There was so much to do and finding staff was relentless, I had to give it my full attention, but it was hatred of the ape that drove me on. It was always there. I had to be successful or he would have conquered me. In my mind it was clear that I'd only get even with him when I had money, real money, but I don't think I had a clue what getting even, actually meant.

A few days before Christmas, Lesley called round, by this time she was living with Dean, a West Indian who was a couple of years younger than her. I'm not sure what his job was and I have no idea how he coped with her. She bought some wine with her and a copy of Kate Bush and Peter Gabriel's record, 'Don't give up,' which I played until it was almost worn out. If Lesley had been royalty she would be described as having the common touch. So many times she nearly bought me to the brink of disaster with her antics and giant gob, especially when she worked for me, but trying to break away from her was like trying to resist hugging a polar bear, who cares about the danger?

She seemed to know, without me going into detail that I was fighting my way through the gates of hell that Christmas; only I wasn't sure which direction I was travelling in. She asked me if I was going to be alone on Christmas day, and of course I lied. I said I was going away. How could I of all people admit to being lonely or afraid? She might have sent for the Salvation Army, and they would have confiscated my whiskey and then I'd have been thoroughly up Shit Street.

She told me that she was getting married at Easter and had applied for and been given a transfer to the Doncaster branch of the building society. She would be leaving in the New Year. I was happy for her, but I felt too low and raw to even smile. Her news just brought home the fact, that another era had come to an end; and even for people whose roots have been snapped off and who know no certainties, endings still bring a sense of loss and an awareness of the passage of time.

Phoenix.

337

Chapter Twenty

Writing to Scarlett, while alone and lonely did nothing to pacify Phoenix's fear, it only reiterated her long held belief that life simply wasn't worth the bother. The words spoken to her by Condon, at her mother's funeral, rang with a new vibrancy in her ears, and the feelings of self hate and disgust they were designed to arouse, bubbled dangerously ever nearer the surface. She had lost her mother without ever telling her the truth, and now she stood to lose Jack, because the same truth refused to be told.

It was inevitable, so why fight it? She took to wandering moodily around the house she had once so passionately loved, wondering what possessed her or anyone to bother with possessions or any of the paraphernalia of life given that it was all so temporary.

One morning, while waiting for Daisy, she turned and catching sight of herself in the tall gilt mirror in the hallway, she addressed it as if it were a person 'Why?' she asked. 'Did I buy you? When I am dead I will have no use for you, you simply mark the passing of time.'

She went about her work looking curiously into the faces of the people around her. Did they simply not comprehend, as fully as she did, how futile it all was? Or were they simply more stoic than her? Was it an open secret that she wasn't privy to, that everyone knew life was fundamentally a waiting game? That far from being lifestyle choices, every activity from shopping, to golf and business meetings were all just essentially, the equivalent of Robinson Crusoe's notch on a stick? Merely rituals to fill in the passing of time.

Jack rang faithfully each morning, but several times when she tried to phone him, fearful of her state of mind, his mobile rang mournfully into the distance.

When she thought of him at night, through a haze of whiskey, the only picture she could conjure up was a vision of the wide grey sea that divided them. No matter how tightly she held her eyes closed, the face of Jack refused to come into focus.

He was staying with his sister Eileen and her family and Phoenix could summon with the blinking of an eye, the cosy image of Eileen's farmhouse, with its range and comfortable, ramshackle furniture. Jack would feel at home there, but she wouldn't, because she was an outsider and didn't belong and yet; as she stood alone in her own immaculate butternut kitchen, she no longer felt at home there either.

When Jack finally returned four days later; the urge to see him had died. He on the other hand, having had time to think, regretted his coolness towards her and was sorry for having left her behind. Eileen had told him on the day of the funeral, how concerned Danny had been for Phoenix. He had spoken of her, the night before he died; urging Eileen to phone Jack and to make sure all was well with her. With mounting unease Jack had listened to Eileen's tale, remembering Phoenix's pleas to accompany him and her protestations of love for Danny. He should have taken her with him, it was her right and certainly, Danny would have wanted her presence.

He returned home, determined to waiver any right to complain should she be angry or cold towards him, but the moment he entered the house, he knew something was very wrong. She wasn't angry, cold or even bitter, just disinterested. She asked about his journey, enquired after Eileen and the rest of the family, but it was all so perfunctory. He had a distinct feeling that he could have answered her in Polish, and she wouldn't have noticed. He declined tea and instead took a bottle of Powers from his holdall. Phoenix taking the cue fetched two glasses and he poured.

'To Danny,' he said and Phoenix raised her glass in a toast.

'Tell me then,' she said 'did he get the send off, he deserved?' She didn't really want to know about the funeral, it was irrelevant, it didn't add or detract to what Danny had been, but she had to say something, anything rather than risk Jack bringing the conversation round to her, or them.

'It was a massive turnout,' he said, 'Even mad Kate was there.'

News of the local mad woman sat uneasily with Phoenix, she didn't want to hear about someone, who had lost their sanity, not when she had a strong sensation, she might be following suit. 'Really?' she said with obvious disinterest.

'She has learnt to drive,' Jack continued, 'but still hasn't managed the knack of reversing; she calls on any old Tom Dick or Harry to do that for her.'

'I wouldn't fancy her chances around here,' Phoenix murmured, bored with this tale about a wild old woman, she didn't know or care about.

'Just as the funeral was starting,' he continued, 'She skidded into the church yard honking her horn, missing this giant fucking flint wall by inches and then she wound down her window, and shouted, 'Will one of ye useless shaggers come over here, and park this contraction for me?' He laughed as he relayed the story of mad Kate, but Phoenix felt his laughter was thin and unconnected to the story he had just told and she shivered, fear making her feel cold.

She wanted to reach out to him and for them to be again the good allies they had once been. But she was handicapped by the memories she had recently uncovered about her own mother's funeral. She felt brittle and unable to articulate any words of interest or comfort. I should feel something she told herself, after all Danny was a good man, he was kind and not old enough, to just die like that, but all I can think is, it happens to everyone, so what's the deal?

'You know something,' Jack said. 'Danny wasn't an old man, he never drank and he didn't smoke, it makes you wonder who the fuck will be next.' He placed his head in his hands, sighed and looked up. 'I can't believe he is dead,' he said, 'and just when Ireland has really taken off.' Phoenix looked up and to her horror; she saw tears in his eyes. And yet still, she couldn't muster words of comfort. She could hear Jack talking but couldn't absorb his words; they seemed to bounce off her like hail off a roof. She opened her mouth to speak and was instantly consumed by a fear that the moment she spoke, all the control she was now exercising would cease. She might say anything; coarse, obscene, hurtful or even funny, anything was possible.

She reached out and placed her hand softly on top of his, and he realizing there was nothing forthcoming from her, spoke again.

'But it was good to be back. I saw the O'Brien's, the youngest has just opened a garage in Bantry, which is fucking amazing, since he couldn't even mend a puncture on his bike.'

He talked on about others he had met and as Phoenix listened, something in the way Jack spoke, struck her as familiar. She listened further and finally, she recognised it; it wasn't just grief, Jack was homesick. He longed for the old days. He wants, she told herself, to be back amongst his own. Suddenly the past looks more attractive, because the people from it are disappearing. 'Christ,' she thought frantically 'I'm fighting on too many fronts, I'm like a lone fireman, fighting a blaze with the one hose, and even that one is leaking.' She took her hand away from Jack's, and in a bid to draw the night to a close, repeated the mantra, her mother had always churned out on the death of anyone, be it a child or a ninety year old

'Well Jack', she said, 'You can be certain, wherever Danny is now, he wouldn't swap places.'

In his first perky movement of the entire evening Jack raised his head and shook it disbelievingly. 'Jee,' he said, 'you must be more pissed up than the urinals at Aintree, because I'll tell you one thing for certain Reverend Mother, he couldn't, even if he bloody well wanted to.' And with that he stood up and made his way, somewhat unsteadily to the door. 'Are you coming?' he asked.

'In five minutes,' Phoenix replied. She waited until she heard his footsteps on the floor overhead, before making her way to the study. There was no way she could sleep right now.

Dear Scarlett,

Sometimes I'm so confused, I don't know if I'm talking or thinking and when I look back on the things I've said and done over the years, I don't recognise the girl in the story at all. For too long, I've acted as if all the unhappy memories were dead, crushed under an avalanche of work and the sheer passage of time. But they didn't die, they simply got buried and now they have risen again like the nettles and briars that appear along with the snowdrops and the bluebells from the hard earth at the end of a long drawn out winter. Certainly all the hate and anger never died; the pair of them just sat and festered, unnoticed throughout the years. Petals are falling and weeds are sprouting even as I sit writing these words to you. I'm not aware of them, but that doesn't make their reality any less real.

Jack has been reminiscing about the old days. He tried to sound dismissive, even ridiculing some of his old acquaintances, but I recognised the homesickness in his voice, I recognised it because I felt the same pang, when I recalled Mom's death. I hate my family for the way they barely scratch the reality of living, refusing to even contemplate that life may not be all it seems. And yet, when I think about them, I long for the days when I was just like them. Life is full of instances, when things happen and you know instinctively that they herald either the beginning or the end of a chapter.

Well this is one of those instances.

When you almost choked on that radish Scarlett, in your desperation to eat something, after your long journey home to Tara, you made a pledge not to be beaten; eating that radish out of pure desperation was the catalyst that spurred you on. I know that Danny's death, so unexpected is making Jack reconsider the life he now leads. I suspect Jack may long for home, home as in Ireland.

Right now, in this house; I have a distinct sensation of a darkness sinking in like an eclipse, gently but unremittingly, stealing away the light.

There was an eclipse a few years ago. How worked up people got about the sun retreating behind the moon for a few minutes on the 11th August 1999, I couldn't understand the excitement; after all, a dark, dank sky in Britain during August isn't that unusual. By coincidence, we were taking a few days break at the time, some guy Jack was working with had a cottage in a place called Looe in Cornwall, and we went with some other friends for a few days. It was crowded though because the South West was reputed to offer the best vantage point in England for viewing the eclipse, and fools desperate to stare the sun out descended en masse into Cornwall.

Warnings were given about mass blindness being a reality, if people didn't act with sense, and of course dire predictions of the eclipse heralding death and disaster were made. This caused one or two people to momentarily consider cashing in all their assurance policies, and ploughing their cash into a monumental piss up in the dark, but generally the freaks were ignored.

Our cottage overlooked the sea and a moronic girlfriend of one of Jack's friends kept banging on about the eclipse being the start of a new astrological order for everyone. She poured out champagne and dished out sun visors, and just as the eclipse appeared, she put on a 1980's hit called 'Total Eclipse of the Heart.' I shivered because the lyrics of that song have a real air of desperation and the sound of it never fails to makes me feel uneasy.

Anyway, as the sky began to darken some watched in hushed silence, others began cat calling and yahooing, but do you know something Scarlett, all I felt, apart from boredom, was an enormous sense of despair sweep over me. ..and as I write this, a feeling of recognition dawns on me. I think watching that eclipse, may have been the start of my present depression. I really think it began that day. Watching helplessly as the world grew gradually darker and realising that there was nothing anyone could do about it, if the sun should choose to remain behind the moon. I was among a crowd of people with champagne sloshing, and squealing cries of 'notice me, notice me,' yet I felt isolated, aware of only one thing, the absolute lack of control anyone has over life.

And if you will forgive the pun Scarlett, the fear inspired by the eclipse was eclipsed itself by New Year's Eve 1999 when most of the world celebrated the leap into the next Millennium.

The same hype accompanied this event. Computer meltdown was forecast; the system, according to the soothsayers would struggle to recognise 00. There were reports of pubs preparing to sell beer at a hundred pounds a pint, babysitters becoming millionaires overnight, hospitals full of patients, but no doctors or nurses, because they'd all be out on the binge. And last but not least, the four horsemen from the Book of Revelation were predicted to come riding in on a cloud, in order to tell the world, to put its head between its legs and kiss its arse goodbye.

None of it happened of course. Most pubs shut down for the night through fear of enterprise, and babysitters remained unemployed as families chose to stay at home and fight each other instead of strangers. Computers didn't catch a hiccup never mind a virus and the four horsemen stayed at home with the telly.

Jack's family, Danny and Eileen and Con and their three children came over from Ireland for the New Year. We stayed for a few nights at a country house hotel in Sussex. It staged a millennium party, complete with a disco and a band and a firework display at midnight. I don't know why Jack booked this break, no one really wanted to be away from home, but we went anyway. With just a few minutes left of the old century, Daisy developed an urgent need for the lavatory and I had to fight my way through the crowd with her in my arms, and queue for what felt like eternity.

When we came out of the cloakroom, I couldn't fight my way back to Jack and the others. The crowd was that preoccupied, with waiting shoulder to shoulder, for Big Ben to give the go ahead for the New Millennium, it would have taken a gun to have dispersed them.

Big Ben chimed and I was almost sick with fear. I stood there with Daisy in my arms, surrounded by a swelling tide of people kissing and hugging each other, as if each and every one of them had just won the lottery jackpot.

But the crowning glory of misery came, when the gross, fat, sweaty jock of a DJ played an appalling record to greet the new dawn. The moment Big Ben slunk away he tapped his microphone and said 'Och aye folks, here we are into untouched territory,' and then he stuck on 'Like a Virgin.'

God, I wanted to vomit. All around me, big red faces smiled and sweaty bodies jostled along out of rhythm, to an anthem for gobshites.

Despair? I was drowning in it.

A New Millennium had started, but everywhere in that overcrowded room the past seemed to be looming up at me. I felt out of place and out of step, it was as if I had taken my child to the toilet, opened the door, and re entered, into the old century. I knew then, there was to be no running away. I had run and I had hit a barrier. The only movement from there on would be backwards.

A thud from upstairs, startled Phoenix and she leapt in fright; half expecting to see Jack staring at her accusingly from the doorway. Hurriedly, she slapped the book shut and flung it into the open drawer. But she had panicked unnecessarily; the noise was only the result of a book slipping off her bed in the room up above.

She stood for a moment, hands held tight to her chest, aware her heart was beating irrationally fast. This was the symptom that frightened her most; the beating, erratic heart; the engine that drove and whipped up the fear and disorientation that caused her to question her sanity.

For the second time since taking Shelby's advice, she had made a breakthrough, a significant one, but there was no euphoria, no relief and no joy. Only anxiety that she was on the precipice of being found out.

Now she had a start date for the fear that dominated her life. It hadn't just evolved or appeared like acne does on the face of an unsuspecting teenager. The seeds had been sown on the day of that eclipse, when she had watched the sun darken, and had considered the possibility of it retreating forever. It had been a replay of the night in Condon's house, when he had taken his wife to the hospital and she had stood alone, watching and wondering if the snow would fall forever.

The fear had culminated on the night of the New Millennium, when she had failed to break through the crowds to be at Jack's side, and that awful, jeering record had been played. In an instant, she realised not even a New Century could protect her from herself. The climatic, astrological events of 1999, had merely confirmed her worst fear. There was no such thing as control.

Chapter Twenty One

June 2001 dawned bright and vibrant, turning out to be spectacularly hot and sunny. The annual sporting crowds poured into
Wimbledon dressed in their summer finery, and with the aid of
the weather, they gave the world a brighter and happier façade
than the one it had worn in the preceding damp and dreary
weeks and months.

Few places in Wimbledon however, could compete with the
riot of colour and gaiety emanating from the gardens of Fuchsia
House. From the moment the Keane's had purchased the elegant,
if somewhat dilapidated building, Jack had arranged for the
creation of a spectacular show of roses in both the front and
rear gardens. They were Phoenix's favourite flower, and in those
love filled early days, nothing had been too much trouble for
Jack, as he pursued making Phoenix content and happy. Just like
Wordsworth's famed daffodils, they grew in every conceivable
place, along the path, beside the pond, beneath the trees,
nodding and bowing their splendid heads in the gentle London
breeze. Now with the added bonus, of sudden unexpected
sunshine, they bloomed even more readily, making the entire
garden, a stark contrast to the dark atmosphere, within the
house itself.

Daisy's fourth birthday arrived, and no time by Jack or
expense by Phoenix was spared in making it a day for her to
remember. Her aunts in Kent despatched sensible functional gift
vouchers to her, and from Aunty Eileen in Skibbereen, she
received an elegant water marked edition of Hans Christian
Andersen's best known fairy tales, full of exquisite ornate illus-
trations. Much as Phoenix admired the artistic merit of the beautiful book, she couldn't bear the icy arrogant features of the
wicked Snow Queen, who stared out at her so accusingly, with
just the hint of a smirk.

In fact, the entire book soon became the bane of her life as
Daisy begged every night for just one more story. Valiantly,
Phoenix unable to muster the concentration required to read the
quaint italic text, battled the confused jumble of ideas in her
head and relayed, a garbled account of a classic fairy tale. And

Daisy, just grateful for the company of her mother, never once corrected the strange, inconsistent versions her mother told of the same story.

Jack's pride in his young daughter soared to new heights and her obvious joy in his gift of a tiny white kitten, went some way to uplifting his own increasingly downcast heart. The feelings of pointlessness, or at least disinterest, which had descended on him since his trip to Boston had not entirely evaporated, and Danny's sudden death had only exacerbated his growing belief that life was too short to squander on the unnecessary. But his resolution to find a more simple way of living was proving very difficult right now.

Phoenix had gone overboard with her child's birthday, buying numerous dolls and toys which Jack felt Daisy neither wanted nor needed. It had been the same with the birthday party. Daisy's simple request to bring two friends home to tea had been brusquely pushed aside by Phoenix, who insisted on taking the whole class, the good, the bad, and in Jack's opinion, the downright foul, to the Italian Café for tea and ice cream.

Several times he had questioned Phoenix about the necessity of what she was doing, but she had turned on him with a viciousness that left him speechless. He began to suspect she was unwell; it even crossed his mind that she might be pregnant, but every attempt to speak or reason with her met with such an out pouring of venom and hate, that he decided to back off. Which was precisely what Phoenix wanted, she had enough to contend with, without taking on board Jack's philosophical whining as well.

When she wasn't doing the things she had to do, there was only one thing Phoenix wanted to do. And that was write to Scarlett.

'Gone with the Wind' had only one fault as far as Phoenix was concerned, and that was the character of Ashley Wilkes, husband of the sainted Melanie. She disliked him with a passion, perceiving him to be a weak, spineless man who had led Scarlett on out of vanity thereby robbing her of the happiness she could have found with Rhett.

Everything about blond honourable Ashley incensed Phoenix. She detested his false notion of honour almost as much as his inability to make a decision and stand by it. How could Scarlett, she asked herself; have possibly loved someone like him, never mind jeopardise everything for his sake?

But life is full of irony, and now when it was imperative that she remained strong, Phoenix found herself in the position of identifying with the irritatingly weak Ashley. Just as he had sought refuge in a world that had disappeared, when he had returned home from war to a way of life, that was beyond his comprehension, Phoenix too, found herself increasingly looking to the past, to a time, when life, though not happy had at least been more straight - forward.

The present had nothing to offer. Her hold on it was too tenuous and as for the future, well, that was a remote frightening country, where all her fears would become reality. Only the past offered anything remotely resembling security. The past was a road she had travelled on, it wasn't pleasant, but it was familiar and that was the best she could hope for right now.

She began to approach her letter writing with a greater sense of ease. Present day necessity drove her backwards, to a time when life was complex, when there had been so many things to juggle, like arranging finance, engaging staff and stealing contracts. By contrast life now was too stark; only one thing occupied her thoughts and though her mind flitted from one anxiety to another, fear was at the root of all of them.

There was something comforting about casting her mind back to the days when she had nothing and nobody to lose and everything to gain. Often when she should have been thinking about the issues of the day, she found her mind drifting back to a particular time or place and it was with a sense of great dread and reluctance that she drifted back to the present time.

She still wrote in secret, but now she was more open about being surreptitious, she merely locked the study door behind her and informed Jack to keep away.

Dear Scarlett,   **17th June 2001**

I'm beginning to wonder, if there ever was a time, when life was
free from worry and anxiety. If that eclipse really was the start
of anxiety controlling me, then I can have some sympathy for
how Jack is feeling right now, because I know how easy it is to
be at ease one minute, and so immeasurably out of place the
next.

There is something indefinably wrong with Jack and I have
more than just a suspicion, that he is seriously contemplating a
move away from London. The very thought terrifies me. How
could I leave the only place I can call home? London gave me
my break. Its vastness covered my lies and got my business
started, lies like telling people in Clapham I had premises in
Acton, safe in the knowledge that while most Londoners might
know their locality like the defects on their own nose, across the
river is alien territory.

Rhett Butler was spot on when he told you Scarlett, that the
destruction rather than the development of a civilisation is the
time to make money. In the 1980's a chill wind of change blew
through Britain, and gradually an old civilisation died. 1979
may have been Iraq's year for scooping first prize in the contest
for choosing Arsehole of the Decade by electing Saddam
Hussein, but it was also, (according to some people) the year
when Britain won runner up position, by voting in Margaret
Thatcher.

I remember the night she won; I thought it was a good omen
of change for the world, but Mom didn't. She hated Thatcher;
she said, 'that woman is God's curse on England,' and when I
said it was great to have a woman as leader of the country,
Mom replied, 'It would be, but the fact is Thatcher is no
woman.'

I don't know what she knew about Thatcher that the rest of
us didn't but she seemed to view her as some kind of hybrid in a
skirt. I wished I had paid more attention to that election,
because there is no doubt in my mind, Thatcher winning was
critically important to me. Without her I would have been lost.

She stood in her blue suit on the steps of Number 10 and
spoke the words of St Francis, words that we had regularly sang

at mass on a Sunday. The only problem was, when Mrs Thatcher spoke those words, 'Where there is discord, let us bring harmony,' they didn't sound calming or philosophical at all. They sounded totalitarian, 'we will have peace, you will not doubt.' It was definitely not a case of 'the meek shall inherit the earth if that's all right with the rest of you.' Her voice was awful and her rendition of that prayer the biggest and best ventriloquist act in history; somebody most definitely had their hand up Thatcher's jacket for that one.

With the advent of Thatcherism Scarlett, the post war era of Britain was gone with the wind. Almost overnight she introduced a new world, a much harsher competitive one, but one that was open to all, provided you were tough and desperate enough to take advantage of it and I owe her a great deal for that.

Now I am older and comfortable and have money in the bank, I can afford to be a hypocrite and say in certain company, 'it's terrible to think what this country lost under Thatcherism,' but the truth is, the only things that are lost, hardly keep me awake at night. I don't cry into my pillow over things like school milk, council houses and Arthur bloody Scargill.

Like the inhabitants of Georgia in your day Scarlett, the workers in Britain under Thatcher's rule had a lot to fear from the Yankees, because it was from them that Thatcher nicked her ideas about change. Things like stream lining, down -sizing and accountability all of them were drafted into Britain from the Yanks, in fact the whole of the bloody 80's was like living on a film set because the only words you ever heard were, 'cut, cut, cut.' Hospitals, schools and banks, they all came in for it. Unemployment went up and words like compassion and sympathy became the new obscenities and it was all carried through under the guise and respectability of Victorian values. Keep the state out and let individuals show their philanthropy. No one even knew what was really happening.

In a way, Thatcher's control of Britain was like a master and dog relationship, because the more kicking's she gave the people the more they loved it. They must have done, because they kept voting her back in, although you would have been hard pressed to find anyone who admitted to doing so. She took a broom and swept the old world away. She picked fights which on the face of it she couldn't win, and she won.

To Lesley's dismay, she beat the miners to a pulp, baited them to go on strike, before crushing them under her stilettos. She was clever, smart, as you would say Scarlett, because she used the police as her battering ram, and sneaked another change through on the side. The cosy image of the friendly village copper, peddling his bike and dishing out cauliflower ears to wannabe vandals was gone forever. Goodbye Mr Plod, Hello Mr Sado Masochistic, complete with helmet and visor, riot gear and truncheon. The miner's strike of 1984 was Thatcher's icing on the cake.

I went about my business oblivious to what was happening a hundred miles away, but poor Lesley whose family had mined for generations was in despair. She stepped her effing up a gear and developed a violent dislike for the police, everywhere we went, she daubed 'Help the police, beat yourself up,' on windows, doors and fences. She told me, in a deadly serious voice one day, that the police horse was an anatomically unique animal, since it's the only one known to have an arse half way up its back.

When I stared at her blankly, trying to visualize a horse, she said, 'What a moron you are O'Connell, no wonder you ended up stockpiling shit for a living.'

Lesley, the one who had ridiculed Fiona and Sally for their interest in South Africa, and the down trodden everywhere, suddenly became a champion of the oppressed. Under Thatcher's rule, she changed, but then so did lots of people, because no one in PAYE felt comfortable with the rug constantly being pulled from under their feet. And then the night came when Thatcher's hotel was bombed. Personally, my suspicion fell automatically on Lesley. I phoned her first thing in the morning, 'Just where were you last night Miss Page?' I asked. 'Is it true you were in the vicinity of Brighton Pier plying your trade?'

She said 'Piss off O'Connell, with a name like yours you should be shitting yourself this morning, anyway it's fucking obvious I wasn't involved, she's still giving out isn't she?'

Lesley certainly had the motivation, but then so did millions of others.

The reality was, no matter how much Thatcher's policies were hurting the likes of Lesley's family, they opened doors for people like me. The people she was putting out of work were the manufacturers, the miners and steelworkers, and the ones who gained under Thatcher were the financiers, the paper pushers and the young upwardly, mobile professionals. People who could afford cleaners and wanted to be employers and flaunt their wealth.

To the new breed of wealthy young Londoners, cleaners were like long haul holidays, only worth having if everybody knew about them. Yes they were good times for me because when did you last hear of a manual worker who had a cleaner that wasn't his wife or daughter? Thatcher systematically took miners out of mining and welders out of shipyards, and instead of building big ships they served Big Macs, because it was the service industries turn on the merry go round.

And when unemployment numbers in the North grew embarrassingly big, one of Thatcher's henchmen told them all to 'get on their bikes and get a job,' (Lesley remembered me saying something vaguely similar once to her and she said, 'See O'Connell? Great fucking arses think alike.')

It was all change on the Western front with Thatcher's hand on the helm, the party that was staunchly aligned with the family broke away from its tradition, and communities that had been intact since the war were suddenly no more. They were dispersed throughout London and the South East to cities whose pavements were lined, not with gold but with fast food joints. It wasn't all doom and gloom though because the migratory workers didn't get piss all, they just got low wages, free food while working and best of all a free uniform. It had the same ring of indecency to it as the great scam in India when they handed men free transistor radios in return for a vasectomy. Hardly a bargain when you really think about it, but by the time anyone thought it through, it was too late to do anything about it, because as Lesley put it 'They 't'were down South having a reet shite time.'

They were the losers.

But there were winners as well. Along with the city gobshites with their red braces sprung a new breed of manhood, a real sucker with nasty thorns and shallow roots. The 1980's British version of the carpetbagger; estate agents! These Scarlett, were mainly male, invariably spotty and always sporting filofaxes. The majority of them had serious speech defects as well, that made them prone to exaggeration with all things concerning size. They were hated by virtually everyone, including their own mothers whom they would have sold for a parking space.

Once, as Lesley and me were cutting through Croydon market, on a Saturday afternoon, a fishmonger held a gleaming red spotted plaice under Lesley's nose. He said to her in a real cockney, lad about town voice, 'fancy a nice plaice, darlin'?

She hated the sight of fish and leapt back in disgust. 'Do you know something?' she said to him, 'You sound like an estate agent and that fucking fish looks like one.'

All those changes that Thatcher ushered in benefited me Scarlett, because like you I read the situation well, and for that I reckon I owe myself a 'round of a claws,' as Daisy would put it. You knew when the war was over that Atlanta would have to be rebuilt, and building materials would sell at a premium, likewise, I looked and saw a society driven by image was being formed and the only way to succeed was to meet it head on.

The new world of the 1980's was the beginning of a materialistic age and the icon of that era summed it all up when she sang 'I'm a material girl.' It was the starting point of widespread belief, that the things you owned, rather than the person you are is what really counts. It was all to do with perception. Thatcher brought bleeding tears to the eyes of every bleeding heart in the country when she declared one day, that there was no such thing as society. When I heard that, I wanted to throw my hands in the air, and scream for joy at the recognition of a kindred spirit. It suited my outlook on life perfectly because it was people who had bollixed me up.

Cleaning boomed and so did counselling as more and more people, myself among them, searched for a black cat in a black room, that wasn't even there. I've still got the contract for 'The

Balmy Evenings' nursing home; I keep it on as a sort of lucky talisman, but to begin with I had to take each and every job I could get hold of, skirt round enormous overdrafts, pilfer Nick Grainger's cleaning materials along with his clients and find something rarer than gold dust. Decent Staff.

When I first started out with my flat mates and Poppy and Patsy; it was like walking on soft-boiled eggs in stilettos, and it wasn't until I was in a position to employ entirely new staff that I was able to pass myself off as Phoenix and not Sinead. We all worked like dogs and I had to pay well over the odds to keep them on board.

I really grew to despise Sally though, she wore a permanent sneer and she came with a list as long as her nose of the things she wasn't prepared to do. She got on everyone's nerves with her constant moaning, if it wasn't one thing it was another, she was Essex's answer to Aunty Phil with her grousing. I would have loved to have told her to piss off, but I needed all the help I could get.

But then, besides being a professional grouser, she was a notorious tight arse as well, always saving for something, double checking her bank statements and crying when she spilled her lager. When Geldof appeared on television to stir up support for his Band Aid concert, he used words to the effect of, 'Get off your fucking arses and do something about it, get your hands out of your pockets and give.' Sally was incensed.

She leapt off her beanbag and stormed out muttering something about there being no call for 'talk' like that. Lesley said it wasn't his language that maddened her, 'Just the fact he was fucking well asking for money.' And she backed her statement up saying, 'But what would you expect from someone who'd buy mushy peas rather than fork out for bubble bath?'

Fiona on the other hand was decent, she didn't relish cleaning bogs any more than Sally did, but at least she didn't complain or count her wages out in front of me.

Patsy was her usual plodding old self, and Poppy; well she was my guardian angel.

You got your start in business Scarlett, via the assets you stole from the Yankee soldier you murdered; and mine came courtesy of Nick Grainger. It didn't take him too long though to figure out why I was so keen to man his phones on a Saturday. He was furious, he effed and blinded and had the fucking cheek to ask who was I working for? It was beyond his comprehension that I was working for myself. I didn't shatter his illusions though. 'Her majesty's Customs and Excise' I said.

He didn't say another word.

Finally there was Lesley, who in fairness did roll her sleeves up, worked hard and kept Sally in some kind of order. Mind you the stress of working with her nearly finished me before I'd even started. She couldn't work without taking the piss, and I lived in fear of her coming face to face with my clients because there was no telling what she might say. In view of this I had to make sure that Lesley and I always paired together. One of my early jobs was the flat of an interior designer (another lot who were on the up in the 80's,) and Lesley almost lost me my first truly valuable contact.

The flat was like a film set, everything in it was immaculate, except for one thing; the dirty knickers left scattered over the bedroom floor. Lesley firmly drew the line at touching them, and one day I caught her lifting them up with the end of a broom handle before dropping them into a laundry basket. When I asked her what she was doing, she replied. 'I'm taking these fucking knickers to a resettlement place because no way, am I touching some slobbish cows breakfast remnants with my bare hands.' So she continued, all the time keeping up a running commentary about Brands Hatch and skid marks.'

I had already told Lesley several times to go easy and to watch her mouth; I lived in fear of people overhearing the state of their knickers or love life being discussed. And of course it happened. The immaculate beanpole walked in to find Lesley carrying a pair of her white knickers on the handle of the broom, waving them about like a flag shouting, 'Make way, cease firing, cease firing.'

The woman looked at Lesley in horror. 'What the hell is going on?' she demanded and my heart sank as I saw my prized contract disappearing down the drain. Lesley wasn't in the least bit fazed, she went over to the woman, put her hand on her arm and said 'God luv, I'm sorry, I was just practising for the finals of my Red Cross exam tonight - it's on combat situations.'

The woman believed her; why else would anyone carry knickers on a broom handle?

When they call witnesses to the trials of the rich and famous they should make the chief one the cleaner, because it's the cleaner who really gets to the nub of what a person is like. They know all about the scrubbed up doctor in his sterile gown and mask who gives a nurse a bollocking for a stray hair, yet keeps bread and cheese sporting forty shades of green in his own kitchen. Or the frigid little set designer with her emphasis on style and panache, who pisses in her bedroom sink, rather than walk bare foot across the cold tiled floor to the bathroom. Some professional people seriously lose their mystic when you see what they get up to in private.

Most of the work I got to begin with was in ordinary private households and some of it was so awful that sometimes I'd think I had backed the wrong horse, should throw the duster in and go back to college and quit while I was behind.

Scarlett I remember reading how you were glad your mother wasn't around to see how you turned out, well that's exactly how I felt the day I picked up a cats turd mistaking it for a slice of Swiss Roll. I was glad Mom was over seventy miles away and couldn't see the daughter who was destined to get an education and a life free from domestic drudgery, literally shovelling shit for a living.

Mind you my education didn't stop when I took up cleaning; it merely went down another track. I learnt an awful lot, especially from the stuff people keep under their beds. When I was a child Mom used to say, 'Go upstairs and clean that filth out from under your bed.' She meant of course, dirty socks and underwear. But cleaning under the beds of London gave a completely new meaning to 'filth under the bed.' Some of the stuff was mind blowing, for the first time the British preoccupation with crime and punishment began to make sense. The whips and masks and handcuffs, well they were unbelievable. I didn't even know what some of the items were.

Lesley of course put me straight in no uncertain terms, but the idea of men paying someone to beat and humiliate them was preposterous. I didn't believe her. I thought she was taking the piss. Lesley however was pragmatic, she said. 'There's great money in it and I wouldn't mind kicking the shit out of an old git and getting paid for it.' It was all news to me, but then I was learning more about everything with each passing day. I rented a garage in Acton, which I used for storage and every penny I made went straight back into the business because its very existence soaked money up.

It was something of an obsession, I had to make it work, but at times it was all so depressing being treated like shit by gobshites. Lesley and Sally and Fiona continued to have a social life, but mine died a slow death. I went up the West End and to the Hammersmith Palias a few times to please them rather than myself, I didn't have the money or the time to spare, but it wasn't just that. All three of them were desperate for blokes and for sex. Lesley simply wanted to clock up a certain number of scores, while Sally and Fiona wanted some evidence of having lived, before settling down with a Harry Enfield look-alike somewhere in the Home Counties.

But I hadn't grown out of my revulsion for men, I couldn't bear the thought of one of them touching me, or delivering some worn out chat up line like 'I'd love to father your children.' Honest to God, this creep in a club actually said that to me. I turned my back on him, but he merely followed it up with, 'Violet's are bluc, Roses are red, Lets cut the crap, and head for bed.'

I said 'No, you've got it wrong, 'Roses are red, Violets are blue, My dog is pregnant, It must have been you.' I nicked that from Lesley, she used to chant it to Simon in the building society and he always thought she was being dead romantic.

There was another occasion in a club near Leicester Square, when a whole gang of blokes descended on us the moment we entered. The one who sought me out was a real slime ball, and trying to shake him off was like trying to wipe shit off a shoe. His mates though were luckier. I saw Lesley and the others at intervals, all flushed and glowing and in need of a comb. The slime ball must have noticed as well because just as we were going, I heard one of his mates say to him, 'how did you get on?'

He replied 'Trust my luck, I picked the fucking dyke.'

That really stung, but do you know something Scarlett? I think he was voicing what most men secretly believe, that any woman who can resist them must be a queer. But frankly, if the choice was between being a dyke or getting off with the likes of slime ball, I'd have my hair cropped tomorrow.

Anyway, Scarlett, that was how it all started. The first year was nothing more than an expensive practise run. I had to learn cleaning techniques, because like everything, cleaning does have a formula, there are ways and means of cutting corners that are not obvious. And I had to learn about staff management.

Using my new name helped, Phoenix Ashton sounded so formal, a thousand miles away from Sinead O'Connell with its aura of candles and incense and life being lived on its knees. I was now living on my feet and God it was different.

I took a lot of stick from Lesley and the others over my new name, 'Why Phoenix?' they asked. I didn't say anything about a glorious resurrection from the ashes of an earlier life, I just said it sounded tough and business like, but Lesley sharp as ever said.

'Wasn't the Phoenix the bird in the ashes? Go easy round the electrics Sinead.' That was a bit too close for comfort, but thankfully she soon discovered my new initials and her mind was diverted, 'Ah, P.A.,' she said, 'now that suits you much better, because I've always known you are a piss artist at heart.'

The new me finally emerged when I got new staff, and didn't have to rely on friends anymore. I knew right back when I first nicked Nick Grainger's work that staff was going to be my biggest problem; if there had been such a thing as convict labour, I would have used it just like you did Scarlett. It's the stigma attached to cleaning that makes it so undesirable, it's just not the sort of job school children aspire to, in reality it's the job of the last resort and few people can tolerate it for long. But you know Scarlett; it's not the job per se that's bad - for every cleaner sweeping out cold and draughty public bogs; there are cleaners like mine, working in scrupulously clean, warm and elegant houses.

Certainly my stint at 'shovelling shit' as Lesley so eloquently described my business, didn't last long; it came to an abrupt end when I moved up market and it certainly isn't the case now. Most of my maids work in houses that are virtually unlived in, because the owners are away, breaking their necks to pay off huge mortgages. Most of them only want a cleaner in the same way they want a Gucci handbag. It is usually a case of want, not need. Lots of them started out as ordinary people, left of centre, chanting for Mandela's release, and somewhere under the power suits a weak heartbeat can still be detected.

They often feel uneasy about having a 'maid,' they do touching little things like, order 'The Mirror' along with their copy of 'The Guardian.' Others are pure working class reared on the mantra 'cleanliness is next to Godliness,' contracts with people like that never last long, because they can't stand the bloody strain of getting out of bed at the crack of dawn, to get the place clean before the cleaner arrives. Others again are jumped up farts, but that's another story.

You can't dismiss cleaning out of hand, it's like any job; it can be good or bad. Teaching is a case in point. I know someone, who skidded past five mangy O'levels, with the handicap of coming from Essex, who now teaches in a plummy public school where the kids are bursting a gut to learn. They rise up and down like a yoyo every time she enters or leaves a room, and generally treat her like God's rep on earth.

But there are scores of others, probably better educated who end up in a duff school in some back passage of a place like Boston, where they have to arm wrestle fat gits, just to get them to take their coats off. And once that's done, listen while the fat gits try to articulate their opinion, that teachers are nothing more than fucking morons anyway.

To move the business upmarket, I had to introduce an element of hard to get. I changed from Phoenix Ashton Enterprises to Phoenix Maids and decked my cleaners out in black uniforms with a white apron, sort of French Maidish without the sleaze. Having a Phoenix Maid had to mean something; a bit like 'I'd only have a Norland nanny for my brat and a Phoenix Maid for my trash.'

Most of my staff back in the eighties were foreign girls; desperate to work cash in hand. Foreigners were easier to keep in line, most of them were just grateful to be working. Looking back, I can say without any real pride or shame, I got where I am today by using a sexist and ageist agenda. I only hired women, since men tend to be useless. The willing but uncertain are painful to the eye, with their little dabs here and little dabs there, touching ornaments as if they're going to bite, and the 'know alls' are a pain in the arse with their, 'No problem, this job won't take me five minutes.' They are dead right, it never does and it shows.

My second rule in the early days; was an upper age limit of thirty. Cleaners over that age I found, have the same affect on other staff, as over ripe bananas do on other fruit. They know all the ruses; how to be awkward within an inch of losing their job; and they spread discontentment and dissatisfaction, better than Billy Bunter could ever dream of doing at a weight watchers convention.

Anyway, besides being easier to handle, young staff were necessary because the emphasis in the eighties wasn't on what you did, but what you looked like. Phoenix Maids were trained to put emphasis on the immediate, they left behind sparkling mirrors and taps and fresh flowers, courtesy of the company. Older women would have beaten mats and turned mattresses, but that wasn't required. When a slip of a girl in a uniform turned up, not a middle aged woman, in baggy tights sporting a hacking cough, the cleaner became something to boast about, a must have acquisition.

Now almost fifteen years later it sounds calculated, tacky and cynical and it was. But it worked. I refined it for the nineties and the New Millennium and it is still a raging success. I'm not going to weep into my whiskey over a bit of tack; all I did was face the world as it really was. The end really did justify the means and it was only fools who sat on a spiked fence thinking, 'ooh I don't know if this is right.'

I cheated with my tax, my VAT, in fact everything and if I used the same staff management techniques today; I'd spend my entire life in front of some tribunal or other. Anyway, it wasn't a case of slow start, then boom, boom. House prices did rocket and thanks to Mrs T, I got my foot well and truly on the ladder. After selling my council maisonette with the aid of a few lies, I was able to buy two flats in Wandsworth, one I lived in, the other I rented out.

It was like a licence to print money. Sometimes I'd think about my family in Kent in their houses overlooking the sea. Fortunes were there to be made, yet vast chunks of the population slept through it all while others became frenzied. Total immersion jobs, head neck and arse in debt, believing against all reason and common sense that the boom was going to last forever. Those property boom years of the late eighties were like a new religion, a tacky one that you might pick up in some beyond the bounds American Evangelical show, stuffed full with promises of money buying undying happiness, all win and no lose, 'Hey punters just show your hand if you want more.' The boom didn't last of course and when the explosion came, the people who had jabbered in pubs and bars about the value of their houses; were silenced overnight.

Recession hit Britain with a vengeance Scarlett at the end of the eighties, and two words, no one under forty; had ever heard before, were suddenly on everybody's lips, 'Negative Equity.'

House prices plummeted and places that were once sought after; were suddenly almost impossible to give away. There was real human tragedy; even I was touched by it. Thousands of people were repossessed; lots of them former clients of mine and they weren't all greedy bastards. Lots of them were families forced to pay extraordinary prices for ordinary homes, because that was the market economy at work. It was too miserable to even think about it, so I didn't.

Some people faced it as it was and sold at a lost, while others held tight and took to working round the clock just to make ends meet. But there were those who took direct action; unable to face total financial ruin they killed themselves. There was a lot of suffering, but very little pity. The great Mrs T been proved right, there was no such thing as society, she got criticised for it, but was found to be spot on, because when individuals began to suffer there was piss all by way of community spirit to help them get it together again.

The nineties hadn't long started when Thatcher got her own marching orders, and joined the expanding dole queues, stabbed in the back by a bunch of taffs. As she left Downing Street, she was photographed with tears in her eyes. There was tears in mine too when I saw her bravely fighting back the inevitable, there is nothing mighty or great or thrilling in watching the downfall of a proud person. No matter the rights and wrongs of Thatcherism, she was owed a more dignified send off than the one she got. Her going marked the end of an era and there seemed to be nobody big or colourful enough to take her place. The gloom and fog of depression merely got worse and reached a crescendo when the grey mouse of a man that took over from her declared to the repossessed and the unemployed, 'If it ain't hurting it ain't working.' When I heard him utter those insulting words, I wanted to poke a poker up his arse and ask him, 'Does that hurt?'

Sanctimonious shites; who had bought their homes way back in the sixties and seventies, came out of the woodwork to gloat about it all. They phoned in old farts on radio shows and said, 'It was greed that did it, back in my day we cut our cloth, not like these young fools today, living the high life with their drink and drugs and running up debts like willy nilly.'

I've never met willy nilly, but I'd sure as hell like to, he sounds quite a character. There was one group though that got it in the balls and received nothing but applause for it and that was estate agents. News of another chain biting the dust was the only thing that brought a smile to most people consumed with debt.

The down turn hit me badly, but I held tight. I figured cleaners were still a necessity, sit it out I told myself, let others go to the wall, and there would be more clients than ever. So I carried on as if there was no recession, only cutting back on my private spending and wheedling bigger and bigger overdrafts. It was a risk but I had to take it. I advertised, kept the profile up and worked around the clock and against the odds it worked.

The fact is, success really breeds success, and no I'm not trying to flog you one of my franchises Scarlett, but the truth is, people had heard enough complaining, they were relieved to employ someone who seemed to be on the up, and not out to make them feel guilty for having survived a recession.

Actually Scarlett, I didn't just survive the recession, I benefited from it, because during it I bought my lovely house in Wandsworth. If it had been available a few years earlier it would have been out of my reach. And like all things, the gloom came to an end, and the mid nineties saw house prices begin to rise again. I had ridden the storm, came out of it with my business intact, a valuable house, a builder to do it up from top to bottom at a fraction of the price he would have charged a few years previously. And to cap it all, I met Jack.

Phoenix

She could have continued writing the entire night, but mention of Jack's name catapulted her swiftly forward to the present. She replaced the top on her pen and locked the book back safely in its drawer.

Closing the study door quietly behind her, she headed for the kitchen with the intention of having one last drink before bed, but was stopped in her tracks, when she saw a shaft of light peeping out from under the kitchen door. She wasn't the only one, who now roamed the house in the early hours; it seemed Jack had also lost his desire for sleep. Unable and unwilling to face a stilted conversation, she went instead to the bathroom and the miraculous shampoo bottle hidden on the top shelf.

Chapter Twenty Two

The fine weather continued well into July and the mood of the country began to lift. The new government was firmly installed with a secure mandate for change and last but not least, foot and mouth finally seemed to be under control. Life in Britain was on the up.

None of this however, did anything to lift the mood of depression that now had such a firm hold on Phoenix. There had been a time, when she had valiantly fought any attempt by her mind, to hold a telescope to the past, when she had buried with a frenzy of work and frivolous thought every accidental glimpse of the dark side of the 1980's. Now the reverse was true. All she wanted; was to rest her mind on the familiar pastures of the past but despite her best intentions, the incessant searchlight of the future turned its beam upon her forcing her to focus on the month rapidly hurtling towards her. And the fear and trepidation associated with September multiplied, as the summer days sped by.

She relied steadfastly on Carolyn to oversee the day to day running of Phoenix Maids; for the few occasions when she did take control, only served to undermine her confidence further. Her mind was no longer as attuned as it used to be and the sense of urgency that had always accompanied her business dealings, had dissipated, leaving many of her clients feeling wary and less confident of the apparently more conciliatory Phoenix. She wasn't unaware of the change in herself, just unable to do anything about it.

Often in the dark of night, she consoled herself with the thought that madness might mean oblivion. If the worst was to happen and she took to screaming obscenities in public or staring into the abyss, at least she wouldn't know anything was amiss. But she couldn't fool herself entirely, she was losing control and far from being comfortably unaware of it, she lived daily with its ugly reality.

There was nothing Jack could do to help Phoenix. His attempts to reason with her; met with either venomous denials of anything being wrong, or cool indifferent shrugs. He felt himself drifting away from her, irritated with what he perceived to be her new persona of ineffectualness. 'How much longer' he wondered, 'did she expect him to chase and cajole her?'

Mid July finally brought about Jack's successful acquisition of Shitlegs O'Carolan's garages. Using a variety of aliases, Jack had made a series of offers on O'Carolan's property, only to pull out at the last moment, causing O'Carolan to panic as his contested divorce drew ever nearer to completion. Frantically O'Carolan had sought a solid, silent buyer and just when both his spirit and the price of his property had plummeted to their lowest ebb, Jack stepped in as he had planned to do all along. 'I'll probably only ever use them as storage,' he told a salivating O'Carolan, 'Although with just pedestrian access, even that might prove difficult'.

He had no conscience whatsoever about purchasing the pipe dream of a council tenant; it was a classic case of speculating to accumulate, with the added bonus of shafting a shifty shyster. The night following completion, Shitlegs O'Carolan turned up slightly the worse for drink on the doorstep of the Keane household. It was Phoenix who answered the erratic knocking on the front door, and she cursed when she saw him for she couldn't bear the sight of the man, drunk or sober. As she watched him swaying back and forth in the evening breeze, the thought crossed her mind that he might have got word of Jack's intentions concerning the recently purchased garages.

'Damn Jack', she thought irritably, 'this is just what I need, a moron kicking up a stink.' She was about to tell him that Jack was away, when he saved her the effort.

'It's all right,' he said throwing his arms up as if he were a conductor in front of an orchestra. 'I don't want them back; I've only come to ask Jack, the name of the firm in Boston that's looking for the plasterers.'

She showed him into the front room and collected Jack from the kitchen. He grimaced when she told him O'Carolan was there, but nonetheless greeted his visitor with a smile of welcome. To look at him Phoenix thought scathingly, you would think seeing O'Carolan was the best news he had received for a year. He shook hands and slapped O'Carolan on the back, urging him to take a seat and turning to Phoenix, asked her to bring in a few bits to eat, since this called for a celebration. She stared at him, as if he had taken leave of his senses, what was he playing at? Ordering her around like a skivey in front of a guttersnipe. Jack returned her stare with a wink and with a sinking heart, she realised, the game concerning O'Carolan still had some running time.

When she re entered the room, Jack was pouring three large glasses of whiskey, he put the bottle down and cleared a space on the table, taking from her some plates of French bread, cold meat and a selection of cheeses. There was a side of poached salmon in the fridge, but she certainly wasn't going to waste that on O'Carolan, she'd give it to Daisy's kitten first.

She watched as O'Carolan stared in confusion at the green olives she had used to garnish the meat. He picked one up and twiddled it between his forefinger and thumb as if he were a jeweller examining an exquisite ring.

'Will that do you Sir?' she asked sarcastically and turned to go, but Jack pulled her arm.

'Come on,' he said 'join us in a toast.' She hesitated for a moment before sitting down in the armchair nearest the door. O'Carolan turned his flushed face to her.

'I'm surprised at your old man here,' he said indicating towards Jack with a jerk of his head, 'He must be losing his grip, those fucking garages are worthless, they are landlocked, just like fucking Surrey.' He laughed, a hissing, blabbing little laugh, like gas escaping from a balloon.

Phoenix flicked her eyes warily across to Jack, wondering if there was going to be a scene after all, but Jack seemed strangely impassive. 'Oh well,' he said leaning back in his chair as comfortably as if O'Carolan had merely passed an opinion on the weather, 'You win some and you lose some, who knows what the future holds,' and with that, he raised his glass towards O'Carolan.

O'Carolan in turn raised his glass and at the same time threw the olive in his other hand into the air, leaping up like a salmon to catch it with his mouth. Seconds later he coughed and spluttered like a choking pig, and for a moment Phoenix feared she

would have to do a good turn and perform a Heimlich manoeuvre on him.

'For shits sake,' he gasped when he finally managed to
breathe again, 'That's the sourest grape I've ever eaten.'

'So far' Phoenix murmured to Jack, who in return fired a
warning look to stay silent. When O'Carolan fully regained
composure, Jack cut to the chase.

'Look,' he said to O'Carolan, handing him a white envelope.
'I've put in all the contact names of firms in the Boston area that
I dealt with, you won't regret the move; the place could have
been designed for you.'

O'Carolan stared at the envelope before picking it up and
hoisting it into his back pocket. 'I'm sure you are right old man,
at least from what you said I'll be able to buy somewhere to live,
all I need to do now, is find a seller as gullible as you.'

'Impossible,' Jack laughed, 'but I tell you, the moment I set
eyes on the place, I thought of you, you'll be welcomed as one of
their own.' Again glasses were raised and eventually O'Carolan,
after a protracted, emotional goodbye left the house. Jack closed
the door on his visitor and returned to the lounge where an
astounded Phoenix awaited him.

'I don't understand you at all,' she said, 'You talk about me
being out of it, yet you just let him walk all over you.'

Initially, Jack said nothing; he sat down on the settee and
drained his glass before turning to his wife. 'I'm surprised at
you,' he said. 'You are usually the ring leader when it comes to
keeping the lid on something hot, but for your information, that
bastard's grin is going to be well and truly wiped off his face,
does that satisfy you?'

'No,' she replied argumentatively. 'What satisfaction is there
in having a creep going around, thinking he pulled one over Jack
Keane?'

Jack leaned back into the settee and raised his feet onto the
table, a habit that annoyed Phoenix. She imagined it was the
kind of gesture he used when he lived with Polly, to signify the
man of the house was back and in need of being waited upon.

'You really aren't as sharp as you used to be, are you Puss?'
he said. 'Do you honestly think, O'Carolan is heading into the

happy ever after sunset, because if you do, you are more out of touch than I realised.'

That was a suggestion that Phoenix didn't like, it merely served to confirm what she already feared, and in a bid to prove the opposite, she became more entrenched, but even to her ears her argument sounded hollow. 'O'Carolan now has money, in a place like Boston he could even buy into a partnership, it just sickens me that you are the one to give him his big break. All he will do is dream on about how he screwed you.'

'Complete bollocks,' replied Jack contemptuously, 'He'll have that money pissed up against the wall before the summer is out and the only chance of him staying put in Boston, is if they sentence him to life, for murdering a fellow shit.' He looked up and smiled at her disgruntled face, and said in a more conciliatory tone. 'No, he'll be back, probably when the first planning notices go up and that will remove the grin off his face.'

But his words of consolation were wasted, because Phoenix wasn't listening anymore. When it came to writing to Scarlett, she could drift on for hours, sinking deeper and more contentedly into the far past, but conversation was a different matter. It had the possibility of weaving out of her control and she no longer possessed the agility of thought to guarantee normal responses. Invariably she found her mind switching off and often she was left fumbling as to who and what she was speaking about.

She reached forward and lifted her glass of the table 'I've got a letter to write,' she said, 'It's one I meant to do earlier.' And before Jack could enquire, she left the room and headed to the study.

Dear Scarlett,   **10th July 2001**

In my last letter, I should have told you how I came to meet and marry Jack; but my courage deserted me. Just telling you about the day I met Jack, acted like a switch, fast forwarding me into the present, the very place I don't want to be.

But his existence in my life is so crucial; that I can't ignore how he came into it. Watching him in action tonight; was like watching a master craftsman at work. He deftly and niftily extracted a man's prized possession and not only was the man unaware of the robbery, he deluded himself into thinking he was the master thief. I have nothing but admiration and a great sense of foreboding.

I met Jack on the 23rd of May 1995, when the first green shoots of recovery were up and truly established. I was on my way to see a very angry client, a hospital administrator, one of the people appointed to put a human face on the NHS. A maid of mine had accidentally broken her lamp. She phoned me up in a fury and demanded that I came personally to collect the broken object with the aim of replacing it immediately.

Naturally, I assured her that we were fully insured and offered my apologies, and in return she told me in no uncertain terms where to put them. She didn't want money; she wanted a replica, and with that she slammed the phone down. No wonder the NHS is up Shit Street.

Her chintzy little flat was stuffed full of useless odds and ends. It was no wonder something had got broken; there wasn't room to swing a mouse, never mind move, without sweeping something or other of a surface. I found the lamp where she said it would be, on the hall table. It was a cheap and haughty nude with an outstretched hand balancing two balls that now lay in pieces at her feet; her left kneecap was also chipped. It made me laugh because I'd been expecting some Grecian work of art. I tucked the nude under my arm and went back to the car.

And that's when I saw him. A tatty warehouse opposite was being converted into luxury water side apartments, and I had taken an opportunity to peep through the barbed wire to see how it was coming along, since new accommodation of this calibre, usually means more business.

Jack was there, talking to the architect and he looked up. When he saw me, he looked over enquiringly, as if he thought I was waiting to talk to him. I immediately scuttled back to my car but he followed me.

'Hello,' he said, 'That's a fine specimen of a pen holder you have there.' His accent was soft and his face open and friendly.

'Pen holder,' I said. 'Where?' He walked across and picked up the statue that I had placed face down on the roof of the car. He pointed to its backside and said.

'That's what you call a pen holder.'

I had to laugh, I told him it made a change from calling it a bike stand and he laughed. 'Don't you think she's very elegant?' I asked.

He picked her up and pretended to examine her carefully, 'Well she's missing something,' he said, and before stopping to think I said. 'Yes, she's lost her balls.'

'Oh yeah?' he said raising his eyebrows, 'then she's a very queer lady and by the look of those knee caps, a very dirty tackler.'

I asked him about the redevelopment across the way, and he told me there were great plans for the place. He asked if I lived locally and I told him I'd just bought a place, in Wandsworth. 'It's on the up,' he said and I agreed. He then said 'If you need a hand with any building work, here's my card,' and began searching his pockets. I knew there was no card in his pocket; it was just a way of extending the conversation and it reminded me of my own fiasco with business cards when I first started up.

'I'd take a bet that's your own business,' he said pointing to my logo emblazoned car.

'And how would you know that?' I replied.

He just tapped the side of his nose and said. 'Oh I know these things,' and then quite abruptly, he put his hand out and said. 'It's been a pleasure meeting you Miss?' and I replied.

'Ashton, same here Mr?' and he said.

'Jack, Jack Keane is the name.' He gave a wave and walked off; whistling the song I will always associate with him, Peggy Lee's, 'Feelin Too Good Today Blues.' I couldn't fathom it, I felt so let down and disappointed when I saw his departing back. I don't know why. What had I been expecting, a date?

I had spent almost my entire adult life, avoiding men, risking all kinds of rumours and innuendo and suddenly, I was desperate for the company of a man dressed in shabby clothes with his own logo of 'I couldn't give a piss,' stamped right across his forehead.

Over the years as the business grew and developed, I had numerous opportunities to meet men. There were advertising executives and sales representatives, not to mention the occasional client. It was pleasant to attend the odd business lunch or dinner date, even though they usually turned out to be nothing more than primal grooming sessions. Greasy salesmen telling me what a fantastic business package I had put together and me telling them, how marvellous their products, or sales strategies had been.

I would have loved to have had someone to go out with, to relax and talk to and laugh with. But the thoughts of sex and the inevitable showdown of birth were repugnant enough to act as a good set of brakes as far as men were concerned.

That was until I met Jack.

Coincidentally, the day I met him was also the day I poached Carolyn. She was working at a bookies in Vauxhall. I knew the man who owned it well; Shay Hickey, a native of Mayo and just about the biggest rogue on two legs. He was as bent as a hairpin and involved in an untold number of betting scams. However his luck ran out and the Jockey Club and a few others caught on to him. I had the cleaning contract for the suite of offices next door to his shop and used to spend the odd occasion chatting with him whenever I was in the area. It was on those occasions that I noticed Carolyn. She stood out like a little flower in a very seedy world.

I did something that day Scarlett, that I am not proud of, but which I don't regret either. I inferred to Hickey that Carolyn was most likely his informer. I did it very persuasively and Hickey believed me. He sacked her on the spot; in fact he was a total bastard about it, and if she had had any cop on she would have taken him to the cleaners for the way he went about it.

Of course I did the decent thing. I immediately offered Carolyn a job, a much better one and far better paid. And she was incredibly grateful to me. I don't feel bad about it, she was wasted on Hickey and I really needed someone I could trust; Hickey after all had a bloody great mob looking out for him. I was alone and in much greater need of someone who wouldn't sell me out to the tax man, or VAT or any of the other black-guards who were chasing my heels back then.

I spent the rest of that particular day sourcing that wretched lamp. Up and down Oxford Street, I went. I tried Selfridges, John Lewis even DH Evans, where a particularly snotty young woman, told me they most certainly did not stock lamps like that.

Finally I went into Argos and spotted a replica instantly. The following day I took the statue and lamp round to the NHS dragon. I didn't have to, but I had a double mission, one of them being the hope that I might by chance, bump into Jack. There was no sign of him and that put me in bad form.

The dragon though was there alright, waiting for me in her den, and she snatched the lamp out of my hands before I even said a word. 'Just tell your maids to be more careful in future,' she said, and started to close the door on my face. She might have been a good administrator, but she was a lousy mind reader. I was furious. I pushed the door back open and told her there wouldn't be a next time. There was no way I was being held to ransom by a pig on horseback.

Like I told you Scarlett, this business brings contact with all sorts of people. Some really are the salt of the earth, and others are pure waste, excrement really, successful, purely on account of who; rather than what they know.

There were benefits of the big crunch up that came with the recession, and one of them was watching the gobshites who had crapped on others on their way up, pulling crap out of their hair on their way down. A few of them could have done worse than ask their cleaner for advice, because it's surprising how much a cleaner notices things. They often have a finger on the pulse of what is really going on in particular places because they are the only ones to slip between the scenes of a business, front and back stage so to speak. I can't tell you the amount of times one of my cleaners has said to me, 'You want to watch Creep and Co, mark my words, they are going down the pan,' and sure enough, within weeks they are flushed out and away.

Anyway, a couple of days after meeting Jack, when my guard was completely down, he phoned me at work. I recognised his voice immediately.

'Can I speak to the proprietor of Dublin city's big park please?' he asked.

'Not if it's Jack Keane speaking,' I replied.

'Oh do,' he said, 'there's nothing I like better than a stroll in the park.'

He asked me out to dinner, a bistro in Wimbledon village. As soon as I put the phone down, I regretted saying yes, and Carolyn soon discovered that Shay Hickey didn't have a monopoly on foul language; because at the age of thirty one I was going out on my first real date and was more fractious than any teenager. I didn't have a clue what to wear or how to act. I so badly wanted to create an image, I had one in mind, but nothing I put on seemed to live up to it. In the end I took Carolyn's advice and settled for a black satin suit. I remember that first date; everything about it, the food, the drink; even the weather.

And Jack.

He swore, he smoked, and he drank and I felt like I had come home, in a very peculiar way. He laughed when I told him that I'd have the same as him, so long as it wasn't pork. He said what was wrong with the poor old pig that so many people had a downer on him. I told him that a few months previously I had eaten some disgusting pork, at a business lunch in Golders Green.

'For God's sake girl,' he said. 'It must have been a dog you ate; they'd never get a pig into Golders Green.'

After the meal we went to a pub in the village. It was one of those calm spring evenings that make London seem so special. The pavement outside the pub was crowded, and we sat until told to go home by the landlord. Jack phoned me the following day, and invited me for a drink at the weekend, but I declined. He persisted though and eventually I agreed to go out with him on the Monday. You see, I had to be in control. I had to be certain he was interested, not just passing time with me.

We went for the drink and followed it up the following week by a trip to the Epsom Derby, that's when I nearly blew us out of the water by having a panic attack on the train.

Our relationship flourished Scarlett because it was based on friendship.

I remember reading how Rhett shared stories with you that you felt weren't quite right for a 'lady' to listen to, but you loved them, because their crudity and honesty was liberating. It was the same with Jack. He told me about some disgraceful things he did when he first came over to London and in return I told him about some of the shadier things I did. He was never shocked or disapproving and telling him was soothing, a bit like going to confession, without the penance. It was perfect, except for one thing. I feared him getting close to me.

Sex frightened me. Every time Jack went slightly further than kissing, I tensed up. I tried to make light of it and I think Jack thought I was being a tease, keeping him waiting. I wondered how long he would continue to think that before thinking, perhaps I just had gonorrhoea and was reluctant to share it with him.

I must have been desperate because in the end I saw a doctor. She was a young Australian, relaxed and to the point. 'What exactly do you mean?' she said. 'When you say you have a problem with sex?'

I couldn't bring myself to say 'Well I've only had it once and that was when I was ambushed by an ape.' So I told her that I found it difficult to relax enough.

'The acid test is,' she said. 'Have you ever had sex that you've enjoyed?'

Well there was only one answer to that, and the end result was her arranging for me to see a sex therapist by the name of Sara Edmunds. And I went. I really did. One of the first things Sara Edmunds did; was ask me; if I had been sexually abused as a child. I shook my head and she then proceeded to ask if I had ever been the victim of a sexual assault.

I answered, No, very vehemently, but I think she knew from the way I shifted in my chair, that I was lying. Why didn't I just tell her the truth? She wasn't a Shelby, she didn't want to know my life history. She was working to a very confined brief, how to get me a sex life of sorts, but I still couldn't do it.

She then asked me a whole series of questions like, how many boyfriends had I had; and had I ever had successful sex, and what did I enjoy doing with my present boyfriend. I wanted to shout, 'Stop the fucking asking.'

I felt like a pervert, listening to an endless ream of unbearably personal questions. She then outlined a programme of treatment for me. She said she could sense that I was very reluctant to speak, and that was a great pity, since fears often disappear when spoken about. The critical point was not to rush things and to learn to love my body.

Creating the right atmosphere, she said, was very important. Calming music and candles were a good idea. We (Jack and me) were to start, by only holding hands, we could progress to gentle kissing and touching of the upper body, but on no account were we to touch genitalia. Scarlett, I sniggered like a dirty school girl when she said that, I thought, why would I want to touch Jenny Taylor, I don't even know her. She made another appointment for a few weeks later and I flew out the door like a trapped bird and nearly broke my neck in the process.

How pathetic I was. She was pleasant, calm and calming and if I had let her, she would have helped me. She would have pointed out the risk and foolishness of keeping such a big secret from Jack and she was absolutely right, I did have a problem with my body, I hated it, it felt dirty and used, not good enough, in fact I still feel like that about it.

I never did go back to her; instead I took her advice about the music and creating ambience, which I achieved by almost drinking myself to oblivion. Everything seems different when approached through a haze of alcohol, but even so, the first time I slept with Jack, Scarlett, it was awful, like being assaulted again; when I think about it. Whiskey had me beguiled. It relaxed me to the point of not caring, but the moment I attempted to put not caring to the test, calmness disappeared and anxiety immediately came rushing back like an anxious parent, wanting to know what the hell was going on.

Sex was reduced to an act of initiation; the admission ticket for joining the normal world. It should have been passionate and loving with just the two of us. But Condon was there, lurking in the shadows, and when Jack spoke to me, it was the ape's words I heard. I wondered if Jack was merely reciting a charm, something to get him through it, because he was getting what he wanted, and it was turning out to be truly fucking awful.

I don't really know what Jack made of that first attempt, but he stayed around and gradually through a mixture of clenched teeth and drink, it got better.

Life was rapidly becoming passable, I had my business, financial security and now good company and then one rainy night, Jack accelerated it further along the new path it was travelling along. He had booked as a surprise, a couple of seats at the Adelphi Theatre; I can't even remember what the play was, because I never got to see it. We went to the wrong theatre, and by the time we realised our mistake it was too late to do anything about it, so we went for a meal and a drink instead and walked for what felt like miles in the rain. When we got back to my place, we were both so wiped out that we fell asleep on the settee. I woke up though in the early hours but I couldn't move because Jack was leaning against me and I didn't want to disturb him. I sat, trapped in the dark, forced to listen to Gene Pitney on the radio; he was singing 'Something's Gotten Hold of My Heart'. I'd heard that song many times before, but for the first time ever, I really listened to the lyrics of that song, and it occurred to me that I too was being led away from safety. My soul and senses were being dragged apart. I didn't find the thought romantic at all, in fact it terrified me and immediately I sat bolt upright, ready to run, because that is what I always do when panic hits me. But Jack suddenly sprang into life and pulled me down on top of him.

He said 'Now that you're a fully ruined woman are you going to marry Jack Keane?'

'Is Jack Keane asking?' I replied and he said.

'Yes.'

I hesitated; just long enough for him to look wary, before replying, yes, I would, so long as he fully understood, that I was fully ruined before I met him. It was a feeble attempt at some kind of honesty; I knew what I meant, even though Jack took it as a boast of a sexual past.

We got married at Clapham registry office, on St Patrick's Day 1996, having known each other less than a year and just like you Scarlett, when you married Frank Kennedy, we called two strangers off the street to be our witnesses. You did that because you were in the process of stealing the groom from his bride to be and so had to act smart, we did it because Jack didn't want his family knowing it wasn't a church wedding, and I didn't want my family anywhere near me.

Afterwards, we held an enormous party at an Irish club in Battersea and practically everybody we knew was there, except family. The following night we left for a fortnight's holiday in Seville, where we got caught up in all the dramatic Easter celebrations of Southern Spain.

My wedding day Scarlett, was almost as good as it gets, but for all the joy there was a terrible ache in my heart. Mom wasn't there to see it. Not just the wedding but the way things had turned out for me. She would have liked Jack, she'd have said, 'God made you and the devil matched you.' I felt the loss of Mom more keenly than I'd ever felt it before. I had achieved, and she wasn't there to see it. I felt bereft. But why worry, it looks as if it might all be over anyway, perhaps it has been for a while, it's just that I've been too busy rubber necking the past to see it.

Did I tell you before Scarlett, about that line from a song in the eighties, 'Life is what happens when you're busy making other plans.' A crank murdered the poor guy who wrote those words, on the 8th December 1980. I was living with the great grey grouser, Aunty Phil at the time. The newscaster on the radio solemnly announced.

'Today is the day; the world lost one of the best lyricists of all time, the great John Lennon.' She leaned over and snapped the radio off, 'Enough of that tripe,' she said, 'Today is the feast of The Immaculate Conception, never mind the death of a four eyed gook who ran round the place in the nude.'

Looking back, I think I've spent too much of my life, seriously overrating the value of protection. First there was the effort to protect the ape's wife from the dangers of the mad house, followed by the need to protect Mom from reality. Now reality is facing me and I'll be the one to end up in the mad house. The motivation to do right has caused me nothing but misery. All too late, I've discovered motivation is never enough; it has to be backed up with knowledge.

By protecting Olga, I merely protected the ape; perhaps if I had come clean, I might have given her the very grounds she needed to divorce him. Payback for all the shit she'd had to put up with, because when I think back to her coolness and frigid little ways, she wasn't a happy woman.

In the same way, keeping quiet bought no peace of mind for Mom, instead of having a figure to pile her hate and fury on; she spent her life wondering who and why. The curse of protectionism didn't end there, Scarlett. The moment I married Jack without telling him my history, I was back on the treadmill again, protecting him from the reality of me and I could have carried that, bad as it was but then Daisy came along.

Jack and I never spoke about having a family; I think he just assumed having a child was as inevitable as the wind blowing, so inevitable in fact, that if was pointless even talking about it. For me there was never any doubt, that I'd never have another baby, you wouldn't believe the lengths I went to ensure it didn't happen.

The best part of twenty years had passed since that awful night on the 11th September 1980 when that child was born, but in my mind it was as vivid as the night it happened. The pushing and tugging, pain and anxiety all for nothing; I vowed never again, never will I go through that humiliation, but in September 1996, less than six months after Jack and I had married, I found it had happened again.

I prayed that it was just a nightmare, but as I walked out of the house one morning to buy some milk, I saw a pink dummy lying in the gutter and I knew it was an omen. I sat down on a bench because every part of me was shaking and as I sat hunched forward, shivering like a jelly, a pair of sandaled feet plonked themselves right in front of me. I heard a woman say, 'Are you alright love, you look very shaky.'

I didn't even look up, I just muttered, 'I'm fine, just a bit hot,' and she replied.

'Ooh I get that, I come over all hot and I shake as well.'

Oh how my heart lifted when I heard those words, I thought, 'oh you stupid bloody woman, you're not pregnant at all, it's probably just a bug that's going round,' but when I looked up to smile my thanks at the voice of salvation, I found it belonged to an old woman, who was as simple as the wind.

She said, 'My doctor says it's to do with the change of life, but you look a bit young for that.' I thought if I am pregnant, that will mean a serious change of life for me.

The thought of a baby ripped me apart, I just couldn't go through with it. It was cowardly but I didn't care, having a baby would simply drag the past into the present, I couldn't let it happen. I abandoned the idea of buying milk, and instead went straight to a chemist, bought a pregnancy testing kit and headed for the station toilets. I literally flew up the concrete stairs only to find that the toilet in the Ladies resembled what Jack would call a typical Lincolnshire pub lunch, being piled high and full of shit. The Gents were out of order.

I didn't want to do the test at home so I headed for an Italian cafe bar that had only recently opened, but being mid morning it was almost empty. I ordered a cappuccino and headed straight for the toilet. From there on the whole procedure turned into a farce. The cloakroom lights were activated by the door opening, but they didn't work, it was like the black hole of Calcutta in there. I was so desperate that I ran into the gents, past the urinals into a tiny W.C no bigger than a cupboard.

Two terrible minutes ticked by and when the result came; it was the one I had been dreading, but expecting if you'll excuse the pun. A light but very definite blue line had developed in the second window. I tried looking at it from several different angles in an effort to persuade myself that it wasn't really there, but there was no disguising it. It was only the fear of humiliation at being caught in the gents that kept me from fainting. I opened the door without thinking and immediately slammed it shut because two blokes were pissing away in the urinal. They were talking about their girlfriends, one of them said, 'She's all right but she's got an arse and a half on her, it puts me off.'

The other guy, a real porky looking thing said, 'Drop her mate, arses don't get smaller, you'll end up having to saddle it.'

I felt like a peeping Tom, peering through a crack in the door, hunched like an athlete ready to run the minute they went out, but when they left, another bloke came in, whistling 'always look on the bright side of life.' How cheery he was, bending and straightening his knees as he peed in circles against the urinal. I begged God not to let me witness anyone doing something indecent, or worse still allow me to see someone I knew.

The cheery fellow was swift, in and out, just stopping briefly to throw a smile at himself in the mirror, but as soon as he went, two more blokes came in. I felt paranoid, where had they all suddenly descended from? One man began firing away; while the other one rattled the door I was hiding behind.

'Oi,' he shouted 'hurry up in there; I'm bleeding bursting out here.'

He began banging on the door and the other bloke, the water cannon said, 'It's probably out of order Mike.'

Mike the moron kicked the door and said, 'lousy bloody spics, I'm going over to the jacks in the station, you get the beers in.'

When they left, I tore out so quickly that I caught up with the pair of them up on the stairs, and they were startled by my sudden appearance out of nowhere. I paid for my coffee and left without touching it. The testing kit had only confirmed what I already knew. I was pregnant for the second time in my life.

When you discovered you were pregnant with Bonnie, Scarlett, your first instinct was to have an abortion. Well just like you, I couldn't face the upheaval of having a child, just when life was beginning to look like it had the potential to be worth living again. You were more honest than me though; at least you confided in Rhett and allowed him to talk you out of it. I didn't want to confide in Jack. I didn't want to be talked out of doing what I knew I had to do.

I remember the last few days of that September, being bathed in sunshine and thinking how all the blossoming I had undergone since my wedding day in March, was being slowly submerged into a terrible gloomy fog. I had blossomed, everybody commented on how happy I looked. I just couldn't face going into reverse.

Apart from the pain of that first birth, I remembered stupid things like fearing the gas and air mask; mistaking it for the apes hand, not knowing how to push and being too tense to be examined and hearing one of the nurses comment 'It's a bloody miracle you got pregnant in the first place.'

But it wasn't just physical things that haunted me. I remembered too clearly those awful days as a pregnant teenager, trapped and reliant on others, I had come too far to ever allow myself to suffer like that again. And there was the emptiness, the feeling of having given so much for so little in return, in fact absolutely nothing and I knew that if I had another baby I'd have to relive it all again, it would simply be history repeating itself.

I was so caught, so confused and so alone. There was no one to talk it over with.

A few days later while silently and constantly praying for a miracle, I found the answer to my prayers. I was coming home on the northern line from a franchise deal I had set up in Barnet. A ticket inspector got on the train and when he said to me 'tickets please,' I was so engrossed in my prayer that I replied, 'Hail Mary.' He leapt back as if I was a lunatic and didn't even bother to check my pass. I felt my face burning as the person sitting beside me, began to shuffle away from me, and in an attempt to appear casual and unconcerned, I flicked my eyes up at the adverts.

And that is when the miracle occurred, I saw one that I'd seen a million times before but had never given a second thought to. It was for an abortion clinic, based in the West End, with lunchtime appointments available. It also offered post abortion counselling.

I took the number down and the next morning after Jack had set off for work, I phoned the clinic from a public box across the road. The girl who answered it sounded young and business like, a bit like Phoenix Ashton did back in the eighties. She asked me if I was definitely pregnant, 'How many weeks?' Had I seen a doctor? She arranged an appointment for half past two that same day. The snappiness of it took my breath away. I couldn't believe what I had done. I had made an appointment with an abortion clinic as easily as if it was a hairdresser, and a thousand times more easily than if it had been a dentist. I could only marvel at how far I had travelled from my upbringing, but wasn't that what I had set out to do? Every fibre in my body told me that what I was about to do was wrong; I really believed that eternal hell fire awaited me, but even that didn't deter me.

I decided to go for my appointment by car, even though the clinic had told me that driving immediately afterwards was not recommended. It would give me more control and though parking would be a nightmare, it would be worth it; not having to face people on buses or trains when it was all over. But just as I crossed Wandsworth Bridge; my mobile began to ring. I cursed it and left it, but it rang again and again and I knew somebody was desperate to catch me.

It was Jack. He needed to meet me immediately at The Plough in Wimbledon. I told him I had an important meeting, but he was adamant, 'Put your foot down girl and turn that car round, I have something here that won't wait'. I thought you are not the only one, but he wouldn't be put off, so I U-turned, sick with anxiety and went back over the bridge and made my way to Wimbledon, to The Plough.

Jack was there, with a shit-eating grin on his face. I told him whatever it was he had to show, had better be good and he said, 'I'll tell you; this is one u-turn that you'll never regret.' We drove in his van towards the common and eventually stopped outside what is now our house. He had struck a deal, a real back hander. We could buy this fabulous Georgian house, set in its own grounds, at a fraction of its markets value. It would mean selling Wandsworth, but this was the chance of a lifetime. If I was up for it, it would be ours, but we'd have to act quickly.

'So this is your news,' I said and Jack replied.

'It is, now top that.'

I said 'That's easy; I'm going to have a baby.' I don't know what made me say it, the words just came out, the way they always do with me. I had just done another u-turn; there was no way I'd be going back to that clinic up the West End because Jacks reaction was incredible.

He picked me up and swung me round, he was ecstatic, he kept saying. 'Are you sure, when did you know, why didn't you say?' I told him that I wanted to be certain before saying anything to him. I didn't say a thing about finding out in the slash room of a rip off café.

He was so overjoyed; I could have cried for him, if I had any doubts back then that Jack loved me, they were quashed that day. As we drove back to The Plough to collect the car he kept squeezing my arm, telling me I was wonderful. But I didn't feel wonderful. I felt like a total shit. If Jack hadn't phoned me, a part of him and me would have been ripped away from us forever. No not quite true, it would have joined the other heaps of guilt already on my back and the terrible thing is, I would have done it not to deprive Jack of a child but to have spared him, me and it from future suffering.

When we got to The Plough, Jack ordered another round, this time he insisted on me having a Guinness, he said. 'It will do you the power of good, trust me, I'm not a doctor.' He then rang Tosh and told him to collect the van from the pub car park and to bring it home later. He wanted to take me out to dinner, but we were turned away from two restaurants in a row, on account of Jack being in his working clothes. It felt like Mary and Joseph being turned away from the inn. In the end Jack said 'Fuck them,' and we went to a fish and chip shop instead. He also bought champagne which made me smile because he hates it, but the occasion called for it, so what the hell.

When Tosh called by later that night to drop the van back, he was instantly suspicious, I had to frown a warning at Jack to say nothing, I was already reaping the rewards of having considered a termination, I was racked with a superstitious belief, that God would take this baby away from me now that I wanted it. He would pay me back. No way did I want Tosh or anyone to know about the baby until I felt completely over the danger zone.

Both Jack and I wanted rid of him and he knew it but he wanted an explanation for the champagne. The new house had genuinely slipped both our minds, but Tosh knew something was up. 'You've won the lottery, haven't you?' he said. There was a real note of fear in his voice when he asked that, he's always been convinced that only the stinking rich or teetotallers ever win it, but it doesn't deter him from playing.

In all his gambling he is an eternal optimist.

Later that night, as we lay in bed, we talked about the house, selling the old one and doing up the new one. But the last thing Jack said to me before falling asleep was, 'Where were you going when I called you, was it anything important?'

For once I was truthful, I said, 'Oh just a bit of business, which I am pleased to have avoided.'

My lovely old house in Wandsworth was sold and I felt bizarrely emotional the day we moved out. That house was my degree certificate for having bucked the trend. While our new house was being done up, we moved into Jack's flat in Battersea, he had never bothered to do it up and it was something of a comedown living there.

Morning sickness hit me badly with Daisy and for a time I wondered if twins were a possibility. Even so, I refused a scan, much to my doctor's irritation. This time I was going to call the shots; it was a real case of 'take your stethoscope off my lawn.'

St Patrick's Night came round, our first wedding anniversary and I was already six months gone. We went to a big gathering at an Irish club in Clapham and lots of Jack's old pals from his early days lined up to congratulate him and the sight of them chilled my heart. I saw their compliments to Jack and general camaraderie as efforts to put me down, rather than as the rallying call of friends building up one of their own. I felt like an outsider; and an enormous surge of resentment flooded through me, against Jack, for taking me there.

My aggravation didn't die with the night either. The next day I told Jack I was going to a conference on franchises in Brighton, one was being held at the exhibition centre on the seafront. I'd had the invitation for months; but had stuck it at the bottom of a pile of other rubbish, with absolutely no intention of going to it.

Jack said, 'That's news to me.' I didn't tell him that it was to me as well and when I told him, that I might stay the night depending on the finish time, he was furious. He said it was ridiculous to be going to Brighton after a late night out, it was asking for trouble. He shouted and swore, but I said 'Kiss my arse Jack,' and went.

Of course it was a childish and immature way to act, but that's what insecurity does to you, it makes you irrational, more likely to be guided by fear than common sense. That St Patrick's night party had made me feel like I was losing control. Jack had looked so confident, so completely at home. What could I give him that he didn't already have? Nothing; except the threat that I could do without him; I had to make him understand right from the start, that if he ever chose to walk out, I'd still survive. The only way I felt I could keep him, was by holding the door wide open for him to leave.

I didn't stay the night, the show was shite. Most of the punters didn't look capable of running a brothel for dogs never mind a complicated business. I left early and spent the rest of the day shopping in Brighton. I went into Hannington's department store where I bought the most wonderful white satin baby dress I'd ever seen. It was too beautiful to resist, if Jack had been there he would have said, 'Put it down and buy something neutral, if it's a boy he'll sue you for that.'

In May 1997, a month before Daisy was born, we moved into our Wimbledon address, SW19. Of all the back handers Jack has ever received, this is the real McCoy. The moment I stepped inside, I felt like phoning my family, just to let them know that I had arrived, really arrived.

I have been partially honest with Jack, about my family. He doesn't like the idea of me being estranged from them. I told him that we had a serious falling out years ago, when they made some crazy assumptions about me and I didn't give care if I never saw them again. I told him that when Mom died, she had left the little she had, not to her youngest child, a daughter in London with on the face of it piss all going for her, but to her youngest son who was a fully qualified teacher.

'That's fucking typical,' said Jack. 'Why do the fucking Irish always have to fight and fall out over money or land?' When I shouted back equally angrily, that the fall out had nothing to do with money or land, he said, 'then what the fuck is it to do with, because I can't think of anything else worth falling out over.'

I should have told him; and by doing so knocked the wind completely out of his sails. But of course I didn't. He had to believe that the 'me' of the 1990's was the genuine article, not just a caricature that had evolved out of hate, self loathing and a need to justify a pointless existence.

But Scarlett, in the early hours of June the fifth 1997, life changed completely yet again. Just as I was about to climb into bed my waters broke. I remember thinking, 'Oh please not tonight I'm too tired,' but within the hour the pain started. I elbowed Jack to wake up and he awoke with a start and flew out of bed with the speed of light and began turning round in circles like a dog looking for its tail.

'What, what' he cried.

I said 'Jack it's the baby.'

'Right,' he said. 'I'll be ready in a tick.'

He was. He put on a shirt, socks and boots and nothing else; opened the door to go downstairs and must have felt a draught, because he stopped, looked down at himself and walked back into the room, flopped down in a chair and took his boots off, and started again.

When my little girl was placed in my arms, later that same morning, I felt too overwhelmed to even breathe and when I looked up at Jack, I saw tears on his cheeks. She was beautiful, so soft and pink with just the slightest smattering of golden down on her head.

'Well,' said the midwife 'What a beautiful fresh little daisy you have to greet the dawn'.

Her words made a real impact on Jack, he said 'You're absolutely right, she's a daisy and that's just what we should call her.'

Later that day, I looked up the meaning of Daisy, in a little book of names Jack's sister Eileen had sent. It said, 'Morning glory, eye of the day.' I knew it was perfect.

I had to stay in hospital for two nights because my blood pressure was slow in returning to normal. I wasn't surprised about that, because my feelings for Daisy were so intense, they unnerved me, I had the urge to hold her all the time and I kept repeating to myself. 'This is my daughter' and those simple basic words of truth made me tingle and a great sense of awe overwhelmed me. It was all too much to grasp.

When I read your story Scarlett, I cringed when Melanie said 'the happiest days are when babies are born,' I thought she was crazy, but those early days with Daisy, confirmed the truth of her words. So many people were kind to me; Carolyn worked round the clock and sent flowers and teddies, as did countless other friends, clients and staff. People visited, bearing gifts and good wishes. I found it incredible, that so many people whom I had treated badly were apparently so willing to forget all in the face of my daughter being born.

The next day, on the sixth; Poppy came visiting with her husband a retired businessman from Suffolk. She bought with her amongst numerous other gifts, a beautiful little book. 'For little Miss Daisy,' she said 'when she get big.' It was 'A Poem For Every day Of The Year.'

Later when all the visitors had gone and the night had crept in, I opened the book and looked up the fifth of June, Daisy's birthday. The poem designated for it was, 'My Luv Is Like A Red, Red Rose,' by Burns. It's not my favourite poem, but it seemed such a happy coincidence, my beautiful baby named after a flower, having a poem about a rose, my favourite flower, on her birthday. It felt like a good omen. If I had then put the book down, all might have been well, but I didn't. I couldn't resist looking up September 11th; that other birthday.

I flicked the pages over and when my eyes set themselves upon the allotted poem I felt the blood drain from my face and the familiar pulse of panic; begin to beat in my chest. I wanted to close the book and yet I was riveted to the page. I remembered my father quoting this very same poem as he shaved in a cold bathroom, when I was about eight or nine years old. Even then the words made me tingle, so haunting and suggestive of hidden meaning did they sound.

And as I read them in that hospital bed, they whispered in my head like an echo from the past. One day I would come face to face with my nightmare, no matter how many barricades I put up, be it distance, time, money, Jack or Daisy, this nightmare would never allow itself to be buried,

'I have spread my dreams under your feet
Tread softly because you tread on my dreams'.

The same old story Scarlett. The most ecstatic moment of my life was weaved through with fear and an unaccountable emptiness. If anyone, apart from Shelby knew I was writing to you, they would dismiss me out of hand. They'd say something like, 'Well, she's always had a screw loose, so what do you expect?' And I wouldn't blame them; I don't treat many people as if they are human, so why would anyone search deep to say something good about me.

But, writing to you makes perfect sense to me Scarlett. If Shelby is right, and reviewing my life in terms of a story unfolding is going to do me any good at all, I can't think of a better person to tell it to. As I read over it, the similarities between us are just too apparent; I just hope I can avoid your ending.

Jack reacted to Daisy's birth in the same way as Rhett did, when Bonnie arrived. He was so proud and watching him as he held and talked to her, made me realise there was a gap in Jack's life and that Daisy had filled it. He collected us from the hospital and for the first time in his life, he drove with care, stopping at red lights and giving way at roundabouts. I came home to find the entire house filled with yellow roses, and when I looked out of the dining room window, I saw McCavity the cat sporting an enormous white ribbon tied in a bow around her neck.

McCavity was a stray cat that had made its home in one of the garden sheds, a big black and white long haired cat, I don't particularly like cats but this one seemed to have taken a liking to me; or at least the shed and before I knew, she had taken up residence there. Jack knew she was a fixture when I gave her a name from a poem I had loved at school. He knew all about T.S.Eliot's 'Cats', but Tosh didn't have a clue.

'Why Macavity,' he asked, 'Does it have bad teeth?'
Macavity went on to have two kittens, which Jack named Shit
and Piss, they eventually found a home, with a friend of Tosh's,
or at least I hope they did.

That first night at home with our new baby, Jack cooked a
meal, chilli con carne, and served it with more panache than a
waiter from the Ritz. While we were eating, Tosh called by to
give Jack a run down on the day.

'Did you know?' he said, sniffing the air, 'Chilli con carne is
an Irish invention?' He then went on to tell a ridiculous story
about a farmer in the Black Valley in Kerry coming home to a
steaming spicy stew after a night rounding up sheep in a
blizzard. 'I've made it hot,' the farmer's wife said, 'Because it's
chilly, Con Carney tonight.' But even aggravating Tosh couldn't
dampen my joy at being home with the only two things in the
world that suddenly mattered.

At Jack's insistence, I wrote to Alice and Eileen telling them
my news, they both sent cards and good wishes. I continued to
work my own hours, but even so I needed someone around, so I
decided on an au pair. Jack was furious; he said an older woman
would be much better, more experienced and more understanding. And that just goes to show how much men know, because
most older women I have ever had dealings with tend to be
easily irritated, set in their ways and judgemental, (Aunty Phil,
Eileen, Alice, need I say more.)

I contacted an au pair agency with Italian links, I knew
exactly what I wanted. A young, pretty girl from a child centred
culture, who would love playing with and dressing up a little
girl.

We got Carmen, very seductive sounding from Venice. She
was young, pretty, child centred and enormously fat. 'Christ
almighty,' Jack said when he saw her walking up the drive, 'This
is going to cost us a new suspension for the car.' He took to
calling her the Egyptian when she was out of earshot, Egyptian
as in 'two ton Carmen.'

She was perfect, ate like a horse, was cheerful and looked
after Daisy with the veracity of a mother goose; even Jack knew
his place in the pecking order. She stayed with us for two years

and when she went back to Italy, I couldn't face replacing her, I'd never be so lucky again. So instead, I shuffled my hours around a bit more; Daisy attended nursery and Helen our house-keeper extended her hours for when gaps needed to be filled. Life went on.

Jack's joy in his child has never diminished and neither has mine, but the truth is Scarlett, Daisy's arrival destroyed the little peace I had. Life was suddenly too good, it could only mean one thing; something was going to derail it, but this time, I wasn't going to be struck by something out of the blue, I knew what was coming, all I had to do was wait. And the waiting is almost over.

I have survived many things, but looking into the face of a boy, sporting the black hair of his father the ape, well that is beyond me. Sometimes, just sometimes, when I hear stories of adoptive children searching out their birthmother, I feel a chill in my heart. I even feel sympathy; an emotion I use sparingly, because it frightens me. I have the knack of looking the other way, down to a fine art because it really is true; what the eye doesn't see, the heart doesn't give a toss about.

But when I come across stories about people desperate to breach the unknown, grown men and women who have grown up dogged not by 'if' but with 'why' well even I, shed a tear. But their story is different from mine; they search and sometimes find a mother who was forced to give up her child by people who should have known better, I can't think of anything worse. If somebody took Daisy away from me, I would die. I'm not as strong as you Scarlett, there is a limit to what I can take, even now when Daisy falls or is late back from a friend's house, I live in fear that God has taken her from me, as payback for the time when I was ready to get rid of her.

My son is not like other adopted children, he was forced on me by a violent act that wiped my girlhood away and with it went all my dreams and ambitions. I lost everything, my mother, my family, my religion; all the things that had been drilled into me as being the most important things in life, one night they were all swept away. I had to face the reality that instead of being protected I was the protector, so many people reliant on me to keep silent as the snow that fell that terrible night. I have remained as still as snow, I have never had the satisfaction of one person saying to me, 'Sorry, I should never have assumed.'

I was killed by a passing snowflake and nobody noticed.

It's too late now to make amends, the people who owe the apology; well I couldn't give a meercats piss for any of them. Like you Scarlett, I set out in my small boat and I dumped overboard all the things I had no use for, things like pity and apologies for people who step on my toes, piety, kindness and gentleness. 'Smile and the world smiles with you, weep and you weep alone.' It's probably true, but save your smile for those who can afford to pay for it.

If Scarlett, I had remained like the Sinead O'Connell who went to the Legion of Mary with Magda, and danced demurely and gratefully with her teacher, I would be living the life of an apologist. I had to change; I'm no good with people on any emotional level. I'm incapable of distinguishing between a compliment and a put down, so I take no chances. It's a fact, those who live by the sword, get killed by those who don't. Why mess about with a machete when a gun will do the job quicker and cleaner?

Sometimes, at night in bed when Jack is sound asleep, it occurs to me, life is just one long process of inevitability. People say if Germany hadn't been left bleeding in the gutter after the first war, if it had been offered a helping outstretched hand, Nazism would never have reared its ugly head. But what if certain things are inevitable? People bang on about atrocities and say 'Never again,' but it's all bollocks, because if some situations are beyond human control or understanding, then the whole process of inevitability will inevitably kick in.

My biggest mistake has been to think that anything really matters, because it doesn't. How can it, when it is all so transient anyway?

Phoenix

Chapter Twenty Three

The summer of 2001 finally drew to a close, but the slippage from summer into autumn was hardly noticed in the Keane household. As far as Jack Keane was concerned, it had been winter, pure and simple since the beginning of June. Several attempts to wean Phoenix out of London; for trips to the sea, countryside; or anywhere that took her fancy; fell on deaf ears. She even refused point blank to celebrate her birthday in August. Instead she remained determinedly morbid, overshadowing Daisy, often to the point of refusing to let her out of her sight.

On a few occasions, she had insisted on taking the child to work, only to return home bad tempered and frustrated, because once there, the child's need for company and occupation had only served to cause further confusion and fuss.

Jack didn't know what to do and in a last ditch attempt to find out what might be wrong with Phoenix; he sought again the confidence of Carolyn. He had initially considered phoning his sister Eileen for advice, but mindful of the mutual animosity between Eileen and Phoenix, he decided against it.

Carolyn though eager to placate him, was unable to reassure him; Phoenix was as distracted at work, as she was at home. 'Has she said anything to you?' he asked. 'Has she ever told you anything that could explain why she is acting so peculiar?'

Carolyn shook her head. 'No,' she said, 'but then Jack, you know Phoenix, she never burdens anyone with her problems, she's very self contained.'

'*Really*,' Jack replied as he wandered over to the desk Phoenix usually sat at. He stared for a moment at the scattered pieces of mail strewn across it, before picking up a few buff coloured envelopes and throwing them down again, when he saw they were nothing more than circulars.

'What about this tax specialist she's been seeing?' he asked. 'Do you think she has let something financial get out of hand?'

Again Carolyn shook her head, 'Not Phoenix, she's too smart for anything like that but...' she stopped and Jack looked across at her. He was about to press her further, when it occurred to him, efficient and conscientious as Carolyn was, Phoenix would never divulge anything shady to her, or to anyone else for that matter.

He decided to take his leave but as he was walking towards the door, Carolyn spoke again. 'Listen Jack,' she said hesitantly. 'Please don't think I'm overstepping the mark or anything, but there is something I'd like to tell you.'

He closed the door and walked with an air of determination towards Carolyn who immediately began to tremble, fearing she may well have already overstepped the mark by delaying him. But there was nothing threatening in Jack Keane's demeanour, only an overwhelming need for reassurance. She stood up and placed her hand nervously on his arm. 'I don't want to alarm you or bore you with details about me, Phoenix has probably already told you about my history.'

'No,' Jack replied, 'she has never said a word.'

Carolyn smiled and squeezed his arm with a rare hint of flirtatiousness, 'That is one of the things I like about her so much, the way she keeps a confidence. I'd love to help her if only she'd let me.'

Jack looked into Carolyn's face with a slight feeling of unease. Could it be possible that gentle, serene Carolyn; was taking the piss, winding him up? Phoenix, keep a confidence, now *that* was news to him, she had never shared one since he'd known her. And as for Phoenix not discussing Carolyn's history; she probably hadn't even being listening to it in the first place, although she would have made all the right noises to indicate otherwise.

He looked searchingly into her face, cringing slightly as he wondered what kind of clichéd observation, this well-meaning, unworldly woman was about to impart, but to his surprise, he didn't see the dull vacant eyes of conformity he had been expecting. Instead he saw compassion and a worrying shadow of pity.

'Well,' he said smiling at her, 'What has your history got to do with Phoenix at this moment?'

Now Carolyn felt uneasy, was she being presumptuous? There was every possibility that unless she was exceedingly careful, Jack might misinterpret what she had to say, and if he did, he would be furious, for never in her experience was there a man more proud of his wife than Jack Keane was of Phoenix. She took a deep breath and turning away from him, spoke gently. 'A few years ago, well, longer than that, I had what I can only call a personal trauma and the result was; I had a breakdown, not a mediocre one either. I was sectioned.'

She stopped for a moment to gauge Jack's reaction and since he didn't appear to be in the least bit perturbed, she continued, an edge more confidently, 'What I am trying to say, Jack, is that I think Phoenix may be having some kind of mental breakdown. I recognise the symptoms, she is so distracted; it's almost as if she is living in another reality, whatever is wrong with her is personal and she needs help, believe me.'

She glanced over at him, and when she saw he looked both shocked and not altogether disbelieving, she moved quickly to pacify him. 'I might have it wrong' she said in a placating voice, 'but I had to tell you, in case I am right, perhaps you could persuade her to see a doctor or a counsellor even.'

He looked up and stared at her for a moment, before giving a bitter dry laugh 'Do you really think, me telling Phoenix, to see a shrink, would work?' he asked scathingly. 'You must be mad.'

Carolyn's face flushed red and she dropped her gaze and Jack instantly realised the implication of his words. 'I'm sorry,' he said. 'I didn't mean to imply anything, but if I so much as suggested a doctor to Phoenix, she would think I'm trying to have her sectioned.' Again he cringed as the word 'sectioned' echoed in his ears. 'Fuck it,' he thought irritably. 'I've had enough of this'.

The conversation was flowing freely as a river does up hill, and he was getting tired and perplexed with it. 'Perhaps both of us are blowing this out of proportion,' he said wearily, 'She might just be getting sick of the whole business or having problems with some regulation or the other.'

'No,' said Carolyn emphatically, turning to face Jack again, 'Nothing at work would ever get to Phoenix, she might get angry, furious even, but she'd never, ever get down about it.' Even as she spoke, Jack recognised the wisdom of her words. The only emotions work ever inspired in Phoenix were anger, pride or greed. Carolyn was right; it had to be something else.

Feeling at a loss as to what to do or say next, Jack turned and stared out of the window, the same one Phoenix stood by when she wanted to take in great gulps of the openness of Clapham Common. He cut an altogether less confident figure of a man to the one who had so self assuredly breezed into the office, determined to find the cause of the ailment afflicting his wife and which was having such a profound effect upon him.

As he stared at the people clad in their summer finery, basking in the sunshine on the common, it dawned on him in a sudden clarity of vision; that the way of life he had built for himself in London, was coming to an abrupt end. From the moment he had left Ireland, the only cause that had really mattered was the well being of Jack Keane. Nothing in the pursuit of making his dream a reality, had been too risky, or too low to contemplate. Even to divorcing a woman whose only crime was to walk out of step with the onward march of the great Jack Keane. On and on he had gone, acquisition becoming easier, as he put into practise all the dubious skills he had accumulated over the years.

There was no denying he had been lucky, not only had he made his fortune and created a lifestyle unthinkable to the young Jack Keane who had left his homeland in the dead of night, he had met someone who was prepared to accept him for what he was and she had given him the child who had completed his happiness. That had been the cue to move on, life was changing and he too should have changed. But he hadn't. Instead he had carried on like a great red fox, always on the chase, on the prowl, taking what was on offer and more besides, simply because he could.

There had been numerous opportunities and reminders for him to change along the way, but he had chosen to ignore them. Even that pathetic excursion to Boston when he had struggled to take on board a dull and intransigent workforce had produced a revelation. It was there that he had caught the first unflattering glimpse of himself as he really was; a grasping high handed man, chasing business he had been advised to steer clear of. Even in that monstrous place and situation, a way to seek some kind of redemption had been pointed out to him. Daisy had been happy and he had recognised the lesson; attention, not possessions were what she deserved, the people in his life were what mattered, he had seen it so clearly.

The same lesson had been further underlined when Danny had died so suddenly, the first warning shot that life can change direction on a single beat of the heart. 'For where your treasure is, there your heart will be also...' He had listened attentively to the words which had accompanied his brother to the grave, resolving in the emotional atmosphere to change and to change quickly.

Turning his head away, as if by instinct, from the bright incongruous summer scene beyond the window, he tried to justify himself. Phoenix had aggravated and exasperated him with her mood swings, her temper and her secrecy. These were the things that had provoked him into wanting to retaliate and this he had done, repaying her with cool caustic comments, and encouraging Tosh to hang around until he himself had become sick of his ganger's presence, it wasn't all one sided. He looked up at Carolyn, as if willing her to confirm his silent attempts at justification, but she wasn't looking at him. Her gaze was fixed on the window behind him and something in the motionless way she stood was reminiscent of something Jack could not put his finger on, yet made him feel distinctly uneasy. The office which had initially appeared cool and shady after the piecing brightness of the morning sun now felt heavy and oppressive with the pall of autumn upon it and he wanted to be rid of it.

He had no justification, Phoenix was ill and had been for a long time and if he had wanted to, he would have seen it but he hadn't wanted to; he had only wanted life to run on without distraction. The impetus had been to get her back on track, with treats and trips, not for her sake but for his; because she was affecting his quality of life. She was spoiling the dream. Only she wasn't, because she was the dream, she was the red headed woman who had turned his life round.

Without her there would be nothing.

Chapter Twenty Four

Brilliant sunshine ushered in September the 10th 2001 and Phoenix remained in bed long after Jack had risen to see to Daisy. She held her eyes tightly shut in complete denial of the yellow sunlight that flooded in through the Georgian window, like a searchlight upon her.

As she lay, slightly huddled on her side, she became vaguely aware of there being something different about the day ahead, but was unable to pin down exactly what this difference might be.

As for tomorrow, that was another story. The inevitability of September the 11th was now final and absolute, but that reality did not make it any easier to bear. She had sought a deep whiskey and valium induced sleep, but the magic charm once so effective in days gone by, had failed to work; on the contrary it seemed her mind had been energised by the cocktail. All through the night, a frenetic, jumbled fusion of thoughts and visions had pursued her, and not once had her mind attempted to filter the vital from the useless. So many people had crept uninvited into her consciousness, Jack speeding away in his car, Daisy in her school uniform demanding a haircut, even Helen the housekeeper had appeared briefly, perched precariously on the roof trying to retrieve a damaged bird. The most frightening visitor had been Jerh Condon. He had appeared out of nowhere, banging on the front door demanding to see his son and the sight of him had caused her to sit upright and cry out in the darkness.

Morning had arrived, but it didn't make the slightest difference to the chaos going on in her head. To get up was to face the day and all the confusion and confrontation it would invariably serve up; while lying in bed offered nothing other than an opportunity to be a sitting target for the thoughts and fancies that skidded through her mind.

Jack meanwhile was downstairs, seeing to Daisy's breakfast. He chatted with his daughter, quizzing her about the day ahead, but all the while his eyes flicked to the door, waiting for the first sign that Phoenix was still in touch with reality. Surely she remembered that Daisy was going back to school and that the pair of them were going to drop her off, before heading out for shopping and lunch in Surrey. He smiled with relief when the kitchen door swung open, though some of the relief evaporated when he saw that Phoenix was still in her dressing gown.

'Daddy, Mommy's here,' Daisy announced.

Jack walked across to Phoenix and kissed her on the cheek. 'Come and sit down Mom,' he said. 'We have just made some toast for you.' He led her rather as one might lead a confused aunt, across the room to the chair beside Daisy and she sat down looking faintly baffled.

Daisy immediately took up the baton from Jack and let forth a barrage of chatter. 'Do you think Mommy, that Mrs Higgins will be as kind as Mrs Carter, Daddy says she's going to be even better.'

But Phoenix was a long way from Wimbledon. Where, she was wondering, did Eileen get the box, the one with the satin inlay of the Regency couple? Daisy tugged at her arm and Phoenix looked down and stared at her child, almost as if she didn't recognise her. 'What do you think?' Daisy persisted.

'About what?' Phoenix replied, bewildered by this apparently open ended question.

'Who's the best,' Daisy said with emphasis, as if addressing someone slightly dense, someone who hadn't been paying attention when they should have been, 'Mrs Higgins or Mrs Carter?'

The question meant nothing to Phoenix, the names didn't even sound familiar; right now the only familiarity was the man in the powder wig, offering the woman in the low necked dress, a short stemmed rose.

'How would I know?' she replied distractedly. This answer baffled Daisy; mothers after all, were not supposed to make their disinterest so apparent.

Jack, sensing Daisy was skidding on dangerously thin ice, casually intervened. 'I think,' he said, reaching across for the butter, 'You should run along puss, and let Mom get on with her breakfast.'

But Daisy refused to budge, something was in the air and she wasn't going to miss out on it. She looked sideways at her mother and noticed she wasn't eating anything. 'Mom isn't eating her breakfast Daddy,' she reported back to Jack. 'Do you think she's not feeling very well?'

'Perhaps Mom isn't hungry,' Jack suggested, wishing that for once, Daisy would just shut up. 'You're building up an appetite for lunch later on, aren't you?' he said to Phoenix, hoping to take some of the intensity out of the atmosphere.

Phoenix looked across at Jack and surveyed him as one might a stranger who enters a local pub. She took in his checked shirt; the hairs on his arms that glistened in the morning light, and the slightly stubbled chin that moved rhythmically as he chewed his toast and sipped his tea. So full of it, she thought, catching the conspiratorial wink he passed to Daisy, so sure of his worth. He looked up and caught her eye, but this time, she didn't flinch under his gaze, she sat staring at him, through him and beyond him.

He felt a frisson of fear as he looked at her. Tiredness had given her face an almost translucent look. 'Tiredness from the exertion of living,' he thought, 'not from lack of sleep'. He reached out and took hold of the limp hand she had placed on the table; but it was as if the hand belonged to someone else, for her eyes didn't even register contact had been made. 'Why don't you,' he said gently, 'Go back to bed, and let me take Daisy to school today?'

At the mention of the word 'bed' Phoenix involuntarily flicked her eyes upwards, back to that room upstairs, the one where she had been pursued all night. He was sending her up there for a rest. Was he mad? She edged sideways slightly, as Daisy jabbed her arm in her eagerness to climb down from her chair and reach Jack's lap.

'If Mom goes to bed, it will be just you and me Daddy,' she cried. 'Can we stop at the shop and buy sweets?'

'We'll see,' Jack replied unaware his daughter's enthusiasm had placed him firmly in the front line of the action. Human shield status had just been achieved. 'What do you say Mom?' he asked Phoenix. 'Will you grab the opportunity for a rest?' For a moment Phoenix said nothing. She stared at the pair of them. She was being airbrushed out of the picture, pushed aside. The arrogance of the man, watch with Mother, as it should be done. Who did he think he was?

'What are you up to Jack?' she spoke quietly, for the intense beating of her heart made the very act of speaking difficult.

'I've no idea what you mean,' he replied, relaxing his hold on Daisy, his whole body preparing for fight or flight.

'I think you do,' she said breathing heavily. 'What are you after?'

He also took a deep breath, like a diver preparing to sink into unfamiliar water. What was the solution, should he attempt to pacify, continue to plead innocence, or agree with her? What would calm her down?' He could tell by the look in her eye, and the low level voice, that this was not the Phoenix he had sparred with in the past. Trying to figure out the best solution to this dilemma was like attempting to fix an electrical fault, with unmarked wires; touch the wrong one and the result could be fatal. After some deliberation, he opted for pacification. Sliding a less confident Daisy off his knee, he said softly. 'I want to help you; I know something is wrong, tell me for God's sake, I'll do anything for you.' In the space of seconds, the fuse was ignited and finding the breath necessary, she turned on him. In an instant Jack knew he had tugged the wrong wire.

'What can you do for me, hey, Jack Keane?' she shouted. 'You, the big fixer fucker, you think you know everything, that you only have to click your fingers and all is well, but you are wrong Jack there are things even you can't fix.'

She looked down at the carefully laid table, complete with the peach roses picked fresh from the garden that very morning, sitting resolute in a crystal vase and with one swipe of her hand she sent the crockery and cutlery helter skelter to the floor.

'For God's sake,' Jack shouted as Daisy fled from the room, whimpering like a kicked dog, 'Get a hold on yourself.'

'For what Jack?' she asked, in a perfectly reasonable voice, as if replying to a request of his for some small change, before continuing in a much more aggressive tone. 'Why don't you just come clean, you're not concerned for me; you never have been. What is it this time, are you thinking of leaving, walking out like you did with Polly, making sure all is smoothed over before you go? I made her breakfast you know, I even took the kid to school, had me eating out of her hand, so she did. But a man on the make has to keep all the balls in the air doesn't he? It doesn't do to have an old wife in the attic, or have I got it wrong, perhaps it's a simple case of some old Bleasdale coming to dinner?'

Pausing for a moment to take a breath, she turned her face upwards and addressed the ceiling. 'What a travesty; Howard is coming to dinner but the wife has gone mad.'

She stopped, and since the ceiling was apparently reluctant to utter an opinion on the situation, she abandoned her pose and walked over to where Jack stood. 'Get a chef in,' she said as breezily as if she was handing over a tip, a piece of well tried advice. 'Ask him to do something typically English for a real old fucker, tripe and onions followed by Birds cream droppings, should do nicely.'

Jack stared across at Daisy, who was now peeping from the safety of the other side of the door. The child looked confused, her mother's words meant nothing to her, but the intonation had been very clear. Mom was not happy.

Stepping on and over the broken glass and china in her bare feet, Phoenix walked to the door, but before making her exit, she turned and faced Jack. 'I will take my own child to school,' she said. 'Don't think for one minute I'll let you take her away from me.'

She turned and walked regally out of the room with great composure; but the moment she entered her bedroom, she clasped her hands to her head, running her fingers frantically through her hair. 'Oh God,' she repeated. 'Oh God, Oh God, Oh God, what is happening to me?' The awfulness of the scene she had just created played itself repeatedly through her mind and while it did so, she caught several camera stills of Daisy's frightened face and Jack's shocked one. She really wanted to care and regain control but a feeling of incredible indifference and resignation overwhelmed her.

There was only one thing she wanted right now and that was to get out of the house, everything about it suddenly presented itself as malicious in her imagination. The walls, the curtains, the windows - all of them were witnesses to her secrets, to her drinking, to her writing and frantic pacing and mutterings. Even the silence of the bedroom seemed menacing and knowing, rather than soothing or calming. She had to take Daisy to school after that performance, but, her inclination was to run and hide from everyone and everything.

She searched in her wardrobe, pulling clothes from it at random; what she needed was something easy to wear, certainly no tricky buttons or fiddly zips, her hands weren't up to handling them. She settled in the end for trainer bottoms and a baggy black top. 'Jesus,' she said as she took a quick look in the mirror. 'I look like a knacker, red haired Mary on her way to the fair at Dingle.'

Her hair was wild and though she tried to tie it back, her hands were too jittery to put it into any order. She also attempted to apply makeup, but again, dysfunctional hands refused to obey commands, instead they trembled and shook and after poking herself in the eye, she called her mascara brush an obscenity and threw it at the wall. A trail of blood from her injured feet followed her frantic pacing around the room, but she ignored their plight and forced a pair of sandals on them. Finally she headed for the door, reaching at the last minute for her bag; she wouldn't get far without her VW.

Jack was waiting in the hallway, with a uniformed Daisy, proudly clutching her brand new school bag, standing beside him. 'There is no way,' he said, barring the front door with his back, 'I am going to let you drive.'

'Drive,' she repeated. 'Why would I drive, when I can walk?'

He looked at her, at the wild hair sticking out behind her head like a turkey cock's feather, and the ashen face with two over bright eyes like smudges on a clear page. Mentally he calculated the route to Daisy's school; there were no major roads to cross; and there were bound to be crowds of other parents and children. He would let her go, but the moment she left he would arrange for Carolyn to come round. If she failed to make any impact on Phoenix, he'd get a doctor, this was beyond him.

He smiled down at Daisy and she returned the smile. She didn't share his anxiety in the least, after all, Mom nearly always took her to school, not usually dressed like a scarecrow, but that didn't matter. Only moments earlier, it had occurred to Daisy that Mommy might be going away, but now that fear had been laid to rest, she was happy for the familiarity of some kind of routine.

As he opened the front door, Jack pulled Phoenix's arm. 'You take care,' he said softly and as if to reiterate his request, he repeated with just the faintest hint of a warning. 'I'm asking you to take care of Daisy.'

'Asking ain't getting,' she thought, 'After all I want the fucking world to end in the next twenty four hours but it sure doesn't look like I'm going to get it.'

Phoenix held out her slightly shaking hand and Daisy grasped it tightly and together they set off.

Immediately their feet crunched the gravel on the drive, Daisy launched into a rapid round of chatter and unbeknownst to her, so did her mother. If he has any sense Phoenix told herself, he will go, he will walk away. Can't he see that's what I want him to do? Or is he determined to stay around and watch me fall apart, he must know that is bound to happen. There is no way out of this; no happy ending, he will find out the truth, he will be repulsed, and I will be shamed.

He'll pretend of course it doesn't matter, but we'll both know it does. No line in the sand can be drawn, Condon's son will arrive but he'll never go, and I will have to tell Daisy about him, and then he can never ever go. It's all a mess, there is no solution. No solution.

She looked down for a moment at Daisy who was tugging her hand, wanting to tell her mother something urgently. Who, thought Phoenix bitterly, would ever have a child if they really knew what was involved? Oh yes, she continued sagely, they warn you off, telling you all the things you are not allowed to do from the moment of conception, they tell you how much it costs, how much it hurts even, but they never tell you about the despair of never being free, of losing the right for all eternity, to simply walk away.

She looked up just in time to see a group of mothers approaching her with an assortment of children, some in pushchairs; others running wild. One oversized child of about four or five was tethered by reins; as his doughty looking mother pushed two other moon faced children in a pushchair. The restrained child looked ridiculous, chomping at the bit, wanting to run free like the other children. He reminded Phoenix of a Victorian cartoon she had once seen of a bear held down by chains, while a moronic crowd baited him. The group moved towards her, surging forward like the geese in Danny's farmyard; their heads leading and their arses following. All heading for the slaughter, part of the same treadmill.

One member of the group; a women dressed in shorts and a printed summer top waved her arm and attempted to speak to Phoenix, but Phoenix ignored her. 'Whatever she has to say, I don't want to hear, she told herself, she probably thinks I should have the decency to let the herd past first. Anyway, she addressed herself firmly, banishing the rude woman out of her thoughts, there is no trauma for Jack; men don't love women, they always get over the loss of one, and if you think about it, it's logical why they should, they don't even like them. They employ one another, prefer the company of their mates, and they invariably remarry when a spouse dies, there is nothing of the swan in men; except vanity. And even that is misguided, because once out of the water, swans are pretty ugly looking bastards as well. No, women in men's lives have the status of spare parts. A new bit can always be found to replace the old.

She looked up and found herself at the entrance of the school gates. Running her hand over her hair in a belated effort to bring it under some control, she turned abruptly and pulled Daisy along, but the child yelled out a defiant 'No.'

Phoenix looked around her, at the parents milling around, some were staring at her and the realisation that she was the object of attention made her feel more agitated. 'Come on Daisy,' she pleaded. 'It is time for school.'

'No Mommy,' Daisy said. 'Not this school.'

What on earth had got into the child? Phoenix gazed around willing a teacher to come forward and take the nuisance off her hands. She didn't have too long to wait, a woman, a tall thin severe looking one, approached her.

'What seems to be the problem?' she asked. 'This is Woodsfield Preparatory; shouldn't this child be at Yew Wood School?'

For a moment Phoenix stared back at the woman without comprehension, taking in nothing but the absolute greyness of her; but a furtive glance beyond the tweedy shoulders made her aware for the first time, of the total absence of Yew Wood's distinctive purple and green uniform. These guys were like canaries decked out in repulsive yellow. She nodded her head and the woman, not quite certain of Phoenix's ability to comprehend, indicated with her hand shaped in a dog leg pose, that to find Yew Wood, Phoenix simply had to retrace the route she had just taken.

As she walked away, with Daisy's small hand tucked in hers, she heard the woman remark, in the rasping voice of the English upper class, 'Really, you'd think some parents would employ carers that can at least speak the language.'

'Language,' Phoenix thought angrily to herself. 'I could teach that streak of piss a thing or two about language.' Hurriedly she retraced her steps to the point where she had met the gaggle of geese, the mothers who had almost ousted her from the pavement with their pushchairs and chatter.

Registration was already under way; when Phoenix finally located Daisy's classroom. She bent down and kissed her daughter on the head. 'I will see you,' she whispered. Then deliberately mistaking the beckoning gesture of the school secretary, she waved and fled the building.

Where could she go? She wasn't going home; she couldn't go there, not after the scene she had created that morning; and besides, if she didn't go home, Jack would be worried and the thought gave her some satisfaction. She had no idea why she wanted to hurt Jack; but the overwhelming misery in her own world dictated that right now, nobody had cause or right to be happy. Going to work wasn't an option either; she couldn't face Carolyn or any of the other old cats there, gloating at the state of her, rejoicing in how the mighty have fallen.

She continued her walk along the road; head down for fear of meeting someone who might remotely know her; when an idea came to her, overwhelming in its logicalness. I'll see Shelby, she thought, I'll see her, there has to be something she can do for me.

Walking hurriedly to the edge of the common, she caught a bus to Fulham Broadway, not once considering the small problem of not having booked an appointment, or what she would do if Shelby wasn't around. She faced the window; her head averted from her fellow passengers, and stared at the transient passers -by.

'Watch it granny', she mentally informed an elderly woman, who pulled a shopping trolley behind her, body hunched forward, 'face any further west and it will be arse over tip for you.'

The conductor, a chirpy, red faced, tin soldier of a man, swung himself down the centre aisle, grappling the rails like a child on the monkey bars in a park. 'Fares please,' he sang, and Phoenix leapt in fright at the sudden intrusion into her very private world. She reached into her bag, fearful for a moment lest she had left her purse at home and handed the conductor a ten pound note and asked for Fulham Broadway.

'Lucky you,' he told her, 'we've had a busy run today and I'm Mr Bags of Money.' He laughed good-naturedly and jiggled the coins in his care. Foolish old man, she thought contemptuously, as he handed her a ticket and a fist full of change, the money in his bag wouldn't fund a meal in a greasy bollocks café in Fulham, never mind a day dream about being super rich.

The bus trundled onwards noisily and jerkily. The constant calling out of the conductor and the ringing of the bell jarred on her nerves and when it came to a prolonged halt at a set of traffic lights, she relished the relative peace it ushered in. Her gaze fell on a sprinkling of customers sitting at a pavement café. One man in particular caught her eye; he was sitting casually back in his wicker chair, one foot gently balanced on the opposite knee, a mobile clutched to his ear. 'What a very clever monkey,' she told herself. 'What other tricks is he capable of, I wonder?'

The bus pulled off again and her mind turned back to Jack. There was no point in her walking away, she was the one who was being stalked and wherever she went, the stalker would follow. She closed her eyes briefly in an effort to imagine where peace might best be found. She knew it wasn't in a place but in a situation, and no matter how she tried to fix various scenarios together; each one appeared more hopeless than the last.

If only Jack would go, leave and spare her the indignity of being found out; leave and whittle down her options. No outcome I can think of is pleasurable, she told herself, but there is one that is worse than the others and that is Jack knowing I deceived him. There are many things I can handle, but being stripped of the identity it has taken me twenty odd years to build up, that's the worst.

But even as the words formed in her mind, she knew they weren't true. There was something else, something too awful to contemplate. An idea, so dreadful that when her mind even ventured near its border lines; an automatic response set off the hounds whose job it was to guard that secret. Chase, chase, chase, they went, and in response, her mind contemplated everything, from the sublime to the ridiculous, anything rather than the truth.

The bus pulled to a halt and the conductor called out Fulham Broadway, before leaning back almost dejectedly against the luggage hold, as if his jovial persona had all been one big act. Phoenix pulled herself out of her seat, and made her way to the exit. Reservation was already beginning to replace her sense of anticipation at the idea of seeing Shelby; but she was here, and there was nowhere else to go.

She set off, a slow moving figure amongst the crowds who moved around her, going over in her mind, what she would do when she met Shelby. She would tell her the truth, listen to her advice, and then leave, safe in the knowledge, she would never see her again. In an effort to calm her fiercely beating heart, she stopped beside a jeweller's and stood for a moment, looking into its enticing window, like a child, watching a shopkeeper measure out sweets for another, luckier customer. Carefully concealed spotlights beamed down on the various diamond encrusted jewels as they sparkled and gleamed in the artificial light.

A male hand, clean, white and hairless appeared out of nowhere and she watched as he slid away the cushion of diamond studded earrings she had been gazing at. They were there and in an instant they were gone. That was life, here one minute, gone the next. No wonder peace was in such short supply, how could life ever be tranquil, when each and every human lived with a sword permanently raised above their heads?

But, bringing the axe down on her own head was not an option, escape routes like jumping off a bridge, or driving into an oncoming juggernaut did not apply to her; such an act would only catapult her fast forward to face a harsh and unforgiving God. Hell, Phoenix believed, was much more likely to exist, than heaven.

She turned her attention away from the jeweller's window, when she heard an excited babble of foreign voices. A group of Muslim women dressed head to toe in black flashed past her, led by a defiant, shiny faced man pressing a book tightly to his chest. 'What a lot of wives to keep,' Phoenix remarked to herself,' of course, he tells the oldest, she's his muse, but you can bet your bloody life, it's the youngest one he screws. And I'm not hostile to them,' she thought, as she continued her way, 'at least there is honesty there.' The world is designed for men, though women may fool themselves into thinking otherwise. A cursory glance at a pavement news seller confirmed this opinion in Phoenix's mind. A range of tabloids decked his counter, each red top displaying woman in various stages of undress. Sport on the back pages and sex on the front ones - the world was tailored to suit men.

She found this thought disagreeable in its truthfulness and intensified her footsteps, trying to step away from the claustrophobic choking sensation that engulfed her as she realised, the world she wanted to exist; was an impossibility.

Shelby Warner meanwhile, oblivious to the fact that she was about to receive a very perturbed visitor, was indulging in a wicked and illicit treat. Standing by her fridge, pinning its door open with her left elbow, she was busily engaged in spooning small, frequent helpings of Mississippi Mud Pie into her mouth, with all the urgency of a sparrow being fed by its mother. The desert had been purchased earlier that same morning, from the American deli around the corner, its original destination being a gift Shelby intended to take round to a fellow New Yorker later that very afternoon. But having a sweet tooth, temptation had got the better of her.

The European attitude to chocolate perplexed Shelby; bitter chocolate in her view, was not only best confined to laxative status, it was an oxymoron. The Brits were now trying to be as suave as the French in declaring on TV shows and magazines their preference for real, bitter chocolate, while continuing to stuff themselves silly with Twix's and Mars Bars.

She was savouring the flavour; when a frantic knocking at her front door caused her to jump. An instinctive glance at the kitchen clock, informed her it was coming up to eleven o clock. 'It's probably the postman,' she thought, closing the fridge door reluctantly. She walked along the hallway, licking the spoon as she did so and the knocking started again, this time even more frantically.

'All right, all right, I'm coming,' she shouted. Reaching the front door, she placed the licked spoon on the hall table, before turning the key and looking out inquisitively. For a moment she looked without recognition at the figure on her doorstep, and slowly it dawned on her, that it was Phoenix Ashton.

'My God,' she said. 'I didn't recognise you, what on earth are you doing here?'

Now it was put into words, Phoenix found herself searching hard for the answer. Just what was she doing, standing at the front door of a shrink? 'I...' she began and stopped. Shelby looked at the dishevelled figure with genuine alarm; she had never placed Phoenix in the stalker cum 'door stepper' mould. She wiped her mouth with the back of her hand, suddenly conscious she might have chocolate smeared around it.

'Come in,' she said, 'you look positively dreadful, what on earth has happened?' She opened the door wider and Phoenix walked past her, knocking without noticing, a dessert spoon off the hall table, before coming to a halt in front of the gilt mirror. Shelby bent down and retrieved the spoon, holding it close to her side, out of sight.

Once in the house, all energy evaporated from Phoenix, and she leaned back against the mirror thinking it was the wall. Shelby grimaced slightly as she saw the mirror sway; just what I need, she thought, a bloody lawsuit, client crushed by mirror.

'Come on through here,' she said sounding a lot more relaxed than she felt and led the way to her private sitting room. Phoenix followed her and once inside, Shelby closed the door. 'Take a seat,' she gestured to a leather Chesterfield, but Phoenix declined. She stood instead by the window, handbag slipped over her left shoulder, hands clutching opposite arms above the elbow, as if she were chilled. 'Well,' Shelby began 'tell me why you've come here.'

The silence was unnerving and for a while Phoenix struggled to get her thoughts together, she wished Shelby hadn't closed the door for the feeling of claustrophobia that had pursued her earlier, had returned again with a vengeance. 'I can't go on any more,' she said. 'I have no way out.'

'Way out of what?' Shelby asked taking a seat herself, 'You will have to be more specific, if I'm to be of any help to you.'

Phoenix turned and faced the window and in short, succinct, carefully chosen words, she related a brief account of Condon's assault upon her. In slightly more detail, she also told about the son who was adopted, who was going to be twenty one tomorrow and who was going to visit her on his birthday.

'When did he contact you?' Shelby asked.

Phoenix shook her head, 'He has never contacted me.'

'Then how do you know he is coming?' Shelby asked.

'Because I know'

'But you can't know that,' Shelby said with all the rationality of an East Coast American, 'That is outlandish; you fear it might happen, but you have no grounds to know it will happen.'

'I know,' Phoenix replied, 'Because I know, I can't explain it any more clearly than that, I've always known.' She spoke as if she was stating the simple, absolute and obvious and Shelby knew there was no point whatsoever in trying to contradict what Phoenix believed as fact. She tried a different tack.

'Do you want him to come back, is this a case of wishful thinking?' she queried.

At this, Phoenix swung round, her face ugly in its fury. 'Are you crazy?' she said. 'I have a husband and a child who don't even know of his existence, tomorrow he will come and claim ownership and everything I have, everything I have built up, will be destroyed. It's all over.'

Shelby said nothing. She felt oddly unnerved by the revelation Phoenix had just made. Instinctively, she had known from the start that Phoenix harboured a secret of some magnitude; she was too hard headed to be traumatised by something trivial. Shelby had been intrigued to know what it was, but the possibility it could be anything as terrifying and awful as the story she had just heard, had never occurred to her.

This, Shelby admitted to herself; was a real dilemma, it went way beyond the issues that made up the bulk of her work; the sulky faced women still itching over sarky, sharp tongued comments delivered years earlier by a jealous mother, or over - zealous teacher, or the defiant divorcees, intent on picking at the scab of a relationship they had fought to end. By comparison, such complaints were trivial. They were the fodder that should make up the load of a less than fully committed bored American psychotherapist floundering in London. For a moment, she felt something approaching guilt, for encouraging Phoenix on such a lonely course of action. Writing about a past that could never really be laid to rest. 'How do you think Jack will react?' she asked quietly, more like a friend than a therapist.

Phoenix shrugged her shoulders. 'I suppose, he'll be shocked, initially he'll say he forgives me, but he will think it over and repulsion will set in.'

'Forgive you for what?' Shelby asked, horrified at the thought that Phoenix might be on the verge of revealing herself as some kind of a closet fundamentalist.

'For not telling him about the child.'

'I see,' Shelby replied nodding her head, relieved that at least forgiveness wasn't being sought for anything else, 'But why repulsion, why should he feel that?'

'For second hand goods,' Phoenix replied.

'Only goods, not people can be second hand Phoenix.'

'That might be true for where you come from,' Phoenix replied, 'But it isn't where I come from; or where Jack comes from either.'

She paused for a moment, but when she saw Shelby was about to contradict or point out the error of her thinking, she continued on a different track; she didn't want to be placated, or reassured that the impossible is actually possible, just so long as you wish hard enough for it. 'I took your advice Shelby,' she said, without the slightest hint of accusation. 'I wrote to Scarlett O'Hara, and I started from the beginning and I stayed with it, continuing almost to the present day, and although I've discovered many things, I've never got to the root of my fear.'

Shelby said nothing. She could have pointed out, that Phoenix hadn't discovered the root of her fear, because she wasn't ready for it, but she didn't. Phoenix had enough to contend with right now.

'All I can do; is wait until tomorrow comes; but I want oblivion, I want to wake up when it is all over, but it can't be over until I face it.'

Shelby sat silent and attentive. It would be too crass to remind Phoenix that she was acting as if her son's return was inevitable, when in fact it was nothing but a remote possibility. She wanted a solution and Shelby had none to offer. 'Phoenix,' she said gently, 'There is nothing you can do other than bow to the inevitable, something you have done all your life and survived. There is no reason to believe you won't survive this.'

Phoenix said nothing. She had sought Shelby out as her last resort, like the woman reaching out to touch the garment, but there was no miracle to be found here. 'I'm sorry,' Shelby said 'I'm sorry I can't offer you anything, other than a small reassurance.' She stopped for a moment to draw breath, for like Phoenix she too felt claustrophobic and trapped; boxed in by a dilemma with no obvious exit signs.

'You are in no danger of going mad,' she continued, 'and I know that has always been your greatest fear, but what happened to you is so truly terrible, to feel anything less than acute anxiety would be a sign of insanity in itself.'

She shook her head and clasped her hands together in the time honoured gesture of defeat. 'No,' she said, 'you are not crazy but you are exhausted and that will need treatment of some kind.'

She stood up and walked across to Phoenix and in a show of friendship, placed a hand on her arm. 'What you must do as a matter of urgency,' she said quietly, 'is tell Jack, tell him as you told me. Perhaps it might be helpful if you showed him some of the letters you wrote to Scarlett, if...'

Abruptly she stopped, as a strange muffled noise filled the air. Startled she looked down at Phoenix's head which seemed to be jerking slightly in tune to the curious noise that was steadily growing louder. Anxiously, she stared more closely and saw to her great surprise that Phoenix was both laughing and crying by turns. With no handkerchief or tissues to hand, Phoenix shook Shelby's hand off her arm and wiped her eyes with the bottom of her baggy tee shirt.

'For God's sake, Shelby,' she said, 'Just where, do you come from? If I showed Jack a letter like that, he'd be out the door so bloody quick, he'd meet his arse coming in.'

'Well perhaps you are right,' Shelby conceded, relieved that Phoenix was at least coherent, 'but promise me this, when tomorrow comes and goes, with no sign of your son, don't be tempted to continue the silence. Don't let him find out. You do the telling, you take control, tell Jack sooner than later.'

Jack was standing in the driveway, looking into the distance when a taxi brought Phoenix home later that same day. He walked along the pavement as the car drew up, increasing his pace, the more certain he became of the passenger in the back seat. Oh he cares deeply now, she told herself, when she saw his worried face, look at him, the prodigal father, no, she hastily corrected herself, it's the prodigal son, but he is like the father, awaiting the return of the wayward son, except there won't be any fetching of sandals, or slaughtering of the fatten calf, when he hears my story.

'Where have you been?' he demanded not caring that the driver was still within earshot 'for God's sake, I've been sick with worry, why didn't you take your phone and why didn't the school give you my message?'

She looked at him with a blank expression and he realised, she didn't know what he was talking about. 'I rang that fucking useless place this morning and told them to ask you to return home as a matter of urgency,' he said, trying to clarify the situation. 'I've spent most of the day searching for you.'

Remaining silent, she walked by his side up the gravel drive. It seemed like another life time, rather than a matter of hours, since she had walked down that same drive, hand in hand with Daisy. The sudden thought of Daisy reminded her that she had made no plans for her collection from school, and a mental picture of her little girl, languishing against a wall, standing forlornly in an empty school yard filled her with panic.

'Where is Daisy?' she asked her voice almost breaking with fear. 'Where is Daisy?'

Jack pushed open the front door, 'She's across the way, playing with Lily,' he said, 'and she is fine; I collected her myself.' Phoenix put her hand to her chest, as if to reassure her heart; that since the worst hadn't happened, it could now take a rest.

Once inside the house, Jack turned to her. 'Someone is here to see you,' he said 'She's been waiting here most of the day for you, so don't attack or bully her.' Phoenix, though had no desire to meet anyone and she attempted to dodge him, but before she could reach the stairs, Jack threw open the door to the dining room.

Sitting there in a chair beside the open patio doors was Carolyn.

Suspicion and fear gripped her when she saw her assistant, and throwing Jack's hand off her arm, she strode towards Carolyn 'What on earth are you doing here?' she demanded. 'Is this your doing Jack?' She turned round to face him, but he had read the signal in Carolyn's eyes and had taken the opportunity for a quick exit.

'Oh Phoenix please don't be annoyed with Jack,' Carolyn cried, distressed at the scene her presence was causing, 'If anything, be angry with me. I told Jack recently that I was concerned for you, and he seems to have taken it very seriously.'

Phoenix looked aghast; it was getting worse by the minute, what on earth was going on, her assistant talking about her, discussing her with her own husband. 'So you thought it fit to talk about me behind my back, who else have you been talking to?'

Carolyn shook her head vehemently, 'You've got it so wrong Phoenix, Jack saw me because he was desperately worried about you and I'm afraid to say, I didn't make him feel any better, I told him I thought you were ill, that you might even be having a breakdown.'

The forbidden, unmentionable word acted like a blow to the back and Phoenix unable to stand such was the weakness she suddenly felt, dragged a chair from the dining table and sat down heavily upon it. Carolyn amazed that one compound word could wield so much power, walked over to her.

'Please,' she said holding her right hand to her chest and extending the other one in a gesture of friendship to Phoenix 'Don't be angry. I only mentioned the possibility, because seeing you look so distracted, so disinterested, reminded me of the time at university, when I was ill and no longer wanted to cope.'

Phoenix said nothing, somewhere in the recesses of her over-crowded mind, a faint memory sufficed of Carolyn telling her about some drama or other. She had hardly listened when Carolyn had bared her soul, dismissing it as drivel. The only thought she had entertained on the subject, was that instead of going mad, Carolyn should have got even. Burning the bastard's house down, would have been a good starting point.

'After Matt finished with me,' Carolyn continued. 'I felt as if I had a sudden insight on the world that others didn't have, everyone has the right to end a relationship if it's going nowhere or is destructive, but he did more than that. He did it so publicly, so vindictively, but you know, it wasn't what he said, that made me ill, it was the pondering of why.'

Phoenix didn't want a sermon and she certainly didn't want to be preached at by someone whose story was so different to her own, but something about the way Carolyn was speaking caught her attention and forced her to listen against her will.

Someone else had once spoken to her in the same tone, telling her something, oblivious to whether she wanted to listen or not.

She cast her mind back, reeling in the past, trawling through the many memories, unearthed from the letters she had constructed so religiously to Scarlett O'Hara. And finally, she realised that this hushed tone and aura of a tale, that needed to be told was reminiscent in its eeriness, of the night, when Lesley, the girl from Doncaster, told her about the death of her sister. The one who had killed herself. She hadn't wanted or expected interruption as she relived the grim details and Phoenix had the feeling it was the same now with Carolyn. She didn't want or expect a response to a story that was still too painful to be picked over or held to the light for consistency, but she did want to be listened to. A faint shiver of fear ran down her spine, as she turned her head and heard Carolyn repeat 'It wasn't what he said that made me ill, it was the pondering of why.'

'The pondering of why,' she repeated to herself and instantly her heart responded, by beating at a furious rate. 'Where?' she thought panic stricken, 'where have I heard those words before?' and in an instant she was on her feet, ready to run, so massive was the panic that was now unfolding. But there was no need for panic, the time when she too had used those self same words were within easy reach of her consciousness. It was when she had written to Scarlett about the plight of adopted children, who spend their life dogged not by 'if' but with 'why.'

She sat back down and looked across at Carolyn and for the first time, some inkling of the person behind the image emerged. Circumstances had made Carolyn what she was, just as they had formed her. There was more behind the mask, than a simpleton who simply smiled and thanked and generally kissed arse.

Her thoughts were interrupted by the arrival of Daisy back from Lily's house. She bounded into the room leaping first on to Phoenix's lap and then on to Carolyn's. 'Where have you been Mommy?' she asked placing her hands behind her back. 'We were waiting for you for ages, where have you been?'

'And didn't you have a boring time, playing all those games and teasing me with all your stories,' interrupted Carolyn, circling an arm around the child's waist and pulling her close, in an effort to distract her. She had noticed a look of harassment flash across Phoenix's face; it was obvious that wherever Phoenix had been, she didn't want to talk about it.

Confusion and light hearted chaos erupted as Jack entered the room with a tray of drinks. An extra bottle of Budweiser, put on the tray for good measure, toppled over as he reached for the table and Carolyn caught it by the neck. Her agility was applauded by both Jack and Daisy and she laughed as she shook the cold beer off her hand.

'Fetch a towel from the kitchen Daisy,' asked Jack, but Carolyn declined the need for one and instead invited Daisy to sit on her knee. He glanced uneasily at Phoenix, wary she might take exception to Carolyn fussing the child, but she seemed either unaware or disinterested.

Taking the civilised atmosphere as a cue to continuing with normality, he handed both Phoenix and Carolyn a glass of Bacardi and Coke topped with ice and lemon, before placing the bottle of Bacardi along with several cans of coke on a side table. Daisy immediately vacated Carolyn's knee, in favour of a vantage point on the floor beside the soft drinks, a move that didn't go undetected by at least two of the adults present.

Carolyn raised her glass in a toast of thanks to Jack, while Phoenix eyed hers distastefully. What she wanted more than anything was something to eat; something to banish the acute emptiness inside her, she hadn't eaten a single thing all day. She sat back in her chair, and listened half heartedly as Jack and Carolyn exchanged banter and light hearted foolish talk. She wasn't interested; she knew the talk was being kept deliberately breezy to avoid exciting her, but even the thought of being patronised failed to rouse her. The only emotion she now felt with any real strength; was resignation.

The ambience was briefly shattered when Carolyn's phone rang out. She answered the call and smiled knowingly across to Phoenix. It was the office; news was out that both Phoenix and Carolyn had been out all day, what was going on?

'I'm with Phoenix now,' Carolyn said to the caller. 'I've just called in, on my way back from Vauxhall, she rang in earlier, she says she's sprained her ankle but from what I've seen, I think it's worse than that, she might even have broken it.'

Phoenix looked across at Jack, taken aback at the ease with which Carolyn had told a lie, and a good one at that. The vexed question of how she was going to excuse herself from work had already crossed her mind but Carolyn had found a solution and a face saving one at that.

She sat back in her chair and watched while Jack and Carolyn teased Daisy, helping her to fish ice cubes out of the jug and laughing when she shattered them on the paving stones outside the window.

It was all so confusing, more confusing than she had ever thought possible.

Chapter Twenty Five

A form of reconciliation was in place when Jack and Phoenix retired to bed late on the night of September the 10th. He didn't mention the scene she had created at breakfast, or query her about where she had been all day and in return; she never questioned his involvement of Carolyn in her affairs. For a short while, Jack lay awake, turning over in his head, the events of the day; the bizarre exit Phoenix had made from the house, his anxiety when she had failed to return and his urgent telephone call to Carolyn. He knew beyond doubt now that Phoenix was ill, but the problem of persuading her to seek treatment still remained and it was the examination of this issue; that finally lulled him into sleep.

Sleep however still eluded Phoenix, she heard the rhythmic breathing of Jack slowly evolve into long, drawn out snores and endeavoured to concentrate on them, hopeful they might hypnotise her into a warm, deep, oblivious sleep. The anxiety that had raged earlier; had calmed down considerably, but she still felt tense and uneasy. She turned over in her mind what Carolyn had told her, it seemed incredible to think soft, meek, compliant Carolyn had once looked upon the world as a thoroughly unpleasant place to be in. Whatever had happened to delude her into thinking that it wasn't? She had always dismissed Carolyn as dull and appeasing by nature thereby denying that there was any merit in Carolyn's undying reasonableness and ability to placate. The realisation that Carolyn also possessed emotions strong enough to hospitalise her, came as something of a shock.

Her mind drifted further back to Shelby, the oracle who never was, she thought, without a trace of bitterness. She had set that woman an impossible task, hinting about but never revealing the secret that tormented her, but Shelby had risen to it. Storybook medicine had been an inspired idea, for although she hadn't found the true source of her anxiety, she had discovered countless other truths for which she was grateful. Especially the one about her mother; the revelation that she wasn't the smug, shamefaced woman Phoenix had feared she might be, was worth all the time and effort alone.

It is true, she thought turning onto her back and staring at the ceiling, everybody needs a hero and Scarlett O'Hara was mine.

In the seconds it took to flutter her eyelids shut, she summoned up a picture of the cold dank room in Kilburn, and the wrought iron bed upon which she had escaped into the world of the Deep South and the O'Hara family. She remembered with a shiver, the chapter above all others that had inspired her to make a new beginning; the one where Scarlett had arrived back at Tara, anxious for her mother, only to find she was dead and the existence she had once known, with all its comfort and grandeur was gone forever. What were the words Scarlett had used? Something about no avoiding the dead end she had come to - the end of the road – with nothing to look forward to other than grinding poverty. The words had struck terror into her when she had first read them; she had seen them as a foretelling of her own future. But she had read on, and like Scarlett she too had recognised, the past had nothing but misery to offer; only tomorrow counted.

The choice had been clear, she could accept a life of servitude, dependent on the charity of others, or start again, and create one of her own making. For a brief moment as she lay in the semi darkness, she felt again the stirrings of confidence those words had once inspired in her. They had worked once before, why shouldn't they work again? And just as Scarlett O'Hara had done, she turned her gaze on those who had gone before her, not just her parents, but their parents and the generation before them. There had been countless rebellions in Ireland and wars and famines - the fact she was around meant she came of a line that had survived them. Surely, she could survive what lay ahead now?

Her perusing of the past though romantic was not reassuring. In the still of the moonlit room, the ghostly shadows on the walls and ceilings spoke for a more fearsome outcome, where did inevitability fit into all of this? What if things happened for no other reason than they were fated to?

She propped herself up on her elbow and leaning over, turned up the volume on the radio and slowly the faint rumble of background noise translated itself, into clearly defined words. What she wanted right now was distraction, perhaps there was something happening in the world that might absorb her, take her thoughts across the sea, to some distant land and people.

She flopped back down on the pillow and listened with rapt attention as the newscaster announced: This is London and it is 0300 hrs Greenwich Mean Time. Today is Tuesday the 11th of September.

Tomorrow had arrived.

Moving carefully so as not to disturb Jack; she lifted back the quilt and slid out of bed and quietly and deftly headed for the stairs, which she descended lightly and at speed. The moment she reached the last step she stood still, unsure about where to go, though her heart continued to beat frantically, urging, insisting she keep moving. She discarded the idea of going into the kitchen, being at the back of the house, it would be too claustrophobic, she needed somewhere with an open aspect with access to the car and the road, should the need to run grow too strong to withstand.

Moving slowly, she headed to the front room, cursing softly as she stood on one of Daisy's toy teacups, and leaving the door slightly ajar, she tiptoed over to the glass fronted drinks cabinet, where she searched in the dim moonlight for a bottle of whiskey. Eventually her efforts were rewarded when she located a bottle, only to find to her dismay that it was unopened. This caused a fresh bout of cursing as her trembling hands struggled with an unfamiliar sealed top. Finally though she succeeded and lifting the bottle to her mouth, she drank from it at length.

With the bottle in her hand, she made her way to the window and there she stood for some time, staring into the moonlit night, conscious of only one thing, she was living out the last moments of normality. Fatigue and an excess of whiskey eventually persuaded her to sit down and leaning back into the settee, she watched as the sun gradually stole the night away.

When she opened her eyes again, Jack was standing beside her with a cup of tea in his hand. 'Christ girl,' he said, 'but you frightened the shite out of me, what on earth made you come down here?'

'I couldn't sleep,' she replied.

'Why didn't you wake me up? I would have joined you'.

She took the cup from him, to avoid answering his question and noted with some surprise that her hands were quite steady. A blue patterned quilt, she didn't recognise, lay in a heap on the floor and she wondered nervously where it had come from.

He saw her look at it and quickly explained its presence. 'I got that from the wardrobe upstairs,' he said. 'I put it over you earlier on, you were freezing.'

He sat down beside her and looked at her enquiringly, 'what am I going to do with you?' he asked, leaning forward and stroking her hair. She took his hand and gazed at it like a fortune teller working out the future and a sudden resolve swamped her. Now was the time to tell him, Shelby was absolutely right, Jack had to know before Joseph turned up.

'Jack,' she said, 'There is something I want to tell you.' He took her hand and pressed it to his cheek.

'Let me guess,' he said. 'You are never, ever going to touch whiskey again?'

'Please Jack,' she said, 'Please be serious and listen to me.' It would never do if Jack insisted on laughing and teasing, she couldn't spring something so dark and miserable into a light and banterish atmosphere.

But he was adamant 'No,' he said. 'I can tell by your face that you are very earnest and very serious, but now is not the time for a heart to heart, not after the amount of whiskey you must have put away in a very short time.'

She stared at him confused 'What do you mean?' she asked forgetting entirely how she had drunk like a race horse just a few hours previously.

'I mean,' he said, 'that empty bottle of Reserve bloody whiskey I bought to give Jim Collins today.'

'Oh that,' she said recognition slowly gaining pace.

'Yes, you old soak,' he said half teasingly, 'If you were going to go on the batter, why not choose Paddy or Johnnie or any of the other gang.' He clasped her right hand in both of his and spoke kindly though very seriously. 'I don't want to talk with you when your poor old brain is fuddled and confused with all that shit. I want to talk when you are calm and rested, because there is something I need to say to you and I want you to listen to me and to be able to understand.'

She listened dully as he spoke, realising the chance to come clean was rapidly diminishing. Could it be, she wondered hazily, that Jack knew she had something momentous to say and simply didn't want to hear it?

'Please Jack,' she insisted.

But he ignored her plea. 'I have left Daisy in bed,' he said, 'So don't go bothering with school today, I will have to see Jim Collins though, about that job in Purley; I've already cancelled twice, but that won't take any time at all. I'll be back and then we will sit and have a proper talk. Is that alright with you?' She nodded her head and he laughed at her woebegone face. 'Go on then,' he said 'Tell me if it is that urgent.'

But the moment had passed. This revelation wasn't something to be slipped in amongst the general agenda for the day ahead and it certainly didn't fit into the role of any other business.

'It doesn't matter,' she said quietly 'It can wait.'

'Are you sure you're going to be all right?' he asked, wary again when he saw how crestfallen she looked. She nodded her head, but Jack was now very concerned. 'Look' he said reaching into his pocket for his mobile phone. 'I'm going to cancel Collins, he can wait.'

'No Jack' she said quickly, 'There is absolutely no need for that, get it over and done with'.

'Will I get Carolyn then to sit with you while I'm gone, or shall I ask Helen to come in today instead of tomorrow?'

She shook her head vigorously, alarmed at his suggestion. 'No, honestly,' she insisted. 'You are fussing about nothing there is no need for anything like that. I'll be fine.'

She put her cup on the floor staring for a moment at the faintly specked red carpet as if she had never seen it before and then stood up and headed for the door. 'I'm just going to take a quick shower,' she said and disappeared from the room.

Jack remained seated, wondering what on earth it was that he had said to make her grow so cool and distant after such a promising start. He pondered to no avail.

She took her shower and as the water splashed upon her she wondered fleetingly how Jack would have reacted, if she had pressed her case and told him the truth. Stepping out, she dried herself and dressed with a good deal more attention to detail than she had done the previous morning, taking care not to choose anything remotely symbolic, nothing black and nothing red.

She left the room dressed in jeans and a white tee shirt and went back downstairs, determined to act as normal as possible. The last thing she needed now was Jack to have another change of mind and decide to stick around. He was in the kitchen folding up some architect plans with Daisy sat beside him, holding open a large envelope, ready for him to pop the plans back in. He wolf whistled when he saw Phoenix, and Daisy sensing the ceasefire ran to her side.

'Is there really no school today Mom?' she asked.

'Really,' Phoenix reaffirmed.

'We can go to the common; we could take a picnic, couldn't we Mom?'

'No,' answered Jack standing up. 'I don't want you to tire Mom out; you are meant to be looking after her for me, remember? You are to be a good girl and do as she tells you.'

Daisy scowled at Jack and ran up to Phoenix. 'Please, say yes Mommy,' she begged and eager to reduce the noise, Phoenix replied with the age old refrain that all children instinctively understand as meaning all is not lost.

'We will see.'

Shortly before half past ten, Jack left the house. Reaching into his pocket he hesitated for a moment before taking out his car key. 'Are you sure you will be okay?' he asked again.

'For God's sake, yes,' Phoenix replied, with much more confidence than she actually felt.

Still not entirely at ease, Jack tried again to establish whether or not it was safe for him to go. 'I will phone soon and if there is any problem I will come back immediately, okay?'

She nodded her head to reassure him and stood on the doorstep to wave him goodbye. Watching the car disappear down the drive, she had a recurring feeling; that everything she did that morning, would be for the last time. Never again would things be the same.

Daisy was ready and waiting for her inside the house with an enormous collection of dolls at the foot of the stairs, all eager to be taken to the common. 'We are not going yet,' Phoenix told her sharply, 'And put some of those guys back, I'm not carting all of them with us.'

Not waiting to listen to Daisy's cries of protest, she made her way gingerly into the kitchen; the first signs of a hangover were just beginning to pierce her head. She stood by the sink, and washed down a few painkillers with a cup of water. As she swallowed the medication, her mind begged the question; how best to spend this never ending day? Staying hidden in the house was not an option; she couldn't hide all day waiting for the axe to fall, quaking every time the phone rang, or a floorboard creaked.

A quick walk to the common; probably wouldn't be such a bad idea after all she thought, but trying to rustle up a picnic was more difficult than she anticipated. Pulling open cupboards at random, she tried to scramble together some odds and ends but concentrating on even that simple task proved almost impossible.

Waterloo Sunset by the Kinks played quietly in the background and Phoenix walked over and turned the radio up; it was one of her favourite records, it reminded her of the early days, when much of her commercial work had been based around Waterloo. The record came to an abrupt end with the eleven o clock news bulletin interrupting its flow mid way, and at the same time, a knock on the front door resounded through the house. Sheer terror rooted Phoenix to the spot and one by one the apples in her hand fell to the ground, scattering in all directions.

Another knock came, just as sturdy as the first one and just as resolute and the echo of it released within her a fresh surge of panic. Putting a hand to her heart, she stood listening to the noise of her blood thundering on its way to her brain.

'Mommy the postman is here, he's got a parcel.'

The sound of her daughter's voice crashed into her consciousness and she leapt in fright at the interruption. It took a moment for her to register what her child was telling her. She bent down and retrieved one of the apples that hadn't rolled as far away as the others, a delaying tactic, for although she had been given the all clear, the front door had suddenly taken on a frightening status.

Slowly she walked along the hallway, patting the back of her damp hair as she did so, and carefully she opened the front door with her hand extended, ready to take the delivery. Only it wasn't the postman. It was the ape. Giving a small whimper, she slammed the door shut and leaned against it, fear causing all her limbs to shake.

The phone on the hall table began to ring, but not one muscle did she dare to move, what if he was calling her on his mobile? The phone continued to call out into the stillness, until eventually the answer phone clicked on. It was Jack. 'Hi my love,' she heard him say. 'I take it you are either in the garden or out on the common, I will try you on your mobile, see you soon.'

No further knocking occurred and Phoenix edged herself slowly towards the side window. She could hear Daisy talking to herself in the dining room and the knowledge her child was so near to this mortal enemy filled her with fierce anxiety. The thought of the ape coming face to face with her little girl was tantamount to looking the 'evil eye' in the eye. It could not be allowed to happen.

She strained her eyes through the small paned window, peering to see around the Georgian column outside the door. The lone figure still stood there, he hadn't gone anywhere; at least he wasn't rooting around the back or peeping into windows. She raised herself up on tip toes and risked one long look at the black headed figure, and saw that it wasn't the ape after all, but it was most certainly his son.

She stared transfixed to the spot as the vision that had haunted her dreams took shape in front of her. An arm stretched out from the dark clothed body that was now standing slightly at an angle and it seemed to her that the knocking on the door every bit as ominous sounding as that of the unicorn, who rapped frantically on the door of the ark, came from another source, perhaps even from within her own head so detached from reality did she now feel. All other noise and existence was drowned out, just the tap, tap, tap of a human hand on a wooden door filled her senses.

Joseph Fox stood on the other side of the door, a small package tucked under one arm, his hands trembling with both fear and anticipation. He was he believed, on the verge of coming to the end of a long and heartbreaking search. When the door had opened briefly, he had seen a woman whose face he recognised immediately. It had even stared out of the mirror at him on several occasions. His spirits had soared only to be dashed, when the door had been abruptly closed in his face. Instantly he had regretted his actions, they were too bold, too confrontational. He knew beyond doubt he had just seen his mother, but she wouldn't know him and she certainly wouldn't be expecting to see him.

He felt half inclined to walk away and try again later, but the thought he may have worried his mother bothered him. Fuchsia House was secluded; she might think he was a burglar or some kind of stalker. No, he decided, he would try again; and slowly and carefully he would reassure her and introduce himself.

When the door opened for a second time and remained open, he could hardly conceal his joy. 'Hello,' he said. 'I am looking for someone by the name of Sinead O'Connell.'

'Hello Joseph,' Phoenix replied.

'Mom,' he said incredulously. 'Mom, you recognise me, you know who I am. How good it is to see you.'

Phoenix nodded her head and held the door open. Her eyes went to the mat on the floor, letters were strewn across it, Daisy hadn't been mistaken, the postman had called, just another of life's coincidences. 'Come in,' she said.

She closed the door and led the way to the front room. It was in a state of some disarray, the quilt Jack had draped over her earlier that morning still sat in a heap on the floor and a trail of toys and colouring pencils circled the room, evidence that Daisy had been at work in there as well.

'Take a seat Joseph,' she said calmly, though her heart thundered within her chest. She sat down beside him on the settee, her hands clasped tightly together.

'I can't believe it Mom,' he repeated. 'I am so overwhelmed.'

The door burst open and Phoenix looked up in alarm as Daisy ran in. 'Hello' the child said looking with interest at Joseph, 'who are you?'

Before Joseph could reply, Phoenix interrupted. 'Daisy,' she exclaimed in a high pitched voice and the child turned and stared enquiringly at her. Phoenix struggled to control her voice, searching for words that would drive Daisy out of the room and away from the nightmare at hand. 'Go and find Old Bear,' she said eventually. 'I'd like to see him.'

It was an illogical request, but her mother initiating a meeting with one of her toys was a rare occasion indeed and one Daisy did not intend to miss out on, so abandoning her interest in the stranger, she obeyed her mother and went in search of the elusive toy.

'Is that my sister?' Joseph asked. Phoenix nodded her head; and gingerly touched the side of her face at the same time, for a sensation of numbness was slowly crawling over her nose and mouth. It was impossible to think this man sitting beside her was actually related to Daisy.

'My parents, Maria and John Fox, told me that you were very young when you had me,' Joseph ventured softly, 'They told me that you fought long and hard to keep me, but circumstances were against you.' Phoenix said nothing, her heart just continued to beat rampantly. 'Now I've seen you Mom, I have some idea of what they were talking about; you still look like a girl.'

There was a slight West Country twang to his voice, and Phoenix remembered for no good reason, Mr Roberts at the building society where she had worked all those years ago, he too had been from the West Country. She kept her eyes averted. 'I can handle this,' she told herself, 'I can handle the tremor in his voice, I'd even handle his hand upon mine, but I can't look into his face; that is beyond me.'

'Has life treated you well?' she asked searching for something to say that wasn't too banal or trivial.

'Oh yes,' he replied enthusiastically, 'The Fox's have been wonderful to me, given me every chance I could ever have wanted, both Maria and John.' At the mention of the word Fox's, a picture of a black snouted creature nosing into a box of straw rooting for hidden eggs flashed into Phoenix's mind, and for no good reason, she felt a sudden surge of enormous irritation.

'Maria and John Fox,' she repeated, before adding, 'He sounds like some sort of Protestant reformer.'

'Oh no Mom,' Joseph laughed, 'Not Dad, he's just about the most level headed, devout Catholic you'll ever come across.' She put her head down, ordinary salt of the earth people; that was what Joseph was describing, people who paid their taxes and didn't cheat on the buses. She felt a stab of envy for a way of life that could have been hers.

He placed his hand gently on top of hers, as if suddenly aware praise for his adoptive parents may have insulted her. She looked down and saw his long slender fingers, so similar to her own. The last time she had seen those hands, they had been curled up in a tiny fist, peeping above a white shawl, given as a peace offering. She felt a tear prick her eye, as she remembered the day the two had parted, when she had taken her leave and the distance between them, reflected itself in her memory, as a long and winding road.

She turned to speak to him 'Joseph...' she said. 'I ...' But the words wouldn't come; she couldn't trust herself to speak. The phone in the hall way rang out, destroying the silence and desperate for space to think, she leapt up without a word of apology and ran to answer it.

It was Jack. 'Hello,' she said struggling to keep her voice together. He asked where she had been and she told him she had been out in the garden. He sensed something was wrong by her short static sentences.

'I'm coming home now,' he said.

Desperation at the thought of Jack and Joseph coming face to face immediately propelled her into action. 'Oh Jack, don't go worrying, I'm a bit out of breath from running in from the garden,' she lied. 'I'm just off to the common with Daisy anyway, but I have got a bit of a hangover.' He was doubtful, but again she reassured him, and in return he told her he would be home as soon as possible.

Returning to the front room, she took a sideways glance at Joseph, who remained where she had left him, sitting on the settee. He stood up as she entered the room and she realised for the first time, that he was actually a good deal smaller than the ape. Only the hair was the same, that dreadful crow black hair. She took her seat beside him again not knowing what to say. Surely she should offer tea or coffee, or something, but she couldn't. There was no guarantee she could keep a steady face for much longer, a faint buzzing noise was echoing in her ears and she felt distinctly disorientated.

He was the first to speak. In his hand he held the small package, the one that had led Daisy to think he was the postman; it contained a small photo album, pictures taken of him when he was young. He saw his mother struggling for composure and the sight pained him; there was no way he could add to her distress with photos from a past that had excluded her. But at least it was true, she had cared and she still did.

'I want you to know,' he said, 'that I understand you have a life of your own; there is no need to tell anyone about me, if you haven't done so already. I haven't come to see anyone but you.'

She nodded her head, still unable to speak. At that moment Daisy came back into the room. 'I can't find Old Bear anywhere Mommy,' she said. 'I think you threw him out, after his leg fell off.'

Phoenix didn't like the sound of Daisy's conjecture at all, it sounded harsh and uncaring and very accurate so she moved quickly, to change the subject.

'Oh he's probably in the loft. Now run along and get ready quickly if you want to go out, the sun won't hang around all day.'

Ignoring her mother, Daisy turned her attention to Joseph. 'Are you coming with us?' she asked, 'to the common, for a picnic?

'I would love to,' he said, 'but I'm afraid I have to go now.'

He turned to Phoenix 'I would love to meet you again soon,' he said. 'If I give you my number, perhaps you could call me, when you are ready?'

Daisy stood back and silently watched the interaction. There was something special about the visit of this man, she could tell by the subdued way her mother was acting, she looked different and Daisy wasn't at all sure whether or not she liked the change. She listened carefully, waiting for her mother to reply to the man's request. But Phoenix was too distraught to speak. Too many questions were demanding answers. How could a stranger be her son? How could her son be a stranger? Her mind toyed with this predicament cutting out all other considerations. She stared down at her hands and shook her head. Joseph seeing her distress; took a pen from his pocket and on the back of a London bus ticket, wrote his telephone number.

'Whenever you are ready,' he said 'Please phone me. I live in London now; I'm at the Royal College of Music.' She took the ticket from him and he stood up; a signal to her he didn't want to prolong her ordeal any longer than was necessary. She too stood up and made her way to the door and he followed.

For the second time in a matter of hours she was watching someone take leave of her and all her senses cried out, don't let him go. He turned to her and speaking quietly and in a voice laden with emotion, he said. 'You know, this could so easily have been the worst day of my life, but it has turned out to be the best.' He put his hand out and she took it, resisting the urge to pull him close to her.

She stood watching until Joseph had disappeared down the drive, out of sight but most definitely not out of mind; then turned and went back inside the house. Pushing the door shut, she leaned her head against it overwhelmed by the ordinariness of it all. It was over. It had happened and she had survived. But where did she go from here?

A harsh ripping noise cut through the silence and turning round she saw Daisy sitting on the second step of the stairs fiddling with her shoes, opening and closing the Velcro straps. Given the strange surreal atmosphere, Daisy knew better than to urge her mother on, a hint would have to suffice.

'I'm coming,' Phoenix informed her daughter and walked into the kitchen. Snatching a carrier bag from a drawer, she shoved into it the assortment of food rooted from the cupboards earlier and opening the fridge grabbed a bottle of soft drink. It is better to be out she told herself as she walked with her daughter in the warm September sunshine, I don't think I could bear being inside one minute longer.

Once on the common, she sat down on a wooden bench and watched as Daisy, safely ensconced in a little dip just beyond her, arranged her toys in a semi circle. Pessimism in the form of a grey fog seeped into her soul as she surveyed through her memory the ruin that was her life. She was too old for a new beginning and probably too young for a sudden ending. As she sat, the realisation came to her that the years she thought had crawled by had in fact flown past. Joseph's arrival back into her life had shined a torch down the anxious weeks, months and years she had travelled through, condensing them into a feeling that they were more yesterday, than yester year.

Her thoughts turned to Jack, travelling home from Surrey, thinking his wife was ill merely through overwork or unlucky heredity. What a shock he would get when he learnt the truth. The desire for the game to be up in its entirety overwhelmed her. She had no doubt that Joseph was a man of integrity, there was nothing to stop her from continuing with the secret, but what she longed for more than anything, was honesty, truth and something she could only loosely define as freedom.

She felt a tear roll down her cheek as she imagined Jack's reaction, his shock and horror, but worse of all, his disillusionment. Like someone caught with their hand in the till, exchanging a tenner for two fivers, who would ever believe that the only person she had set out to deceive was herself? Jack had never known her as anything other than ruthless, headstrong and determined, but now he was going to be presented with an image of her as weak and shrill and the thought made her burn with shame. Certainly he knew nothing of the gormless teenager, running and fetching, eager to please and justify her existence to a mother who hadn't expected or wanted another child at the age of forty six.

And what would he make of the trapped and hopeless creature who had lived with the wicked fairy in Kilburn? Jack had no inkling of any of this; she wasn't the only one for whom September the 11th was going to be a day of revelation.

Her thoughts were interrupted by an elderly man, who sought her attention by tapping his walking stick on her bench. He addressed her in an authoritive, querulous tone, and although she had no desire to listen to what he was saying, she did catch the gist of 'belong to you?' Immediately she leapt to her feet, Christ she thought in a panic, another catastrophe, when would it ever end 'Yes,' she said frantically to the old man, 'where is she?'

He gave a grunt of disgust. 'People like you are a bloody disgrace to dog owners I've been watching that dog of yours crap its way round the common.'

Phoenix looked at the old man as if it were he and not she who were mad; then walked slightly forward to see more clearly the dip where she had settled Daisy to play; Daisy was thank God, still there, engrossed with her dolls.

'Look,' the old man insisted, pointing with his stick, 'pissing its heart out against the litter bin.'

Phoenix followed his gaze and saw a little black and white mongrel furiously sniffing the bin it had just fouled against. 'That dog is nothing to do with me,' she said to the old man.

He gave her a contemptuous stare 'That's a likely story,' he replied. 'I've a good mind to report you to the dog warden; that would give you something to worry about.'

A violent desire to seize the old man by his scrawny neck tore through her; did he she wondered, have a death wish? Turning to him, she said in a fury. 'I've a good mind to report you to the police, anyone who spends the day watching a dog crap should be locked up, you......'. A piecing whistle stopped her in her tracks and she looked over to see the little mongrel bounding its way over to two enormous black guys, one of whom bent down and attached a lead to its collar.

She turned back to the old man 'Fancy giving them a lesson on dog ownership?' she asked, but he ignored her and began to shuffle away. 'Cowardly old bastard,' she shouted.

The brief encounter left her feeling aggravated; there was no escape, no peace to be found anywhere. She walked over to the dip where Daisy sat and called the child to her. Daisy scrambled up the tiny hill brandishing a bottle of Budweiser. 'Look what you put in my picnic Mommy,' she said. 'I thought it was Tango.'

Phoenix bent down and took the beer from the child. 'Save it for Daddy,' she said poking it into her handbag. 'Though I have a feeling he will need something stronger than this.'

'Like a cup of tea?' Daisy suggested.

'Yes,' Phoenix replied. 'Like a cup of tea.'

Jack was already home and Phoenix's heart sank when she saw his car parked haphazardly outside the front door. If only she had a little more time to think things through, if only she had taken Shelby's advice and had told Jack the truth as a matter of urgency. She looked down and caught sight of Sleeping Beauty's perfect head, peeping out of Daisy's arms. If only the fairy at her christening, had given her something more useful than the gift of hindsight.

He was in the kitchen, sitting at the table with a newspaper spread open in front of him and most unusually for Jack, the television was on. He stood up when she came in closing the paper as he did so. 'So you made the common,' he said. 'Did you take a picnic?'

'Yes,' replied Daisy, 'but silly Mommy took a bottle of beer instead of orange.'

'I don't think that is silly at all,' Jack replied walking over to Phoenix. He pulled her to him and kissed her on her forehead. 'It looks as if the fresh air has done you some good,' he said, 'you have a touch more colour in your cheeks.'

'Can I play outside?' Daisy asked. Phoenix nodded her head by way of agreement and sat down on the chair vacated by Jack.

'Will you have tea?' he asked.

'Yes,' she replied and watched as he proceeded to fill the kettle from the tap.

'Jesus,' he said with his back turned to her 'but that is some terrible news today isn't it?'

She hardly dared to speak, as alarm spread through her with more rapidity than spilt ink travelling across a silk sheet. What on earth was he talking about? 'What news?' she asked falteringly.

He spun round. 'That for God's sake girl,' he said indicating with his head towards the television. 'The world is in uproar; some arseholes have attacked America and blown the Twin Towers up.'

Was that all? Well, she could handle that.

'I've been out all afternoon,' she explained. 'I haven't heard any news.'

'Well get ready to hear more,' he said. 'This story is going to run for weeks; it's some fucking mad business.'

'Where is Daisy?' she asked, deliberately looking away from the television. She couldn't make out what was happening, a building seemed to be on fire and all she could detect from the scene was a frenzy of mass panic and it unnerved her.

'Where she said she would be outside.' He made the tea and bought it across to her. 'Forget everything else,' he said swiping the news away with one deft aim of the remote control and pulling out a chair in order to sit down beside her. 'How was your day?' It was such an innocuous question, one he had asked and she had answered countless times before with no regard to consequences. How different it was going to be this time.

She looked up at him, into his tired, concerned looking face and though she was sorely tempted to follow the road more travelled, she steered herself with resolve to the alien one, the narrow path of truth. 'Jack,' she said starkly 'I feel as if my life ended today.'

She stopped for a moment and he looked across at her knowing instinctively she was about to say something momentous. 'I've got something to tell you,' she said looking down at her hands. 'I wanted to tell you this morning; in fact I've wanted to tell you for years.'

Silence reigned, save for the distant cries of Daisy as she played in the garden, and the jerky rhythmic ticking of the damaged cuckoo clock.

'Just say, what you have to say.'

'A long time ago, I had a child. He came to see me today.'

She didn't want to meet his eyes, but she knew she had to if she was to retain any credibility. But to look into them was almost too painful to bear. She saw the shock upon his face and the realisation hit her, that she had been too preoccupied with how Jack would react to her, rather than how he would react to the consequences for himself. She had the benefit of knowing for years that this day would come; Jack on the other hand, was being immersed without warning into news that had the capacity to change his life forever. He was owed more than a bold admission.

She stood up and walked to the sink, her back turned to him and her eyes focused upon Daisy, playing in the garden beyond the window. 'I want to tell you the truth,' she said. 'I want to tell you what I should have told you years ago, and then you will have some idea of what is going on, why I've gone to pieces and why none of this is any fault of yours.'

Taking a deep breath and like an introverted performer who finds solace in the blinding brightness of stage lights, she concentrated on the world outside and slowly told him her story, starting with the night of the school disco, when the snow had fallen, burying beyond recovery the girl she used to be.

She spoke factually and without emotion about how Condon had frightened her before fooling her into thinking he was benign. She recounted his violence and the venomous words he had used as he set about ruining her and about the retreat she had made in the snow. Pausing only briefly, she gave a description of the haranguing she had received at the hands of her family and the unknown fear that insisted on her remaining silent. With bitter words she recalled her days in Kilburn, right up to the day when she had taken her leave from Joseph.

Without any embarrassment, she told a deeply pragmatic Jack how a work of fiction had inspired her to form a new life for herself. All the grimy details she laid bare. There was no longer a reason to hide anything from him. And not once did he interrupt, he listened as one might listen to the tale of an ancient traveller, who through magic and mystery takes one down paths unknown, to a world beyond comprehension.

By the time she had finished her tale, night had begun to fall and turning around finally to face him she saw Daisy tucked in his arms, subdued into sleepiness by the surreal atmosphere of her mother talking into the darkness and her father listening.

'What more can I say?' she said shaking her head, 'you were right to doubt my state of mind, I am close to breaking point, but your sympathy and concern is misplaced. I have bought it on myself.'

He said nothing. He continued to look past her for a moment, before standing up and walking abruptly to the door with Daisy in his arms. She heard his footsteps disappear down the hall and the slam of the front door as it closed behind him. Making no attempt to move or to discover where he had gone; she stood with silence echoing in her ears. It was too late to chase, to cajole and persuade. It was over.

She closed her eyes and flinched slightly as her memory without warning fixed on an image from the archive in her head. She saw clearly, a picture of herself on the day she had handed Joseph over; slumped against the wall in the public toilets of Paddington station, contemplating the reality of a long unremittingly bleak future with everything that mattered stripped away from it. The only thing she had been able to visualize were the long empty years, stretching ahead until she was finally released from the misery of it all.

She was back from where she had started. There was no life to be had with him and no life worth living without him. Now, she knew without doubt, she was in the dead end that Scarlett O'Hara had talked about. How stupid she had been to think rape and the death of her mother were the worst things to bear, they were as nothing compared to the loss of Jack and her child. Insanity was no longer something to be feared; she wished with all her heart it would descend upon her, consume her, overwhelm her to such a degree, that all conception of reality would be blocked out for ever. Life was a sickening, useless, exercise and she no longer had any more desire for it.

As if from nowhere, Jack's voice spoke through the gloom. For a moment she thought she was imagining it, until she turned and saw him standing in the doorway. 'I've taken Daisy to Rebecca's house for the night,' he said and the serious dull tone in which he spoke, sent a chill through her heart, destroying in an instant the momentary lift in mood that had occurred upon hearing his voice. 'I think we need some proper time to talk.'

She nodded her head and gestured with her hand to the table.

'No,' he said tiredly. 'I've been driving all day and those chairs hurt my arse; we'll go into the front room.'

She followed him, unsure what the nature of their talk together was going to be, her heart beating in trepidation. She wanted neither recrimination nor reassurance both would be equally beyond endurance; all that consumed her now was a devouring sense of irrevocable remorse.

'Jack,' she said anxiously, as she sat down beside him on the settee, but he waved her silent with a brush of his hand.

'What I don't get,' he said, coming to the point without any preamble, 'Is the silence, why didn't you tell someone. How could you let the fucker run free?'

She threw her hands up in a gesture of helplessness. 'How can I explain it to you?' she said, shaking her head. 'I wanted so much to tell my mother, even though the shame was fierce and I almost did, until he walked in with the news about his wife.' She paused for a moment. 'When I discovered I was pregnant, it was too late, who was going to believe me? I felt as if it had all been taken out of my hands, everything conspired against me.'

He leaned back in the chair, a hand raised to the side of his head as if he were in pain. 'But why the silence with me?' he asked and before she could reply, he spoke the single fact that pained him most. 'Why so little trust in me?'

She shook her head, 'It was never a question of trust Jack. If I was going to tell you it had to be right from the start and that would have been ridiculous, telling a stranger my life story'.

'Then you could have told me a little later on'

Again she shook her head, this time in exasperation. 'You don't understand, as time passed it became more difficult and anyway, it was all about self delusion, I had portrayed a false picture of myself to you, telling you ...'

'I told you about Polly,' he said not waiting to hear her explanation in full.

She got up and walked to the window, clearly now greatly agitated. 'It's not the same Jack; it's not even in the right ball park.'

'That's you, isn't it?' he said, a touch of bitterness adding salt to his words. 'You always underestimate others, you rubbish Carolyn as a fucking clown because she never puts you straight; but you never acknowledge how she runs your business without a hitch. Has it ever crossed your mind how I felt, still feel even about that divorce? It was over twenty years ago, there wasn't even such a thing as divorce in Ireland. I told you in the full knowledge that you might leave, because for all that you weren't a practising Catholic, you had all the hypocrisy of one and you've never been renowned for your charity, but I took the chance.'

'It is different Jack,' she said tilting her head back in order to face the ceiling, as if imploring a spirit from beyond, to inspire her with words to convince him that the comparison was innocuous, 'Divorce is about making a mistake, what happened with me wasn't a mistake, it's not even about something I did, it's about something that was done to me. It's about self esteem, are you incapable of grasping that?'

He leapt up, insulted by her easy dismissal of his own grief and the insinuation that he lacked the refined ability to under-stand something subtle and rushing across to her, he pulled her by her shoulders so that she had no option but to turn and face him.

'Take your hands off me,' she cried shrinking away from him. 'I don't ever want to be touched by you or anyone again. Is it any wonder I never told you? There is no comparison between a man getting divorced by choice and a woman being raped by an animal, having his child and being forced to live like a leper.' She had done it, she had used the dreaded word; the one she could not bear the connotation of with its suggestion of defilement and ruin. The word which until now she had supplanted with 'assault' or 'attack' anything rather than the one with the capacity to lift up the rug of reality and lay bare the true nature of what Condon had done.

She dropped her head and swallowed hard in an effort to keep her voice steady.

'Why are you dragging this out for me anyway?' she asked bitterly. 'Can't you understand; I never told you because I knew the moment I did, it was over?'

His hands slid off her shoulders and he took a small step backwards. 'Why?' he said. 'Why should it be over?'

Turning her head aside, she placed the back of her right hand to her left eye as a sudden sharp pain forced her to blink. From her point of view the conversation had now turned around; pacifying Jack by leaking the truth out slowly and carefully was no longer the issue. There was no disguising what she was and she wanted no part in a cover up and most certainly, as sorry for herself as she now felt, she didn't want his pity.

With great difficulty, she turned and faced him. 'Do you think?' she said her voice breaking slightly. 'Do you think I could ever live or sleep with you again, now that you know how I was used and thrown aside like a piece of shit, by a piece of shit.'

She turned away again, having delivered the opening shots in her quest to destroy forever the image Jack had of her. It was as if by not facing him she could detach herself from the truths she felt duty bound to deliver.

'Think back to when you first met me, you didn't have a clue about the agony I went through every time you came near me, remember how I used to fight you off, you thought it was a game of playing hard to get. Did you ever wonder why I had to drink so much? And the reality is Jack, if you had known the truth; you would have run a million miles away'.

She paused a moment and when he made no reply, she took his silence as evidence that she had hit upon the truth. Not wanting to hear the rejection that would surely follow, she turned and faced him, choosing her words carefully so as not to leave him in any doubt, that she fully understood his feeling of repulsion.

'Not a night has passed Jack, when the thought hasn't occurred to me, that if you knew what this body had been through, how its been manhandled and thrown aside; you would surely run a fucking mile, rather than have anything to do with it.'

The level of despair in her voice frightened him, for self loathing was something he had never experienced, and he felt himself lost in a territory he knew nothing about. Contrary to what Phoenix believed, Jack had done things which he had gone on to regret, but he had never punished himself the way Phoenix was doing now to herself. He stepped forward unable to listen as she consigned their marriage and her integrity to history and without warning, he grabbed her arms and pinned them fast to her sides.

'Why are you doing this?' he shouted. 'Why are you telling me things that will only make you hate me for hearing them? What purpose does it serve?'

She tried to break free from his grasp writhing backwards and forwards but he held her arms in a grip she couldn't escape from. 'You wanted the truth,' she shouted back. 'Now you are getting it and you don't like it, but it's the truth and nothing you can say will change it'.

'It's bollocks,' he told her angrily, his temper beginning to rise despite his best intention to keep calm. 'Don't even dare to tell me what I think or feel, I never demanded any of this from you, but now you've had your say, I will have mine'.

She tried once again to slip her arms out of his hold but he was too quick for her. 'Keep still,' he ordered, in a much quieter tone. 'Listen to me and then make any decision you want.'

She quietened down and even though she stood motionless, he held fast, suspicious of her calmness. 'Can't you get it into your head; that when that old fucker preyed on you, you were a child? You weren't the woman you are now.'

Was that all? Were these his great words of wisdom? Did he really think, she was going to say, well now, that puts a new light on everything? But he wasn't finished.

'You might have turned the events of that night over in your head a million times, but since you've never told anyone, the only perspective you have on it is that of a teenage girl.' He paused for a moment, contemplating just how much she would despise him for what he was about to say. But Jack Keane's ability to estimate was legendary and he knew that Phoenix's mind was made up. He couldn't lose her with what he had to say, he could only draw her back to him.

'Looking at it from a man's point of view, that bastard probably intended sleeping with you from the moment he set eyes on you. That night was just too good an opportunity to miss, wife away and Christmas. He tried drink and chat and when that didn't work, he helped himself, rape wasn't the preferred option.'

'It makes no...' she screamed.

'But more than that, he had you sussed, not just you but your entire bloody family, he knew exactly which way you would jump, he knew just the way to play it.' He paused, before adding very quietly, 'Do you really believe his lousy, shitty wife had a breakdown?'

Phoenix remained silent and he asked again, this time much more aggressively. 'Do you?'

She shrugged her shoulders, as if unable to contemplate Jack's line of reasoning. 'Yes, I suppose she did.'

'Then how naïve you still are,' he said dismissively. 'He is a classic fucking abuser, who wouldn't have left anything to chance. I'd put money on it that he raced round to that hospital and confessed to an affair with you. She could put up and shut up like she'd probably done on countless other occasions.'

He paused and squeezed her arms gently, aware that much of the fight had deserted her. 'Puss ever since I've known you, you have worked on instinct and it has never let you down, it was instinct that kept you silent. She would have backed him to the hilt rather than have the shame of being married to a rapist.'

As his words resounded in her ears Phoenix felt her body go limp. She recalled the way Olga Condon had looked at her on the two occasions when their paths had crossed following that terrible December night. There had been the coolness at the baby's christening and the iciness on that cold Christmas morning, when Olga had glared at her through the ring fence of priest and parish worthies. Stupid young girl that she had been, she had dismissed those looks as nothing more than Catholic Olga's disapproval upon hearing on the grapevine, that quiet demure Sinead O'Connell was really a dark horse, who had indulged in teenage sex. It had never occurred to her that the looks belonged to a furious wife who thought she was staring at her husband's latest trollop.

Jack's conjecture now seemed the more likely scenario.

Jack opened his mouth to speak, but stopped at the last minute staring down at the ground instead. He knew she was now facing the reality that the option of coming clean all those years ago, had never really existed. Condon and his wife would have been allies and together they would have buried her integrity along with her good name. He kept his hands on her arms, although he knew there was no spirit left in her and realising that he had a captive audience, he made the decision to keep the momentum up.

'Didn't Condon tell you that he would get the boy on the next go?'

She nodded her head dumbly, as a new sickening realisation hit her, he did get a boy, just not a kosher one.

'Well, tell me this,' Jack enquired. 'Were there any more children?'

She shook her head. 'Of course there wasn't, that was the price he paid for buying her silence, she'd probably turned a blind eye to countless affairs over the years, just grateful to have the bastard taken off her back. But a baby was something she wouldn't have forgiven easily.'

He dropped his grip on her arms and walked over to the settee, sitting down on it with a sigh. 'After dropping that bombshell, he would have to have gone elsewhere for it full time. He's probably got bastards all over the place.'

Phoenix winced at the mention of the word 'bastard'. It suddenly sounded so harsh and uncaring, even though it had previously served her very well as an adjective to describe everything from her car to her colleagues.

She stood arms loose by her side, and stared across at him.

If only, she thought bleakly, if only she could disappear, go somewhere a million miles away and, not start again - just finish this existence off in some kind of peace and solitude.

He looked up and returned her gaze. 'Do you remember the day we met?' he asked.

She nodded her head 'Yes, by those flats in Wandsworth.'

'When I looked across at you, you looked so lonesome. I remember thinking; there's a woman who's probably just been walked out on by some bloke. I couldn't think of any other explanation.' He paused, waiting for a reply and when it didn't materialise, he stood up and walked back to her. Taking her hands in his, he tugged them slightly in an effort to encourage her to raise her eyes.

'Within minutes of speaking to you, I knew I had to have you and though you will probably never believe me and think I'm just a crass bastard, but hearing the real reason for that lonesome look makes no difference, I don't want to lose you. I only want to take care of you, the way someone should have done, all those years ago.'

She knew he was speaking the truth, but his words of comfort and love far from comforting her, only made her feel more desolate. For years she had cultivated the personality of an abuser, fearing anything less would place her in danger of being once again, the abused. Now slowly, Jack was peeling away the layers she had wrapped herself in, revealing the person she wanted to keep hidden.

It was all too much and placing her head on his shoulder she cried, and though he too was suffering at the sight of her in so much pain, he ignored his own agony and coaxed and soothed her, urging the tears to stop, but they continued to flow. They flowed for both shame and regret at not having told Jack the truth earlier, and for something else, something, indefinable.

He led her to the settee and disappeared to the kitchen returning quickly with a towel, a bottle of whiskey and two glasses pegged together between his fingers. He placed the bottle on the small side table and poured two enormous measures before turning to her with the towel. 'Here,' he said patting her face as if she were a distraught baby, 'Let's have a drink and you tell me about this boy Joseph.' She sipped from the glass he gave her, wiping her eyes and nose in turn with the back of her hand and the towel Jack had handed her.

'Oh Jack,' she said snorting like a child in her attempt to bring her crying under some control. 'When I saw him through the window, I thought it was the ape, but when I looked at him properly, it was only the hair that was the same.' She took another sip of the whiskey and sighed; shuddering as she did so. 'How will I tell him?' she asked.

'Tell him what?'

'About his father being a rapist.'

He slapped his glass down on the side table and turned to her aghast. 'You're not serious,' he said, 'you can't do that.'

She turned her open mouth away from her glass, stunned by his words. 'Why?' she said, 'why not, for too long I have shielded Condon, why shouldn't he go through what I suffered today?'

He edged himself forward on the settee, in order to look her full in the face. 'You can't do that, not to the boy, you can't wreck his future.'

She picked up the towel and began wiping her face furiously for the tears that had abated slightly, once again began to flow freely. 'Why not Jack, why must I always be the one to pay?'

He threw his hands in the air 'Because, the boy is innocent, no matter what the father did, he is innocent.'

'But the truth Jack,' she cried. 'What about the truth?'

He leaned further forward and took the glass from her hand 'What about the truth?' he asked gently, 'Anyone with a drop of Irish blood in them knows that the truth is too important to be dragged out for any old occasion.'

She stared at him, not sure if he was serious or joking. 'You sound like Scarlett O'Hara's father,' she said. 'Except he said something about love of the land and the Irish.'

He refused to be waylaid, 'No one,' he said, in dead beat seriousness, 'Really knows the truth concerning their own conception,' and she looked at him, not recognising the tone he spoke in. 'Why?' he asked softly, 'should Joseph be an exception?'

She took her glass from him and raised it to her mouth, draining out the last of it. 'Why' she repeated 'Always why.'

They sat together in silence, no murmur of the radio, no ticking of the clock to disturb them; only the occasional sniff as Phoenix fought to regain control of her tears. 'Where do I go from here Jack?' she asked suddenly. 'I can't even feel the desire to start again, and even if I did, it would be too late. All I've ever wanted is to belong.'

She placed her glass on a little Italian sewing table, tucked in beside the settee and brushed her hands through her hair. 'When I was young, some teachers at school used to call me the red haired Irish girl, and when I told them I wasn't Irish; they would click their tongue, and say 'there is no need to be ashamed of it you know.' I didn't understand what they meant. I wasn't ashamed; it just seemed stupid to say I was Irish when I was born in England. I grew up neither one thing or the other and the same contrariness showed up numerous times in Ireland. I remember once when I cheered on Kerry in a hurling final, your sister, Eileen turned to me and said, 'It's so funny when the English act as if they are at home in Ireland.'

He placed his glass on the floor and turned to her with a smile on his face. 'Well,' he said lightly. 'Supporting Kerry while you were in Cork, was asking for trouble,' but when he saw that she didn't catch on to the intended joke, he became serious again. 'Does it matter so much, what people think, or say beyond these four walls?' he asked.

She shrugged her shoulders in a way that was quickly becoming habit forming. 'I would like to say it doesn't,' she replied, 'but that wouldn't be true. There are so many things I want to believe, right now I want to think there is hope, but I know tomorrow I will wake up full of despair, and I'll see the idea of a new beginning for what it is, a pointless, meaningless, gesture. I can't grasp why people think life is so precious, it passes, everything passes'.

'All anyone can do,' he pointed out, 'Is get through it the best way they can and you are wrong, life is special, think of the grief caused by the death of a baby or young child, all the focus on the missed opportunities and dreams that won't be realised.'

'No,' she said shaking her head vehemently, 'The grief is about losing someone that is loved, not on what the dead are missing. I want to know the point of it all, where does it lead to?'

He removed his arm from around her shoulder and sat back slackly against the chair, a gesture that made her feel unaccountably uneasy. She was only just beginning to realise how vital his support was and the thought that the warmth and vibrancy of it was about to diminish, filled her with a new despair.

'You are not the only one to question what it is all about,' he said. 'I've never questioned anything; I've always done what's suited me at the time, but do you know when all that changed? It was after that lousy trip to Boston.'

She looked across at him and nodded her head slowly in agreement. 'Yes, I can believe that,' she said quietly. 'You did change; I thought you were just shame faced at having got it so wrong.'

He laughed, just a tad too dryly for her liking 'See, you do have a talent for underestimating. Yes I got it wrong, but it wasn't that, I got a sudden glimpse of myself, chasing money for no good reason other than the chase, and I could handle that, but, you know, it was Daisy who made me think twice. I think those few days in that shit hole, were the happiest I've ever seen her.'

At this preposterous thought, Phoenix leaned forward and shook her head vigorously. 'No, I don't think that's true,' she said emphatically. 'I really don't, not at all.'

'Oh but it is,' he replied, 'For the first time, she had the two of us united and together, if only in joint intense hatred of a place and its people, but united all the same. Don't go worrying though, I'm not about to preach a life style based on deprivation, but it is a fact, all the things we give her are pointless, in comparison to attention.'

Phoenix said nothing; she thought back hazily to that strange week and apart from a dim recollection of a harassed Jack, she couldn't recall one incident of Daisy playing up, there had been no sulks, no tantrums thrown. Perhaps Jack was right.

'What really bought things to a head though,' he said leaning forward and pouring more whiskey into his glass, 'Was Danny dying so suddenly, it was like a warning, get things together while you can. I think Danny was the only truly happy person I've ever known, and you know how much he cared about money.'

She nodded her head. It was true, Danny had been happy and money had meant less than nothing to him. 'He didn't need money Jack,' she said, 'because he was secure in himself; and I suppose security is all money really means to anyone.'

'Don't fret,' he said reaching out and patting her knee 'You can hang on to your fortune, I'm not about to pull a Christ like stunt and tell you to go sell all you own, but both of us need to think things through.' Both of us need to think things through. His words hung in the air and she rejoiced in them. They were inclusive and strangely reassuring, they had to work together.

It wasn't up to one or the other to set the record straight.

As the last minutes of September the 11th slowly ebbed away, Phoenix leaned back in her chair and considered some of the things Jack had said. For the first time she began to grasp how little she knew or understood about him, and how much he knew and understood about her. He had grown with the relationship and she hadn't. Having him around had been enough; she'd never made any attempt at a deeper understanding of him. And he had her sussed, she did underestimate people; she never gave credit where it was due, she always suspected an ulterior motive.

As she sat in the cool darkness of a September night, when the order of both her world and the one around her had just been irrevocably changed forever, she analysed that characteristic. And for the first time, she saw that it wasn't the attractive, hard headed, sharp thinking business like virtue, she had once believed it to be. It was in fact, closed, narrow and suspicious, all the characteristics she hated and despised in others. Christ how her head ached, there was too much running through it, too many revelations.

I won't think about it about it now, she told herself, unintentionally repeating the mantra of her heroine; I'll think about it tomorrow.

Chapter Twenty Six

When the year 2001 finally drew to a close, all the scandals, murders, disease outbreaks and political intrigues, which had captured the headlines during the twelve unfolding months, were buried beneath the avalanche of bad news occasioned by the events of 9/11 which September 11th became known as.

The incessant talk regarding that particular day, made Phoenix feel despairing at times of ever surmounting the task of coming to terms with her own moment of reckoning. She listened, often very glumly as people spoke of the event that changed the world and felt nothing but guilt. As much as the events in America had shocked her, they couldn't compete in her own heart for the trauma that September day had unleashed upon her.

Since Jack now knew about Joseph's existence, deception was no longer a burden to be carried and she did her utmost to walk more lightly. She even took the unprecedented step of seeking help from a doctor. What was more, she even took the prescribed anti depressants, and bore with fairly good grace the kindly advice offered (though privately the idea of swapping whiskey for essential oils in times of panic struck her as plain foolish and bizarre.) 'Ancient Chinese medicine was all very clever,' she thought, 'but it was at least two thousand years out of date.'

Yet in spite of this particular progress, a great sense of foreboding continued to oppress her as she tried to find some benefit from her new found freedom. She pondered in the secrecy of her heart, all the things Jack had said and told her on the night of Josephs return. And on this basis, finally came to the conclusion, never to tell her son, the truth about his paternity. Unfortunately, the aura of peace and goodwill she had expected to descend upon her in return for this positive gesture, failed to materialise. On the contrary, bitterness and frustration at the unfairness of Condon once again escaping justice almost overwhelmed her and for a long while the vision of the villain going to his grave without meeting his nemesis cast a dark and dreary shadow over her.

'There's not a lot I can tell you about your father,' was what she told Joseph, 'Other than he was Irish and a business man. We never had a proper relationship.'

The carefully constructed words had echoed in her ears as she had delivered them, causing her to frown, she had contrived them as a placating lie, but unwittingly, they had relayed the truth. There was truly, very little she knew about the real Condon. 'I could succinctly sum him up in three little words,' she had thought, 'but since I've resolved to be a better person, I'll keep silent.

With much trepidation she telephoned her family in Kent and told them about her son's reappearance. She knew that while her brothers would be indifferent, neither of her sisters would be overjoyed with her news; for them that shameful event of over twenty years ago was history, something to be buried or rewritten. Black sheep were all very well as far as the O'Connell's were concerned, so long as they belonged to another time and place; preferably before the Great Famine.

On two occasions, she hung up the phone when she heard her sister's voice on the other end of the line. She would gladly have passed the opportunity to tell her news, but Jack sensing closure would remain elusive for Phoenix, while loose ends concerning Joseph still remained, was adamant that the call had to be made. Alice took the news with slightly bated breath, pausing just a little too long, in a bid to disguise her unease.

'And how has Jack taken to all of this?'

'With delight,' Phoenix had exaggerated, slightly put out by what she perceived to be the adversarial response of her sister.

'Well, well,' Alice had replied, before abruptly changing the subject, preferring to talk instead about her son, who had just taken up a position as a teacher in one of the local schools and the builder who was taking forever with her new conservatory.

Phoenix, perplexed at her sisters reluctance to accept the enormity of her news, had moved swiftly to end the lack lustre conversation and Alice, perhaps sensing that a new chasm was about to open up, had interrupted her sister's farewell with what she had considered to be a shocking snippet of local gossip.

'Oh there is a bit of news down here, you might be interested in,' she had said with all the mystic of someone about to reveal the third secret of Fatima. 'Do you remember the Condon's?'

'Vaguely,' Phoenix had replied coolly.

'Well, the eldest daughter, the one you used to baby-sit, her flat was raided last week for drugs, and it turns out she is living with another girl; she's a lisbon.'

Upon hearing this useless piece of information, Phoenix had stifled both a smile and a grimace simultaneously, it was the 21st century and her sister still didn't know the difference between a dyke and the capital of Portugal.

'And not only that,' Alice had continued, oblivious to the silence on the other end of the line, 'But poor old Jerh was set upon by a gang of thugs. They attacked him on his way home from work with hockey sticks. They told a passer- by to pass on the message that the beating was a belated thank you for an unwanted Christmas present, from many years ago.'

'How do you know all this?' Phoenix had asked; terror stricken at the thought of what else her sister might reveal.

'Because Guy was on duty in the hospital when he was brought in,' Alice had replied, her voice suggesting there had to be some perks to being married to a sad arsed doctor. 'Jerh refused to comment on the whole affair; he wouldn't even let the police interview him. Don't suppose do you that he is something of a dark horse?'

'Possibly,' Phoenix had muttered before hanging up leaving Alice both bewildered and disappointed at the lack of excitement her astounding piece of news had aroused

There was no doubt in Phoenix's mind, that Jack's labourers were behind the assault and that the sticks in question were not hockey but hurleys. The thought hadn't filled her with delight either, for although there had been a time when the thirst for revenge had almost burned her in its intensity, she was now wiser and in full possession of the knowledge, that there is no such thing as a quick fix for anything of consequence.

When Joseph visited for the second time, he stayed at the request of Phoenix for a long weekend. He came to see his mother and throughout the three days, she searched for what could only be described as the soul of her son, taking care to always sit or stand in the best vantage point from where to analyse him. She took in the shape of his head, the texture of his skin and the mannerisms he used to distinguish him as an individual. Once again, she had felt overwhelmed at the prospect of a complete stranger, being so tightly bonded to her. This was the child who had lived in the shadows of her life, made real.

His eyes, which she still refused look into, were reminiscent of her mother's, in their slate greyness and ability to suddenly light up when he smiled or told a self deprecating joke. 'He is more like me than I could ever have imagined,' she had thought to herself as she had waved him good bye. And instantly she had corrected herself 'Well more like I used to be, easy going, fearful of giving offence and eager to please. She had noticed how he invariably waited to be asked to take a seat, cleared up after meals and had never once hinted that he was tired or bored with Daisy's incessant demands for his attention.

He had spoken with affection about his life in the West Country; his parents owned a souvenir cum teashop in the heart of rural Devon and had two children of their own. From all accounts it was an idyllic childhood, full of horse riding and country walks; hell on earth Phoenix thought privately, though she could see the attraction from a child's point of view. He told about his life at the Royal Academy and his obsession with all things musical. The flute was his instrument and he had made a fortune the previous summer, busking in the London underground.

As she listened to this particular piece of news, a light had shined upon her soul. Her father had apparently been Kerry's answer to Count John McCormack and more importantly, the only one genuine thing, she knew about bloody Count Dracula Condon, was that he was totally and hopelessly tone deaf.

When the weekend visit concluded; a depression like a cold front, moved forward and settled over Phoenix; leaving her with an unaccountable sense of loneliness. Wintry thoughts and doubts drifted through her mind and she was at a loss to address any of them. Night time bought no relief either, for the dream concerning attached money which had once haunted her in Kilburn, came back with a new ferociousness, turning up every night and leaving her dejected and frustrated.

She turned to Jack, frightened by the intensity of her feelings, fearful that she was returning to the neurotic days that had preceded Joseph's return. She begged him to take her away to a place where she could finally lay to rest, the sore that continued to fester within her. Much as she loved Fuchsia House it was proving to be no Tara for the peace and contentment she had once derived from it was no longer to be found. Fuchsia House had provided balm when her heart's desire could be assuaged by something material. Now her longing was for something far more intangible.

Jack listened both anxiously and attentively to her description of where she thought peace might be found and after much deliberation, took her to Ireland; to Skibbereen and the house on the headland left to them by Danny. The West Cork farmhouse which in Danny's day had always been accompanied by smoke permeating from its stout chimney pots together with chickens scratching a living around its permanently open back door, now stood lonesome and empty. It had once served as a family home, but years of careful neglect had gradually whittled it down to being a basic abode, finely tuned for the needs of a bachelor farmer. Now just one acre of land surrounded the house, the rest having being shaved off and left to Eileen and her family who farmed in the surrounding area.

Believing as he did, that the essence of a person cannot be confined to bricks and mortar, Jack had drawn up extensive plans for the renovation of the cottage, but upon hearing of his plan to take her to Ireland, Phoenix begged him to keep it the way it was, for just a little while longer. She didn't fully understand this request and would have dismissed out of hand, any suggestion of it coming from a secret hope that something of Danny's peaceful and contented spirit might rub off on her if she was to live as he had lived, even for a short time.

An explanation was sent to Daisy's school regarding urgent business interests that needed to be dealt with in Ireland and with that done, the Keane family set sail for Ireland in July.

Life can imitate art. Just as Scarlett O'Hara was cajoled into selling her off her beloved saw mills at the behest of a husband concerned for her health, Phoenix crumbled under pressure from Jack, and gave rather than sold; her south London franchise to Carolyn, although the brand name of Phoenix Maids remained under her control.

Giving up the right arm of her mini empire, the one which had seen the birth of her business tore at her heart; with it went so many memories, but there was an upside to the ordeal. The poaching of Carolyn, or rather the manner in which she had carried it out, did weigh heavily upon her.

She was still a long way from wanting to realise her childhood ambitions of saving the world, but she had learnt enough to recognise the value of Carolyn. Far from being an unthinking insipid mope; she was a loyal and faithful servant, having depths of character that she herself could only dream of possessing. Giving the franchise to Carolyn, at least served as some form of benediction

In the peace and tranquillity of the cottage overlooking Tragumna beach, Phoenix turned a searchlight upon her life, and set about seeking for the source of the regret that pinched her heart and stole the glory of each passing day. With the exception of her foray into poaching, she remained adamant, that there was very little she would change about the way she had operated her business and by that she meant her life. Yes, perhaps she would have been a little kinder, more understanding even, maybe, but nothing else. She didn't want to end her days, wracked with regret, like a withered old feminist or porn star. She had taken a stand against conformity and nothing would ever persuade her, that life would have been better, if she had remained passive and compliable.

The gospel story of the Sheep and Goats had always struck a particular resonance with her; clarifying as it did, that it wasn't the things you did that sent you to hell but the things you didn't do. Such a belief left a lot of room for manoeuvre. But the comfort she had once found in her youthful theory had dissipated along with her ability to think with clarity, focusing even on the most simple of ideas, was now proving to be as complex as keeping track on a single snowflake in a blizzard.

She had a sense of being driven back to basics and that meant having to face the question of faith and where it belonged in her life. There was a time, when she had consciously believed that she had been born with life -long immunity from the afflictions that troubled other mortals. Her mother wouldn't die, no one she knew, would ever be murdered, or appear in disgrace on the front page of a national newspaper and although she might brush against the wings of catastrophe, she would never be ensnared by it. It was only a question of daring to believe and frequently she had taken the dare. Never had she been let down. Never until that night, in Condon's house.

In the hinterlands of Skibbereen, though inner peace was in short supply, external peace and tranquillity were available in abundance. If the weather was fine, she walked the jagged headland, drawn in fascination by the surging Atlantic. The water with its ever changing façade mesmerized her. What a very different scene it was to the seaside of her childhood. As she remembered back in fragments to childish days at the seaside, she saw an image of a sea whose sole function was to attract the day tripper from London. It pictured itself in her imagination, as a static sea, sitting awaiting the visitor. By contrast the sea shaping the wilderness of West Cork appeared mysterious, wild and grasping, infusing in her a reckless energy.

Sometimes Jack and Daisy accompanied her, but mostly they left her to walk alone. Though she never objected to their company, both instinctively felt her drift far away from them as the walk progressed and since neither enjoyed walking in silence, father and daughter made excuses and left her to it. And their instincts were right, once out in the open, be it along the headland, or along a winding fuchsia fringed country road, Phoenix turned her thoughts to the busy process of inquisition.

She questioned and interrogated both herself and the very nature of the world around her. At one point she even considered talking to a priest, but dismissed it on reflection, as pointless. On the real issues that mattered, nobody knew more than anyone else; there was no record of anyone dying and coming back to report on what lay ahead, or what had started it all in the first place. When it came down to it, it was a case of her guess being as good as the next.

She remembered abstractly, the faith her mother had entrusted in the priest who had attended her dying father. He had arrived late at the scene, yet still had the arrogance to state with authority, that it didn't matter, since the soul did not depart the body until an hour following death. The memory made her seethe. How did he know? Who told him? Why did the church persist with the nonsense that it held all the answers when plainly it didn't. The notion of free will was a case in point, why did the church preach this concept with the aura of fact? It was a ridiculous idea. Free will if it did exist was extinguished the moment someone else put theirs into practise. Jerh Condon had acted freely and by doing so had taken her destiny out of her hands.

But bizarrely more than anything, it was the relationship between the sexes; that obsessed her, the blatant, crass, unfair cruelty of it all. Such was the profusion of thoughts that crowded her mind that she began to regret more bitterly than ever, her lack of education. Surely if she was educated, she would have the ability to discipline and decipher her thoughts, rather than be confused by their dubious veracity. Just who was deluded? Was it her? Or could it be the rest of the world? Such a notion was on the face of it crazy, taking the idea of 'to the power of one' to the limits but the evidence in her favour, was overwhelming. Was it the case that most people knew the awful truth about the structure of life, but turned a blind eye to it in the interest of world stability? Turned a blind eye to the unpalatable fact that the two combatants, who formed human existence, were so unfairly matched? Was this how it was all meant to be? If it was, then how did other women square the circle? How did they bear the cruelty of it all?

The world demanded physical perfection from the female; yet it was women who aged quicker, got fatter and lost fertility. Her disillusionment did not stem from an inflated view of women. On the contrary, women irritated her with their foolish ideas and fancies. Women lacked many of the qualities men had and

Phoenix envied, such as decisiveness and loyalty. Loyalty in her opinion was a rare phenomenon amongst the female gender. No 'old school' network could ever exist amongst women. There would always be one who wanted to curry favour and do what no self respecting male would ever do, and make exceptions for the opposite sex.

The glamour industry was the only one that featured women in leading roles and that entire industry was dependent on women betraying their sex for a price, after all beauty has a shelf life; and what then? Even the skinny city slickers, in their pencil skirts and tailored jackets with just the right amount of cleavage peeking through, would end their days; overweight, or wizened, plucking hairs from a stubbly chin and remembering their glory days when men had turned to look at them.

There were enough stupid ideas and assertions peddled by men designed to denigrate women without women throwing in ridiculous ones of their own, such as the nonsense that men matured while women aged. Rather than rebutting such talk, women connived with it, some being willing to suspend disgust and sleep with, (even marry provided they were rich or famous enough) foolish, withered, diseased ridden old men. And no one, she thought grimly, remembering for no good reason her own sisters, was faster than a woman at hurling the first stone against another woman who played the same trick, with a younger man.

Men are cleverer as well, she conceded at protecting their interests, they share a tacit agreement; that only shirt lifters pose in the nude; and they would boycott anything that attempted to reduce them to the level of a commodity. In fact men resorting to the sex industry; as in front of the camera rather than behind it, was the stuff of tragic- comedy; like The Full Monty.

Men, be they in the form of government ministers, law lords or chiefs of industry, were the ones to set the agenda and they were the loudest to complain when the agenda failed to deliver. Geldof along with a whole shower of professional Rent a Gob's saw fit to protest on behalf of fathers shunned by the courts. But they kept strangely quiet about the babies who failed to be born, on account of fathers, washing their hands of involvement in anything other than their conception. Parental concern as shown by men, she thought grimly, could usually be translated into meaning a wrangle about possession.

On and on bitter thoughts raced through her head, as an inexplicable hurt pierced her heart. The bleak unaccountable cruelty of the world loomed in front of her and though she sought peace of mind, something within; something in the core of her being, refused to be pacified, peace was being withheld. Sometimes she returned home resolving to be optimistic, counselling herself that there had to be exceptions to the rule and her good intentions held sway, until a random newspaper article, a stray word or report on the radio triggered off the despair again.

And this was the case one day, when she sat with her sister in law, discussing the local National school Daisy might attend if they decided to remain in Ireland for any length of time. As Eileen spoke of the proximity of the school bus, Phoenix found her attention drifting towards the discussion on the radio concerning the plight of baby girls in China. She had looked up into Eileen's eyes and a feeling of isolation and confusion had surrounded her. She had no doubt, that if asked for her views on what was happening in China and elsewhere, Eileen would reply it was a dreadful state of affairs altogether, and she would mean it, but she wouldn't dwell on it. She wouldn't apply it to herself or her daughters; she wouldn't think it was symptomatic of what was wrong with the world. Why then Phoenix asked herself, do I?

Was she fighting a rearguard action, against the way things were meant to be? Was it really the case, that for all the talk of women being champions at multi tasking, in reality they only served one function? After all it was universally accepted that successful men deserved trophy wives. Even some religions concurred with the idea that women were chicken shit in comparison to men, necessary only for procreation. Surely though, this wasn't how God intended things to be. But every now and then, a sneaking fear possessed her; that things were as they were, precisely because that is the way it was ordained to be.

If that was the case, she thought, perhaps the Islamic world had it right. Perhaps in those far off countries, where technology wasn't king, the people were more in tune with the earth and so acted and lived accordingly. Such a belief could justify a lot of things such as highflying women being publicly ridiculed and dismissed in favour of a sapling of a male in the City. Even the rape of women or girls in darkened railway stations in the pitch of night, or in broad daylight by pupils in a storeroom in an inner city school could be justified. It was simply nature kicking in, for women were destined to be kept fully wrapped, hidden away; safe at home, away from men, who couldn't or shouldn't be expected to restrain themselves from their natural urges.

But, her mind cried out, the history of the world was littered with examples of men and women who loved and cared for each other. The problem was, at this particular moment, she couldn't bring any to mind and living in a modern material world, where the virtues that really mattered weren't marketable, wasn't helping the situation.

As she passed the church on her way back from Eileen's, she caught a glimpse of the elderly priest, as he made his way down the steep stone steps. She hurried away, not wanting to come to his attention and as she did so, she wondered about him. Did he ever feel lonely or adrift from the world of his parishioners? Was he like the rooks that congregated in the church yard, part of the scene, yet fundamentally without worth? As her thoughts centred on the priest, it occurred to her, that human need was most aptly demonstrated, in the clandestine affairs women have with the clergy. Invariably such women were deeply unhappy; she couldn't bring to mind a single case of a young, vibrant, thrusting woman having an affair with a priest. Scandals in the press concerning errant priests were always accompanied by incongruous photos of dowdy looking women usually in head-scarves or anoraks. It was always, the lonely and distressed, the divorcee seeking hope. They seek a priest she told herself, because what they really desire are the virtues associated with the priesthood, care, compassion and loyalty even unto death. This very tall order was the attraction, certainly not the priest himself.

Though not fully aware of the extent of Phoenix's distress, Jack knew things were far from resolved for her and sometimes when far away on business, an image of the rocky headland edging the Atlantic would flash into his mind, causing him to panic. What if she had a relapse and decided to end it all? The headland was an invitation to someone like Phoenix, who couldn't even swim.

While Phoenix fretted about the world and the men in it who disliked women so much, Jack made great plans to take her and Daisy around the globe. He wanted to put a gap between themselves and the tumultuous year that had passed and in the process, set about realising for Phoenix some of her dreams. They would go to America and travel in style from coast to coast and then perhaps, move on to Australia and all the Pacific Islands.

The grief he felt for her was real and he worried about his capacity to really understand her. The only thing he knew for certain; was that he wanted to make up in some way, for the lost years of her youth. It was obvious to him, that all the wealth she had been driven to create, had never compensated her for the freedom she had lost as a young girl, to be mistress of her own fate. It wasn't possible to wipe out the past, but it was possible to make the present a better place to be. He wouldn't even mind Joseph coming, if that was what Phoenix wanted. Once Christmas is over he told himself, I'll broach the subject.

Chapter Twenty Seven

For all the turmoil going on in Phoenix's mind, on an external level life in Danny's farmhouse was almost tranquil in its simplicity. Even the lack of heating, didn't really bother her, especially when Jack was around and able to coax the old Stanley to do its business and warm the house to the rafters. The peaty smoky smell from the ancient stove reminded her of days gone by, when Danny had acted as host, boiling up enormous saucepans of spuds, most of which ended up being fed to his dogs.

The sense of tranquillity was enhanced by the fact that Daisy was so patently happy. The minimalist living agreed with her, she loved the painted wooden stairs that echoed her footsteps as she descended them two at a time, almost as much as she loved the view of the sea from her bedroom. The novelty of living in close proximity to relatives who were always pleased to see her, hadn't worn off either. There were a lot of small pleasures that filled Daisy's days. But the one she loved most of all, was shooing out with the aid of a broom, the nosey hens given to her by Aunty Eileen, who ventured too deeply into the house at every given opportunity, pecking and scraping on the concrete kitchen floor.

On the morning of 17th December 2002, another variety of feathered friend paid a visit, and Phoenix was not at all pleased to see him. She had entered the kitchen to find an enormous, black crow, throwing itself at the closed window. The backdoor had been left slightly ajar, probably by Daisy who made a ritual of throwing bread to the birds early every morning and although the crow obviously had no trouble locating the entrance, he was struggling frantically to find an exit.

Taking the heavy bristled kitchen broom and gritting her teeth Phoenix had poked and prodded the air randomly around the bird in a bid to guide it towards the door and when it finally flapped its wings on its way to freedom, she stared after it shivering with fear. She hated crows, they were big, evil, greasy looking birds, insolent in their daring and movement, surely one in the house was a bad omen?

Immediately after the birds departure, she had searched the kitchen in a bid to eradicate any evidence of its appearance, but since there was none to be found, she came to the conclusion, it hadn't been as frightened as her. The ordeal of the crow gradually receded from her mind as the day progressed and by the time she had finished putting up the Christmas decorations with Daisy's assistance, all thoughts of the big ungainly bird had virtually disappeared.

Mother and daughter stood hand in hand and together, admired their handiwork. A room reminiscent of an illustration from the world of Hans Christian Anderson had painstakingly been created. Streams of multi coloured paper chains criss –crossed the wooden ceiling, dancing gently in response to the draught caused by the stove and as if to order, a smattering of snowflakes with perfect timing, drifted lazily past the window, shaping to perfection the idyllic Christmas scene.

'Oh Mommy,' Daisy cried, looking at the scene above her head, 'isn't it beautiful, won't Daddy love it.'

When she saw the child's joy, Phoenix was glad she had made the effort; she knew Jack would be delighted as well, for she was conscious that he was eager to read signs of normality in everything she did. It was going to be a busy Christmas, with relatives for the first time, literally on the doorstep. Joseph was coming for the New Year and Phoenix sensed that Jack was secretly planning something big. His many acts of random kindness, which once aggravated, now touched her and in a peculiar way caused a new hurt to burn in her heart. Her sordid secret was out and in return she had expected some liberation from having finally told the truth, but so far it wasn't working out that way. An iron grip still had a hold on her heart, acting like a dam and preventing the love within it from flowing out to those who mattered.

She was standing on a chair, fixing balloons to the ceiling when Con, Eileen's husband, drove into the yard. She wasn't expecting him; he was in fact, meant to be collecting Jack from the airport that very afternoon and she watched anxiously as he strode towards the house.

'My God,' he said, smiling as he entered the gaily coloured room, 'but you've made a grand job here, Danny always went to town with the Christmas decorating, he'd be proud of you.'

Phoenix smiled at him and her worried face visibly relaxed when she saw no evidence of bad news being responsible for his visit. 'Well,' she said feeling slightly embarrassed at the thought of being seen as a woman with time on her hands, 'It seemed like a good idea at the time.'

'I was wondering,' Con asked, 'If you would like to take a spin to Cork, I have to collect a piece for the old boiler from the city, so I thought I'd do it at the same time as collecting Jack.'

Phoenix shook her head 'That's kind of you, but after all this palaver,' she said pointing to the bits of broken decorations that clung to the floor and chairs. 'There is a lot of clearing up to do before Jack gets back.'

'Fine anyway,' he said but as he walked to the door, Daisy ran to him.

'Please Mommy,' she pleaded, 'Let me go with Uncle Con.'

Phoenix waved her hand in a bid to silence her daughter, but Con intervened. 'It will be no trouble at all,' he said, 'You would love to see the city wouldn't you Daisy?'

The child nodded her head vigorously and Phoenix looked at Con warily. 'Are you sure you don't mind? It would be easier for you to go alone.'

'Not at all,' he insisted.

She walked into the hall and snatched Daisy's coat and scarf off the clothes peg from behind the door and suddenly for no apparent reason, felt inexplicably anxious again. Wrapping the scarf slowly around Daisy's neck, she turned to Con and said nervously. 'Oh please take care on the roads won't you? There was snow earlier on and...' she hesitated before owning up to her real fear, 'it's just that a horrible black crow flew into the house earlier and it's made me feel uneasy.'

He laughed good naturedly and shook his head. 'Oh for God's sake girl, look at that sky, there is hardly any snow to be had from that and sure there's no harm in the old crow, wherever they are, life is, so it goes.'

Phoenix rolled her eyes upwards. 'Maybe, but I don't like the idea of a bird in the house, I'm sure it is unlucky.'

He laughed again, tousling Daisy's head as he did so. 'It is winter and the birds have to eat, the crow will track food down wherever he can find it.'

She too laughed, feeling suddenly a bit foolish, the woman from the city across the sea acting like a bog man. 'Oh well,' she said. 'You drive carefully anyway,' and leaning down she kissed Daisy on the head.

She waved from the window until the car was out of sight then turned and stared around her, wondering where to start. The absence of childish laughter and enthusiasm, suddenly struck her as being at variance with the cheerful, gaily coloured decorations, and she immediately became conscious of the silence that now seeped in through every crevice

Turning her gaze away from the closed door, it fell by chance upon the oil cloth on the basic wooden table before sweeping up and taking in the old fashioned press and the smoke stained ceiling. She felt drawn, almost against her will to look around, and as she did so a sense of unreality descended on her. What on earth was she doing in a farmhouse in the back of beyond, making a fire like a caveman, when she had a luxurious house sitting empty in London?

She walked slowly over to the old settle that nestled beneath the small high window and sat down, all the time continuing to look intently around her, at the frugally furnished room. By coming here, to this cottage, she had unintentionally gone full circle back to her parent's roots and the worrying thing was, it didn't feel at all peculiar, just eerily familiar.

In the second it took for a beam of December sunlight to pierce the small room transfiguring it with a blast of winter whiteness, she saw with a blinding vision, that essentially, she was no different to the person she had always been. Circumstances had made her fight with all the tenacity she had inherited, to ensure survival. She glanced into the bold face of the dining room clock and wound her memory back to the night before Joseph reappeared, when she had found strength in thinking of the ancestors who had gone before her to escape war and famine. The times were different but the cause wasn't and neither was she. She had used the façade of Phoenix Ashton, to get her life back on track. The mistake I made, she told herself, standing up and walking towards the little mirror on the gable wall, is that I really believed I was brash, secular Phoenix Ashton, not merely Sinead O'Connell masquerading as her.

Staring into the mirror, she remembered back to another occasion when she had sought her reflection. The time in Condon's house, when emerging from the bath, she had looked into another mirror, much bigger and grander than this little token one left behind by Danny, but just as truthful. It had shown the face of a frightened, hopeless teenager. That girl would never have survived the London of the nineteen eighties, she had needed a minder and who better than someone like tough, don't tread on my toes, Phoenix Ashton?

She dropped her gaze and returned to the wooden settle, sitting down on it with a sigh like Danny used to do, except his ritual always involved him hanging his cap on the carved top and brushing his sparse hair down with the palm of his hand. You can live and die she told herself, without ever being aware of a simple, single fact that could turn your life around, if you only knew of its existence. Mom did. She encouraged me to live her dream, because her life was so full of regret. She was so certain life would have been better if only she had been educated, but the truth is; it would have been different, but not necessarily better. It wasn't lack of success that made her unhappy, it was her marriage, but she wasn't allowed to think, never mind say that.

As she sat, alone and calm in the winter sun, her thoughts became more lucid and from the depths of her being, she summoned the strength to admit the inadmissible. Like the tectonic plates gliding into place under the earths crust, she could almost hear as well as feel, the grinding of her brain as it braced itself for the inevitable showdown of life regaining the track it had been derailed from so long ago.

She had to do it. She could of course continue going through the motion of living, she had done that for over twenty years, proving one thing at least; that it is possible to learn to make a living without ever learning to live. Now she wanted to change, really change and it could only happen with the freedom that truth would bring her. There was no guarantee of happiness, but that wasn't what she was after, she wanted peace, the absence at least of conflict.

Standing up, she walked calmly towards the wooden table and lifting the flap of oil cloth up at one end, she pulled open a little drawer and extracted from it, a pen and a child's school exercise book.

For a moment she stared at the closed book, pausing to consider whether or not to go ahead with her idea and then quickly, almost as if she feared a loss of courage, she walked back to the settle and sat down with the book balanced on her knee:

Dear Phoenix,

So many letters I've written and all those words only for the eyes of someone who doesn't exist, a character from a book, who I wanted to be like, because I so disliked being me. What a clever disguise you were Phoenix, formed in part from Scarlett O'Hara and tough talking Lesley who proved to me all those years ago, that nothing silences people like a tongue sharper than a machete.

For years I have fooled myself about so many things, one of them being that if life had only gone to plan, what a top class lawyer I would have made.

What a delusion.

It took a life shattering incident and meeting Jack to make me see that for most people life is never straightforward. There is a difference between an arse and an elbow and a lawyer who doesn't know that is dead from the ankles up, or destined to be a judge. What better evidence have I got than my own brothers and sisters, who in world terms are neither bad nor stupid, but who are without exception smug and sanctimonious, simply because nothing serious enough has ever persuaded them to be otherwise.

As for my marriage to Jack, it only goes to show I have the skill of underestimating down to a fine art. In my heart I've always looked down on him; dismissing him as a chancer or as Rhett Butler would have put it 'a Mick on the make.' Never once have I given him credit for all he has achieved. Life could have been better for Jack, if only he had been given the opportunity, but since there was no other way, other than by sheer hard dirty graft; he grasped what he could and made a go of it.

The list of people I have trashed could go on for eternity, but it is not other people I am bothered with right now. The only person I ever over estimated was the ape, believing for one minute the story he gave out about Olga going into the madhouse. It took Jack minutes to understand what I never figured out in over twenty years. The ape had me sussed; he knew the shame was far worse than the pain, in all its forms.

Right from the day when I decided to live by rules other the ones I was reared on, the need to shun sympathy and avoid the grief of others was critical. I lived in fear of the sympathetic word or touch that would make me cry out. But the history of the world is scarce on people, who denounce the wrong they have done. There is no record to my knowledge of Hitler or Stalin or any of that crowd putting their hand up and saying 'I got it wrong.'

But I must. I must if I want to live. I must acknowledge it now and shout it from the roof tops if necessary. For weeks and months I have driven myself to the brink of madness, thinking about the big issues of the world, the insolvable ones, when really it is only the issue within me that has to be addressed.

My biggest torment wasn't the rape, or the family estrangement or Mom dying without reconciliation; or even the hiding of a secret from Jack. It was handing Joseph over in the first place. Admitting a need for that baby felt tantamount to saying I had asked to be raped. But I needed that child, because he was all that I had that was mine. I lost my family and with them I lost everything that mattered, but there was still something that belonged to me.

So many times, as I wrote to Scarlett, memories would trickle into my consciousness more artfully than a stream winding across a valley, but I closed my heart to them. Things like the awful giving out I gave to that social worker who arranged Joseph's adoption, the frustration of being in a process I couldn't get out of, finally spilled over with her. And the hatred I felt for Aunty Phil when she pointed out Joseph's hair in the hospital, when she said 'that's pure O'Connell,' making me recognise that it was more likely pure Condon. I hated her for giving me a reason to turn my back on my baby. How could I still want him when it was so clearly pointed out where he had come from? And those memories of how I used to search the bed, thinking the baby had been born during the night. Some of the emptiness and the futility of it all, would sweep over me like the darkness of a starless sky. The biggest irony of all was Mom going against all her instincts, all her beliefs, bargaining with her own eternal peace, sacrificing Joseph, to buy me what she never had. A rich and comfortable future full of the happiness and peace she believed it would deliver. The regret never faded; instead it grew stronger with the passing years, changing into denial when it became apparent that it could never be assuaged.

I was certain Joseph would return on his twenty first birthday. I was certain because I knew instinctively, that if he didn't return then, he never would and a great unacknowledged wrong would never be put right. But now I can acknowledge it and by doing so, find enough peace to want a future. Finally, I understand my refusal to look into Josephs eyes. I couldn't do it, because I felt like a Judas; I had betrayed the innocent and cloaked the guilty with secrecy...

She put her pen down and stared straight ahead for a moment as the thought occurred to her, that although the betrayal was wrong, the secrecy wasn't. Thank God she hadn't told Joseph the truth about his father. For the first time in her life, she recognised the absolute supremacy of mercy over justice, with all its beguiling promise of peace through revenge.

Pushing the book aside, she clasped a hand to her heart. It was done, the truth was out and she hadn't collapsed with despair, or faced with too much reality gone mad; as she had often feared she might do. She glanced slowly around the room as if in search of something that might reassure her, and finally her eyes came to rest on the picture of the Sacred Heart that hung on the gable wall. A similar one had hung over the fireplace in the dining room of her childhood home. This one contained beneath its prayer of intercession, the names of Jack's entire family. The parents and two children were now deceased, Danny of course and a child, a little boy James who had died in infancy. Such was life; the duty to live it to the full was constantly being passed on to the next generation. Feeling something of the pain that infant death must have inflicted on the lives of Jack's less than happy parents, she instinctively got down on her knees, uttering as she did so the first genuine, heartfelt prayer she had made since that night in Condon's house. 'Thank you God,' she whispered, 'Thank you for the many gifts you have showered on me, thank you for carrying me throughout the years. I've spent so much time looking upon the things I lost, that I've never taken time to see the things I found.' She got up from the floor and walked over to the window, knowing intuitively that the peace she felt was for real, and not the by product of any substance she had taken.

A sparse scattering of intermittent snowflakes, floated and drifted dreamily past the window and as she stared after them, it felt to her as if they were beckoning her to come and join the dance. With only a momentary hesitation, she headed for the hallway from where she grabbed her heavy coat off the peg before opening the front door and setting off for the headland.

Just for a moment, she wanted to capture this perfect picture of snowflakes in the sunshine ending their days in the relentless sea. It was colder than she had imagined it to be and as she walked, she pulled her coat tightly around her, telling herself she wouldn't stay long.

Finding a vantage point on the rocks, she looked down, and the sea stretching ahead to infinity mirrored back to her some of the openness of heart she now felt. The snowflakes had dwindled to almost nothing but the waters of the Atlantic swarmed forth in abundance, tirelessly trying to breech the sea wall only to fall back repeatedly into the ever oncoming swirling waves.

Like the tide, she could never give up. In the same way an acorn can only grow into an oak tree or a downy, fluffy gosling into a fierce and hissing goose, she knew she could only ever be Sinead O'Connell. 'I'm finished with tinkering with the past,' she told a passing snowflake; 'It is the only thing in life that is permanent, so why bother trying to change it.' Even as she uttered the words, she knew she was expressing a hope rather than reality; there would still be moments of anxiety, but there would never again be the black despair that had shadowed so much of her previous life. She would never overcome the injustices of the world, but she could find something worth living for in the confines of her own world, with the people she loved.

She turned to go, anxious suddenly to be home and rid of the thoughts that were deeper than the water beneath her, but as she turned, her foot slipped on the wet rock and she fell, face down, sliding several feet nearer to the cliff edge.

Beneath her left ear clamped to the dirty, grassy ridge, she heard only silence, while with the other; she heard too clearly the swish and smash of the hungry sea. Stricken with fear, she attempted to pull herself up, but the rock she tried to grip onto was wet from the recent snow and her hand slithered clumsily over it. Down her hand slipped until it met another rock, equally wet, equally slimy. Again she dug her fingers in, but her coat and boots were heavy and the strain fighting the downward momentum was getting almost too much to bear. 'Oh God,' she cried. 'I don't think I can hold on much longer.' Her arms throbbed with tiredness and she tried to ignore a surge of despair as her feet searched desperately for a foothold that didn't exist.

For one very brief moment she was almost tempted to bow to the inevitable, but the vision of her note book on Danny's settle sailed through her consciousness like a yacht on the horizon and the letter it contained echoed in her head as a suicide note. Filled with superstitious terror, she remembered the times when she had wished death upon herself, now it seemed her wish was about to be fulfilled, but she couldn't let it happen. Seizing upon a strength that had come to her once before in an hour of desperate need, she clung more urgently, once again reaching up in what she knew was her last bid, grasping at a jut of rock; steadfast and strong enough for her to hold onto, while her strength returned. Slowly, inch by sliding inch, she made her way to the top, not once daring to hope or look back on what might have been.

Safe once again on the grassy banks, inhabited by Eileen's Friesians during the summer months, she stopped to catch her breath. Painful spasms from her bruised ribs were making breathing difficult and her finger tips were both raw and red. The sky had lowered, but the snow had ceased and she stood, shocked and slightly hunched, pausing to orientate her thoughts. In the distance smoke from the farmhouse chimney was busy travelling into infinity and a car trundled stoically on its way to Skibbereen. There was nothing to suggest that Sinead O'Connell had almost made her final exit amidst so much terror.

For a moment her thoughts turned back to the ordeal she had just survived, to consider what might have been, but she disciplined herself sharply. I won't think about that now she told herself, there is something else I have to do first. She began to walk, not at all briskly for she was still in the grip of pain, but with a purpose, back towards the cottage.

'When Daisy sends her letter to Santa up the chimney tonight', she told herself, panting with the exertion of walking in the frosty coldness, 'I too will throw in all my letters, every single one of them. There is going to be a hell of a blaze, as Sinead O'Connell finally burns her bridges with the past. I'm through with it.

After all, as the woman herself said 'tomorrow is another day.'

THE END